Daily
Guideposts, 2000

THOMAS NELSON PUBLISHERS®
Nashville

Published in Nashville, Tennessee, by Thomas Nelson Publishers, Inc.

ACKNOWLEDGMENTS

All Scripture quotations, unless otherwise noted, are from *The King James Version of the Bible*.
  Scripture quotations marked (NIV) are from the *Holy Bible, New International Version* Copyright © 1973, 1978, 1984 International Bible Society. Used by permission of Zondervan Bible Publishers.
  Scripture quotations marked (RSV) are from the *Revised Standard Version of the Bible* Copyright © 1946, 1952, 1971, by the Division of Christian Education of the National Council of Churches of Christ in the U.S.A. and are used by permission.
  Scripture quotations marked (NAS) are from the *New American Standard Bible*, © 1960, 1962, 1963, 1968, 1971, 1972, 1973, 1975, 1977, by The Lockman Foundation. Used by permission.
  Scripture quotations marked (TLB) are from *The Living Bible*, © 1971. Used by permission of Tyndale House Publishers, Inc., Wheaton, IL 60189. All rights reserved.
  Scripture quotations marked (NKJV) are from *The New King James Version of the Bible* Copyright © 1979, 1980, 1982, by Thomas Nelson, Inc., Nashville, TN 37214.
  Scripture quotations marked (NLT) are from the *Holy Bible, New Living Translation*, copyright © 1996. Used by permission of Tyndale House Publishers, Inc., Wheaton, Illinois 60189. All rights reserved.
  Quote by Dag Hammarskjold found in the October 24 devotional is from *Markings* by Dag Hammarskjold, trans., Auden/Sjoberg. Copyright © 1964 by Alfred A. Knopf Inc. and Faber & Faber Ltd. Reprinted by permission of the publisher.
  "All Things New" series, which appears at the beginning of each month, was written by Elizabeth Sherrill.
  "A Place of My Own" series was written by Van Varner.
  "The way of the Cross" series was written by Pam Kidd
  "Unlooked-for Blessings" series was written by Marci Alborghetti.
  "Grandma Remembers" series was written by Mary Lou Carney.
  "A Christmas for the Heart" series was written Marilyn Morgan Helleberg.

www.guidepost.org
Designed by Holly Johnson
Artwork by Gary Halsey
Indexed by Patricia Woodruff
Cover Photo by © Fotopic/Omni-Photo Communications, Inc.
Typeset by Allentown Digital Services Division of R.R. Donnelley & Sons
Printed in the United States of America

ISBN 0-7852-6994-0   2 — 2000

Table of Contents

TABLE OF CONTENTS

Introduction

Welcome to *Daily Guideposts, 2000.* Are those words as astonishing for you to read as they are for us to write? For a long time, we've seen this year ahead of us in the distance. And now it's here, and with it comes a new decade, a new century and a new millennium.

A very special year needs a very special theme, and for *Daily Guideposts, 2000*—our twenty-fourth edition—our theme is taken from the promise of Jesus, recorded by John in the Book of Revelation, "Behold, I make all things new." We don't have to fear what a new millennium will bring, because our God is there ahead of us, waiting for us in the twenty-first century as surely as He walked the roads of Judea in the first century and sustains us with His Spirit today. Yesterday, today and tomorrow, God is always new for us and always ready to make us new in Him.

We invite you to travel through this momentous year with fifty-three friends, old and new, who are waiting to tell you how God has been working in their lives to bring renewal and hope. In the pages of *Daily Guideposts, 2000,* you'll find insights and inspiration to renew your mind, your heart and your spirit.

At the beginning of every month, in "All Things New," Elizabeth Sherrill will tell you about those special moments when she has discovered God's newness in her life: in reading the Bible with new eyes; in experiencing the wonder of God's ever-new provision of our daily bread; in finding the renewal on the other side of pain. She'll help you see God at work making your own life new every day of the year. During Holy Week, Pam Kidd follows Jesus on "The Way of the Cross" through the streets of Jerusalem to the Easter miracle of the empty tomb. Seven inspiring stories of faith, hope, sacrifice and love explore the meaning of those two-thousand-year-old events for life in a new millennium. In June, *Daily Guideposts* newcomer Marci Alborghetti will tell you how God used a diagnosis of malignant melanoma and an uncertain future to renew her life with "Unlooked-for Blessings." For a week in October, in "Grandmother Remembers," Mary Lou Carney shares the precious memories—of home and school, of church and answered prayer, of long-ago Christmases— her mother left as a legacy to her grandchildren. In "A Christmas for the Heart," Marilyn Morgan Helleberg draws on the memorable Christmases of her life to help you make the birth of Jesus a reality in your own heart. And throughout the year, watch out for a glimpse of a New York cityscape. It will tell you that Van Varner is ready to invite you into his Upper West Side apartment to share a story of God's presence in the Big Apple.

The future is richer for the wisdom and experience we bring into it, and we're especially happy that so many of our beloved *Daily Guideposts* friends—Marjorie Holmes and Fred Bauer, Marion Bond West and Rick Hamlin, Ruth Stafford Peale and Oscar Greene, among so many others—are here again to share their lives with us.

And we're happy to introduce some special new friends alongside Marci Alborghetti, a reporter and writer from Hartford, Connecticut. Dave Franco, an advertising copywriter and father of two from New York City, shares his prayerful search for a new job and a new home. And Sharon Foster, an educator and mother from Glen Burnie, Maryland, tells you how she left a high-pressure business career to find renewal with her two small children in rural North Carolina.

You'll also find the extras you've come to look forward to in *Daily Guideposts:* the "Fellowship Corner"; the "Reader's Room"; and our handy indexes, including once again the popular Scripture Reference Index. And this year, artist Gary Halsey has drawn some very special pictures to make your walk with us even more rewarding.

So let us greet this amazing year together as a family, with faith and hope, confident that, as He has promised, our Lord will be with us every day, in every moment, to strengthen, to inspire and to challenge us as He proclaims, "Behold, I make all things new."

—THE EDITORS

A SPECIAL NOTE

Next year, in 2001, *Daily Guideposts* will be celebrating its twenty-fifth anniversary. To make our silver anniversary celebration a truly special occasion, we need your help. We'd like to know how *Daily Guideposts* has helped you over the years, and which particular devotionals have meant the most to you. Please write us at the address below, and let us know!

> *Daily Guideposts* Editor
> Box 25
> Guideposts Books
> 16 E. 34th St.
> New York, NY 10016

JANUARY

And I saw a new heaven and a new earth: for the first heaven and the first earth were passed away; and there was no more sea. —REVELATION 21:1

S	M	T	W	T	F	S
						1
2	3	4	5	6	7	8
9	10	11	12	13	14	15
16	17	18	19	20	21	22
23	24	25	26	27	28	29
30	31					

1

S   *But, beloved, be not ignorant of this one thing, that*
A   *one day is with the Lord as a thousand years, and a*
T   *thousand years as one day.*   —II PETER 3:8

When I was a child, my Aunt Cass used to tell me how blessed I was because I would be around to see the new millennium. "You'll be part of history!" she would declare. I wasn't quite sure what the big deal was. The only handy point of comparison that came to mind was the odometer on my father's 1960 Bonneville turning over.

One thing bothered me, though. I would be ancient by the turn of the century—forty-six! I couldn't imagine being forty-six. I'd be too old to celebrate. The more I considered it, the more depressed I became. So I just stopped thinking about the millennium.

Of course, millennium fever has infected all of us these past several years. No one seems to agree on anything. Millennium purists maintain the Big Day doesn't technically arrive until January 1, 2001. But a majority of people like the sound of the nice round number 2000. Then there are the killjoys who get perverse satisfaction pointing out that many cultures don't follow our calendar anyway, and besides, any ordering of the years and centuries is necessarily arbitrary. Theologians generally accept that Christ was born in 4 or 5 B.C.

Well, here we are in that arbitrary year 2000. I am forty-six, just as I feared. It's not so bad, really. I've discovered I'm not too old to celebrate. And as Aunt Cass pointed out, I'm a part of history, and I rather enjoy it. All of the millennium arguments aside, the world seems to have agreed to celebrate this particular year as a milestone of human progress, the year when all our odometers turned over at once.

Lord, Your love is eternal; we all live in Your time.

—EDWARD GRINNAN

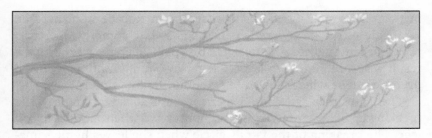

ALL THINGS NEW

"Behold, I make all things new" (Revelation 21:5). As we stand at the threshold of a new year, a new century, a new millennium, the excitement of new beginnings is in the air. Every year, every day, in every aspect of our lives, God is at work renewing, reviving, making new. Elizabeth Sherrill, at the beginning of each month, remembers moments when she has been aware of this newness breaking into the routines of her life. The promise of Daily Guideposts, 2000 *is that we can learn to discern this process at work in our lives, each day of the year.* —THE EDITORS

2 | S u N | Starting Anew

Though our outward man perish, yet the inward man is renewed day by day. —II CORINTHIANS 4:16

She's a tall, slender seventeen-year-old with long, blond hair—and an erect, graceful carriage. But our granddaughter Lindsay did not come by that perfect posture without pain.

She was twelve when we first noticed that one hip seemed a little higher than the other. Scoliosis, the doctor called it, an S-shaped curvature of the spine, which, he warned, would only get worse if uncorrected. He prescribed a body-encircling chest-to-hip brace to nudge the still growing spine into alignment.

Lindsay went into the brace in October 1994. For a Miami youngster, the rigid plastic casing was a hot and itchy torment. She wore it uncomplainingly for almost two years, but the scoliosis was no better. "The gradual approach hasn't worked," the doctor said. "We're going to have to give the spine a brand-new start."

A new start. . . . How much breaking of the old those words imply! In this case, they meant that Lindsay's back must literally be broken, in two places, and a metal-alloy Harrington Rod be implanted on each side of the newly straightened spine. The complex operation took place in August 1996, followed by a pain-filled recovery. But the result was stunning. "I'm *two inches* taller, Gran!" Lindsay reported over the phone when allowed to stand for the first time.

There are other "breaking" experiences still ahead for Lindsay. The breaking up of her close-knit high-school crowd when she goes to college. The breaking of the family circle when she leaves home someday to start a family of her own. But, like the trauma of her surgery, the pain of rupture must take place before new growth can come.

When breaking old molds hurts, Father, give me the faith that looks ahead to new beginnings. —ELIZABETH SHERRILL

Editor's note: God is calling us all to renewal as we begin this amazing year 2000. We hope you'll take time out to record the ways God is working in your life in "My Renewal Journal" at the end of each month.

3

M
O
N

Now the Lord of peace himself give you peace always by all means. The Lord be with you all.
—II THESSALONIANS 3:16

How mind-boggling it is to step over the threshold of not only a brand-new year, but a whole new century! With all the hullabaloo of celebrations all over the world, it seems insipid that my husband and I mark the turn in what has become our happiest state of being: cozied up in front of the crackle of a pinecone-fed fire in the simplicity of our own living room.

Both separately and together, we find ourselves refocusing into a mindset we call "Escape from Affluenza!" It's not that less is more, it's just that less is more than enough, which brings with it the soul-satisfying freedom of an unencumbered state. We ask the children, please, no gifts we'll have to put on a shelf and dust, no gewgaws that will sit in cupboards while we continue to use familiar things that may be out of date but are so very much a part of all we are.

We are still years behind in all the new technologies. "E-mail, Mom. You gotta have e-mail," the children tell me.

"Someday," I reply, "but till then write me a letter. One to read over and over again."

We're finding pleasure in little things: a full moon; summer rain; a hummingbird's nest outside our bedroom window; homemade soup with homemade bread; a car pulling out of a parking space just in time for us to take it. Best of all, we're finding more pleasure in each other.

Blow the whistles, bang the drums, ring the bells. Let others do the razzle-dazzle. We'll share a kiss, sip hot chocolate, listen to Mozart and quietly pray for an end to all violence to welcome what we hope will be a century of peace.

Lord of all our days, give peace as only You can give to heal a hurting world.　　　　　　　　　　　　　　　　　　　　　　—FAY ANGUS

4

T
U
E

I will lead them in paths that they have not known. . . . .　　　　　　　　—ISAIAH 42:16

My plane landed at the Raleigh-Durham airport at 9:00 P.M. With luck, I'd be in my hotel and in bed by ten. At the transport desk a burly fellow grabbed my bag and pitched it in his van. "Come on," he yelled, "we're ready to go!"

I sat next to a woman who held her hands clasped tightly in her lap. "It's my first trip to North Carolina," I said. "I'm here for the chaplains' conference." She didn't answer. We passed miles of forest. "I don't see any lights anywhere," I said. Again she didn't respond. I shrugged and looked out the window. I tried to watch for signs and began to feel anxious.

I was on the point of checking with the driver when the woman spoke. "I'm sorry," she said, "I didn't mean to be rude." Her soft voice commanded my attention. "I'm here for treatment at the clinic. The doctors don't know if they've caught it in time. The cancer, I mean."

Suddenly, the need for getting to bed seemed trivial. I patted her hand. "Please don't give up hope," I urged her. She took my hand and looked into my eyes.

The van stopped. We were in Durham. "Would you pray for me?" she asked.

"I will," I promised. She squeezed my hand as she got out.

"This is the last stop," said the driver.

"Aren't we going on to Raleigh?" I asked.

"No," he said. "This is the Durham van. We'll have to go back to the airport. I'm sorry, miss, but you won't get to Raleigh before midnight."

"That's all right," I said. "I don't feel sleepy anyway. I'm going to move up there so we can talk on the way back."

"I'm glad you're not angry," he said. "I sure would be."

"If it hadn't been for that woman who sat next to me, I probably would be mad," I said. "But now I know I was here for a reason."

Dear Lord, may I follow Your path, wherever it leads.

—SUSAN SCHEFFLEIN

5

W E D

For it is God which worketh in you both to will and to do of his good pleasure. —PHILIPPIANS 2:13

I picked up our Christmas photographs at the grocery store and flipped through them as soon as I got to the car. *Egads!* I cringed. *Who is that puffy-looking person wearing my clothes? It's time for a diet,* I resolved as I drove home. I had plenty of motivation. Our son Derek had announced his engagement, and the wedding would be in five months. *Wedding pictures last forever,* I warned myself, *and I don't want to go down in family history looking like a puffy penguin.* As a reminder of my resolve, I taped one of the bad pictures on the refrigerator.

Reluctantly, I joined a weight-loss program at our church, but I didn't have much hope. I've started plenty of diets under similar circumstances. I tape some unflattering picture of myself on the refrigerator, force myself to give up most of the stuff I like and dread the daily weigh-ins to check my progress. After a few discouraging weeks, I quit and begin to accept myself as the person in the picture on the refrigerator door.

I soon learned that this program was different. There are no weigh-ins, success isn't measured by the numbers on the scale, and motivation doesn't come from unflattering pictures. It focuses instead on faith and encouragement to become the person God created me to be. "Find a good picture of yourself, and tape it on your refrigerator," I was told. "Look at that picture every day and know that is who you are becoming."

So I've taken the bad picture off the refrigerator, and in its place is one that I like. Will this work? I don't know. I'm only at the beginning, but I'm starting with a positive picture of the person I think God created me to be, and faith that He will help me become that person.

Father, strengthen my resolve to become more like the person You created me to be—inside and out.   —CAROL KUYKENDALL

6

T
H
U

Nations shall come to your light, and kings to the brightness of your rising.   —ISAIAH 60:3 (RSV)

I often wonder what happened to the gifts of the Magi. After a particularly moving Epiphany service, I like to think about the people those gifts may have touched.

How did Mary, Jesus' young mother, view that sudden unexpected wealth? Had she been awestruck? Had she expected it? Had she put it aside, planning some day to use it for Jesus' studies with a rabbi, or for the family she hoped—like any mother—He would have? What of Joseph? Had he been forced to use some of it on the flight to Egypt and, later, on their return to Nazareth? Had the people he'd paid to help them found themselves blessed by some miracle or shining memory?

In the time I spent imagining all the goodness worked through those gifts of gold, frankincense and myrrh, my mind opened to other wonderful questions about stories in the Bible. What happened to the little boy who brought Christ the few fishes that fed five thousand? How did he feel when he heard his Miracle Worker had been crucified? After the Samaritan woman at the well brought Jesus to her town, did her life change? Did the villagers still view her as an outcast, or did she win their respect and a chance for a new start?

Usually, I put away my manger on Epiphany, but this year I'll leave it up a little longer. Maybe all year. It makes me think. What did that awestruck young shepherd tell his wife the next morning? Did that wealthy astrologer kneeling before a penniless Child treat his own servants differently when he returned home? And, if he did, did they, in turn, become gentler with their own families?

What wondrous questions come to your mind when considering Christ's life?

Lord, as I imagine how Your every act affected others, help my acts, in their small ways, to do the same.   —MARCI ALBORGHETTI

7

F
R   *He that abideth in me . . . the same bringeth forth*
I   *much fruit. . . .*   —JOHN 15:4

One of our family mottoes is "We don't cancel picnics because of dark clouds or the forecast of rain." More often than not, on occasions when we've been tempted to postpone family excursions, we've gone ahead and gotten positive results. Sometimes the weather improved dramatically by the time we reached our destination; at other times, even when the clouds cried on us a little, we made do and still had a good time.

I think there's a lesson in our picnic experience: If we always wait for perfect conditions before embarking on any endeavor, we will miss many of life's grandest opportunities. Perhaps it's faith that I'm talking about. It doesn't take faith to accomplish a sure thing. Faith is needed when the outcome is in doubt, when the odds are long, when our chances of failure make us white-knuckled and wobbly-kneed. But it is in weakness, uncertainty and insecurity that God shows us His true colors, and we often succeed beyond ourselves, accomplishing what a short time before may have seemed impossible.

A few years ago I got caught in a January snowstorm in Pennsylvania on my way to a speaking date. The roads got worse and worse, and traffic finally came to a halt at one particularly steep and slippery mountain. Some people gave up and turned back. I was tempted to do likewise, but a few "we don't cancel picnics" drivers carefully inched upward, and I joined them, eventually reaching the summit. There the clouds suddenly dissipated and the valley below glistened in sunlight like diamonds.

I got to my speaking engagement on time, but I didn't tell my listeners how close I'd come to turning back—perhaps because the subject of my talk was "Never, Never, Never Give Up."

> *Teach us, O Lord, when roadblocks appear*
> *To lean on You—and to persevere.*   —FRED BAUER

8

S   *I had a dream which made me afraid; as I lay in bed*
A   *the fancies and the visions of my head alarmed me.*
T   —DANIEL 4:5 (RSV)

About a week ago, I visited my brother Jay and his wife Adrienne in San Diego, California. Usually a night owl, I woke up very early my last morning there—shaking myself awake from a horrible nightmare, frightened and a little sheepish. I knew I was safe, yet my heart was thumping and I couldn't dispel that feeling of dread.

The early morning light seemed to hush and soften everything. Stacy, another visiting friend, was stretched out on the couch across the room, serene, snoring softly. One of my brother's cats was curled at her feet. One paw twitched in a dream, probably a happier one than mine. The Christmas tree, still celebrating the New Year, twinkled happily by the window. I took a few deep breaths and wished I could find a place in the peaceful scene.

Slipping out of my sleeping bag, I distracted myself with morning duties . . . finding the other cat, washing some dishes, helping Jay choose four giant scrambled-egg burritos at Humberto's Café. Then we settled down in front of the television to watch a movie and enjoy our burritos and tea.

The Christmas tree still twinkled, but now the cats were batting at ornaments as the movie drew us in. Stacy and Adrienne told old jokes over lulls in the plot, and Jay and I joined in their laughter. Several times, the telephone rang, and Jay leapt over scattered sleeping bags and empty tea mugs to answer it. When it was someone we all knew, he paused the movie and we passed the phone around for a friendly chat.

I found peace, not in the quiet beauty of the early morning, but in joyful noise and comfortable everyday chaos. In this warm nest of friends, I let go of my nightmare and let it be just a dream.

Lord, sometimes I still have bad dreams. Please free me from last night's fears and yesterday's worries. I want to make the very best of this new day!
—KJERSTIN EASTON

9

S
U
N

"So you also must be ready, because the Son of Man will come at an hour when you do not expect him."
—MATTHEW 24:44 (NIV)

"Next Sunday will be Judgment Day," the announcer's voice boomed from my television. I stopped lacing up my boot and looked to see who was privileged to have such information. It was a sports announcer. "The four top teams in football will meet in competition. Judgment Day will be preceded by Preparation Week."

I clicked off the TV as I headed out the door for church. Judgment

Day. What would I do if I really knew this were my last week on earth? Be a little less cynical. A little more generous. Laugh more; complain less. Read my Bible. Sing. Hug lots of people. I resolved to ask myself that question every morning.

I didn't know about those football teams, but I had a feeling it was going to be a very good "preparation" week for me.

Each day, Father, is a tangible extension of Your grace. Help me to be a good steward of the time You've given me.

—MARY LOU CARNEY

10 | M O N *Listen . . . unto me. . . .* —ISAIAH 49:1

I have two friends who've launched highly successful businesses. The first runs a chain of clothing stores in the Southwest. A plaque on my friend's desk captures her philosophy:

PLAN YOUR WORK. WORK YOUR PLAN.

She told me once that she sets targets for each week, each month, even each decade. She's right on schedule, too, her clothing empire steadily expanding. Yet the turnover among her staff is high: No manager stays more than two or three years. "It's pressure, pressure, pressure," an ex-employee told me. "She is driven by her own goals."

How different the mood in the office of the other friend. He and his family own a publishing company that is the envy of the industry. On a recent visit I found the gigantic warehouse humming to fill a big order from a nationally known department store. Employees, from clerks to top executives, stopped me to describe their work with pride.

Impressed, I asked him how much time he spent planning.

"Oh, I don't plan," he said. Then, seeing my puzzled look he added, "I listen."

I listen. How different, I thought, from trying to mold events toward some preset outcome. My second friend prays, then stays flexible, holding each decision up to God to hear what He may be saying.

We can all learn to hear God in our undertakings—but only if our own plans take second place to His.

Help me today, Father, to submit my agenda to Your perfect planning.

—JOHN SHERRILL

11

T
u
E

Trust in him at all times. . . . —PSALM 62:8

The waiting room was filled with parents, most of whom were doing no better at masking their anxiety than we were. It was 6:30 A.M., but only the babies looked sleepy. The little ones are first on the pediatric surgery schedule, perhaps because it's hard to expect a child under two to go without breakfast for very long.

We distracted ourselves by entertaining John. Aunt Beth had thoughtfully sent two "pocket trucks" for him as a special treat. As he happily rolled them over a child-size table, my thoughts zigzagged between noticing a stain on the carpet and fear over what lay ahead.

Our name was called. John was weighed, measured and dressed in hospital jammies at least five sizes too big. Andrew and I put on surgical gowns, joking as we put on caps that we now had blue hair. John giggled in delight. The anesthesiologist came in to ask questions. John climbed into a big toy car and happily bumped his way between beds in the empty recovery room. And then it was time.

In the operating room, I held John and sang to him. He panicked only when the mask came over his nose and mouth. I tried to keep my voice and his body steady. Then, in a half-minute that felt like forever, I knew the sickening sensation of feeling his little body go limp in my arms. I laid him down on the operating table. We were gently escorted to the door.

In the hallway outside, Andrew and I broke down. This was the hardest thing we'd ever done. Yet it was straightforward surgery, and we had a superb surgeon, one who obviously cared deeply about his patients and his work. Still . . . skill is nothing compared to the will of God. God can say no. Would He?

We waited.

Seventy excruciating minutes later, the surgeon appeared. "John's doing fine. The cyst was quite large, more complicated than we expected. But he is doing well."

Lord Jesus, whatever You ask of me, I must give You. Help me give it with trust that You know what is best. —JULIA ATTAWAY

12

W
E
D

May the Lord show mercy to the household of
Onesiphorus, because he often refreshed me. . . .
—II TIMOTHY 1:16 (NIV)

In a Bible study many years ago, I came across the name Onesiphorus and the simple statement of Paul, "He often refreshed me." I'm blessed these days to have a wonderful Onesiphorous in my life, an elderly lady called Sister Booker.

The other day, when I was feeling particularly tired and discouraged, the telephone rang. I picked up the phone and heard Sister Booker's voice, joyful as always, saying, "Brother Weary, God has chosen you as an eagle. An eagle has sharp vision and powerful wings. An eagle is one who rises above his troubles."

Sister Booker seems to have a knack of knowing when I'm down. Then she calls me and reminds me to use the powerful aid of the Holy Spirit to rise above my circumstances and trust Him—to be like an eagle. Her messages are always uplifting and filled with a spiritual excitement all her own. Like Paul's friend Onesiphorus, Sister Booker has the gift of encouragement and is willing to use it for the benefit of others.

We all have special gifts from God, gifts He's given us to use for the good of the entire body of Christ. When we don't use them, the body suffers. Today, I want to make a commitment to use my gifts to brighten someone's life.

Lord, thank You for Sister Booker and all those like her who use their gifts to help others. Help me to be like them.   —DOLPHUS WEARY

13

T
H
U

Do not neglect to show hospitality. . . .
—HEBREWS 13:2 (RSV)

Last night we had a wonderful Senegalese dinner, and an equally wonderful lesson in hospitality.

When we first arrived here in French-speaking West Africa, I offered to help people at the office with their English. Marc, the day watchman, immediately took me up on it. During our daily hour together we have developed a comfortable friendship. So when Marc invited us to his home for dinner, my husband Harry and I jumped at the chance.

Marc led us up the stairs and down the long hall of the big, concrete-block apartment building to the last door on the right. As we walked by an open door I glanced into the community bathroom, shared by the twenty other families living on that floor. Hanging on the wall outside the bathroom was a large sink, used by everyone for dishwashing and laundry.

Marc's wife Josienne opened their door with a smile and welcomed us into a cozy, one-room apartment. Squeezed into the twelve-square-foot room were their double bed, a dresser, a small refrigerator and a dining room table with six chairs. A tricycle perched atop the clothes cupboard, and family photos and pictures decorated the walls.

Two-year-old Thierry made himself a delightful nuisance while we happily downed glasses of the favorite local drink, *bissap*, a sweet, cranberrylike juice made from dried flower blossoms. From her tiny kitchen, a three-foot-wide balcony open to the street below, Josienne produced a wonderful dinner of garlic chicken, couscous with raisins, a sweet onion stew, salad and a dessert made of yogurt, coconut and millet. With our French-English dictionary, we stumbled our way through a delightful evening of conversation. As we left, Marc and Josienne gave us gifts: dried bissap blossoms and homemade juice, a fresh coconut and recipes for Senegalese dishes.

Before that evening, we had been ashamed to invite anyone to our small, sparsely furnished house in Dakar. Yet Marc and Josienne, who had so little in contrast to our abundance, had made us feel welcomed and loved. It was time for us to do the same.

Lord Jesus, help me to welcome people into my life and my home.

—MARY JANE CLARK

14 | F R I | *Has not God chosen those who are poor in the eyes of the world to be rich in faith . . . ?*

—JAMES 2:5 (NIV)

One very special event in my life last year was a trip to south Asia. Visiting India, Nepal and Bangladesh was enriching, challenging and thought-provoking. Like many Western visitors, I was struck by the difference in basic living conditions. Many things that have become necessary to my daily living are unknown to vast numbers of people in developing countries. Things like supermarkets, cars, indoor plumbing —even regular meals—are not a part of their everyday existence. A permanent home is unknown to millions of people who live in moveable lean-tos or tarps set up along railroads and highways. I was overwhelmed by pity for the people living in these conditions.

Then one day, I was riding on a train past miles and miles of lean-to villages. At one point, the train slowed, and we passed close to an empty field where dozens of children were playing soccer by kicking around a battered plastic soda bottle. A goal was scored, exuberance erupted, and the engineer tooted his whistle. Suddenly, all the children turned toward the train, every face radiant with a smile.

Though I spoke not a word of Hindi, I got the message: No matter how difficult life is, joy comes not from outward but from inward possessions. In those moments, my heart emptied itself of pity and was refilled with love and an awareness of how much my new friends had to offer me, even as I sought to be helpful to them.

Father, keep my heart open to the needs of others, and open my eyes to the wonder of hope and faith in the most difficult places.

—ERIC FELLMAN

15 | S A T

Behold, how good and pleasant it is for brethren to dwell together in unity! —PSALM 133:1

Just before she died in 1955, my mother told me a story of my early childhood that showed me some of the unconscious graces with which I was raised. Although the words we use to describe ethnicity have changed since then, I'll tell it exactly as I remember it.

"You were three years old," she said. "We lived on Green Street in Philadelphia, and I took you with me when we went to the corner drugstore to shop. The store was crowded, but the only other little girl was a Negro child whose mother had brought her along, too.

"We were waiting for the druggist to wait on us. You went right up to the little girl and said in a really loud voice, 'I know why you're that color.'

"Everyone in the store froze, including the druggist. I was terrified what you might say next. The Negro woman looked at me with an expression that might have been fear. Except for her and her daughter, everyone in the drugstore was white.

"'Why?' demanded her daughter.

"You said, 'Because your mommy's that color. And I'm this color because my mommy is.'

"People laughed, and the Negro woman smiled at me. Then the store went back to business as usual."

I've thought about that story a lot in the years since. We are what our parents make us. And underneath that, we're all what God makes us. God and my parents made me loving. Even at three, I knew why a little black girl and I were alike, despite our different colors.

We've come a long way in the last fifty years, Father. As we remember Dr. Martin Luther King, Jr. today, give us the will to continue walking in his footsteps.
—RHODA BLECKER

R E A D E R ' S   R O O M

"Each day a blessing on an idea comes to me as I read the *Daily Guideposts*. A victim of multiple sclerosis, I am well aware of His strengthening power. The healing journey helps me emotionally and spiritually. Here are some thoughts I had: 2/9/98—I am thankful that in this 'me' centered world there are still those that think 'you' (God) first. 2/21/98—God accepts us flaws and all. 3/10/98—Answers to prayers and I haven't even uttered. 4/13/98 —The word *hope* was shaped at the Cross."
—*Margaret McAbee, Portland, Indiana*

16

S U N

The Lord gave, and the Lord hath taken away; blessed be the name of the Lord. —JOB 1:21

When I stepped into the large, nearly windowless sanctuary of our church last Sunday, I encountered unexpected darkness. "The power's out," an usher whispered. I stood in the doorway expecting to hear him say that the service was canceled, but instead he directed me to a pew in the dim inner twilight.

How can church go on without electricity? There won't be any organ music, I thought. Just then, two men wheeled in a piano, and the sanctuary filled with music. *I'll never hear the minister without a microphone,*

I fretted. The minister stood in the pulpit and apologized for the lack of electricity in a clear, loud voice. I heard every word. *The choir won't be able to see a thing up there in that darkness,* I decided. At anthem time, the choir filed down from the dark loft and arranged themselves on the chancel steps, where sunlight drifted into the sanctuary from the side door.

As we stood and repeated the Apostle's Creed from memory, I felt a sudden burst of understanding. *My fellow churchgoers haven't let what's missing keep them from worshiping. The electricity may have been subtracted from the service, but it has only emphasized the deeper things that run on their own power. God's presence is here all the more powerfully, not despite the darkness, but because of it.* I had always assumed that God makes things new by adding something. Now I understood that things can also be transformed by subtraction.

During the offertory, the choir sang "All Hail the Power of Jesus' Name." I heard a loud whoosh as the heater fan and the lights pulsed once, twice and then stayed on for good. Perhaps I wasn't the only one a little disappointed.

Lord, as the subtracting goes on in my life, help me to add up the ways it transforms me into someone wonderfully new. —KAREN BARBER

17

M
O
N

Bless our God, O peoples, let the sound of his praise be heard. —PSALM 66:8 (RSV)

The twentieth century had barely begun when I was born in 1910. But during the almost ninety years I've been lucky enough to live, there have been more major and significant changes for the comfort, convenience and pleasure of people than ever before in human history. For example, we've gone from a world of silence to a world of sound.

When I was a little girl, the streets and houses in our small town were usually quiet, except for the shouts of children or the sounds of pianos and people singing around them. The telephone had just been invented, and not everybody had one. When you used it, you had to turn a crank and call Central, where an operator would ask, "Number, please," and get it for you. Victrolas were also new and for the privileged, and radios were almost too exciting to be real. All the movies were in black and white, and silent, except for a pianist, who tried to convey the mood of the story that the stars were pantomiming. I was in college before we actually heard their voices, and discovered that some of them, like Gloria Swanson, could sing!

Now we live in a world full of sounds: TV and radio, stereo boom boxes and portable CD players. Great music is easier to listen to than ever before in history, and a sermon or hymn is as close as the nearest portable radio or cassette player. But all this progress has had its price: It's hard to find a quiet street in our cities and towns, and birdsong isn't so easy to hear on a summer's day. And now, as then, when we want to talk to God, it's best to sit in silence.

Lord, thank You for the feast of sounds You give us to enjoy. No matter what else I may listen to, help me always to listen to You.

—MARJORIE HOLMES

18

T
U
E

Ye shall do no unrighteousness in judgment . . . but in righteousness shalt thou judge thy neighbor.
—LEVITICUS 19:15

Louise, who lives next door to me, is something of a recluse, keeping pretty much to her house. She had always been cordial when I caught her in her yard, but my visits to her house were few, confined to the kitchen area via the back door. When I found out that she was in the hospital, I didn't visit. She had told me that when she was sick she preferred to be left alone—no visits, no phone calls, not even cards. Her husband and sons confirmed this every time I asked after her.

So just let her live in her house, I told myself, and I'll live in mine. If she doesn't want to be a good neighbor, I won't bother her.

Then winter arrived, and Louise came home from her long hospital stay. A few weeks later, my morning paper began appearing on the front porch, rather than at the end of my driveway, folded and laid flat against the front door. I'd tried to thank the early-morning walkers in our neighborhood, but they all denied doing it.

One cold, rainy morning I rose much earlier than usual and headed toward the front door. As I opened it, I saw Louise in her robe and slippers headed toward the porch, my paper in her hand. "So you're the one!" I called to her. "I wondered who was being so thoughtful of me."

She shrugged slightly and smiled. "I go out to pick up my paper," she said, "and I just get yours, too. I know you sleep later than I do. It could get soaked, or a dog might take it."

How lightly she treated it! This dear woman, whom I thought cold and unneighborly, was quietly adding a bit of comfort to my life. Just because she wasn't an outgoing person, I'd failed to see—or even imagine—the sweetness of her spirit.

Father, help me open my eyes and my spirit to the goodness with which You surround me.   —DRUE DUKE

19

W
E
D

He changeth the times and the seasons: he removeth kings, and setteth up kings. . . .   —DANIEL 2:21

When it comes to modern technology, I'm something of a Luddite. I have no tolerance for the small, portable cell phones that people use everywhere. *Can't they enjoy a little peace and quiet away from the phone?* I wonder.

Then came a midwinter's day when I was taking a train from Manhattan out to a suburb on Long Island to tape a TV show about prayer. Unfamiliar with the route, I became alarmed when the train slowed to a crawl between stations and came to a complete stop. We remained there for half an hour with little explanation. "We hope to be moving shortly," the conductor kept saying.

Dear Lord, how can I let the people at the TV station know where I am?

As the agitation of the crowd increased, the gentleman sitting next to me took a cell phone out of his briefcase. He stepped to the back of the train. "I'm sorry," I heard him say, "the train seems to be having some trouble. I'm going to be late."

Swallowing my pride, I asked him, "Can I borrow your phone for a minute?"

"Sure," he said.

I, too, stepped to the back of the train and called the TV station. I was quickly reassured that there would be no problem. I could be picked up at the next stop.

At least I'll have a good example for our discussion on prayer, I thought. *And maybe a little more tolerance for modern technology.*

Help me, Lord, to see the difference between a modern nuisance and a modern convenience, and not be controlled by either one.

—RICK HAMLIN

20
T
H
U

Is his mercy clean gone for ever? —PSALM 77:8

One day back in 1995, I told God that I didn't see how I could endure caring for another family member with cancer after my first husband Jerry had died of the disease in 1983. Now my mother's cancer had recurred after nearly ten years, and she'd come to live with my husband Gene and me. It wasn't just my fear of losing Mother, it was the battle I dreaded. Cancer just doesn't fight fair. I asked God for a word of encouragement. He often seems to speak to me when I run. As I turned the corner and headed down the road, a word popped into my mind and sat there as though it belonged: *Gone.*

"No, Lord. I hate that word. It's scary."

Gone.

"That's such a final word, Lord. I wish You hadn't given me that word."

Gone.

"Lord, why are You giving me that unmerciful word. . . ."

Gone, Marion, as in "The cancer will be gone." All gone.

I stopped running, and still breathing hard, looked up into the cloudless sky for a sign, confirmation, some signal—anything to let me know that what I'd heard was from God. Cars zoomed by me, and all I saw was a dot of an airplane disappearing silently. Had it been my imagination? Was it wishful thinking?

Mother didn't progress with radiation as well as the doctor had hoped, and she flatly refused chemotherapy. Amazingly, a bone scan in 1997 showed a reduction of her disease. Her walking still wasn't very good, though, and I so dreaded the bone scan in 1998 that I didn't even call the doctor to ask about it; his nurse called me. "Hi, Marion," she said. "Your mother's bone scan shows no cancer."

"You mean no new cancer?"

"No. No cancer. We will need to treat the arthritis that's showed up, but the cancer appears to be . . . gone."

O merciful Lord, I had no idea that gone could be such a wonderful word. Thank You. —MARION BOND WEST

21

F
R
I

My voice shalt thou hear in the morning, O Lord; in the morning will I direct my prayer unto thee, and will look up. —PSALM 5:3

Whenever I'm tempted to skip my morning prayer time, I think about making gumbo. A good seafood gumbo, chock-full of shrimp, crab meat, okra and bay leaf, is a favorite dish around South Louisiana where we live. Its rich, full flavor can be achieved in only one way. My mother told me the secret the first time I asked her how to make gumbo: "First you make a roux."

Like all Southern cooks, my mother knew that a rich, dark brown roux is the basis for a good pot of gumbo. And she also knew that a roux can't be hurried. Here's how you make it: Heat a little oil or lard in a heavy cast-iron skillet. Add an equal amount of flour, then stir slowly and constantly until the roux is a rich, dark brown color. It takes about an hour.

My early pots of gumbo reflect the impatience of my youth. My sister Sandi and I attempted to make our first pot of gumbo together. We stirred and stirred, waiting anxiously for the roux to turn the desired color. Our impatience got the best of us. We moved on to the next step and ended up with a gumbo that looked like chicken noodle soup. We telephoned our mom. "What did we do wrong?"

"First you make a roux," she said. "A dark brown roux. If you want a good gumbo, then you've got to take the time to make a good roux."

My prayer in the mornings is a lot like a roux, full of color. When I give it the time it deserves, it makes my day rich. It gives me the patience I need to teach 150 high school students each day. It gives me gratitude for a family that will be clamoring for dinner in the evening. The time I spend in prayer is the basis for my entire day.

So when the thought of the tasks ahead of me tempts me to skip my prayer time or end it too quickly, I always hear my mother's voice: "First you make a roux."

Loving Father, getting up early to talk with You is a small price to pay for peace I carry with me throughout the day. —MELODY BONNETTE

22 | S A T

The Lord said to Moses . . . "Tell the people of Israel to go forward." —EXODUS 14:15 (RSV)

My little blue airplane trembles in the cold January breeze, like a frightened butterfly sitting on a freeway. I'm ready for my solo flight. The runway stretches out before me, a millennium long and as wide as the world. Powder-sugared with fresh snow, it's almost too pretty to ruin with tire tracks.

I run through my preflight checks. The propeller flips slowly around with a *chuppeta, chuppeta, chuppeta,* and my heart beats in syncopation.

Forty years I have longed for this moment, made mountains of model planes as a boy and devoured dozens of aviation books. Now that the moment is here, I am tormented with doubts. *Do I have the right stuff for this? Can I afford these lessons? Can I justify the expense? What if I crack up a thirty-thousand dollar machine? What if I get lost and have to land on a busy highway? What if I fail the flight test?*

I whisper a prayer, palm the throttle knob and shove it firmly to the panel. With a throaty roar, the plane weaves down the runway and claws at the sky. As the earth drops away, so do my doubts, driven out by inexpressible joy that I—with no help from anyone—am flying an airplane!

You've been there yourself—at the springboard of success or the drop-off of disaster. *Should I marry this man or not? Should I sign up for this class? Shall we have another child? Shall I accept this job promotion?*

"Look before you leap" is good generic advice, but if I look too long I may never know the joy of soaring on the wings of resolution. Like the ancient Israelites, I find that the sea parts for me only when I go forward.

Here I go, Lord. Hold on to me as I go forward with faith in You.

—DANIEL SCHANTZ

23 | S U N

"Bring my sons from afar and my daughters from the ends of the earth—everyone who is called by my name, whom I created for my glory, whom I formed and made." —ISAIAH 43:6-7 (NIV)

I was sitting in our prayer group one Sunday after a week of especially grim news stories: murders, child abuse, corruption in government. Our tiny circle felt weighed down by these and by all the problems we ourselves had brought into the room. In despair, I said glumly, "How does this world keep going? It seems like all these problems would overwhelm it."

A middle-aged grandmother leaned forward, eyes suddenly sparkling. "Why, we're forgetting how large our circle really is. There are millions of us who follow God, who each day, in His name, pick up the jobs we've been given and do them to the best of our ability. All over the world, this very minute, people like us are sending up prayers. There are more of us than you think when you're reading the papers."

Her reminder brought sighs of relief. The mood shifted. Our load had lightened. We smiled at one another, fellow laborers in a world where God still reigns, despite the bad news.

The next time I feel outnumbered, weighed down and weary, I'll remember this truth. And when I read the paper, I'll keep the bad news in perspective.

Lord, help me to do my part and leave those who don't do their part to You.　　　　　　　　　　　　　　　　　　　　—SHARI SMYTH

24
M O N

I will put a fleece of wool in the floor; and if the dew be on the fleece only, and it be dry upon all the earth beside, then shall I know. . . .　　—JUDGES 6:37

"You're crazy staying in Nashville," my colleague was saying. "If I had an offer from a New York investment firm, I'd be gone like a shot from a gun."

Maybe I'm wrong to stay put, I thought to myself. *I like my clients, and I care about what happens to them. But I could really advance in the business if I went to Wall Street.* Then I remembered a sermon my dad had preached from the sixth chapter of Judges.

"Gideon faced a difficult decision," Dad had said, "so he asked God for a sign. Even today, there are times when God will make a path as clear as a flashing light, and other times when God doesn't mark one choice because many choices are acceptable. It's up to us to be faithful and invite God into our choices. Pray. And then listen."

So that's what I decided to do: Like Gideon, I asked God for a "fleece." "God," I prayed, "I'm asking you to send me a sign. Send someone to guide me through this time of uncertainty."

Just two days later I received a phone call from John Beasley. John has worked on and off Wall Street in the investment business for more than twenty years. "I'll be in Nashville tomorrow," John said, "and I thought we might get together for lunch." The next day, I found myself sitting across a table from him. I voiced my concerns, and he responded with just the right questions. Seeing my work from his perspective, I realized how much I liked being exactly where I was.

You might call John's phone call a coincidence, but I don't think so. I believe his visit was God's answer to my "fleece." The truth is, I don't always know what's best for me, but God does. And if, as my dad says, I pray and then listen, God's answer will come.

God, thanks for listening to me. Thanks for answering.

—BROCK KIDD

25 | T u E   *The Lord is near to the brokenhearted, and saves the crushed in spirit.*   —PSALM 34:18 (RSV)

When my daughter was married two years ago, I discovered a reservoir of sadness over my own failed marriage. At the time, God provided friends to help me cope with my pain, and I thought it had gone. But my middle child Phil is to be married this summer, and my pain, I'm discovering, is still there.

When I was a child, my sisters and I were each given a large chocolate pencil. I hadn't had mine long when it broke. I was disconsolate. When my father came home, I went to him in tears with the two halves of my broken treasure. He sat me on his lap and, when I was all cried out, told me to fetch the matches and a candle from the mantel.

"Why?" I wanted to know, sniffing through my lingering tears.

"Watch and see."

Dad melted the broken ends of my pencil over the flickering flame, then quickly pressed the sticky chocolate together. A few slow spins over the flame and he was able to smooth the lumpy joining. When he handed me back my pencil, it was wondrously repaired and, though not as good as new, all the dearer to me. What had once been broken, my father had made whole.

Today, while praying again for the healing of my sadness, I remembered my father and that chocolate pencil and I prayed:

Heavenly Father, I bring You the pain of broken dreams, knowing that whatever is broken, You can make whole. —BRENDA WILBEE

26 | W E D

There is a way that seems right to a man, but in the end. . . . —PROVERBS 14:12 (NIV)

"I never dream about Chase. I dream about Lanea, but I never dream about Chase," I told my friend Portia over lunch, Chinese food with green tea. My daughter Lanea was eleven and my son Chase, three. Divorce and death had taken their fathers from their lives. During Lanea's earlier years we had spent significant time together. Chase, however, had to compete with a job that held me in its grasp sometimes ten or twelve hours a day.

"I don't think I'm spending enough time with him. I'm always tired. I'm always nervous. I'm always cranky. I'm always getting sick. If I could quit, I would."

"You can," Portia said.

I had my life all planned. By the time I was twenty-nine, I had already achieved my major career goal. After two years, I could not think of a single individual on my side of the corporate web who was happy. Smiles and calm, peaceful demeanors were in short supply. "Is this all there is?" I asked, paraphrasing a popular song.

I listened to Portia—and to the still, small voice speaking within me. Boxing up all our things, packing away my fears, we moved to rural North Carolina. We lived in a small trailer in the middle of the woods, with farms all around us. Poor in possessions, we grew richer in love. And we learned about one another.

When we returned to the city two years later, we returned with stronger faith, with the ability to find pleasure in small, simple things. We carried with us the personal relationship we had each developed with God. My career isn't what it was before I moved to the country, but I smile a lot more.

My children, I believe, are more assured of my love and more courageous. They're less impressed with brand names and labels. And at night, when I dream, I dream of them both.

Lord, help me to hear Your voice and follow You. —SHARON FOSTER

27 | T
H
U

Give thanks to him and praise his name.
—PSALM 100:4 (NIV)

When my wife Barbara and I knew that our trip would take us through Oklahoma, we decided to see our longtime friends Wilbur and Gladys Lewis, who lived in the greater Oklahoma City area. They had served for several years as medical missionaries in South America and then returned to Oklahoma where Wilbur built a successful surgical practice and Gladys finished a Ph.D. in English literature and joined the faculty of the university.

Recently, tragedy had struck them while they were in Colorado, combining a medical meeting for Wilbur with a family skiing vacation. In a freak accident, Wilbur's spinal cord was severed. He was rushed to the trauma center in Colorado Springs, where he lingered at the point of death for days. Though he was finally stabilized, extensive tests held no hope that he would recover the use of his arms or legs.

Wilbur's hospital bed was in the center of the living room so people who came by could sit with him. He insisted that visits from friends were good medicine. It was midafternoon, and Gladys made what she called a "British tea"—little sandwiches, cookies and steaming cups of tea. When she set the tray on the stand beside his bed, Wilbur said that he wanted to say grace, so we bowed our heads for prayer. He thanked God for the day and for our being together again. But he caught me totally off-guard when he added, "And we thank you for the health that each of us enjoys."

For a moment I couldn't even speak. Then, as we shared the refreshments, I replayed his words in my mind. They come back to me each time I'm tempted to complain about something in my life.

Lord, help me always to find joy in praising You, whatever the circumstances.
—KENNETH CHAFIN

28

F
R
I

What? Know ye not that your body is the temple of the Holy Ghost . . . ? —I CORINTHIANS 6:19

I was an outdoor walker for more than thirty years. Two years ago, weather and work cut my walking sessions from five times a week down to three . . . then two . . . then sometimes to none. I felt guilty, but decided exercise wasn't really that important. In a few years, life would slow down and I'd start walking again. Then I attended a health conference where a leading researcher targeted "sedentary lifestyle" as the major threat to the health of Americans. "You"—the speaker looked right at me—"can add years to your life, help prevent a variety of diseases and save medical resources by exercising for thirty minutes three times each week. It's the most important thing you can do for your life, health and pocketbook."

My co-workers urged me to find a different method of exercise. "Join my aerobics class," Sandy said, but my travel schedule made that impossible. Helen suggested weights, but I despised them. And my husband's exercise bike was boring and hurt my knees.

Then I stepped on my sister Amanda's treadmill. Walking again felt great, and two weeks later I bought a treadmill of my own. It has ten preset workouts ranging from steady progress to interval training. There is a program to test my fitness. I can also design my own workouts—fast or slow, uphill or level, or any combination. Best of all, I can choose my age and weight! It's amazing! By going nowhere, I'm actually traveling the road to a healthier heart, more strength and stamina, and a trimmer body. And because the treadmill sits in my air-conditioned, electricity-lit bedroom, it's never too hot, cold, windy or dark to walk.

Are you going nowhere in your quest for better health? Try a dance class, aerobics, handball or even a treadmill. One of them will be just the thing for taking care of the temple God has given each of us.

Lord, You gave me my body just as surely as You gave me my spirit. Help me give glory to You by keeping fit. —PENNEY SCHWAB

29

S
A
T

Thou shalt love thy neighbor as thyself. . . .
—LEVITICUS 19:18

Early on a Saturday morning, my husband and I woke up in a lovely, old-fashioned bed-and-breakfast room. We were due at a prayer breakfast in what seemed a very short time. I took the plunge, jumped out of bed and ran over to the window. There was snow—lots of it— and our car, parked beneath the window, looked like an igloo. "Edward, get up," I urged. "We don't even have a scraper."

We began to get ready in disgruntled haste, not at all the right frame of mind for gathering to pray. And I was responsible for the opening words.

Suddenly, I heard an odd rhythmic noise, like a distant lawn mower. Hairbrush in hand, I walked over to the window. There below me was the hooded figure of a fellow guest whose acquaintance we had made only briefly the night before. As quietly as he could, he was cleaning the snow off our car windows. He had already finished his own car parked next to ours.

I drew a deep breath as I let the curtain fall into place. Someone, almost a stranger, without fuss was smoothing our path that early morning. Scraper in hand, he was loving his neighbor in practical fashion. Clearly he planned to drive off unseen. I had no difficulty with that day's opening prayer, entitled, as it happened, "For Others."

Dear God, bless those who care for others in so many ways and ask for no reward. —BRIGITTE WEEKS

30

S
U
N

God saw all that He had made, and behold, it was very good. And there was evening and there was morning, the sixth day. —GENESIS 1:31 (NAS)

I have been a pastor for twenty-four years. As I write these words, I blink in disbelief. It seems like only yesterday when I was ordained at age twenty-three in a small rural church in Kentucky.

Over this last quarter-century I've written a lot of sermons: 576, to be exact. If there is one thing in my life that is constant, it is that weekly Sunday sermon. I've almost always enjoyed the experience of preaching. I have a passion for this task. But the preparation for preaching is another matter. How many times on Saturday have I buried my face in my hands and said, "Lord, I need one more day! One more day before Sunday!"

The fact is that all of us lead busy lives. Seldom are we prepared to perform our tasks to the extent that we would like. But morning comes and we must go to work: perform the surgery; face the jury; teach the class; cook the dinner; sing the aria; plow the field; parent the child; brief the general; coach the game; preach the sermon. Despite our lack of preparation, the show must go on.

I used to feel guilty about not being as prepared as I believed I should be. After all, hadn't my preaching professor said that I should spend an hour in the study for every minute in the pulpit? That's twenty hours a week on a short-winded Sunday! But what about all the other things that demand my time and attention?

I've come to see that excellence is found in the balance between doing the very best I can do and accepting the fact that there will always be more to accomplish at the end of each day.

The Book of Genesis tells us that God created the world in six days and "it was very good." But God was not finished. He is still working. Still perfecting His creation. Still in the process of bringing history to its culmination and the imperfect to perfection. If God is still not through, perhaps there is hope for me, too.

Dear God, in my quest to do my best, help me to be patient with myself.
—SCOTT WALKER

31 | M O N | *But the godly shall flourish like palm trees, and grow tall as the cedars of Lebanon. . . . Even in old age they will still produce fruit and be vital and green.*
—PSALM 92:12,14 (TLB)

When my daughter Julia turned twenty-eight in 1999, she whined about her age. "I can't believe I'm this old!" she said wistfully. "I think I'm going to start counting backward. I'm telling everyone I'm twenty-six. In two years I'll be twenty-four."

I started thinking about the fact that Jeanne, my oldest daughter, would be thirty years old three weeks later. Then I started feeling old. How could I have a thirty-year-old daughter? Where did the years go?

Not long after that I received a printed invitation to my friend Alice's jubilee celebration. On January 30, 1999, she celebrated her forty-ninth birthday, which to Alice meant that she was gloriously stepping into her fiftieth year . . . her jubilee year. She invited more than a hundred women friends to a hall for dinner and a program. More than seventy of us were able to attend.

The room was decorated with brightly colored balloons and flowers everywhere. After dinner, Alice talked with grace and deep appreciation about the women who had been the most influential in her life. There were hugs, tears, laughter and prayers. Then she darkened the room and lit a candle, and as each woman in turn lit her candle from the candle of the woman next to her, we all mentioned one, two or three women who had been the most positive influential forces in our lives. Many mentioned their own mothers or favorite aunts. Others named famous women—poets, writers, politicians, Mother Teresa.

By the time we left Alice's jubilee celebration, we were so happy to be alive that I practically flew home on the tail of one of those brightly colored balloons. Alice had made us feel wise and cherished and, most of all, appreciative of the age we had each attained.

Personally, I can't wait until October 2000 when I turn fifty-five.

Lord, thank You for the strength to age gracefully. Help me to make each year a wiser one.   PATRICIA LORENZ

My Renewal Journal

1 _____

2 _____

3 _____

4 _____

5 _____

6 _____

7 _____

8 _____

9 _____

10 _____

11 _____

12 _____

13 _____

14 _____

15 _____

16 _____

17 _____

18 _____

19 _____

20 _____

21 _____

22 _____

23 _____

24 _____

25 _____

26 _____

27 _____

28 _____

29 _____

30 _____

31 _____

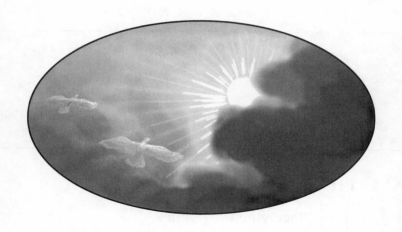

FEBRUARY

And God shall wipe away all tears from their eyes; and there shall be no more death, neither sorrow, nor crying, neither shall there be any more pain: for the former things are passed away. —REVELATION 21:4

S	M	T	W	T	F	S
		1	2	3	4	5
6	7	8	9	10	11	12
13	14	15	16	17	18	19
20	21	22	23	24	25	26
27	28	29				

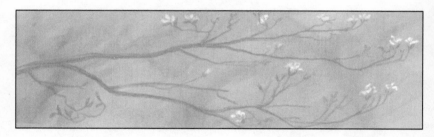

ALL THINGS NEW

1   T   **Receiving Provision**
      U   *I have showed thee new things from this time. . . .*
      E   —ISAIAH 48:6

Years ago, I was given a copy of the Lord's Prayer in French and got a new look at the phrase *Give us this day our daily bread.* To me there'd always been something unappealing in the word *daily*. Ho-hum, the same old thing, each day a repeat of the day before.

The French translate Jesus' words slightly differently: *Donne-nous aujourd'hui notre pain de ce jour.* "Give us today our bread for this day." For *this* day alone, I thought with new understanding. A day I've never lived before, when God's provision will be as unique as the unforeseeable demands of the next twenty-four hours.

Then I went to live in France and discovered how literal the phrase *bread for this day* actually is. From my apartment window in Normandy, it seemed to me that every passerby was carrying a long, crusty loaf: the laborer on his bicycle; the housewife with her mesh carryall; the schoolboy running his *baguette* along the iron railing. Bread for that day—and that day only, as I discovered when I tried to buy a supply ahead, as I'd always done at home, and next morning threw away some loaf-shaped rocks.

It was no hardship to buy bread fresh each day, for a bakery was always nearby. From almost every corner came the aroma of loaves hot from the oven.

Today's bread—what an apt image of God's provision! Given as we need it, close at hand, ever new.

Father, give me new bread for this new day.

—ELIZABETH SHERRILL

2

W
E
D

Thorns and thistles will grow up and cover their altars. . . . —HOSEA 10:8 (NIV)

One of our friends helps run a ranch in south Texas, where the country is rough, dry and immense. Pastures don't provide lush grazing for cattle, but they are full of prickly pear, a type of cactus that is rich in protein and water. To the cattle, who like the cactus, the prickly thorns pose a real problem—they hurt their mouths! So cowboys with portable butane burners ride horseback through the fields and burn off the thorns. The cattle hear the butane burner and come running. They know the "good stuff" is now available.

Sometimes when life gets thorny, I wish I could make the problem go away so easily. I much prefer the good stuff without the pain. Yet as my husband Joe's and my parents age, we have found that the good times are laced with some prickly problems. And the process of raising our teenagers is not without its barbs. But God hasn't promised to remove the thorns. He has just promised that there is good stuff underneath.

Father, thank You for Your Word and Your presence to keep us going when times are rough. And thank You for the blessings that hide under thorns. —MARJORIE PARKER

3

T
H
U

To live is Christ. . . . —PHILIPPIANS 1:21

Many years ago, on a snowy winter's day, I interviewed the late Dr. Karl Menninger at the famous Topeka, Kansas, clinic that bears his family's name. I remember several things about my all-day visit, particularly his concern about my frosted hands and feet (the first thing we did was share a cup of hot chocolate by the fire) and his graciousness in giving so freely of his time. But what sticks with me to this day is the answer the revered physician gave to my question, "What do we need to be whole, fulfilled, healthy-minded individuals?"

He leaned back in his chair and pondered my query for some time before responding. "Everyone needs two things. First, we need a work to do that we consider important and someone to assure us that our efforts are indeed worthwhile. And second, we need someone to love who loves us in return."

I find a beautiful simplicity in his answer, one that synthesizes the hopes and dreams all people harbor, and I've shared his words with many others over the years, particularly those struggling to find purpose and meaning in their lives. And though this "secret of well-being and happiness" seems uncomplicated enough, finding a work we love or a long-term relationship anchored by love are, for many, frustratingly elusive.

I thought about Dr. Menninger's words the other day while reading Romans 8, which includes St. Paul's answer to the question, "Who shall separate us from the love of Christ?" "Neither death, nor life," he writes, "nor angels, nor principalities, nor powers, nor things present, nor things to come, nor height, nor depth, nor any other creature, shall be able to separate us from the love of God, which is in Christ Jesus our Lord."

Teach me, God,

> *Not so much to ponder life, but live it,*
> *Not so much to seek love as to give it.*

—FRED BAUER

4 | F R I | *Then Jesus told his disciples a parable to show them that they should always pray. . . .*
—LUKE 18:1 (NIV)

Even though it was seven years old, our shiny "new" van was a vast improvement over our battered fourteen-year-old four-wheel-drive utility vehicle. It started, even in cold weather, never stalled when turning and shifted into reverse without complaint. It never leaked oil or smelled of gasoline. The radio, tape deck and air conditioner all worked. I could even haul my three children, plus a friend, each in comfort. With its glossy paint and an uncracked windshield, we nicknamed the handsome van Silver Belle.

I had been enjoying Silver Belle for a week or two when I noticed I no longer prayed while I was driving. While I owned the older vehicle, I had invariably started my morning with petitions: *Lord, please let her start! God, don't let me get stuck in the driveway! Lord, let that noise be something harmless and that gas smell be from somewhere else!* After the old vehicle grudgingly sputtered to life on the ninth or tenth attempt, I would mutter a quick prayer of thanksgiving, then head to my substitute-teaching job, continuing to pray about other matters. Now that I drove a vehicle that started, I forgot to pray at all!

I've had to jump-start my prayer life. Instead of asking my heavenly Father for help when I buckle my seat belt, I remember to say, "Thank You, Lord, for a safe vehicle." Most days I can easily think of more blessings to acknowledge: my healthy children; the day's work; the dramatic Wyoming vistas on the way to school. I still ask God for help when I need it, but I try to remember to say thank You even when I don't need to say please.

Lord, let me always be grateful for answered prayer.

—GAIL THORELL SCHILLING

5 S A T *I sought the Lord, and he heard me, and delivered me from all my fears.* —PSALM 34:4

Some people can take tragedy and heartache and overcome them with determination and a loving spirit. My friend Naomi Wilden, who passed away in 1999, was one of those special people. A few years ago, when she was battling a devastating illness, she wrote us this letter:

> During the last year I have had three operations for cancer, the last one involving the amputation of my right arm and shoulder. I have been so thankful for God's presence during this time.
>
> I had quite a struggle deciding whether to let the doctors do the extensive surgery they felt was necessary. I read the chapter "How To Use Faith in Healing" in *The Power of Positive Thinking* several times and prayed for guidance. I came to the conclusion that the best thing to do was to let the doctors do all they could and trust God for the rest. Once I was able to put myself completely in His hands I found peace and was able to go to the operating room without fear.
>
> I made a very rapid recovery and now, eight weeks after surgery, am making preparations to be fitted with an artificial arm. I have been amazed at the way I have been able to accept this handicap without bitterness and depression.

We may not have to undergo trials as daunting as Naomi's, but whatever cross we're called on to bear, we can do nothing better than to put ourselves "completely in His hands."

Lord, may I have sufficient courage and faith in You to pass through adversity when it strikes my life. Amen. —RUTH STAFFORD PEALE

6

S
U
N

Thou art there. —PSALM 139:8

One Sunday morning, while visiting a friend's church, I was intrigued by the pastor's method of creating a children's sermon. Each week he asks a child to take home the Sermon-in-a-Box shoebox and put something inside. The following week the pastor opens the box and builds his children's talk around whatever is inside. This particular Sunday, a couple of toothpicks reminded him of the story of David and Goliath. My friends told me he's made children's sermons out of everything from fresh fruit to teddy bears.

I marveled at what seemed to be a unique gift for finding God in the mundane and everyday. But then I began to think perhaps the gift is not in finding God in everything so much as in looking for Him. Anyone can find God's awesome power in the Grand Canyon, but do I even think to look for it in the lovely roses that bloom every spring outside my front door? Or in the moment when I'm thinking of a friend with whom I've been out of touch who suddenly calls to say she was thinking of me too?

Once I began looking for God in all things, especially the tiny moments, I discovered He is everywhere in my life—in the reliable instincts of the little cactus wren who's carefully building a nest inside the tall saguaro in my front yard; in the emotional power of a sculpted angel at a nearby retreat center, such stunning beauty magically brought forth from a hunk of rock that I must stop to admire it; in the friend who offers just the right words of encouragement on a tough day. These small discoveries of God's constant presence bring great comfort. Now I try to see God every day in some small thing, and as always, He does not disappoint me.

Where can I find You, God? In all things, if I only will look.
—GINA BRIDGEMAN

7 | M
  | O   *To give . . . to the young man knowledge and*
  | N   *discretion.*   —PROVERBS 1:4

One evening a friend invited me to attend a basketball game between two junior high school teams. The game was exciting, and I marveled at a six-foot-four-inch player on the winning team. I asked my friend his name. "That's Chad, and he's only fourteen!"

A few days later, the telephone rang. "Mr. Greene, this is Chad's father," the caller said. "Are you a counselor?" I explained that I had been a youth worker at a community center and that I had taught Sunday school, but I wasn't a counselor. "Would you talk to Chad this afternoon?" he asked. Hesitantly, I agreed.

In a little while, Chad and his dad arrived. When we were alone, Chad told me his story. He enjoyed school and was a straight-A student. On the basketball court, he worked to polish his skills and improve his play as a member of the team. Everything had gone well until a few months before, when Chad was asked to join a gang. When he refused, the gang members grew threatening. Chad said nothing to his parents or the school officials about the harassment. Then one day at school, the gang leader threatened Chad with bodily harm. Chad lashed out and knocked his tormentor unconscious. He was suspended from school for ten days.

Chad's world crumbled. He was worried that he wouldn't be accepted back by his teachers, his classmates and the basketball team. And even more troubling was the knowledge that he had used his strength to harm another. Chad felt all alone. We talked for two hours. Before he left, I gave him a copy of a story I had written about my own struggles to overcome prejudice.

A few weeks later, I got a letter from Chad. He had returned to school jittery about his reception. But the teachers and his classmates greeted him warmly, and the principal hugged him. He was home!

Chad and I learned something from each other: With God's help, a hurting experience can increase our inner strength, and it can lead to victory.

Lord of all, thank You for Your gifts of listening and learning—and for fine young men like Chad.   —OSCAR GREENE

8

"This time I will praise the Lord. . . ."
—GENESIS 29:35 (NIV)

A few weeks ago my husband Bill and I took a deep breath and invested in a new computer. His old desktop was a 386-speed, and my laptop had only eight megs of memory. Using the new computer was like going from the Wright brothers' flyer to the 747 jumbo jet.

I soon found that there were several ways to get to the specific program I wanted to use. The "shortcut key" quickly became my favorite method. This key is actually a small picture at the bottom of my screen. All I have to do is put my mouse arrow on that picture, click once and up comes the program, ready to go. Other procedures work, but this is by far the fastest one.

A few days ago I found myself worrying over something I couldn't do anything about. I quickly became frustrated. From years of experience, I know that sooner or later, I will break away from the fear and fight through into the peace of the Lord. I also know that there are several ways to get there: confession, reason, Scripture, prayer— all will eventually work. This time I was impatient with the process.

"Lord, I need a 'shortcut key' to get from worry to peace!" I prayed.

Almost instantly, one word popped into my head: *Praise!*

I began to thank God for all the little things I could think of: the hummingbird on the window feeder; the green of the woods behind the house; something wonderful that had happened in my son's life that week. Then I thanked God for the ways He had always delivered me from worry and fear before.

In a very few moments, the worry was gone. The shortcut key of praise had opened me up to God's presence and peace. I was on my way again.

Lord, thank You that sometimes You have a 'shortcut key' that will help me soar over the details and get to Your heart.

—ROBERTA ROGERS

A PLACE OF MY OWN

Do you sometimes think you have to get away from home if you want to be closer to God? Do you go on retreats to secluded places or make pilgrimages to hallowed shrines? We all sometimes feel as if God will be more available to us over the next hill or in the big church in the next town. But the signs of God's presence are all around us every day, and if we often take them for granted, all we have to do is learn to look at them with newly opened eyes. Over the course of the year, Van Varner invites us to share seven stories of the people and things that have turned his apartment on New York's Upper West Side into "A Place of My Own." —THE EDITORS

9 | W
  | E | *And he that sent me is with me: the Father hath not*
  | D | *left me alone. . . .* —JOHN 8:29

The apartment house I live in has twenty floors inhabited by a vast spectrum of people, of varying careers and a mix of religions. During the long years of my residency, I have seen babies grow into adults, strong men and women turn rickety with age, the whole picture of life and death. Yet, if I meet a fellow tenant in the elevator, we will exchange only a few thoughts about the weather. On the street, I will always get a friendly nod, but that is all. Nothing more. That I have never been invited to his apartment or he to mine is a matter of New York living. In a community as densely populated as ours, privacy is paramount.

A few years ago I had a stroke and was hospitalized for a month. It was then that I reevaluated my notion of neighborliness, for one day in the hospital I had a most unusual visitor.

"May I come in?" said a lady whom I recognized as Mrs. Lieb, who lives in the apartment above me.

"Yes," I blurted out. "*Yes.*"

She asked me how I was getting along, let me know the news "back home." We talked a bit about her delving into photography, and then, as she was leaving, she said sweetly, "We have missed you." I was overcome.

The next day, Mr. and Mrs. Kornwald from the nineteenth floor came to see me. I was equally surprised. From that time on, gradually, the cards and notes from the apartment house made me realize, at last, that privacy was paramount—up to a point. For twenty-five years, I hadn't been living alone at all.

Today, if I see a fellow tenant, say Mrs. Lieb, I'll say something about the weather or ask how the photography is coming along, then she goes her way and I go mine. I am happy with all the residents here, and am just as glad that I still have not been invited into anyone else's apartment.

You and I know, Lord, that I have never lived alone. —VAN VARNER

10

T
H
U

How beautiful upon the mountains are the feet of him who brings good tidings. . . . —ISAIAH 52:7 (RSV)

When I had a house full of small children in the sixties and seventies, I desperately longed to communicate with adults. One small daily ritual helped to keep me going: the arrival of the mailman. I watched eagerly for him while folding diapers, peeling potatoes or giving a baby a bottle. The squeaking of brakes, followed by the sight of the white truck trimmed in blue and red, never failed to give me hope. I'd just begun to write articles, and I dreamed that one day the mailman would leave me a letter of acceptance. Despite the many rejection slips, I continued to write and watch.

When at long last letters of acceptance began to mingle with the rejection slips, I was ecstatic. Even better, readers began to write to me! Other mothers had the same problems I did: I wasn't the only one who was lonely. Overjoyed to think that I didn't have to go any farther than the mailbox at the end of the driveway to communicate, I began to think of it as a miracle box.

One gray, endless day when nothing good had come in the mail for weeks, I left a cup of hot chocolate inside the box for my mail-man. I was delighted with his hurriedly scrawled, "Thanks, Mrs. West," and even more when he brought the news that I'd been cho-sen to go to the Guideposts Writers Workshop.

Later, when I was a widow, another loyal mail carrier brought three or four letters a week from a sociology professor in Oklahoma I'd never met. It wasn't unusual for him to find me standing by the mail-box waiting for the arrival of another letter from the man who would soon be my husband.

None of my friends understand why I don't have a computer and the convenience of instant e-mail. The truth is, I'd miss that certain sweetness, the longing and fulfillment I find when waiting for the mailman. It's kind of like waiting for spring.

Lord, please bless and encourage every single mail carrier today. Amen.
—MARION BOND WEST

11 | FRI

He shall cover thee with his feathers, and under his wings shalt thou trust. . . .   —PSALM 91:4

My three-year-old son Julian and I were sitting on a bench, waiting for the subway, when another family came and sat nearby. Their daughter, about four years old, was sitting in a stroller, holding a doll and brush. Julian rushed over to play with her, but she showed no interest. I motioned for him to return to the bench and told him that maybe the little girl wasn't in the mood to play. Just then she took her doll and repeatedly moved it toward Julian, then pulled it back toward her chest, as if to say, "Look at my doll. Now don't look at my doll. Look. Now don't look." Julian took the bait. But as soon as he got close, the little girl tucked the doll under her arm, stared him in the eyes and calmly started brushing her hair.

Julian was perplexed. He turned to me with a look on his face that said, *But she . . . didn't she? Aren't I supposed to. . . .*

The opposite sex, I thought. *Oh, dear.*

Remembering how girls had scared and baffled the daylights out of me, I decided then and there to pray for my sweet son, for what's coming in the years ahead: the confusion; the fear; peer pressure; in-fatuation; heartbreak; the struggle for self-control. I prayed that the Lord would help keep him pure. And while I was at it, I prayed the same prayer for the daughter my wife and I were expecting, and for Julian's friends, Jack, Wes, Adelle and Natalie, and for my two nephews who are just entering their teenage years. It was one of the longest, most emotional and most gratifying prayers I've prayed in quite some time.

Lord, help me remember to pray for the children in my life, for their trials that are ahead. —DAVE FRANCO

12

S
A
T

I urge, then, first of all, that requests, prayers, intercession and thanksgiving be made for . . . all those in authority. . . . —I TIMOTHY 2:1-2 (NIV)

Last year our Sunday newspaper ran a story about the decreasing importance of politics and politicians in our lives. It was illustrated with a series of cartoons showing a backyard barbecue at a suburban house. As people in shorts and slacks talked about the important things in their lives—their children's education, their jobs, housing costs, the stock market—little figures in suits and ties, about calf-high, prattled on unheard about health care, Social Security, defense policy and public morality.

As I looked at the cartoons, I suddenly remembered my eighth-grade class trip to Washington, D.C. We had taken an after-dinner tour devoted to Abraham Lincoln, beginning at Ford's Theater and the house across the street where Lincoln died. A short bus ride took us to the Mall. There, a brilliant white against the nighttime darkness, was the Lincoln Memorial. I walked up the steps and looked at Daniel Chester French's great seated statue of Lincoln. How immense he seemed! I stared into his huge, craggy face, determined yet kindly, with more than a hint of sadness in the deeply shadowed eyes. As I stood there looking, I came to understand a little of what his contemporaries meant when they called him "Father Abraham"—a giant of a man, with a compassionate heart and steely resolve, who led the nation through its greatest agony, and at the last hour gave his own life as its greatest martyr.

I shook the memory out of my head and went back to the newspaper. Our leaders often seem to do their best to diminish themselves, but when I demean them, or when I forget all I learned in civics class about my own responsibilities as a citizen, or, worse, when I forget to pray for them, I make them smaller still. We won't see giants like Lincoln in public office very often, but if we're governed by pygmies, we've no one to blame but ourselves.

Dear Lord, as I celebrate Lincoln's Birthday, renew my commitment to be an active, praying citizen.   —ANDREW ATTAWAY

13 | S U N

Who, when he had found one pearl of great price, went and sold all that he had, and bought it.
—MATTHEW 13:46

Buy a cultured pearl anywhere in the world, and chances are good that the heart of that pearl came from Tennessee. It's an industry about which few people know, even in my home state. More than a thousand licensed divers and independent fishermen work the rivers of Tennessee, gathering mussels and selling them to world pearl markets such as Japan.

No one's ever accused a mussel of being pretty! But plant a grain of sand inside the mussel, and it begins to excrete a protective coating around the foreign substance, and before you know it, a lovely, round, iridescent pearl is born.

The pearl story holds a particular lesson for me because I'm just about as plain as one of those old river mussels. But like the mussel, I have the power to make something beautiful.

It's Sunday morning and church has just ended. A group of friends are gathering to go to lunch. I walk toward the coat closet to gather my things. And, suddenly, there's Maggie. She's three years old and, for some reason, she's taken a fancy to me.

"Hi, Miss Pam," she says, throwing her arms around my legs.

I stop, pick her up and twirl her around. "Hi, Maggie! You have new shoes. They look like dancing shoes. Do they make your feet dance?" Maggie giggles as I set her down. I turn to go.

"I *can* dance, Miss Pam. Wanna see me?" I lean against the wall and clap as Maggie pirouettes across the hallway.

"Pam, we're waiting," a friend calls. I turn to go.

"Miss Pam, I know my ABC's," Maggie says softly.

I'm hungry, I'm thinking about lunch and friends and a pleasant afternoon. But I stop again. "No, Maggie, you can't be *that* smart!"

"Yes, I am. A-B-C-D-E-F-G"—Maggie is bursting with pride—"H-I-J . . ."

"Pam, come on. You're wasting time." My husband David is here to fetch me.

"No, I'm not wasting time." I laugh as I give Maggie one more good-bye hug. "I'm making pearls."

Father, use my time, form my words to turn Your children into pearls of great price.
—PAM KIDD

14 | M O N | *I looked for the one my heart loves. . . .*
—SONG OF SOLOMON 3:1 (NIV)

On Valentine's Days past, like many people I have prayed for the "right" person to show me he cared via the "right" card or gift. But then my mother told me a story that showed me that there are other ways to let someone know I care.

One day (which happened to be St. Valentine's Day), my mother went to get a permanent instead of her usual monthly cut and set. My stepfather, who of course wasn't familiar with the ins and outs of beauty salons, had no idea that while a cut takes less than an hour, a permanent takes about four hours from start to finish.

After two hours had passed, my stepfather began to feel uneasy. Where was my mother?

After three hours, he realized that he didn't even know the name of her beauty salon.

At three and a half hours, he got out the Yellow Pages and began dialing hairdressers. He began with the A's, asking if a customer named Elaine had come in.

An hour later, her fresh curls bouncing, my mother walked in. By then (this was in New York City—there are a lot of hair salons!) Joe was only up to the D's. "I was so touched," Mom said. "But my hairdressing shop is William's, so he would have had a long way to go before he got to it."

Joe complimented her on her new perm, and the two of them glanced at the phone book—now a symbol of Joe's caring for my mom.

Today, God, let me accept and value love as it comes to me, even if it isn't exactly as I had envisioned it!
—LINDA NEUKRUG

15

T
u
E

Glory ye in his holy name. . . .   —PSALM 105:3

It was a subzero night during the first winter after my marriage ended. A blizzard was raging across the Great Plains, downing power lines, stranding motorists, breaking tall trees, isolating families in their homes without heat behind walls of drifting snow. Wind moaned through the crack between my front door and its frame, as brittle branches slapped against the windows and snow rose in great swirling drifts. When the lights went out, I picked up the phone to call my daughter Karen to see if the power failure was citywide. No dial tone! The phone line was dead. Never had I felt so cut off from other people and the world.

I went to my prayer chair, snuggled up in Mother's afghan and tried to make contact with God, but even that connection seemed to be severed. The prayers I spoke into the silence seemed to hang suspended in the empty darkness like fragments of lint, without substance and having nowhere to go. I tried to call on God, but all the names I knew Him by seemed to fail me now. "Heavenly Father" felt remote; "Almighty God" seemed overpowering; "Holy Spirit" seemed too untouchable for my arms that ached only to hold and be held that night. Even "Dear Lord Jesus" couldn't seem to reach beyond my walls.

Discouraged, lonely and cold, I got up from my chair and got another blanket to wrap around me. From somewhere unknown, in the starkness of that winter night, came a name I'd never dared to call my God before. "Beloved," I whispered into the night, "my Beloved One." And in the heartbeat of that moment, the longing within me became a loving embrace. No further words were needed. Only those. I was not alone and never had been. Since then, Beloved has been my warmest name for God. It never fails to bring me home to Love.

Beloved, my Beloved One. . . .   —MARILYN MORGAN HELLEBERG

READER'S ROOM

"During last month, 'My Healing Journey' has really been a walk of discovery. I have always had such high expectations of others, even about needs of my own heart. I would be devastated if one of my children forgot to send a Mother's Day card or forgot my birthday. This went for friends, too. I needed so much to feel loved. God is changing that and, through prayer and finally listening, I find I'm not so hurt, but pleased at the terrific things people do. Love doesn't have to be a scheduled event, I'm finally discovering. I still have my moments, but there's an awareness growing. It's also been a healing discovery in my life that maybe God isn't calling me so much to do as to pray. You hear that a lot. So did I. But it never really hit home. It took a fly-ball to conk me on the head, in a sense, and, boy, is life much easier."

—Kathy Thomas, Tucson, Arizona

16 WED

As the Father hath loved me, so have I loved you: continue ye in my love. —JOHN 15:9

Soon after I made a serious decision to surrender my life to God, I heard that the job of a Christian father was to teach his children how to live. So at the dinner table, when my daughters talked about what was going on at school and with their friends, I told them (tactfully, I thought) how they should handle things.

As the years passed, I noticed that when I tried to "help" them in this way, their expressions would change or they would shake their heads in exasperation, and they left the table as soon as they finished eating. And when they became teenagers, my children *really* changed: They just didn't seem to want to be around me when I was in my "helping" mode. I was baffled, and I prayed that they would change or that we could get through those awful teenage years as quickly as possible.

Then one day I overheard one of my daughters talking to her mother. "Why does Daddy always try to control what we do? He doesn't even seem to hear our side." At first I felt ashamed, then angry. Then hurt and rejected. *After all, I thought, I give them advice to help them avoid the mistakes I've made, and some of the pain, and to help them succeed in life. And when they don't even want to listen . . .* I was pretty miserable.

Later, I learned that separation from one's father is a necessary, even crucial part of everyone's growing up—the children and the parents. But it wasn't until years later that I discovered that I hadn't really been listening to my daughters. My need to make them in my own image had pushed them further away than was necessary in their passage to adulthood.

Lord, thank You for letting me be the father of my kids. Now that they're grown, help me put them back in Your hands and turn them loose. Let me just love them—the way You seem to love us all.

—KEITH MILLER

17

T
H
U

Praise ye him, sun and moon: praise him, all ye stars of light.
—PSALM 148:3

It is a sunny winter morning, and I am sitting here in front of my old Corona (am I the last man on earth to use a manual typewriter?) trying to think of an item that might be suitable for *Daily Guideposts* and having little luck. In fact, no luck at all.

The problem does not bother our jet-black cat Muffin, who is sitting in a patch of sunlight on the floor near my desk, washing her face industriously with one of her paws. First she licks her paw, then she rubs it across her ears and cheeks until, finally satisfied, she stretches out in the warm sunshine and blissfully closes her eyes.

Muffin is at peace with the world. And why? Because ninety-three million miles away, a stupendous mass of flaming gases is sending her a message. It takes that message several minutes to reach my office window, but when it does, it brings light and warmth and radiance to one of God's small, trusting creatures. And also to me.

Why do we have to seek for miracles when they are all around us all the time? I share this one with my friend Muffin. And her friend, the sun.

Thank You, Father, for the wonders of Your creation.

—ARTHUR GORDON

18

F
R
I

Train up a child in the way he should go: and when he is old, he will not depart from it.

—PROVERBS 22:6

The phone rang at about nine o'clock last night. It was our son Derek, who has just moved to Portland, Oregon, and is looking for a job while waiting to get into graduate school in social work.

"Mom, I'm so discouraged," he said. "Nothing seems to be working out, and I'm starting to wonder if I'm going in the right direction."

As I listened to him, I found myself facing a familiar challenge: How can a parent help a child—even an adult child—through a place of discouragement?

Just then, I looked up at a collage of family photographs I'd taped to the wall above my desk. In them, I saw a determined, honest, sensitive boy growing into a faithful, perceptive, compassionate young man. There he was at age six, tenderly helping his barefoot little sister across a prickly meadow; at age ten, passing the soccer ball to a teammate at a tournament; at age sixteen, wearing his high school basketball uniform and a bittersweet smile in the midst of a frustrating season; at his college graduation, surrounded by the loyal friends who were a part of his Bible study group.

Suddenly, I knew how I could help Derek through this place of discouragement. I could be a reminder. I could remind him of the goodness God had planted in him, the strong qualities imprinted in his soul, which have been growing since his childhood. I could remind him that God promises to complete His unique "interior" design in His children's lives. And I could remind him of how God has helped him grow through other discouraging places in his life.

So after listening, I tried some reminding. And when we hung up a few minutes later, I prayed:

Lord, may I be a reminder of the goodness You have planted in this child. Please seal those reminders in his heart, where they may help him through this discouraging place. —CAROL KUYKENDALL

19

S
A
T

Thy youth is renewed like the eagle's.

—PSALM 103:5

My hobby, my passion, is a sport called dek hockey, where grown men play without skates. It's just like ice hockey, with a regulation-size rink, dasher boards and referees, except you don't need as much equipment or money or common sense.

Dek hockey games combine a thirty-minute aerobic workout with sticks and screaming—Jane Fonda meets Attila the Hun. I'm quite facile at screaming, but I am not good at the aerobic part. Now in my late thirties, I rank as one of the elder participants in a sport clearly designed for a generation too young to remember Gerald Ford.

I wasn't always this old. I peaked in 1975, but I can still remember it like yesterday, playing three-hour games in the blazing sun or subzero cold, taking breaks only when someone lost an eye or broke a bone. I remember how my body responded then—my vision was better, my reactions quicker, my breathing easier. Nowadays, my body has betrayed me.

So why do I do it? When I drag my iron-poor blood and bones onto the deck twice a week, I just want a chance to play. As betrayed as I feel, there are those rare magic moments when everything goes magically right. My arthritic joints and myopic eyes occasionally combine to remind me of what I once had. Suddenly, I'm breaking in on the goalie alone, me and my retro-body, and it's like hearing a favorite song after twenty years and still knowing all the words. I drag my stick for a second, gathering momentum for the shot, then snap the puck away in a single motion.

After that, nothing matters. If he makes the save, then good for him. It's not the goal that counts (though that would be nice), but just the chance to shoot—to reclaim, if only for a second, the sense of my body acting as it once did, and still can: a holy and united sum of its parts.

Lord, as time slows my body, quicken my spirit to new life in You.

—MARK COLLINS

20 S u N *He opened the rock, and water gushed out; like a river it flowed in the desert.* —PSALM 105:41 (NIV)

Esther came to me after church one Sunday, put her arm around me and said, "I just want to thank you for being an encouragement to my daughter." The tears spilled down her cheeks, and she reached into her handbag for a tissue to wipe them away. "Forgive me for crying," she said. "It's just that I'm planted so close to the water."

What a lovely way of explaining to someone that you cry easily, I thought. While I do care deeply, I seldom shed tears in public. The environment in which I was raised taught me to take a very stoic approach to life, and despite the changing times, my social tear ducts are still dried up.

I thought about the difference between Esther and me as I watered my houseplants yesterday. The impatiens, given copious amounts of water for its size, blooms profusely day after day. In sharp contrast, the cactus right beside it thrives only in bone-dry soil. Neither plant will flourish if I give them the same amount of water. I know. I've tried.

So why do I wish for the "impatiens" of Esther's tear ducts when I'm a "cactus" by nature? God has planted her "close to the water" for the same reason He has planted me "in the desert"—to help fulfill His divine purposes in His own ways.

Dear God, thank You that the local nursery devotes one entire corner to desert plants. It tells me there are people who actually like cacti just the way we are. —ALMA BARKMAN

21 | M O N | *Above all, love each other deeply, because love covers over a multitude of sins.* —I PETER 4:8 (NIV)

I'm struggling to be at peace in our church. I'm struggling to adjust to the new pastor and many changes, as well as the departure of beloved friends. I feel God calling me to stay and work through these problems, but it's painful.

Today I found God's help in an unexpected place—reading stories about Presidents Washington and Lincoln.

Washington's meticulous account books show tremendous generosity. He lent thousands of dollars to people with no expectation of repayment, and in his last will he canceled all debts owed to him. Lately I have felt wronged, hurt and angry. I feel people owe apologies, the new pastor owes us more help in reconciling, and on and on. *Cancel those debts, and give love generously without expecting return.*

Lincoln visited his friend General Pickett, who took up arms for the South, and forgave him. I need to reach out to fellow parishioners. *Forgive, then strengthen individual relationships.*

Once General Washington came upon a corporal not helping his troop fell trees and make a bridge. Rather than criticize him, Washington himself stepped in and worked with the troop until the job was done. I've been criticizing some parishioners for not helping out enough. *Instead of complaining, do whatever work I can do.*

During the Revolution, Washington was found praying on his knees in the snow. When Lincoln led the country through the Civil War he often called on people to pray. I've been doing more stewing than praying. I'll try to catch those troublesome thoughts and turn them into prayers. *In times of strife, pour on prayer.*

Thank You, God, for such examples of love and integrity—and for providing help in all my troubles.　　　　　　　　　—MARY BROWN

22

T
u
E

Be watchful, stand firm in your faith, be courageous, be strong.　　　　—I CORINTHIANS 16:13 (RSV)

When I was a child in a rural school in the Missouri Ozarks back in the 1930s, Washington's Birthday was a big event. Grades one through four shared the same room, and each year all of us students colored mimeographed pictures of Washington's profile—always the same picture—which we then bordered with sketches of hatchets and cherries. Washington, for me, was a hero larger than life who thought noble thoughts, did noble deeds and never wavered in his resolve to create the United States of America.

Only after I studied history in college did I realize how flawed and human Washington had been and how often the outcome of the war had hung in precarious balance. The image that remains with me now is not Washington's strong profile, but Washington on his knees in the snow at Valley Forge, humbled and praying for guidance.

Yes, he was courageous, but most of all he was faithful, to his men, to his principles and to God. A good example to keep in mind as we honor the day of his birth.

Lord, help me act with courage and faith as I move forward through this day. Amen.　　　　　　　　　—MADGE HARRAH

23
W
E
D

The Lord is a great God, and a great King above all gods. —PSALM 95:3

My wife and I used to have a continual argument about the nature of God. My point of view could best be summarized in the old adage, "God broadens the back to bear the burden." She adhered to the philosophy that "God tempers the wind to the shorn lamb." It took the biggest snowstorm of recent memory to resolve our conflict.

Three years ago, after Mother Nature dumped twenty-eight inches of snow on New York City, Carol decided to dig out the car. "But there's no place to go," I said. "I want it ready when we need it," she responded. For four days she shoveled, creating an exit in the wall of snow surrounding our Subaru. During that time I don't doubt that God broadened her back, physically and metaphorically. And yet on the fifth day the winds blew from the west, bringing a warm spell and a driving rain. After eight hours of constant rain, most of the snow had completely washed away, making my wife's labors needless. While bemoaning the futility of all human endeavor, I asked her if she regretted all the work she'd put in.

"Not at all," she said. "I enjoyed the shoveling. It was great exercise."

"But I have to point out," I said, "God *did* send a tempering wind."

There lies our compromise. God broadens the back *and* tempers the wind. After all, a God big enough to send a snowstorm of twenty-eight inches and a rainstorm to follow it can use any means to come to His people's aid.

Good Lord, when You've finished broadening my back, send me a tempering wind. —RICK HAMLIN

24
T
H
U

"How often I have wanted to gather your children together as a hen gathers her chicks beneath her wings. . . ." —MATTHEW 23:37 (TLB)

We all have down times when the going gets pretty rough. The year 1989 seemed to be one of those years for me when everything went wrong. My oldest daughter Jeanne was caught smack-dab in the middle of one of California's most devastating earthquakes. Shortly after that, my ex-husband died of leukemia, a devastating loss for our son Andrew, who was only nine years old at the time. Then a woman named Sonny, whom I'd met only once in my life, moved to Milwaukee, Wisconsin, from Georgia, and decided I was going to be her best friend since I was the only person she knew in the whole state. And quite frankly, I didn't have the energy to be anybody's best anything that year.

I had to find a few other good friends for Sonny. That's when I used what I call the "goose principle" and formed a group of women called the SWILL Gang. SWILL stands for Southeastern Wisconsin Interesting Ladies League.

The goose principle is this: Scientists have discovered the reason that geese fly in a V formation. As each bird flaps its wings, it creates an uplift for the bird immediately following. When a goose falls out of formation, it feels the drag of trying to do it all alone and quickly gets back into formation to take advantage of the lifting power of the bird in front. Geese even honk from behind to encourage those up front to keep up their speed.

In addition to being friends for Sonny, all of us in the SWILL Gang flew in formation with each other. We laughed, cried, consoled, prodded, jabbered and generally lifted each other out of whatever doldrums any of us were in at any given time. We found so much healing in our laughter and conversation that we're still meeting seven or eight times a year.

Father, when I'm lonely, hungry for companionship or feeling stressed out, give me the courage to reach out to others and fly in formation.

—PATRICIA LORENZ

25 | F R I
Weeping may endure for a night, but joy cometh in the morning. —PSALM 30:5

My grandmother died, unexpectedly and away from home, in August 1985. For me, there was a deep feeling of loss and a lack of closure. She had always been there when I needed her; now she was gone, and I hadn't been able to say good-bye.

A few days after the funeral, my sister Debbie came across a letter Grandmother had written to me. It was a single handwritten page, with no indication of when it had been sent. But to me, the words seemed to have come from heaven:

Dear Libbie,
I miss all of you down there. Not that I'm lonely or home-sick; every day is a good one. Everyone is so helpful and kind.
Just remember, when you are blue or lonely, you are not alone. Just stop for a moment and thank God for all things as they are, for they are working out something beautiful in your life. You may not see it today, but tomorrow is coming, and the sun will rise and shine down your path. Keep sweet. God loves you, and I love you.

Your grandmother

Neither Debbie nor I really knows when this letter was written. I think Grandmother sent it to me in 1981, while my husband Larry was away for a year in Okinawa with the U.S. Navy. I have no memory of receiving it, and it doesn't matter now. What really matters is that God knew it would comfort me, and He saw that it was delivered right on time.

Father, You really do work in mysterious ways. Thank You for the wonders You perform in my life.   —LIBBIE ADAMS

26 | S A T   *Feed me with food convenient for me.*
—PROVERBS 30:8

My grandsons recently flew in for a visit. During the forty years since my own two sons were the ages of these three kids, I'd forgotten how much boys eat. I'd expected my oversized casserole of chicken, cheese and rice to last at least two meals, but it disappeared in less than ten minutes.

The youngest spoke for his too-polite brothers. "Grandma, we're still hungry." I dug out a huge bag of potato chips I was saving for a picnic. It disappeared, too.

It was baffling. The boys were slim as spaghetti before they ate; just as slim afterward. *Even a snake bulges when it swallows something, for pity's sake.*

After the boys ate everything, then topped it with ice cream on pecan pie, I suddenly remembered my college chemistry class eons ago. *If what these kids put into their stomachs was put into a test tube instead, it'd blow up.*

It made me wonder if the Lord had boys in mind when He wrote about our bodies being "fearfully and wonderfully made" (Psalm 139:14). My grandsons' ability to consume food probably isn't news to God, but it always is to me.

Lord, help me make my hunger for the food You supply at Your spiritual table just as strong as that for the food at my earthly one.
—ISABEL WOLSELEY

27 | SUN

"There will be no more death or mourning or crying or pain. . . ." —REVELATION 21:4 (NIV)

When I was a young girl, Mabel Duke was my Sunday school teacher, and an extraordinary one at that. I remember her telling us that no matter what our situation in life, God could use us for His glory.

Then when I was in high school, the unthinkable happened. Mrs. Duke was diagnosed with a malignant brain tumor. One Saturday afternoon at the hospital where I volunteered as a candy striper, she was a patient on my ward. I was pitifully short on confidence as I clumsily filled Mrs. Duke's plastic turquoise pitcher with ice.

But even though she was gravely ill, there was a sense of purpose to her every gesture. "Roberta," she asked, "I was wondering if you would be so kind as to shave my legs?" Her gasping breath slowed to a whisper. "The hairs, they're so scratchy," she confided, "and I've been too weak to do it myself."

Several minutes later, armed with a basin, a razor, some shaving cream and a heap of prayers *(Please, Lord, don't let her know how scared I am, and please, please don't let me cut her!)*, I began the task. All the while, Mrs. Duke reassured me. "I just know you're going to make the best nurse ever, Roberta. I've been praying for your future, you know, ever since you were a little girl in my Sunday school class."

In college, whenever I doubted my aptitude for nursing, the memory of Mrs. Duke strengthened my determination. It would have been so easy for Mrs. Duke to have pretended to be asleep that afternoon or to have sent me away. But she had one more lesson to teach me.

Dear Lord, thank You for the lives and lessons of our Sunday school teachers.
—ROBERTA MESSNER

28

M
O
N

Thine own friend, and thy father's friend, forsake not. . . .
—PROVERBS 27:10

Books are very special to me, and over the years I collected so many that I had shelves in every room of my house. They were crowded, and they were a mess. One day recently, after I spent an hour looking for a book I knew I had, I said, "Enough!" It was time to clean house.

The next day I began early, climbing on a ladder to reach the highest shelf. I had a sturdy box ready to receive my discards and a dust cloth to clean the books I would keep. Funny, but after two hours, there wasn't a single book in the discard box. Each time I picked up a book, I lingered over it because it brought back memories.

There was the first book I ever owned: a copy of Charles and Mary Lamb's *Tales from Shakespeare*, versions of the Bard's plays written for children. It had been given to me by a favorite aunt when I was ten, and I felt very grown-up owning it. Another was a copy of James Herriott's *All Creatures Great and Small*, which an adorable puppy had used for teething, now held together by a stout rubber band. I came across a collection of favorite seventeenth- and eighteenth-century writers—Pope, Dr. Johnson, Dryden—from my college days, and some poems of Elizabeth Barrett Browning, which my husband and I used to read aloud to each other.

As I went on, I found so many treasures I had forgotten I had: books by Peter and Catherine Marshall, Dr. Norman Vincent Peale, C. S. Lewis, Marjorie Holmes. And my great-grandmother's Bible, with her carefully written records of births, marriages and deaths. I found a complete collection of Beatrix Potter books, little gems with lovely illustrations of Peter Rabbit and his friends. I took time out to read one of them and enjoyed it every bit as much as I did when I was a child and my mother read it to me.

At the end of the day, my books were dusted and perfectly in order. The discard box was empty. Yes, my bookshelves remain crowded, but it doesn't matter. We can never have too many friends.

Thank You, Lord, for the books that bring us close to so many wonderful people. Amen.
—PHYLLIS HOBE

29

T
U
E

*My son, do not despise the chastening of the Lord,
Nor detest His correction; For whom the Lord loves
He corrects, Just as a father the son in whom He de-
lights.*   —PROVERBS 3:11-12 (NKJV)

Leap Year Day is basically a correction. A small tweak of the calendar, without which the entire world would soon be in chronological
chaos.

I've noticed that corrections are easy to make if I catch my errors
while they are small. "A baby's hand could stop a leak, which, neglected, would require a bulldozer to correct," a preacher friend used
to say.

When I was learning to fly, I enjoyed it so much that my attention
often wandered from the compass. I can still see my instructor's
stubby hand tapping the compass firmly. "Watch your heading," he
would growl, "watch your heading." I would glance at the compass
and think, "Two degrees off? Nothing to worry about." Until one day
when I was making a solo flight to Kansas City, Missouri. Two degrees for two hours, at 120 miles an hour, and I missed the entire
city!

My Sunday school teacher used to emphasize the importance of
making small corrections in our character. "The sheep may drift
from the fold," he would say, "but they never drift back. They have
to make a conscious effort to come back." He was a patriotic man,
and he was seriously concerned about changes he saw in our country. "We are drifting, drifting, drifting . . ." he would say.

Today, when the calendar is being corrected, would be a good time
for me to take stock of my character and the direction of my life. Now,
while it's easy. I will ask myself the following questions:

1. Am I ethical in my business dealings?
2. Am I faithful to my wife and my children, or do I neglect them?
3. Is my faith in God real, or do I fake it?

*Help me, Lord, to amend my life every day, while it can still be
corrected.*   —DANIEL SCHANTZ

My Renewal Journal

1 _____

2 _____

3 _____

4 _____

5 _____

6 _____

7 _____

8 _____

9 _____

FEBRUARY 2000

10 _____

11 _____

12 _____

13 _____

14 _____

15 _____

16 _____

17 _____

18 _____

19 _____

FEBRUARY 2000

20 _____

21 _____

22 _____

23 _____

24 _____

25 _____

26 _____

27 _____

28 _____

29 _____

MARCH

And he that sat upon the throne said, Behold, I make all
things new. . . .   —REVELATION 21:5

S	M	T	W	T	F	S
			1	2	3	4
5	6	7	8	9	10	11
12	13	14	15	16	17	18
19	20	21	22	23	24	25
26	27	28	29	30	31	

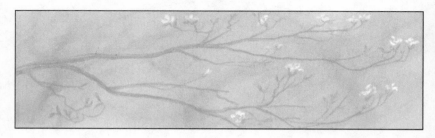

ALL THINGS NEW

1

W
E
D

Acknowledging Sin

We were buried therefore with him by baptism into death, so that as Christ was raised from the dead by the glory of the Father, we too might walk in newness of life. —ROMANS 6:4 (RSV)

In the *Book of Common Prayer*, there's one petition I especially love: *Grant that we may ever hereafter serve and please thee in newness of life.* Newness of life—life forever fresh as morning, wonder-struck as childhood.

But, oh, dear! These words so full of promise are only part of a prayer that also contains some of my least favorite phrases. For years I sped hastily over this segment: *We acknowledge and bewail our manifold sins and wickedness, which we have most grievously committed, by thought, word, and deed.* Why focus on negatives? I wanted to hurry on to the new life, not get stuck at old defeats.

Then one Lent, I noticed that every Bible reading in my daily lectionary dealt with repentance. I decided that all those verses had to be there for a purpose. I noticed, too, that when a biblical figure repented, it was always for a specific sin. Not just "manifold sins and wickedness," but the time yesterday when I crossed the street to avoid meeting a woman who talks for half an hour (she lives alone). The resentment that flared last night when I saw a commercial for a certain department store (the billing error it refused to correct happened twenty years ago).

Making repentance specific, current and daily, I've come to appreciate the wisdom that shaped that ancient petition. When I recall and confess the unkind thought, the careless word, the selfish deed "most grievously committed," I'm allowing it to fall away and be buried. And out of this prepared ground, God brings newness. New warmth in a relationship. New tolerance for failure, my own and others'. New freedom. God makes new, not by ignoring my sin, but by shining the light of His forgiveness upon it.

Grant that I may serve and please You this day, Father, in newness of life.
　　　　　　　　　　　　　　　　　　　　—ELIZABETH SHERRILL

2　T　*But by the grace of God I am what I am, and his grace*
　　　H　*to me was not without effect. No, I worked harder*
　　　U　*than all of them—yet not I, but the grace of God that*
　　　　　was with me.　　　—I CORINTHIANS 15:10 (NIV)

Every Thursday, Mission Mississippi sponsors a prayer breakfast. The breakfast includes some time to get to know one another, a light meal, a five-to-ten-minute presentation by the host group and time for small-group prayer. The idea is to have the breakfast at a predominantly African American church one Thursday, and at a predominantly white church the next, so that people can have fellowship across racial lines.

One particular Thursday morning, a man in his mid-forties stood to speak. "I am from a family that owned slaves," he said, "and we were taught from generation to generation that this was okay. I belong to a denomination that found a way to justify slavery and injustice in the light of an open Bible. I have no earthly reason to be a part of this reconciliation movement."

He paused a moment, and then added, "Because of the work of Christ in my life, I am eager to work for the unity of His body."

Paul's words in I Corinthians 15 immediately came to my mind. In that man's honest words, I saw God's grace working to provide a clear view of the past and hope for the future.

Lord, let me help me to be a grace-bearer as I work for renewal in my life, my church and my community.　　　—DOLPHUS WEARY

3　F
　　　R　*Where your treasure is, there will your heart be also.*
　　　I　　　　　　　　　　　　　　　　—MATTHEW 6:21

I riffled through my desk drawer looking for an eraser. I was helping my friend Joan with a loan application, and I was exasperated. "If you hadn't loaned your sister that money, you wouldn't be in

this mess now," I complained. "You have to look out for yourself."
She tried to hide the hurt in her eyes. "I thought I was doing the
right thing," she said. "My sister is more important than money."

"I'm sorry I snapped at you," I said. "It's just that I hate to see you
with this burden." I jumped. My hand had fallen on a piece of gray
metal that had been knocked off my car when I'd had an accident
the year before. I had thrown it in the drawer and forgotten it.

"What is that?" Joan asked, taking it from my hand. The metallic
chunk of bumper gleamed in the lamplight. "Why would you keep
that old thing?"

"It was supposed to be a reminder," I said.

"Of what?" she asked.

"What you just tried to tell me," I said sheepishly. "My husband
and I could have been hurt in this accident. Instead, we just had a
crushed bumper. I saved it to keep me focused on what really counts.
People are more important than things."

Lord, make me ever mindful of what my real treasures are.

—SUSAN SCHEFFLEIN

4 | S
A
T | *For since the creation of the world God's invisible*
qualities—his eternal power and divine nature—have
been clearly seen, being understood from what has
been made. . . . —ROMANS 1:20 (NIV)

The other day my friend Patsy invited me to go with her to an art show.
I readily accepted, even though I don't know much about art, and even
less about the abstract kind. But Patsy is an art teacher and a painter,
and I figured this would be a great learning opportunity for me.

Paintings in vivid colors hung on the white walls, and clusters of
mixed media sculptures were arranged with careful abandon on the
floor. As we wandered slowly around the spacious room, Patsy
pointed out some basic principles of color and design. After a while
I turned to her. "This stuff is really interesting, but titles like *Patterns
in Purple, No. 4* and *Orange No. 2* aren't very helpful to me," I complained. "I wish they would print a little blurb beside each piece that
tells us what the artist was thinking, the point he intends to convey."

Patsy looked at me, astonished. "It's already here in the art. He's
said what he wants to say, now he wants us to try to hear what that
is by looking and thinking about what he's done."

That day's lesson keeps coming back to me as I think about how God shows Himself in the world. Not all the things around me come with labels; sometimes they don't seem to make much sense. That's when I have to step back, look and pray, and give myself a chance to hear what the Artist is telling me in His work.

Father, open my heart and my mind to know You in the world around me, in the Word of Scripture and in Your Son Jesus Christ.

—MARY JANE CLARK

5 | S U N | *Thomas said to him, "Lord, we don't know where you are going, so how can we know the way?"*
—JOHN 14:5 (NIV)

During the first year I taught at seminary, I was asked to speak in chapel several times. Each time I spoke, I tried to deal with some aspect of the Christian life with which I was struggling. After I spoke, I replayed in my mind what I had said, thinking of ways I might have been clearer, making plans for improvement.

The following year, when I received a memo assigning me to speak again, the dean said to me, "Would you accept a word of advice about your messages?" I was surprised but assured him that I'd appreciate any help he might give me. We were good friends, and I had great respect for him.

"Kenneth," he said, "you're interesting, and students like to hear you speak." I was flattered, but I knew this wasn't what he meant by advice. He paused for what seemed like ages, and then said, "You raise lots of questions when you speak that you don't answer. You need to plan your presentation so that you wrap everything up, so there are no loose ends." He elaborated for a few minutes, and I thanked him for his suggestions. I left with a lot to think about.

I still struggle with his advice. I try to deal honestly with life in all its complexities and to communicate clearly and helpfully with others. But I've discovered that there are some questions for which I don't have easy answers. I grow as a person neither by pushing aside hard questions nor seeking simplistic answers for them, but by living with them prayerfully.

Dear God, help me to trust You with all the things that I do not yet understand.
—KENNETH CHAFIN

6

Set your affection on things above, not on things on the earth. —COLOSSIANS 3:2

After twenty-nine years in the same house in Princeton, New Jersey, we are moving to another one in southwest Florida, on the Gulf of Mexico. It is a smaller place, to be sure, but the surf and sand out our door are a good trade-off.

Our job right now is to dispose of tons of family junk (make that *treasures*; my wife Shirley will read this). All the stuff we have accumulated simply won't fit in our new quarters. So books and bikes, clothes and furniture, tools and travel souvenirs will have to go—to our kids, to the church rummage sale, to charities or to storage. That's the bailout option. If we can't make up our minds on some items, we can store them until the rental space fills up.

For some people, getting rid of things is a no-brainer. But for an old pack rat like me, it's hair-pulling. I still have matchbooks from the 1964 World's Fair and campaign buttons from the 1952 presidential election. One keepsake of mine (Shirley thinks it's dispensable) is a large, framed, Grade-B painting of a seascape. We got it early in our marriage to fill a space over the mantel of a rental apartment. It cost ten dollars. I remember because it was a big financial decision.

Whether we possess things or they possess us is always a question we need to ask ourselves. Jesus directed a rich young ruler who had kept all the commandments to "go and sell that thou hast, and give to the poor . . . and come and follow me" (Matthew 19:21). But, we are told, the man went away "sorrowful: for he had great possessions" (Matthew 19:22). The young man's problem was not riches, but his absorption with them. They held first place in his heart.

Maybe you've got the same problem, a voice inside whispers.

"Nah, I don't worship the things I'm weighing," I answer, echoing the rich young ruler. "I'm only having trouble parting with them."

School us, Lord, in the art of traveling lightly.
What to hold loosely, what to love tightly.

—FRED BAUER

7

T
U
E

The splendor I had given you made your beauty per-fect, declares the Sovereign Lord.
—EZEKIEL 16:14 (NIV)

I was born with naturally curly hair, and when I was in high school and college, I used to hate it. I did everything I could to make it sleek and straight, like the hair of most of my friends. I used commercial straighteners until I burned my scalp and frizzled the ends of the hairs. I ironed it. I wound it around a metal coffee can and slept with my head hanging over the edge of the bed. Nothing worked.

After I had been out of college and in the working world for a few years, I just resigned myself either to going to the beauty parlor for sets that my hair would reject after a day or keeping it cut really short, so that the more egregious kinks and whirls didn't have a chance to develop.

Earlier this year—long after I had given up on having really at-tractive hair—I found I didn't have time to get a needed haircut. My hair was getting longer than usual and therefore becoming unman-ageable. One morning I got up very early, worked out on the tread-mill, and showered and washed my hair before leaving for the office. My blow-dryer shorted out when I plugged it in, so I had to leave for the office with my hair wet.

To my astonishment, the first person I encountered at the office said, "Wow, what a great 'do!"

"It's just wet," I said.

Three more people in the course of the morning complimented me on my hair. I finally went into the ladies' room and looked in the mirror. My hair was curled attractively around my face in a way I'd never really noticed before. All along, God had selected a better hair-style for me than I had ever managed on my own.

Lord, when I'm dissatisfied with myself, remind me of the beauty I can find in everything You have made—including me.

—RHODA BLECKER

8

W
E
D

He who conceals his sins does not prosper, but who-ever confesses and renounces them finds mercy.
—PROVERBS 28:13 (NIV)

It was a flawless summer day in the Berkshires . . . save for the flash-ing blue and red lights in my rearview mirror. I braked and veered slightly onto the shoulder of Jug End Road, hoping, but not quite believing, that the sheriff would zoom past me on the way to whatever emergency had summoned him. But, no, he pulled over right behind my car, then stepped out of his cruiser, brandishing that thick, black ticket book.

I hadn't gotten a ticket in nearly twenty years. I'm a great driver. The road was deserted, and I was merely building up momentum for the steep drive up Mt. Washington to our cabin. Nobody drives the speed limit on this road. Besides, there's no sign, and I couldn't have been going that fast anyway. What's the big deal? *I'll talk my way out of this. I wasn't really doing anything wrong.*

"Sir," the sheriff said when he got to my window, "do you know what the speed limit along here is?"

I confessed I did not.

"Do you know how fast you were going?"

Again I confessed my ignorance.

I winced when I heard the discrepancy between the two figures. *Maybe he'll give me a break.*

But do I deserve a break? I wondered as he scrutinized my license and registration, then scrutinized me. I *had* been speeding. Why was I trying to wriggle out of it? Here I was, caught red-handed breaking the law, and I was turning cartwheels in my mind trying to justify my actions. It was an almost reflexive reaction: I didn't want to admit I was in the wrong. Taking responsibility is something we demand from our children, our colleagues and our elected officials, yet I still sometimes find it hard to own up to my own blunders and transgressions.

By now the officer was finished writing. "It's a perfect day," he said, handing me the ticket. "Why ruin it? Drive safely."

I would—and more wisely, too.

Lord, on this Ash Wednesday, help me to take responsibility for the wrongs I do.
—EDWARD GRINNAN

9 T H U *"But I have prayed for you that your faith may not fail; and when you have turned again, strengthen your brethren."* —LUKE 22:32 (RSV)

I first met Annette when my daughter Elizabeth was six months old. At the time, Annette wasn't sure exactly how to explain how old her son Tommy was. He was seven months, but he'd been born more than three months early. A miracle baby.

We quickly figured out that we had a lot in common. We were both "in-the-sandbox" mothers: the type who get down in the dirt and play with our kids. Our philosophies of discipline were similar. Our one big difference centered around faith: neither Annette nor her husband had any.

A few weeks before Tommy's first birthday, I ran into Annette as she came home from meeting with Tommy's doctor. Tommy had just been diagnosed with cerebral palsy. "What does this mean for my son?" she grieved. "What will his life be like?" There was no way of telling, at that point, how severe the CP might be. Tommy might never walk. Or sit up unassisted. Or feed himself. Or take care of himself at all. Annette was looking down a long, dark, terrifying road, filled with unpredictable bumps and turns.

There wasn't much I could do to help. I gave her a hug and held her for a minute. I reminded her that Tommy was still her beloved Tommy, charming Tommy, miraculous Tommy, and he and his life were still gifts from God. But I went home stunned. That night I had a long argument with God. After pouring out the ache in my heart, I became really angry. "How can You do this to people who have no faith to support them?"

The answer I received was not one I expected to hear: Annette might not have faith, but I did. That was why we had met, so I could pray for her.

Tommy is now a bright, cheerful, "I-think-I-can" four-year-old. He sits up for brief periods unassisted and works unbelievably hard at learning to walk. Annette still does not have faith. But some day she will.

Dear Lord, please grant Your gift of faith to _____.
(LIST NAMES)

—JULIA ATTAWAY

10 | F R I | *A man finds joy in giving an apt reply—and how good is a timely word!* —PROVERBS 15:23 (NIV)

Not long ago I was asked to do what no one wants to do—deliver a eulogy at a good friend's memorial service. Judi's death from a sudden heart attack hit everyone who knew her hard. She was an ebullient woman, full of life, with a talent for making beautiful crafts, as well as a gift for making people laugh and feel loved.

I built my talk around her many talents, her generosity in sharing them with everyone and how much I admired her for it. After the service, one of our mutual friends thanked me for my words about Judi. "She would have loved what you said, but I bet she would have been surprised," he said. "You know how we all liked to kid each other. She probably had no idea you felt that way about her."

I thought about his comments often in the following days. My family and friends know I love them, but how often do I actually tell them what I appreciate or admire about them? So I tried it. I complimented my mom on her ability to find such beautiful things for her new house. I mentioned to the room mother in my son Ross's class that she'd done a great job with the kids' activities this year. And I told my best friend something I've long thought but never said, that she's one of the most generous people I know. They were all taken aback by my praise, but were definitely pleased.

I regret that I never said such words to Judi, but I'm determined not to make that mistake again. Now when I appreciate particular traits in my friends or family, I tell them; I don't silently file away the compliment. From their surprised-yet-pleased reactions, I'm learning that it always feels good to hear encouraging words. I've discovered it feels good to say them, too.

Father, help me to speak the kind thoughts in my heart, so they might encourage others.   —GINA BRIDGEMAN

11 | S
A   *"The Lord is my strength and my song. . . ."*
T   —EXODUS 15:2 (RSV)

As I changed clothes in the locker room after my swim, I recognized the woman with whom I'd just shared a lap lane.

We struck up a conversation, and I learned that eleven years ago Margaret had been in a car accident and injured her shoulder so badly that the doctors gave up on a cure. Looking for a way to strengthen the shoulder, she started to swim. She swam a mile every day, six days a week, and in time got back the use of her arm and shoulder. Today, transportation is a problem, so she's limited to swimming twice a week. This may have slowed her down, but it hasn't stopped her.

"I've swum all the way to Hawaii, and I'm on my way back!" she told me proudly. "Right now, I'm two hundred and eighty-three miles out to sea!" We both laughed. "You know," she confided, "I *was* going to go to Guam, but it's just too far. And you know, I *am* getting older."

With that, she picked up a cane I hadn't noticed and hobbled out of the locker room, swim bag slung over her "bad" shoulder.

Dear Lord, each day let me look for ways around my limitations.

—BRENDA WILBEE

12 | S u N *Mercy triumphs over judgment!* —JAMES 2:13 (NIV)

Very carefully, I brought home the clay figures my Sunday school class had made. These first-through-third-graders took their projects seriously, and I didn't want to damage a single one of them. They needed to be baked, so I carefully set the temperature, placed the figures on a cookie sheet and slid them into the oven. There was a Noah's ark, a Baby Jesus in the manger, a rainbow, a dinosaur and an exquisite Ark of the Covenant. Next Sunday the children would paint them.

The figures came out of the oven, and I lined them up on the kitchen counter to cool. An hour later, I heard a curious thump and hurried to the kitchen. Chaucer, my enormous golden retriever, was on his hind legs, chewing up the clay. What he hadn't eaten he knocked to the floor and broke in tiny pieces. "Oh, no! Bad dog!" I shrieked. Head down, tail between his legs, Chaucer slunk out of sight. I cleaned up the mess and wondered how I'd face my class on Sunday.

On the dreaded day, the children arrived expectantly. "Where's our clay, Miss Shari?" they asked as they came into the room and sat in a circle.

When they were all there, I said, "I don't know how to tell you this, but my dog ate your clay."

"All of it?" Hillary asked in disbelief.

"You mean, chewed it up and swallowed it?" Derek mused.

I nodded, feeling a lump in my throat. There was silence. Then Hillary started to giggle. Derek joined in. Their laughter spread through the circle. "We'll make them again," they said.

Later, as they were remaking their figures, Alexandra looked up. "Tell us again, Miss Shari. The whole story about how you found your dog eating our clay." So I did, to more laughter.

"Did you forgive him?" Alex asked.

I nodded yes.

"Good," she said. "Tell him we forgive him, too."

Lord, may I always have a childlike, forgiving heart.

—SHARI SMYTH

13 M O N *So David triumphed over the Philistine with a sling and a stone. . . .* —I SAMUEL 17:50 (NIV)

Crunch, crunch. Scratch, scratch. Crunch, crunch.

"Mommy, what is that?"

My two children and I huddled together, peering at the heating vent in the floor. The sounds continued. *Crunch, crunch. Scratch, scratch. Crunch, crunch.* Something was trying to get into the small trailer we shared with a long-time family friend.

"Portia, do you hear that?"

"What could it be?"

Soon, there were four of us huddling there, watching and waiting for something huge and hideous to attack us.

"It's a wood rat," our pastor's wife told us days later when we described the sounds to her.

"A wood rat?"

"Yes, and you all be careful of that thing. Don't corner it. It will fight you like a man!"

Each night the rat continued feasting on the innards of our trailer. Every day we talked over our fears. "It must be at least two feet tall, maybe three. What will we do when it gets in? How can we fight such a beast?"

Suddenly, one night there was silence. Then another. A week went by. Our dreaded foe, we surmised, must have found tastier digs elsewhere.

Sometime later, we happened upon a wood rat outdoors. Not two or three feet tall, but more like five inches. It looked more like an unkempt guinea pig than the beast we had imagined. Portia and I stared. Then we laughed at all the fear that little rodent had caused us.

Lord, help me to keep my fears from turning little problems into imaginary giants.   —SHARON FOSTER

14

T
U
E

But thou, O Lord, shalt laugh at them; thou shalt have all the heathen in derision.   —PSALM 59:8

As I write this, I'm looking at a head-and-shoulders bust of a young boy that sits on a table nearby. At first glance, its face has an expression of innocence, but when you gaze a little longer, you discover a hint of mischief in it. People say, "Ah, it's you," when they first see it, but before they get past the look of angelic goodness, I say, "Sorry, it's my dad. I don't go quite back to the turn of *that* century."

Did I say "hint of mischief"? That was unmistakably Dad. A practical joker, a fun boy all his life, Dad never bothered to grow up. My mother despaired, but she, along with men, women and kids, could not resist his charm. Charm it was, and his carefree approach to life was infectious. I have never known what he was named at birth, for early on he said, "Call me Joe"—Joe was a man he admired—and everyone did. He didn't read books or many newspapers, but he was amazingly well-informed, and it used to astonish me when he would recite the names of the books of the Bible straight through, from Genesis to Revelation. And when it came to the Bible, he chose a time to laugh over a time to weep (Ecclesiastes 3:4), or Job listening to Bildad tell how God would not cast away a good man but would fill his lips with shouts of joy (Job 20–21). That was the way he thought. Never down, always up.

Dad died of a heart attack at the age of fifty-two, young perhaps, but he went out joyfully, swinging at a golf ball. How his bust came to me I don't remember, but this much I know—if my day is gloomy and I need a tonic, I look for him on the table. I always get a laugh. You would, too, if the bust suddenly winked an eye.

Lord, forgive my dad his faults; he made a lot of us happy by just being.   —VAN VARNER

15 | W E D

A word fitly spoken is like apples of gold in pictures of silver. —PROVERBS 25:11

I attended a funeral today, feeling a bit baffled about my place in the small gathering of people who were there. My puzzling relationship with the deceased woman began shortly after my own mother died almost fifteen years ago. "I'm going to be your surrogate mother," she told me in a phone call. "I'll be your encourager."

Through the years, she did just that. When I taught a class or had some writing published, she would call me up. "I'm so proud of you," she'd say. "You're doing great." She wrote me notes of encouragement, and sometimes we sat together in church, but she didn't get too close. She never shared much about her own personal life. I knew she had grown children, yet they were estranged. One of her daughters did many of the same things I did. She was a teacher and writer in a nearby community.

During the funeral, the minister alluded to the difficult relationship this woman had with her own children. It sounded like one of those problems that starts out as a little bump in a relationship that continues to grow bigger until no one knows quite how to fix it, in spite of the pain. As I sat there listening and praying, I had the strange but strong feeling I should talk to this daughter. I wasn't sure what I would say, but at the end of the service, I sought her out.

I took her hands in mine and looked right into her eyes. "I don't know if these words will come out right, but for years your mother encouraged me and gave me compliments, and now I realize they were meant for you. So today I'm here to give them back to you . . . where they always belonged."

"Thank you," she said, her eyes filling with tears. "You don't know how much I needed to hear that today."

I didn't know, but obviously God did, for He placed me there and gave me the words to say.

Thank You, Father, for the privilege of being Your messenger.

—CAROL KUYKENDALL

R E A D E R ' S   R O O M

"The end of June my husband suffered a stroke, which left him vision-impaired and with short-term memory loss. On January 3, I suffered an occipital stroke and became vision-impaired also. I am grateful to say that in spite of our circumstances I have only suffered small periods of depression. Yes, oh, yes, God does provide! A dear friend found five men that took a day a week to drive my husband to his exercise classes. Four women friends took one Tuesday a month to help me with business errands or just to lunch out, and another took over the transportation for some household help once a week. My son or his wife from North Carolina came every other week for doctor's or dentist's appointments, haircuts, etc. Has God not taken care of us during this transition year? He is faithful and His people are faithful, to give help and hope to people like us."

—*Regina M. Walters, Bristol, Tennessee*

16

T
H
U

"Should we accept only good things from the hand of God and never anything bad?"...

—JOB 2:10 (NLT)

A number of financial setbacks preceded my trip to south Asia last year. First, one son and then another added a ticket to their driving records, sending my car insurance costs into the upper atmosphere. Then the transmission in my venerable pickup truck decided to expire. College tuition increased at twice the rate of inflation, just as we began to contemplate having to pay three colleges next year. All this kept a cloud in the back of my mind as I traveled.

Coming into Bangladesh, I had little time to think of my problems as my traveling companions and I were confronted with the utter devastation caused by the worst floods in ten years. Whole villages had been washed away, and almost half of the crops would never be harvested. As we flew over the country, we saw little islands of high ground covered with villagers huddled together, awaiting the relief supplies being brought by helicopters and small boats.

When I commented on the awful results of the flood, I was stunned by a government worker who said, "Oh, but let me tell you the happiness of the flood. Each flood, and we have one every year, replenishes the soil by the silt it leaves when it recedes. Without the flood, our farmland would be worn out in just a generation."

Her comment stayed with me throughout the trip and return home. For the "happiness of the flood" recognizes that difficult times are necessary to survival and thriving. In a modest way, the financial setbacks in my family are an opportunity to cut back in ways that hurt but that allow for new growth: to make sacrifices for college educations that will set our boys' futures on a firm footing.

Floods come every year in Bangladesh, and the people receive them prepared for hardship and struggle and with thanksgiving for future crops. What is the "happiness of the flood" in your life?

Lord, help me to remember that difficult times come more to make me rather than to break me. —ERIC FELLMAN

17

F
R
I

Obey this commandment, to love one another. . . . Anyone who says he is walking in the light of Christ but dislikes his fellow man, is still in darkness. But whoever loves his fellow man is "walking in the light". . . . —I JOHN 2:8-10 (TLB)

It is a long way to Tipperary. I should know, as I've just come back! I've fallen in love with Ireland: the brilliant green, the like of which I'd never seen before; the black-faced sheep; the lilting music; and, perhaps most of all, the centuries of tradition in the cathedrals and castles.

My most memorable moment came in St. Patrick's Cathedral in Dublin. Standing under heraldic banners hanging from awesome Gothic arches, I was suddenly drawn to a small, rough-hewn wooden door with a narrow slot in its center. "This is the Door of Reconciliation," the guide told me.

In 1492, two noblemen were battling. Besieged by the Earl of Kildare, the Earl of Ormonde took refuge in St. Patrick's. Kildare, hot on his heels, decided that to continue the feud was folly. He thrust his spear through a small side door of the cathedral and cut a slot. Taking the fearsome risk of having his arm severed, he put it through the slot in a gesture of reconciliation. His hand was grasped by another hand inside the church. The door was then opened, and the two leaders embraced.

As I ran my fingers over the stones framing the arch of that small door, I thought of all the anger, misunderstandings and hurts—the battle wounds that get us feuding with each other. I was nursing such a wound, a falling out with a friend that had led to years of painful estrangement. At the Door of Reconciliation I prayerfully decided to reach out my hand and see if my long-lost friend would take it. I would have to risk rejection: a phone hang-up at the sound of my voice, a letter returned unopened.

I wrote to her from Ireland. She grasped my hand; on my return we met and embraced. The healing will take time, but the process has begun.

How special is the love and peace that comes with reconciliation, Lord.
Give me the courage to risk my heart as I extend my hand to those
from whom I have become estranged.   —FAY ANGUS

18

S
A
T

It is not for man to direct his steps.
            —JEREMIAH 10:23 (NIV)

I got to fretting when it was time for our high school-aged son Chris to decide where he wanted to go to college. One morning as I sat down on the sofa to think about Chris's future, an odd image came into my mind: the Black Hole. The Black Hole, an unexcavated bank of dirt enclosed by a foundation wall, had been created in a new house we bought years ago by the cost-conscious builder in place of a basement room. We had spent an uneasy night of tossing and turning after we put a contract on the house, worrying because our house-to-be wasn't perfect.

On the very day we moved into the house with the Black Hole, a dark-haired woman with sparkling blue eyes knocked on our door. "My name's Margaretta, and I live up the street," she announced. "I've come to invite you to our neighborhood Bible study." As she left, she added, "Before your house was built, I walked down this road in the new development each morning and prayed over every lot."

As I closed the door, I felt a sweep of relief that we *had* made the right decision. It wasn't totally dependent on our wisdom; it had been shaped by the unseen prayer of a stranger. Not only did Margaretta and I become prayer partners and great friends, but even the Black Hole turned out to be perfect after all—as a rugged mountainside setting for the boys' electric train set.

I settled back on the couch. The only sensible thing to do about life's uncertainties was to do as Margaretta had done: simply pray, giving God room to work silently. My heart calmed as I closed my eyes and began to pray over Chris's college decision.

Lord, it's scary to make a decision that will affect my future. Help me to trust You to guide me wisely. —KAREN BARBER

19 | S u N

"With your blood you purchased men for God from every tribe and language and people and nation."
—REVELATION 5:9 (NIV)

My mother is a fantastic cook, and when I was a youngster she loved to prepare international dinners. Dad's job was to come up with authentic music to set the mood for whatever cuisine—Greek, Japanese, African—was taking over our kitchen. I was just a little guy when I mastered chopsticks, and I'll never forget the time we ate goat meat and vegetables Eritrean-style, pinching bites of food between pieces of flat bread.

So last Sunday, when I announced that dinner was on me and gave Dad a choice of any restaurant in town, I wasn't too surprised when he answered, "There's a new Korean restaurant that I'd like to try. It's supposed to be very authentic."

From the outside, the restaurant wasn't exactly impressive. It was located in a little building on a side street on the rougher side of town, and I'll have to admit that I had something a bit showier in mind. But as soon as we entered the restaurant, my doubts disappeared. Colorful Korean art filled the walls, and a beautiful young lady in native dress was waiting to guide us to our table. She smiled broadly as she introduced our waiter as her brother. It turned out that the restaurant was a family business. And though none of the family spoke great English, they genuinely appreciated our visit.

As we struggled with the Korean custom of wrapping fresh-grilled beef in lettuce leaves (no utensils allowed), the father of the family appeared to welcome us. "You are honored among your children," he said to Dad, with a grin of camaraderie.

"This is really good," Dad said, looking around to include the restaurant and the people and the food. It was then that I realized what he and Mom had been trying to teach me all along: The food at God's table is plentiful and as varied as the people who gather there.

"Yes," I answered, "it's *very* good."

God, You have set a feast of plenty before me. Keep me open to learning the ways of all Your children. —BROCK KIDD

20 | M O N | *If when you do right and suffer for it you take it patiently, you have God's approval.*
—I PETER 2:20 (RSV)

One of the hardest things to do in life is to go ahead with something that you know in advance is going to fail.

You go into a basketball game against a team of giants, and your best player is out with injuries. You're going to get pulverized.

You are forced to present your company's budget video after two powerful competitors have shown videos that would rival *Gone with the Wind*.

Or you have to tell your wife that you accidentally cracked up her dream car.

Recently I was in an auto parts store, looking for windshield wipers. I found a large display of them, but when I reached for a box, the entire display groaned and sagged in the middle. I let go, but then the display sagged in the other direction. I was hoping no one had noticed me, but in my lemon-yellow sports shirt I was about as inconspicuous as a strobe light. Since I couldn't prevent this disaster, I decided to have fun with it. I spotted a nearby display big enough to hide me, dashed behind it and peered out. Great was the fall of the Wiper Empire. Row after row of the boxes dropped off, like lemmings falling off a cliff. It was a sight that will linger in my mind for the rest of my life.

In these no-win situations, I think it helps to look for the humor. If I can't win the basketball game, I can play for fun. Or I can dwell on how much pleasure my inferior video is bringing to my competitors. As for my wife's wrecked car? May God have mercy on my soul.

Lord, I can't always win. Teach me to take my share of suffering with a smile. —DANIEL SCHANTZ

21

T
u
E

Sing unto the Lord a new song. . . . —ISAIAH 42:10

"Bill, I am quite certain that I do *not* need this!"

My husband slid the enormous box marked "Microwave Oven" onto the kitchen counter. It was 1981, and all I knew about microwave ovens was that if you didn't poke a potato, it blew up in huge chunks and destroyed the cathode tube, or whatever it was. Needless to say, with four boys approaching their teens, when starvation and sports schedules made mealtime any moment in the twenty-four hours, I soon mastered the microwave and found it to be the best kitchen device ever invented.

But later I understood how overwhelmed my mother felt when, at eighty-eight, we encouraged her to take the secondhand computer my niece offered and learn to get on-line and send e-mail. As I had had to learn a whole new way of cooking and the concepts that went with it, so now my mom faced a whole new world of buttons to push and terms to assimilate. I knew she'd made the transition to the twenty-first century, however, when I called her on the phone one evening a few weeks later.

"Hey, Mom! Your e-mail today said you weren't feeling good. How are you doing tonight?"

"Nothing to worry about, just a stuffy nose." She paused a moment. "Actually, I think I caught a computer virus!"

Lord, help me stay flexible and willing to move, with laughter, beyond the frustrations of learning new ways in technology—and life.

—ROBERTA ROGERS

22

W
E
D

Let her own works praise her in the gates.

—PROVERBS 31:31

Five blocks north of my house, at the end of Avenue I, there's a little boy named Johnny. Though I don't know the boy or his family, I visit Johnny often. His gravestone reads: "Johnny Dale Baker, 1959–1966." The date pulls at my heart because it's the year my own son Paul was born, and I never pass by Johnny without giving thanks for Paul's life and health. I like to walk in the cemetery because it's quiet and beautiful and full of trees and because, in connecting me with the fragility of life, it helps me to value each moment.

Johnny's grave stands out among the rest because of the decorations. In spring, there are huge, overflowing buckets of lilacs, or tall tulips in slim vases, or cherry blossom branches in a sand pail. The flowers are always fresh, as though placed there daily by one who remembers. On the Monday after Easter, my heart almost burst when I saw a large pink and green basket filled with colored eggs, and a soft blue bunny tucked in the center. A few days after Christmas last year, I put on my coat and braved the eleven-degree weather for my morning walk. I was not surprised to see a shiny black and red toy truck on Johnny's grave, surrounded by a holly wreath.

Then one morning in March, I saw who it was who cared for Johnny's grave. Her hair was gray, and her coat looked worn. She wore a green scarf around her head with earmuffs over it, as she placed a candled cake on Johnny's grave. I couldn't read the inscription, but I knew what it said. I wanted to say something, to tell her I had a son born the same year, to let her know how deeply her love and care had touched me. But it was her moment with her son, and I walked quietly by, marveling to myself: *Thirty-four years of faithful remembering!*

When I got home I called my son, who will be forty-one next month, as Johnny would have been. A few words were all I could manage. "Every day I thank God for your life." Paul probably thought, *Mom's getting senile,* but I didn't worry about it.

Thank You, loving God, for creating humans beings with such great capacity for faithfulness.
　　　　　　　　　　　　　　　　—MARILYN MORGAN HELLEBERG

23

T H U

For I say. . . to every man that is among you, not to think of himself more highly than he ought to think. . . . —ROMANS 12:3

Choir practice at St. Paul's Episcopal Church in Nantucket, Massachusetts, was not going well. Three times we'd rehearsed *Dominus Regnavit* by the Renaissance composer Josquin Desprez, and still our director, Richard Busch, was shaking his head.

"You're not together," he said. "Remember, you're a choir, not a group of soloists. This time sing it through very, very softly. Just a whisper! *Pianissimo.*"

We followed Richard's instruction, and now at last he was smiling. "Don't you see?" he said. "When you sing your own part softly, you can hear the other voices."

The next time I am with any group that's having trouble reaching consensus—a family get-together, a business meeting, a political gathering—I will tell the story of the rehearsal at St. Paul's where we whispered and learned to sing together.

Father, help me to lower my own voice so that I can hear what You are saying through others.　　　　　　　　　　　　　—JOHN SHERRILL

24

F
R
I

You have been my help; do not abandon me nor forsake me, O God of my salvation!
—PSALM 27:9 (NAS)

About twenty years ago I began corresponding with a woman I'll call Ryan. We didn't actually meet until about five years ago, when she moved to the Atlanta area. We met for lunch and occasionally dropped each other notes. After a while she mentioned almost casually in a letter that for some time she'd been sleeping in her car.

Her needs were overwhelming. My initial reaction was to put some distance between us, but I tried to do the best I could for her. I made countless calls trying to find her a place to live and help of some kind. I continued to write to her, enclosing what assistance I could. It's very difficult to share the little happenings of everyday life with someone who's living out of a car.

Ryan always answered my letters in her beautiful handwriting, insisting that God was meeting her needs. When her children were small, her minister-husband had left them. Later, a horrific storm had taken away her house and belongings. But she insisted that God was still with her and took care of her. "I'm sleeping in the Waldorf-Astoria of parking lots! A policeman—or maybe he's an angel—watches over me." One note said, "What you sent was just what I needed today." *What about the other days?* I wondered.

My help was so insignificant and my sense of discomfort so great that I thought about not writing. Then a letter came. "I don't tell people how I live anymore," Ryan wrote. "They are too uncomfortable with my situation and turn away."

Whenever I had read the story of Jesus' Crucifixion, I had always felt anger at the disciples who ran away and hid. *I would have been there with John and the two Marys,* I had thought, *not hiding in the court-yard like Peter.* Now I knew better. I went to my typewriter and wrote, "Dear Ryan . . ."

Lord, as I stand with those who are troubled, I am standing at the foot of Your Cross. Help me not to turn away from them. Amen.

—MARION BOND WEST

25 | S
A   *And whoso shall receive one such little child in my*
T   *name receiveth me.*   —MATTHEW 18:5

I can't let a year pass without offering prayers of awed thanksgiving and sharing the good news with all the knitters and crocheters who are a part of our *Daily Guideposts* family. It was on March 25, 1996, that readers first learned of the small part I had played in a program to create warm sweaters for needy and cold children around the world. One thing led to another, and the Guideposts Sweater Project was born.

Knitters who responded from across the country were soon joined by crocheters (seven times more numerous than knitters in this country, I learned to my surprise), who demanded, and received, their own version of the simple pattern we were offering.

More than thirty thousand sweaters have passed through my office since that day in 1996. Imagine thirty thousand sweaters! They make a wonderful, gloriously multicolored mountain as we ship them out every week in ever widening circles—to agencies that work in Appalachia and Mongolia, Ecuador and Africa, Minnesota and New York City, China and Chile.

The sweaters have come from individuals, families, churches; from the Natterers in Boulder, Colorado; the Nimble Thimbles in Newark, Delaware (whose work was acknowledged by their state senator); the Knit Wits of North Carolina; the Knotty Knitters of Indiana; an Episcopal priest in Orlando, Florida, who carries her knitting with her wherever she goes; Leslie in Laurinburg, North Carolina, who is knitting sweaters for the children in honor of her friends as gifts for the Christmas season; and from Sister Monica Maria, a contempla-tive nun in Holland!

The stories are endless. For me, no day passes when the spirit I have received from the knitters doesn't make some chore seem less monotonous and a thorny problem easier to solve. The wonder in the faces of those who put their heads around the door to see the always changing collection makes me deeply proud of the Guideposts family—every day.

Dear God, let us give thanks for the works of many hands, love that is shared and prayers said. —BRIGITTE WEEKS

26 | S
U
N

What does the Lord require of you but . . . to walk humbly with your God? —MICAH 6:8 (RSV)

I wrote about my young friend Andrew in *Daily Guideposts, 1997.* An acolyte at our church while he was in high school, Andrew is now a senior majoring in electrical engineering at the Massachusetts Institute of Technology.

When Andrew returned to church from college last year, I greeted him warmly and told him how proud of him I was. He listened, but showed little enthusiasm. "I don't know," he said. "It's the same old stuff!" Then, noticing my expression, he explained. "I didn't mean it that way. I'm a senior, and in June I'll be out in the real world."

"Are you worried?" I asked.

He nodded, and said, "But then, I was fearful when I entered high school and again when I entered college. It's the same old stuff." Then he brightened. "So everything will be all right."

Andrew couldn't have known how I once feared the future. For eight months I agonized before retiring. I was riddled with doubts. Was I ready to retire? Would I miss my co-workers? Could I handle retirement emotionally? Like Andrew, I faced an unguaranteed future.

Slowly, I came to see that it wasn't retirement that troubled me, but the fear that my dreams for my retirement would fail. I had made all my plans, but I'd neglected to pause and pray. So I put the future into God's hands, where it belongs. And when I did retire, I was amazed at the support awaiting me. Things came unexpectedly and surprisingly from others, far beyond my expectations.

Andrew sees the future through his own plans and expectations, and the times of transition in his life bring anxiety about whether or not those plans will succeed. But God has a wonderful future in store for Andrew, too.

Lord, You give me the freedom to make my own choices. As I face the future, let me entrust it to You.   —OSCAR GREENE

27 | M O N | *Holy, holy, holy, is the Lord of hosts: the whole earth is full of his glory.*   —ISAIAH 6:3

When I lived on the coast of South Carolina, I fell in love with dolphins. I always smiled when I saw them arching and diving in the ocean. But my first encounter with these playful creatures was not so pleasant. One day, while swimming in the ocean, I looked up to see a fin cutting through the water not twenty feet from me. Thinking that I was soon to be dinner for a shark, I froze. My companion, an accomplished surfer, looked at my horrified face, then at the fin and burst into laughter. I had not yet learned to recognize the distinctive difference between a shark's triangular fin and a dolphin's rounded one. Some lessons, once learned, are never forgotten!

Somewhere along the way, the dolphin also became a meaningful symbol of God for me. Every time I walk on the beach, I want to see a dolphin. But dolphins don't appear on command. When I do see one, it's often a fleeting glimpse: a gleaming gray back breaking the surface; the trace of a fin above a wave; or just the distinct wheezing sound of a dolphin breathing through its blowhole. Whenever I see a dolphin, I feel that I've received a gift.

Late this afternoon, I saw a blazing Texas sun dipping toward the vast horizon, silhouetting an arid land in dark, muted beauty. For an instant I felt the tingle of God's presence. Then the sun dropped behind the hillside and I was left with a residue of joy.

God is never on the surface for very long. Although He is always with me, His ways are often hidden; His face cannot be seen. But I am thankful for those precious fleeting glimpses of His wonder.

Dear Father, open my eyes to see You in the simplest of things. May I be grateful for every vision of Your grandeur.   —SCOTT WALKER

28

T
U
E

"Let your light so shine before men, that they may see your good works and give glory to your Father who is in heaven." —MATTHEW 5:16 (RSV)

For a long time I wished we could afford a new rug for the living room. For more than eight years we'd been living with a serviceable but extremely dull gray remnant I had picked up at a discount store. What I would have given for something with color and design.

I don't think I ever told my friend Scott, whose own home is filled with warm, understated and welcoming rugs, how I felt about that rug. Scott, in fact, runs a small business that makes custom-designed handwoven rugs. It's no surprise that he often recycles his products at home.

The other day I was helping him clean out some boxes in his basement when I noticed an antique hooked rug rolled up in one corner. "Do you want it?" he asked casually.

"You mean as a loan?" I said.

"No, to keep."

Our living room now has a beautiful beige, green and gold rug with a subtle floral design. It goes really well with the sofa and makes the room look a hundred percent better. Whenever I walk on it, I'm reminded of my friend's generosity. I've even attempted to match that generosity. For a start, I offered the gray rug to a friend who said it would be perfect for his beach house. I hope so.

Thank You, Lord, for friends who by their generosity guide me closer to You. —RICK HAMLIN

29

W
E
D

A wise woman builds her house, while a foolish woman tears hers down by her own efforts.
—PROVERBS 14:1 (TLB)

One night at a meeting of the SWILL Gang (Southeastern Wisconsin Interesting Ladies League), we got on the subject of pet peeves.

Debbie said procrastination drove her crazy. "I hate it when I put something on my boss's desk ten days before it's due and then it sits there for two weeks before she even looks at it."

Jean said her pet peeve was people who misuse personal pronouns. "I hate it when they say, 'Me and him are going shopping' instead of 'My husband and I are going shopping.'"

Marjorie said her pet peeve was people who constantly crack their gum.

I said I disliked it when people make you take off your shoes before you enter their homes just so they can keep their carpets extra clean.

Sharon said people who grumble about everything really irritate her.

The next day I wondered what we'd accomplished by our round-table on pet peeves. Had we fallen into the category of people in Sharon's peeve? At the next meeting, to redeem myself, I suggested we each mention one human characteristic that we value the most.

Kay said, "I value a friend who has a sense of humor even in down times because that shows joy and faith in God's love."

Sherry said, "I value people who can smile and reach out to people and make them feel welcome. I think a genuine smile really comes from God."

Jean, a clinical psychologist, said, "I think empathy, the capacity to be sensitive to the feelings and needs of others, is the most crucial human quality."

I felt much better after the SWILL Gang left that night, knowing we'd given each other some positive goals. I, for one, am working on a genuine smile. And if I'm asked to take off my shoes when I enter someone's home, I'll flash my best grin, be more empathetic and enter joyfully.

Lord, let me concentrate on all the good qualities of those around me. And help me to polish up some of them for myself.

—PATRICIA LORENZ

---

30 | T H U

We know that we have passed from death to life, because we love our brothers. . . .

—I JOHN 3:14 (NIV)

My brother, my father and my mother all died before I turned twenty-eight. I planned funerals and tried to console the ones who remained. And I spent a lot of time thinking about why God allows His people to be plagued by sickness and death.

One day, shortly after I became a Christian, I was getting into my car to drive to work when I noticed absentmindedly that our four-year-old daughter was playing near the driveway with her dolly. But my mind was already at the office as I started the engine, looked in the rearview mirror and backed the car out of the garage. Suddenly, I heard a snapping crunch, then a scream. My stomach knotted and my throat tightened as I jumped out of the car.

My daughter was standing beside the car, her shattered doll in her arms, sobbing her heart out. And through her tears came rage, hurt and frustration. "You've killed my baby!" she shouted. She would not be consoled by the promise of another doll or by anything I could say. It was her first encounter with irreparable loss.

I thought about it all on the way to work. As painful as it was, it would give my daughter some of the experience she would need to deal with grief as an adult. But now, all she could grasp was the tragedy in her arms. Maybe, I thought, from God's perspective we adults are like four-year-olds, and perhaps a first-hand knowledge of sickness and death is necessary for us if we are to have the sensitivity and loving-kindness to enter into the sufferings of others.

The evils in life are a grim riddle that can't be solved with a neat formula or analogy. But the more loss and suffering I've experienced in my own life, the closer I've felt to others. And gradually I've learned to trust the Guide Who's promised to lead us from death to life.

Dear Lord, thank You for the Cross, through which You have shared— somehow joined me—in my suffering. Help me to use my own crosses to grow in love. —KEITH MILLER

31 | F
R   *Bear ye one another's burdens, and so fulfill the law*
I   *of Christ.*   —GALATIANS 6:2

Jonathan is the son of very dear friends, and I've loved him since he was born. He was always a good kid, but—well, he was lacking in responsibility. Everything came easily to him. He was intelligent, he had wonderful athletic talents, and he was charming. He just didn't work hard at anything. He couldn't be bothered with homework, he didn't show up for team practice, and when he was old enough to get a driver's license, he bent every fender of every car he drove. His parents Joe and Carla tried desperately to awaken a sense of purpose in Jonathan. They had long talks with him, they laid down rules, they assigned him chores around their house—mowing the grass, taking the trash out. The talks were great, but the grass got awfully high and the trash piled up.

Then one day Jonathan read a newspaper article about a horse that had been abandoned by its owner. The poor animal had been rescued from starvation by the local animal shelter, and its fate was uncertain. It was an old horse and needed lots of tender care, but no one was offering to take it. On impulse, Jonathan asked his parents to adopt the horse. "I'll be responsible for it," he said. "I promise!"

Joe and Carla looked at each other, torn between hope and doubt. Finally they agreed. "But you really must take care of it," Joe said.

Now, two years later, the horse is still with my friends and has filled out beautifully. Jonathan built a stall for it next to their garage, and every day he cleans it thoroughly. The horse is too old to ride, but Jonathan walks it regularly. He pays for its food by working part-time at a supermarket. He's very proud of his friend.

But something else has been happening. Jonathan has been doing his homework and getting better grades. He's on the basketball team and never misses practice. He even finds time to cut the grass. Next year he hopes to go to college and wants to be a veterinarian. "How's that for purpose?" Joe says.

Maybe the best way for any of us to become responsible is to start helping someone who needs us.

Even if I am not very strong, Lord, lead me to someone who needs to lean on me for a while.
                                                            —PHYLLIS HOBE

My Renewal Journal

1 _____

2 _____

3 _____

4 _____

5 _____

6 _____

7 _____

8 _____

9 _____

10 _____

11 _____

12 _____

13 _____

14 _____

15 _____

16 _____

17 _____

18 _____

19 _____

20 _____

21 _____

22 _____

23 _____

24 _____

25 _____

26 _____

27 _____

28 _____

29 _____

30 _____

31 _____

APRIL

I am Alpha and Omega, the beginning and the end. I will give unto him that is athirst of the fountain of the water of life freely.　　　　　　　　　　—REVELATION 21:6

S	M	T	W	T	F	S
						1
2	3	4	5	6	7	8
9	10	11	12	13	14	15
16	17	18	19	20	21	22
23	24	25	26	27	28	29
30						

1 | S
A | *You should be known for the beauty that comes from*
T | *within. . . .* —I PETER 3:4 (NLT)

When the new hairdresser finished trimming my hair, she handed me a mirror and spun the chair around so I could see the back.

"Well," she said proudly, "What do you think?"

I stared in disbelief. "What did you do to my hair?" I asked, my voice rising in panic. The back of my head was closely shaved all the way up to my ears. Why, it was the shortest haircut I had ever had!

"You don't like it?" she asked weakly.

I didn't.

Back at home, I stared at my new hairstyle in the mirror. "What will I do?" I moaned to my husband Roy. "I look awful! I can't go anywhere looking like this!"

"Maybe it's time to practice that new idea you read about last week," Roy said. Offered as a way to accept our over-forty looks, it suggested asking "How do I feel?" rather than "How do I look?" when we view ourselves in the mirror.

I looked in the mirror again and asked myself, "How do I feel?" I closed my eyes and thought. Actually, I felt okay. It was a lovely spring day and I had plans to work in my flower garden all afternoon. For the rest of the day, every time I passed a mirror I looked at myself and simply proclaimed how good I felt instead of bemoaning my different look. It worked! By that afternoon I had a garden full of flowers and a heart full of peace. Why, I was actually planning some humorous responses for school tomorrow when my teenage students would surely ask, "Like, what happened to your hair?"

About that time a neighbor walked over and looked at me curiously as I was finishing up outside. "There's something about you that's different," he said. "I just can't put my finger on it."

I could. It was much more than the short haircut.

Today, God, I choose to practice acceptance. Help me to accept myself and my circumstances. —MELODY BONNETTE

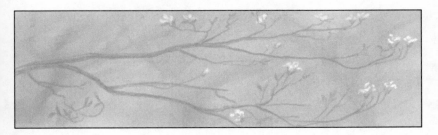

ALL THINGS NEW

2 | S
U
N | **Beginning in Darkness**
And they found the stone rolled away from the
sepulchre.   —LUKE 24:2

I grew up in a nonchurchgoing family. But there was one Sunday each year when we did go to church: Easter! The day to me meant chocolate rabbits, colored eggs and lamb with mint sauce for dinner. And while the lamb was cooking, that once-a-year church service filled with a blue-robed choir singing:

> Christ the Lord is ris'n today, Alleluia!
> All creation joins to say, Alleluia!
> Raise your joys and triumphs high, Alleluia!
> Sing, ye heav'ns, and earth reply, Alleluia!

If anyone had asked me what the Alleluias were for, I would have said, "Spring, of course." Weren't the crocuses popping up in our yard? Didn't I have a new white-straw hat? Darkness played no part in these joyful rites.

It was a quarter-century later that I attended my first Good Friday service. A bare church, the tolling of a bell, not a flower to be seen. The opposite, it appeared, of Easter gladness.

But, of course, it wasn't the opposite; it was the preparation. The new life in Christ, the Resurrection life we celebrate at Easter, I knew by then, was only possible on the other side of death. New things, God's new things, began in the darkness.

"Christ the Lord is risen today!" Not zooming up in a space ship like Buck Rogers in my comic books, as I pictured Him when I was a little girl in a new hat; but risen after bleeding and dying and descending into the dark. Charles Wesley's great hymn, which I first heard on those long-ago Easter Sundays, ends with words that bewildered me then, but fill me today with joy:

Ours the cross, the grave, the skies, Alleluia!

Teach me to look in every death, Father, for the seeds of Your new life.

—ELIZABETH SHERRILL

Editor's note: What new things has God been doing in your life? Take a few minutes to look back at what you've written in "My Renewal Journal," and let us know some of the exciting changes this year has brought. Send your letter to *Daily Guideposts* Reader's Room, Guideposts Books, 16 E. 34th St., New York, NY 10016. We'll share some of what you tell us in *Daily Guideposts, 2002.*

3 | M O N

For to him that is joined to all the living there is hope. . . . —ECCLESIASTES 9:4

A friend of mine who does counseling was recounting a recent experience with a patient who had been sentenced to life in a wheelchair as the result of a serious auto accident. Though understandably devastated by his prognosis, the injured man had made excellent progress.

"You mean physically?" I asked.

"No, mentally and spiritually." The psychoanalyst explained it this way: "My first question was, 'Do you want to live or not?' The guy had lived a very active life, and the thought of a sedentary existence left him disconsolate. I told him that if he didn't want to live, I couldn't help him. If he did, we could explore his possibilities together." The paralyzed man decided he did, indeed, want to go on with his life, and today he is studying engineering.

I was surprised by my friend's stark question about wanting to live, but in retrospect I see that it was a crucial one. Unless we say yes to life, the human spirit cannot triumph. Half-hearted living is no living at all. It's something like lukewarm faith. Fortunately, God has planted a strong survival instinct in each of us, a life force that resists to the end. The mystery is why it so often takes a life-threatening crossroad to discover life's absolute preciousness and its real purpose.

How can we thank You, Father, above?
Only by sharing Your infinite love. —FRED BAUER

4 | T
U
E | *And he called the multitude, and said unto them, Hear, and understand.* —MATTHEW 15:10

Elizabeth sat curled under my arm on the sofa as I read aloud from *Little House on the Prairie.* Twenty-month-old John played happily on the floor nearby with his beloved trucks. The chapter I was reading told about the Ingalls family's neighbor, Mr. Edwards, who spit tobacco juice.

"What's tobacco juice?" Elizabeth asked. I stopped to explain.

Suddenly, John's head popped up, and he raced over. Jumping up and down, he shouted and gestured wildly. *Why is he so excited about tobacco juice?* I wondered. I'd rarely seen him so worked up.

Then John's words became clearer. "*Backhoe* juice? *Backhoe* juice!" he crowed as he ran to pick up his beloved yellow excavator. As if to say, "But, Mommy, why haven't you ever given me any of *that?* You know I love trucks!"

Elizabeth and I laughed for a long time about John's misunderstanding. It's funny how we sometimes hear what we expect to hear, instead of what's really being said. Even in our prayers.

Dear Lord, help me to listen for Your voice instead of settling for an echo of my own. —JULIA ATTAWAY

5 | W
E
D | *If the Son therefore shall make you free, ye shall be free indeed.* —JOHN 8:36

A *Daily Guideposts* reader wrote me from the Oregon State Penitentiary in Salem, pleading, "Please come to see me. Nobody ever does."

Remember the Scripture in Matthew where Jesus encourages His people to visit those in prison? It's always made me uncomfortable. But I took a deep breath and phoned the institution to ask for permission to visit. They requested my driver's license number for a background check.

On the appointed day, I approached the formidable gray-rock walls, topped with searchlights and armored turrets. Inside the entrance, a receptionist requested my identification and then handed me a form with Oregon's official seal at its top. Below the seal was my name, with "No Record" stamped in red ink beside it. The receptionist said, "Permission has been granted," and nodded to a security officer who escorted me through surveillance devices and one barred gate after another.

Each metal gate opened, *CLANG.* And closed, *CLANG.* The *CLANG*s reverberated and echoed down corridors marked by thousands of bars. *CLANG. CLANG. CLANG.*

What if I can't get back out!

To keep from panicking, I had to remind myself continually of that red "No Record" stamp beside my name. Even so, after the conclusion of my visit, I was greatly relieved to be out again. As I drove home, I thought, *Inmates are in there because they broke at least one of our laws. What if I were put in prison whenever I break one of God's laws? I'd never get out!*

Then relief swept over me. I remembered I had another "No Record" stamp, sealed in the blood of the King of kings. Now, that's freedom!

Dear Jesus, You submitted to death to wipe away my sins and heal my guilt. Thank You for the freedom You've won for me.

—ISABEL WOLSELEY

6
T
H
U

Thanks be to God for his indescribable gift!
—II CORINTHIANS 9:15 (NIV)

As Parkinson's disease continued to devastate my husband Bob, we realized we would need an electric hospital bed at home for him. They're far from cheap, and with other medical expenses taking a big chunk of our income, purchasing one seemed impossible.

"We can't give up," our daughter Emily said during a winter visit. "Let's all pray for a way to be opened for him to have one."

No change in our circumstances occurred until a day in April. A fellow employee in the insurance company where Emily works called her into her office. "This is Mrs. Walton," she told Emily. "I think you two have something in common. You need an electric hospital bed, and she has one she wants to get rid of."

"How much are you asking for it?" Emily asked.

"I don't want to sell it," Mrs. Walton answered. "I want to give it to someone who can use it. It was my husband's, and since his death, I've been looking for someone to give it to."

Emily recognized the bed as a gift from God. That's what she called it when she phoned to tell us about it. And when a truck from Emily's office brought it to our house, I knew it was, too.

Almighty God, thank You for the love and mercy with which You supply Your children's needs. As I face this bright, new century, let me proclaim loudly my praises for You. —DRUE DUKE

7 | F
R
I *He giveth grace unto the lowly.* —PROVERBS 3:34

Growing up, I remember an inexpensive set of steak knives with plastic handles meant to look like wood. There was one bent one, its handle heat-warped by the dishwasher. By decree of some sort, Saturday night was steak night at our house, and you knew it by the fact that Mom set the table with the steak knives. Invariably, the bent one was at her place. Typical mother behavior, I always thought.

The number of table settings diminished through the years as my siblings grew up and moved out—I am the youngest—yet every Saturday, the same humble, deformed utensil would appear at Mom's place. When I teased her about always choosing the bent knife, she would say she felt sorry for it, the way I suppose she felt sorry for household spiders whom she'd scoop up in her hand and sneak outside before my father could dispatch them with a rolled-up section of the *Detroit Free Press*. It's true, Mom always loved the underdog.

Shortly before we had to move her into an Alzheimer's unit, a number of years after my father died, I showed up while she was eating dinner alone in that house once so full of children. It wasn't steak night, but, yes, at her place setting was the old bent-handled knife.

Typical mother behavior? Maybe. But Mom certainly wasn't egoless, far from it. She was proud, fiercely proud, of many things—her family, her children, her own sharp, restless, independent mind. She was known to brag a bit, that is true. But as I grew older I understood how hard my mother worked at practicing humility. She saw humility as a *spiritual* discipline, a redemptive one, a reminder of her role in God's world. After all, this was the woman who walked around on Good Friday with a sharp pebble in her shoe to remind her of Christ's suffering. No doubt that knife reminded her of something, too: that even in our smallest, humblest choices we can honor God.

Teach me, God, a lesson in humility, a lesson in serving You.
—EDWARD GRINNAN

8 | S A T | *The Lord watches over you. . . .*
—PSALM 121:5 (NIV)

Last week I went to a rummage sale held in a cavernous gymnasium in Las Lomas High School. I'll admit I was a bit startled when the twentyish man behind me in line told his daughter, who appeared to be about five, "You can go play in the toy section while Daddy looks at the tools. I'll come and find you when I'm finished."

In this day and age? I thought. *After everything you read in the paper?* But the girl nodded happily and skipped off without a backward glance. Still, I was troubled. And although I wanted to say something, I didn't have the courage to tell him he should keep an eye on his daughter.

But I decided that I would do just that, without saying a word. So instead of looking for old books and bric-a-brac, I spent the next thirty minutes watching from a distance as a five-year-old girl I'd never met before nearly fell off an exercise machine, tried on a pair of shoes with stiletto heels and a big purple flowered hat and then talked to her reflection in a big gilded mirror, and played with a set of checkers, another game and three toy trucks. Finally, when her dad—carrying a big box of nuts and bolts and a rusty lawn mower—came by to get her, I breathed a sigh of relief and got back to my junk hunting.

I had to smile to myself at how strange the whole experience had been. After all, though the two of them didn't know I was watching her, I *was* watching her. If she had gotten into trouble or fallen, I would have made sure she was all right. And then I thought, there is Someone Who is always watching me, whether I am aware of it or not.

Thank You, God, for Your constant loving watch over me. Even when I forget that You're there, You're there.
—LINDA NEUKRUG

9

*Come, let us bow down in worship, let us kneel be-
fore the Lord our Maker; for He is our God and we
are the people of his pasture, the flock under his care.*
—PSALM 95:6–7 (NIV)

When my husband Alex has to be away on weekends, I find it a huge
challenge to get myself and the kids to church on time on Sunday
mornings. Last Sunday Alex was away, we had stayed up late Saturday
night watching a movie and I was sorely tempted to let us all sleep
in. Then I thought of my dad and wondered how he did it.

I was eight, Sue was six, Carol, four, and my brother Bobby a tender two years old when our mother died. One day, after battling a vicious virus for three weeks, she was gone. Dad did his best to take
care of us. He had to work long hours to keep his struggling business
afloat. Yet he kept up family times, like picnics and Sunday afternoon
drives, visits to Grandma and Grandpa, even camping trips!

One thing Dad made sure we didn't miss was church on Sunday.
It was a tough task, getting four young children dressed and ready to
go. In his rush to get us all in the car, he locked himself out of the
house a few times. Then it was little Bobby's job to crawl through a
basement window, come up and open the front door so Dad could
go back in and get the car keys. Often we weren't on time, but somehow we made it to church every Sunday.

As I watched Dad kneel in church, his head leaning wearily on his
folded hands, I sensed the burden he was carrying. And it must have
been there that he found the strength to go on, the grace to keep
working and parenting and trusting God for the future.

*Father, thank You for reminding me to come to Your house to be cared
for by You and Your people.*   —MARY BROWN

A PLACE OF MY OWN

10 | M
     | O   *And God created . . . every winged fowl after his kind:*
     | N   *and God saw that it was good.*   —GENESIS 1:21

Scratch, scratch. At first I thought the sounds were something wrong with the air conditioner just outside the window where I was working at the computer.

Scratch, scratch. No, the sounds were caused by something else. I opened the window and tried to see, but the air conditioner was too high. There was a cul-de-sac created by the overhang of a carved angel, part of the building's carved relief, and the sounds were coming from in there. I asked around, and finally the doorman said all-knowingly, "Swallows." Then he added, "Want to get rid of them?" He intimated he knew how.

"No," I said, and I meant it. I went back to work pleased that, although I couldn't see them, at least I knew they were there.

A few days later came a different sound: *Cheep, cheep.* Babies! I was triumphant. Now those country-lovers who decried my way of living, who were always telling me about nature in the raw, had nothing on me. In the middle of New York City I had provided these birds with an air conditioner for a home, and a fine one, as fine as that of the Psalmist who rang forth, "Yea, the sparrow hath found her an house, and the swallow a nest for herself, where she may lay her young" (Psalm 84:3). Then it came to me how alike we really were. It was life, and I was part of it. It was transitory, for weren't we both on lease?

That was a long time ago. They have come every year, have had their offspring and then moved on, only to return. No, I don't know if they are the same swallows. After all, I've never seen them in their nest. Maybe, just maybe, that overhanging angel, that guardian angel, has been protecting us these many years.

How good it is, Father, that I have the fowl of the air beside me.

—VAN VARNER

11

T
U
E

My soul thirsteth for God, for the living God. . . .

—PSALM 42:2

I felt soul-weary when I woke up this morning. Kind of like a crumpled-up juice box, sucked dry and empty, with nothing left to give anybody or anything. Still, I had to drag myself out of bed because I'd promised to attend an early-morning breakfast meeting in town.

At the end of the breakfast, my walk back to the car took me by a park, and though I was thinking about all the tasks ahead of me, the sights and sounds of children caught my attention. On a whim, I took a detour through the park and plunked myself down on the grass, leaned back against a big, warm rock and looked around.

Across the lawn, a young man threw a Frisbee for his golden retriever. A little girl tucked herself into a ball and did a series of somersaults down a hill. A circle of giggly children played "Duck Duck Goose." A young mother pushed her little boy on a swing. A yellow butterfly fluttered across the lawn, a bee buzzed into a bright red flower, and the marshmallow clouds billowed against a brilliant blue sky.

I simply sat there and drank in the surroundings. Then I got up, walked back to my car and drove away.

I'd "lost" a whole hour of the day, but it was the best investment I could have made. I'd refilled the juice box . . . to the brim.

Father, You quench me with Your goodness.   —CAROL KUYKENDALL

12

W
E
D

Now the God of patience and consolation grant you to be likeminded one toward another according to Christ Jesus.   —ROMANS 15:5

My father taught me to drive when I was fifteen. I was not an apt pupil. The first time I put the car into reverse, my foot slammed down on the accelerator and stuck there. Backing wildly through the yard, I mowed down two wooden clothesline poles. When the car finally came to rest, my father sat in silence, staring out the window. At last he said quietly, "I believe we need to work on this some more."

Blessings on my father for his patience. I often think of him whenever I get exasperated with someone around me. Like Sue, with whom I once served on a planning committee for a statewide women's organization. Sue argued every point and backed her views with lots of information, most of it incorrect. There were times when, as chair of the committee, I wanted to yell, "Sue, be quiet!" Instead, remembering my father, I'd take a deep breath and say, "Thank you, Sue, but I believe we need to work on this some more."

The Bible speaks of our heavenly Father's patience and says we should be like-minded toward one another according to Christ Jesus. That's not always easy, but it's a good goal to strive for.

Father, please give me patience today as I work with others. Amen.

—MADGE HARRAH

13

T
H
U

Out of Zion, the perfection of beauty, God hath shined.
—PSALM 50:2

The conversation with the man sitting next to me on the flight from Atlanta was a bit unsettling. When he found out that I'm a Christian, he said, "My wife's into that sort of thing, too. No offense to you, but I think religion's just a security blanket. No one has ever been able to prove God exists, and there's no evidence that anything lives on after death."

I wanted to argue with him but thought it would be futile, so I turned to look out the window. The view was only solid gray, unbroken clouds, an emptiness void of everything. It had rained the whole week I was in Atlanta, coloring my mood as gray and opaque as today's sky. After an hour or so of depressive inner grumbling, I reminded myself that blue sky, sun, patchwork earth, trees and houses still existed, despite their invisibility to me. Finally, near the end of the flight, I turned to my seatmate and said, "You know, no human being has ever been able to weigh and measure love or show where hope resides in the body. Yet every day the stirrings of the heart make their invisible presence known. They testify to the reality of the unseen."

"*Um hm*," mumbled the man as he returned to his newspaper.

Then, startlingly, the gray veils parted as we began our descent into Omaha, Nebraska, revealing April-green fields, brown rolls of hay, blue water and buglike cars on plaid streets, all testifying to the reality of that which was so recently invisible and unproveable. As my seatmate gathered up his things, he glanced past me out the window, smiled and said, "Just look at all that sunshine! Have you ever seen anything so beautiful?"

It would be wrong to read too much into his parting remark, but for me, that moment still shines with the essence of the Divine, like newly polished gold.

God of all creation, please keep me aware this day of Your shining presence in all things.   —MARILYN MORGAN HELLEBERG

---

14 | F R I | *O Zion, that bringest good tidings, get thee up into the high mountain. . . .*   —ISAIAH 40:9

One of the toughest things about shifting from working in a big organization to being a consultant and volunteer is trying to set priorities among all the activities that come at me every day. Once the office schedule set my schedule and the organization's goals set my goals. Now clients, all with different agendas and different needs, make constant demands without regard to calendars or time zones! New friends in Asia are ten or twelve hours ahead, so when they have a concern at 3:00 P.M., my cell phone will ring at 2:00 A.M.!

Flying with a friend into Katmandu, Nepal, I gained some insight into setting priorities. As we approached the city, I was stunned by the beauty of the snow-capped Himalayas. I'd flown over the Rocky Mountains many times, but they seemed like foothills in comparison to the vast range that contains Mount Everest. Turning to my companion, a native Nepali, I asked, "How do you even keep track of which is which?"

"Oh," he replied, "we don't even bother to name them unless they are taller than twenty thousand feet. Once you climb above twenty thousand feet, you can look down on all the others and they fall into place in relation to the higher peaks."

Do you, like me, have a jumbled agenda that crowds your days? Pick out the highest peaks—the items most important to you, your family, your co-workers, your life. Name them. Focus on one thing at a time; tackle each one, and see everything else in perspective. I'm calling it the "Himalaya Method." I'll let you know how it works.

Lord, keep me looking for the highest and best, and help me focus my energies on those things that are most important. —ERIC FELLMAN

15 | S A T

"Give to Caesar what is Caesar's, and to God what is God's." —MATTHEW 22:21 (NIV)

For twenty years, the whole length of my nursing career, Peggy Fox prepared my income tax return. She began an ambitious new business as a tax preparer after retiring from her career as a math teacher.

Every year, Peggy's staff allotted me a two-hour time slot so we could catch up on moments and milestones as we went through my records. There was something about reviewing all those canceled checks and receipts that made me analyze more than just where my money had gone. In her teacherly way, Peggy always seemed to turn the subject to goals. "This time next year, you'll have that doctorate, Roberta," she would mutter as she talked back to her computer.

Come every April 15, I hadn't just given an account to Caesar; I'd also given one to Peggy. As we talked, I would make a mental note to try to be more frugal and I would sheepishly thank God for the many reminders of His grace logged in my check register.

As the years flew by, Peggy began to nudge me toward preparing for retirement. Never mind that she was busier in her golden years than ever before, serving an amazing number of hours as a volunteer and mastering the computer as she neared her eightieth birthday.

This year, I faced April 15 without Peggy, but she will forever be alive in my memory and in my approach to tax time. She taught me that it wasn't a day to dread, but rather a cause for celebration. Tax time need not be a bother: If you do it Peggy and God's way, it's about blessings.

Dear Lord, there's no line on Form 1040 to itemize the graces You have given me, but they are truly my treasure. —ROBERTA MESSNER

THE WAY OF THE CROSS

Have you ever wanted to spend a Holy Week in Jerusalem, walking in the very streets through which Jesus carried His Cross? Since the time when the Roman persecutions of Christians ceased in the fourth century, believers have longed to visit the places hallowed by their Savior's presence, to touch stones that may have been warmed by the sun on the morning of the Resurrection. At the dawn of a new millennium, Pam Kidd invites us to join her in Jerusalem as she follows Jesus along "The Way of the Cross." We'll meet some of the remarkable people who have helped her to a new and richer understanding of the drama of our Redemption. —THE EDITORS

16 | S u N | Day One: Palm Sunday

Jesus took the Twelve aside and told them, "We are going up to Jerusalem, and everything that is written by the prophets about the Son of Man will be fulfilled." —LUKE 18:31 (NIV)

At the beginning of Holy Week, I find myself looking past pretty woven baskets, soft furry bunnies and egg hunts, even past those small worries about what I'm going to wear or whether I should serve lamb or rolled roast this year. I want to set my sights higher and farther, on Jerusalem, the distant city where so many of the stories that made our faith unfolded. Here an angel stayed the hand of Abraham as he drew it back to slay his son. King David chose this place to build his palace-fortress, the City of David, and here his son King Solomon built a great temple in which dwelt the glory of God. Here, nearly two thousand years ago, a Man rode through the city gates in triumph on a donkey's back and six days later walked back outside the city carrying a Cross.

This Holy Week, let's go to Jerusalem and travel the famed Via Dolorosa, the Way of Sorrow, the path Jesus walked to His Crucifixion. We'll follow in His footsteps over stones washed by the tears of saints and polished by the feet of pilgrims for almost two thousand years. In all, there are fourteen places to stop and pray along the Via Dolorosa, the traditional Stations of the Cross. Our trek through the city this week will take us to seven of them, so join me in setting aside a few minutes of devotion and prayer during each of the next seven days. What better commitment could there be than this: to walk along beside the Man Who carried the Cross that set us free?

Lord, as I begin the way of the Cross, renew my hope and strengthen my faith.
—PAM KIDD

17

M
O
N

Day Two: Jesus Is Condemned to Death
When Pilate saw that he could prevail nothing . . . he took water, and washed his hands before the multitude, saying, I am innocent of the blood of this just person. . . .
—MATTHEW 27:24

Jesus had been set up long before He was brought to Pilate. His words had been turned into accusations that ran from "subverting our nation" to "claiming to be a king." The Romans and their collaborators had worked the people into a frenzy, and the crowd's fury rose like an angry tide. So Jesus stood on the fine limestone plaza of Jerusalem's legendary Royal Portico, at the first Station of the Cross, as the great struggle He had unleashed between God's way and the world's way was about to reach its climax.

"Pam, everyone in the auxiliary is sick and tired of Mildred's preoccupation with that delinquent girls' home. For years we've been giving every cent of money we raise to her pet charity and, frankly, it's hurting our image. We never make the paper, and we haven't seen a city-service award in so long I can't remember. Somebody's going to have to step up and do something that gets us a little PR. Now Mildred's going to be absent next meeting, and we're going to use that as an opportunity to get her out of the president's chair. And, Pam, we're going to count on you to help."

So, do I go to the meeting and stand up for Mildred and the little-noticed but badly needed work she does for neglected children? Do I stand with the crowd? Or do I simply "catch a bug" and stay home?

I find it very easy to point a finger at the crowds who egged Pilate on to sentence Jesus. But every time I bend His teachings for my convenience, I am one of the world's crowd shouting, "Crucify Him!"

Jesus, the way of the Cross leads to a new world ordered by Your teachings. Help me apply Your lessons to my life.   —PAM KIDD

18
T
U
E
Day Three: Jesus Takes Up His Cross
So the soldiers took charge of Jesus. Carrying his own cross he went out. . . .   —JOHN 19:16–17 (NIV)

The streets of Jerusalem are narrow. Arches bend low and corners turn sharply from one rough cobblestone lane to the next. Jesus has been flogged, beaten and crowned with thorns. Now, at the second station, the rough-hewn, heavy Cross is placed on His shoulder. There's a song about the "ten thousand angels" He could have called to rescue Him from that burden, but instead He chooses to carry its terrible weight down these twisting streets.

Faith Horner is one of my heroes. She is a true Nashville aristocrat. Several years ago, when the plight of the Vietnamese "boat people" first broke across the nightly news, a little group of people from our church got together and decided that we had to do something about it. Faith was in the lead.

After exploring several options, we decided that we would renovate a carriage house and garage on the church property as a home for refugees. Faith and her husband were more than generous with their financial support. But what we really needed was labor. So early every workday, Faith would drive up in her tidy Mercedes. She would twist back her blond hair into a bun and pull on her work gloves. When we had no one skilled enough to run the table saw, Faith learned how. When no one wanted to volunteer to tar the roof on a sweltering day, Faith was the first one up the ladder with a bucket of pitch. Anyone for stuffing itchy insulation into a tight attic space? Faith was ready.

Faith could have been content to give her money to our project, and we would have been grateful. But she did much better: In sharing our burdens, she gave us herself.

Jesus, on this third day of Holy Week, I will prepare for whatever gift of self You may ask of me. Help me to be astute enough to recognize the opportunities You send. —PAM KIDD

19 | W E D | Day Four: Simon of Cyrene Is Forced to Take Up the Cross

As they led him away, they seized Simon from Cyrene, who was on his way in from the country, and put the cross on him and made him carry it behind Jesus.

—LUKE 23:26 (NIV)

Three of the four gospels say the same thing about Simon from Cyrene. The soldiers "pressed," "seized," "made" him carry the Cross for Jesus. We meet Simon at the fifth Station of the Cross after we have traveled a good way through the streets of Jerusalem. Already Jesus has fallen under the cross's weight. But until the soldiers pull Simon from the crowd, no one has stepped forward to help.

It's Sunday morning and our church congregation has gathered for communion. Just as the elders step forward to receive the elements, I hear the buzz of an electric wheelchair entering the sanctuary. It is a multihandicapped man in his thirties who lives in an apartment on our church grounds. Since birth he has been disabled by cerebral palsy, and he has little control over his body.

Oh, my goodness, I think to myself, *how will Jerry ever take communion?*

My heart skips a beat. He is parking his wheelchair next to my pew. I look around, hopefully. On another occasion I have seen a fine old gentleman rise up from his pew and help Jerry with communion. He's not here today.

The elder distributing the bread is drawing near our pew. My hands feel sweaty, the blood pounds in my head. *I have to do this,* I tell myself.

The plate comes. Jerry glances over at me with his big brown eyes. I take two pieces of bread.

"The Bread of Life," the minister says. Jerry opens his mouth like a baby bird and I put the bread on his tongue.

So far, so good. *Oh, no! The grape juice . . . in those tiny glasses.* Again, I take two. "The Water of Life."

Jerry leans back and I pour the juice into his mouth. He smiles at me. I smile at him. Serving another, whether by chance or by choice, feels very, very good.

Jesus, on this fourth day of Holy Week, help me prepare myself for the frighteningly beautiful opportunity to serve. —PAM KIDD

---

20 | T H U   Day Five: Jesus Is Nailed to the Cross

And they crucified him. —MARK 15:24 (NIV)

Jesus' long journey ends at Golgotha, the place of the skull. Here the stench of burning garbage wafts through the air as the soldiers nail Jesus' hands and feet to the cross.

What awful heartbreak humankind has imposed on God. Everything might have been different if we had lived in faith from the beginning, if we hadn't kept straying away from the light and choosing the dark. And, suddenly, I am very, very sorry that Jesus has had to go all the way—for me.

Jesus' arms are stretched wide, His breathing grows shallow. I long to take the pain in His place. I long to have the kind of faith that would make His misery worthwhile. I retrace His steps through the streets of Jerusalem, remember His words, recall His story. "The Son of man came not to be ministered unto, but to minister, and to give His life a ransom for many," Matthew 20:28 tells us.

Haven't I hung on the sidelines long enough? I've glimpsed faith and stuck my toes in its shallows. Now it's time for me to dive in and become a part of God's story.

Our friend Don Beisswenger recently retired as a full professor at Vanderbilt University. "So, what are you going to do now, Don?" I asked at his retirement party. "Write a book? Travel? Take up fly-fishing?"

"Well, first I'm going to go down to Atlanta and live in a shelter with some homeless people. I'll be there for six months," he answered. "Then I'll see what I'm called to do next."

On this fifth day of Holy Week, Lord, help me to receive what You are dying to give and to give myself to You in return. —PAM KIDD

21 | F | Good Friday: Jesus Dies on the Cross
| R | *Jesus said, "It is finished." With that, he bowed his*
| I | *head and gave up his spirit.* —JOHN 19:30 (NIV)

Finally, Jesus has given all He had to give. He calls out to God the Father, gives a loud cry and dies. Beneath the Cross we stand in shocked silence.

My husband David and I have been in Jerusalem for several days. We are on the edge of a swelling crowd flowing through a huge church bedecked to the hilt with ornate silver doodads. From there we're carried along into a narrow, winding street, through alleys, down a long series of stone steps and onto a broad plaza that overlooks a big wall.

"This," says our guide, "is the Wailing Wall. Its foundation dates back to King Solomon's Temple. Here people from around the world gather, as in centuries past, to pray."

After our tour ends, I walk across the plaza and stand in the area reserved for women who wish to pray. I reach out a bit self-consciously and touch the wall. It is as smooth as satin. It has been polished by millions of prayers.

I see hundreds of thousands of tiny papers stuck in its indentations—the scribbled prayers of wives and mothers, young girls and old women. What hopes and dreams, what pain and suffering, what thanksgiving and praise mortar this wall?

Strangely, my hand finds an imprint in the wall that fits it perfectly. I sense my kinship with these women of many faiths standing and sitting and kneeling around me. They are chanting, wailing, singing and praying in Hebrew, French, Arabic, Japanese and German.

"Our Father, Who art in heaven . . ." I surprise myself as I begin praying out loud. Today, on day six of this Holy Week, I see the meaning of Jesus' sacrifice in this great swell of humanity who seek Him. He lived and died, they tell me in Russian, Chinese and Italian, for all humankind.

Jesus, people come in throngs from around the globe to walk the way of the Cross with You. I see You in their faces and I know what You know: It was worth the price You paid. —PAM KIDD

22

S
A
T

Day Seven: Jesus' Body Is Taken Down from the Cross

So Joseph bought some linen cloth, took down the body, wrapped it in the linen, and placed it in a tomb cut out of rock. —MARK 15:46 (NIV)

This is the darkest Station of the Cross, the time when hope gives way to despair. The old age is finished just as surely as the temple curtain was torn in two from top to bottom in the moment Jesus died. And still there is no indication that the new age is about to break over Jerusalem.

How black that night of unkept promises must have been, and yet one man, Joseph, "a man who looked forward to the Kingdom of God," wasn't afraid to approach Pilate and ask for the body of a condemned criminal.

Just how brave is brave? I ask myself, considering the chance that Joseph took to provide Jesus a proper burial before the onset of the Sabbath. Or was it faith? Might Joseph have already believed the as-yet unbelievable?

I was only a little girl when I knew Ma Peace, but I will never forget her. She had the reputation of being a godly woman. My mother often talked of her kindness, her goodness to others, her steady faith.

And then one day, we heard terrible news: Ma Peace's daughter and her little grandchildren had all been burned to death in a house fire. I remember how my mother cried for Ma Peace, as if she would be lost as surely as her family had been lost. And yet, soon after, we paid her a visit and she was the same: a kind, good, faithful woman. And all her life she never changed: serving, loving, looking ahead.

When death is the only reality and no promises have been kept, how brave is brave? On this seventh day of Holy Week I long for a faith that holds true even in the darkness.

Jesus, Your story is the light that overcomes the dark. Make me brave in its knowing. —PAM KIDD

23 | S U N | Easter Day: Jesus Rises from the Tomb

"Don't be alarmed," he said. "You are looking for Jesus the Nazarene, who was crucified. He has risen! He is not here. See the place where they laid him."

—MARK 16:6 (NIV)

The fourteenth Station of the Cross brings us to the Church of the Archangel. Here a fragment of rock marks the spot where the angel is supposed to have sat when he spoke those words to the women who had come to the tomb. Beyond the rock the sepulchral chamber waits. It is empty.

Jesus' disciples were reluctant to go to the empty tomb after the women bounded in with the angel's news. "They were afraid," a favorite Easter litany tells me, "of finding nothing . . . or of finding God."

I was at a meeting of the outreach committee at our church. We were discussing the plight of the homeless in Nashville. We had decided to raise some seed money, buy an old, run-down house, then restore it. The house will become a home for a woman who has never had a home of her own.

In the weeks ahead, we heard every reason imaginable for *not* going ahead with the project. "The house is past fixing." "Where's all that money coming from?" "How about fixing our own buildings first?" But the committee moved forward because, well, the tomb was empty and we had to do something! People began showing up to work on the house. We ripped out the walls, tore off the roof. We ran out of money and raised more. We started building, hammering, sawing, painting. Six months later, on a sunny spring day, the woman stood on her new porch and looked straight into our faces and sang, "I'm gonna lay down my burdens with the Lord."

It was Easter, once again. The tomb was empty. Fear nothing!

Considering what Jesus has done for us, shouldn't we take each chance He hands us and sign the good work that follows with His name?

God, the Father of all, I am just now at the beginning. Your Son Jesus has shown me that the way of the Cross leads beyond death, past an empty tomb, then home to You. I step out into tomorrow fearing nothing.

—PAM KIDD

R E A D E R ' S   R O O M

"We had just missed the celebration of one year of marriage by one week when we separated. That first year was a troubled one: money problems, health problems and especially spiritual problems. The wedding ring I'd been so happy to have put on my finger broke in half the day of Grandmother's funeral! I think she would have said, 'There's nothing broken that my God can't fix. You look to God, granddaughter.' So that's just what I did. I placed phone calls to those who love us most to begin a prayer chain. The next day was Sunday and church felt especially good. God was at work, and the prayer chain was paying off. My husband made many attempts to talk with me that day. Here we sat one day after our first anniversary, talking, crying and listening to each other's hurts. I look down at the newly reinforced wedding band on my hand now, made stronger by a jeweler's infusion of more gold, and think about how it is sturdier, stronger and has a better foundation. My heart fills with the spirit it once filled with before as I realize my own foundation is sturdier, stronger and worth more than any gold a jeweler has infused into that wedding band. It's as if I can hear my grandmother say, 'There's nothing broken my God can't fix.' "

—*Geneva Sanders, Abilene, Texas*

24

M
O
N

They were taking their meals together with gladness and sincerity of heart, praising God. . . .
—ACTS 2:46-47 (NAS)

The young minister had challenged us to celebrate Easter a little differently, and so very early in the morning on the first day of the week, I found myself driving to church in the predawn darkness with two quarts of milk, a dozen eggs and three bags of pancake mix. I confess, I wondered a little about those early Christians whom we were supposed to be emulating. Had they also marked the occasion of Easter by gathering together for breakfast?

Maybe they, too, had been so busy mixing the pancake batter that the sun burst forth upon them before they were really ready for the day. Tossing aside my apron, I hurried out of the church kitchen to join the sunrise celebration. The Peters and Jameses and Andrews of our small congregation were already gathered on the lawn of our little suburban church. I quietly tiptoed out to join the circle of believers, my footsteps crushing icy crystals in the grass.

With no musical accompaniment, we began to sing, "Jesus lives! Thy terrors now can no longer, deaths, appall us. . . ." Our voices sounded weak and unsteady. Perhaps it was the latent moisture oozing into my shoes that was giving me cold feet, but I was sure these old Easter hymns must sound like idle squawking to disbelieving neighbors on either side of the church. Why, even a nearby crow was poking fun at our voices.

Or, as the young minister suggested, perhaps the crow really had been sent to help us make a "joyful noise unto the Lord." With my face warming to the sun, my soul was rising to the message: "Jesus lives! Our hearts know well naught from us His love shall sever. . . ."

The sunshine was glinting off the puddles in the unpaved parking lot as we scraped the mud from our shoes and reentered the church. The kitchen was no longer dark and gloomy, but a warm inviting haven filled with friends and fellowship and the tantalizing smell of fresh coffee. Somehow I think even the apostles would have appreciated my pancakes.

Father, thank You for the truth of Your Resurrection, and the celebrations with other believers that make it all the more meaningful.

—ALMA BARKMAN

25

T
U
E

All that the Father giveth me shall come to me; and him that cometh to me I will in no wise cast out.

—JOHN 6:37

Our friends Billy and Melissa Bachman were ecstatic when they learned that all the paperwork was complete and they could fly to Russia to adopt two children whom they had never seen but already loved. When they returned with seven-year-old Denis and four-year-old Yulia, they gave us a set of photographs documenting their trip.

I couldn't seem to look at the pictures long enough. There were Billy and Melissa boarding the plane in Atlanta, their faces filled with anticipation and a touch of anxiety. Other pictures showed the first meeting of parents and children: Denis seemed eager, as if he understood immediately that he now had a family. But little Yulia stood with her eyes downcast, her shoulders scrunched up and her hands clasped tightly together. Even as Billy and Melissa reached out to her, her response was reserved and apprehensive. I could almost read the thoughts of her little heart: *Will you keep me or cast me out?*

Pictures of the new family arriving back in Atlanta revealed intensely joyful if weary parents, a happy, slightly tired little boy and a beautiful, dark-haired little girl looking timid and hesitant. Another picture showed the children in their new home, examining toys with their smiling parents in the background. Then there was a picture of Yulia trying on brand-new dresses and seeing her carefully made new bed for the first time. The next to last picture showed a smidgen of hope on Yulia's serious little face. And the unforgettable last picture revealed a radiant little girl who had decided, *I'm going to risk loving you and letting you love me.* Delight shone from her face as she and Melissa looked intently into each other's eyes.

I cry every time I look at that last picture. Seeing the joy in that little girl's eyes, I remember a young woman who, after many doubts and hesitations, had finally trusted Jesus to love her as she was.

Lord, forgive me for ever doubting Your amazing love. Amen.

—MARION BOND WEST

26 | W E D | *Thou art worthy, O Lord, to receive glory and honor and power: for thou hast created all things. . . .*
—REVELATION 4:11

My garden needed attention. Most of all, it needed some color. So I drove to a nearby road stand where my friends Pat and Andy Stauffer were setting out the hundreds of plants they had started in their greenhouses during the winter.

Andy saw me coming and, remembering that I liked petunias, pointed toward a table filled with them. "Got any purple ones?" I asked.

"I think so," he said and headed toward a greenhouse behind the road stand. He came out carrying a pot of beautiful purple petunias in each hand—and suddenly he froze in place.

"Is something wrong?" I said. Then I saw a bee circling one of the pots and laughed. I couldn't believe a farmer would be stopped in his tracks by a little bee.

Andy smiled and watched the bee, not moving. "No," he said, "something's right." Then he explained that because of the cold spring, everything had been slow to bloom. "That bee is hungry, and if she doesn't get something to eat, she's not going to last." Very carefully he put the pot of petunias on a table and left it for the bee, who landed on one of the flowers.

"Now maybe that bee and some of her friends will fly over to my fruit trees and pollinate them so we'll have a decent crop this year," he said.

"And if she doesn't?" I asked.

"No fruit. No vegetables. It's as simple as that."

Andy had stopped out of respect, not fear, and that taught me something. Never again would I kill a bee or brush one away when it settled on anything in my garden. I would simply step aside and let it do the job God created it to do.

I praise You, Lord, for the many miracles of Your world. Amen.

—PHYLLIS HOBE

27 | T H U

Grace and peace to you from God our Father and the Lord Jesus Christ. —EPHESIANS 1:2 (NIV)

I lurched the car onto the interstate, the broken vacuum cleaner bumping the back of the seat, my irritation growing. I'd started the day by dropping a potted plant on our new beige rug. Then I went to the closet for the vacuum, only to remember that I'd meant to get it to the repair shop the day before. After stopping at the local self-service filling station to gas up the car, I was on my way. But why was my wallet on the front seat? *Oh, no!* I'd forgotten to pay for my gas! I'd been in such a stew that I'd filled my car and driven off without paying.

How could I have been so stupid? How would I explain when the police stopped me, as surely any minute they would. That it had been a mistake? That right now I was speeding as fast as I dared to get to the next exit and go back? Nine miles; it seemed like ninety. Finally I pulled into the little station and raced inside the building.

The clerk was waiting on people as if nothing had happened. The manager in his glassed-in office didn't even look up when I walked in. I stood in line. When it was my turn, I said, "I forgot to pay for my gas. I came right back—"

The clerk held up a hand, laughing. "Relax. It's not the end of the world. You could have finished your errand and paid on the way home."

The manager strolled over, smiling. He handed me an ice-cold cola on the house. "Don't think you're the only one. Other people forget and drive off. We have the license numbers, but we rarely have to use them. Most people come back and pay."

Back on the interstate, vacuum bumping against the back of the seat, sipping my cola, I eased into traffic, refreshed by the taste of grace. My irritation was gone.

Lord, help me to drink forgiveness today from the inexhaustible well of Your grace.   —SHARI SMYTH

28

F
R
I

For we know that if our earthly house . . . were dissolved, we have a building of God . . . eternal in the heavens.   —II CORINTHIANS 5:1

I've always known that sooner or later I would have to come to terms with my own mortality. It's just that I would have preferred it to be later, rather than this much sooner. The doctor's voice was serious. "Get in here immediately. Your blood tests show an alarmingly low platelet count. We need to run more tests, and maybe even a bone marrow scan."

With the possibility of a terminal blood disease looming over me, the next few weeks were grim. That is, until the morning I was snuggled in my robe, nursing a cup of coffee in my favorite chair in the garden, and I suddenly found my gateway to heaven! It came early, as dawn pushed a crescent moon back into the sky and filtered soft light through a break in the bushes that separate our property from the large estate next door. It flickered shadows through a canopy of oaks and danced rainbows across the field of dew-drenched grass where deer come to graze. Caught up in the glory of the beckoning light, my heart followed it, up the river rocks that frame the curve of the driveway, beyond the screen of trees to the big house I knew was there but could not see. Around that bend, the light diffused, beyond the limits of my vision.

"Look, darling," I said as my husband came out to warm up my coffee, "there, through the bushes. That's my gateway to heaven!"

"What?" he mumbled, fiddling with his glasses.

"Sit down a moment with me. Listen. When the Lord takes me home, think of me walking through those bushes, across the grass, up the driveway and then to the house we know is there but cannot see."

He poured my coffee, then got up to go. He doesn't much like talk of heaven, this large, stoic, hard-on-the-outside-but-soft-as-mush-on-the-inside man. "No, stay. Listen. That's what you tell the grandkids, hear?" He said nothing. Then, as his eyes followed the rays of morning light, he silently nodded his head.

Thanks be to God, my sooner turned out to be later after all. My platelets were clumping, easily fixed. But someday, I know I'll be walking through my gateway to heaven and the beautiful house I cannot see but know is there.

I'm not in a hurry, Lord, but I am excited to see what the eye has not seen, and to hear what the ear has not heard. When the time comes, I know You'll take my hand and lead me softly as the morning light.

—FAY ANGUS

29 S A T *We conducted ourselves in the world in simplicity and godly sincerity. . . .* —II CORINTHIANS 1:12 (NKJV)

When I'm bewildered by the future, I often take a drive to the past—to Amish country, southeast of our town. There I putter down country lanes, passing draft horses that are as big as my car. Teams of these dinosaurs plow fertile fields without noise, smoke or fumes, their only fuel a good meal of oats and hay.

I pass an Amish house, a large vanilla box with dozens of windows to capture natural light. Mother is mowing the lawn with an old reel-type push mower, while her bonneted little girl chops weeds with a small hand-scythe. Two suspendered boys thunder past me in a Ben Hur-type of chariot, homemade of roofing tin and wood, and powered by a shaggy, sweaty pony. I smile at their creativity and enthusiasm.

Handmade signs everywhere point to products for sale: SUGAR SNAP PEAS, HOMEGROWN POPCORN, WOOD CRAFTS, QUILTS. I stop at

BAKERY and watch plump grandmothers working in a lantern-lit kitchen. On the counter are stacks of glazed doughnuts as big as the wheels of a nearby wooden toy wagon. I pick up a loaf of bread, and it's as heavy as a dictionary. I salivate at the sight of a tray of peanut brittle, as crisp as plate glass.

I cruise past a one-room school and wave at boys and girls playing softball in the front yard, then the air fills with the fragrance of seasoned oak as I near a sawmill. Dark-clad men work with the precision of a military drill team, surrounded by dunes of sawdust and mountains of logs. Their wide-brimmed hats catch the sun like little umbrellas.

From the Amish I learn that although lifestyles may change, certain values will go with me into the future: self-discipline, teamwork, creativity, simplicity and integrity. I find courage from these who hold tenaciously to good ideas.

Lord, help me to pass these values on to my children and grandchildren.   —DANIEL SCHANTZ

30
S
U
N

He that believeth shall not make haste.
—ISAIAH 28:16

As usher-in-charge at our church during Holy Week, I was on duty for the services on Maundy Thursday and Good Friday. On Holy Saturday, I joined the altar guild in preparing for the Easter services. On Easter morning, I was there to greet our regular Sunday congregation and the Easter visitors. After the services, I tidied up the pews, changed the numbers on the hymn board and locked the church doors.

I was looking forward to the Sunday after Easter; I'd have a chance to stay in a pew to hear the sermon and reflect on it. But as I was leaving for church that morning, I learned that some dear friends of ours were being honored at a church nearby. Their celebration would begin at 11:30, and the adult forum I was conducting at our church would end at 12:15. I'd have to hurry if I was to get there before the celebration was over. Then, when I arrived at church, the assigned usher was not there. I had to fill in for him and then rush over to the parish hall for the adult forum.

After introducing our guest speaker, I sat down, my stomach

churning. Was I going to be on time for the celebration? Then I noticed the speaker holding an elastic band.

"Is this your life?" he asked as he stretched it to the limit. Then he relaxed one side of the band and increased the tension on the other. "Do you complete one task and then stretch yourself to the limit on another?" I leaned forward. "Why do you always have to be busy?" he asked. "Take some Sabbath time, time to retreat, recall, reflect and remember. God is with us. You don't have to strain to find Him. Just listen for Him."

I leaned back and took a deep breath. The only voice I had been listening to was my own, urging me to hurry. It was time to slow down. I would go to the celebration, but unhurried and in the Spirit.

Father, when I feel I have to do it all, remind me to rest awhile in You.
—OSCAR GREENE

My Renewal Journal

1 _____

2 _____

3 _____

4 _____

5 _____

6 _____

A P R I L   2 0 0 0

7 _____

8 _____

9 _____

10 _____

11 _____

12 _____

13 _____

14 _____

15 _____

16 _____

17 _____

18 _____

19 _____

20 _____

21 _____

22 _____

23 _____

24 _____

25 _____

26 _____

27 _____

28 _____

29 _____

30 _____

MAY

And he . . . shewed me that great city, the holy Jerusalem,

descending out of heaven from God. . . .

—REVELATION 21:10

S	M	T	W	T	F	S
	1	2	3	4	5	6
7	8	9	10	11	12	13
14	15	16	17	18	19	20
21	22	23	24	25	26	27
28	29	30	31			

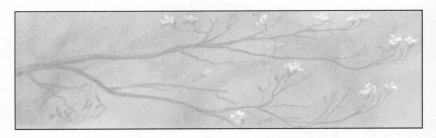

ALL THINGS NEW

1 | M   **Watching Jesus**
       | O   *Let us fix our eyes on Jesus, the author and perfecter*
       | N   *of our faith. . . .*   —HEBREWS 12:2 (NIV)

It was a humdrum meeting in the rector's study at St. Paul's Church, Nantucket, Massachusetts, and my eyes kept wandering to the computer screen behind the desk. Five words continually marched across it from right to left. Now along the top of the screen, now across the middle, now down at the bottom. From where I sat I couldn't make out the words, only that they ended with a question mark. Curious, as the gathering broke up, I stepped closer:

What would Jesus do today?

Rector Andrew Foster was smiling. "What do you think of my screen saver?" he asked.

Instead of a random pattern, he'd chosen these words, he said, to keep himself focused on Jesus. "I can get so bogged down in small stuff, I lose sight of Whose work I'm about. They lift even routine chores out of the ordinary—make each one a little part of His ministry here on earth."

So, of course, I tried it. Not on my computer (with my old machine you save the screen by turning it off), but on notes around the house. *What would Jesus do today?* on the calendar in the kitchen, on the bathroom mirror, on the dashboard of my car, wherever the daily round took me. And I made the discovery people always make when they keep their eyes on Him: His assignments are always new. On His agenda there are no routine chores, no humdrum meetings.

Father, what would Jesus do today?   —ELIZABETH SHERRILL

2

T
u
E

I am their inheritance . . . I am their possession.
—EZEKIEL 44:28

It had been forty years since I'd driven those back roads, and memories flooded back when I spotted the once proud house I recalled from childhood days. Amazingly, it still stood. Suffocating weeds clambered its gingerbread-topped porch pillars, and holes sprinkled its back-broken roof, and clapboard siding gaped to accommodate nest-seeking raccoons.

A vignette from twenty years before suddenly appeared on my mental screen: Ella, weather-beaten even then, stood behind a screen door that had a flapping dish towel drying on its spring. She squinted out to the yard, where an auctioneer was beginning his spiel. "What am I offered for an old-fashioned afghan? Thirty, thirt, thirt. . . . Going, going . . ."

The drone went on—"Forty, fort, fort. . . . Do I hear fifty?" Ella's husband Jeb had been born in that house eighty-three years before. But Jeb had died, and his widow was forced to sell their lifetime of belongings. Suddenly, the scene became too personal, too intimate to watch, and I had to turn away from the auctioneer and the bargain hunters who'd clustered like crows to pick at the remnants of a couple's half-century of labor.

Now, forty years later, I viewed the house again—dilapidated, beaten by the elements—and reminisced about the long-ago couple's lives.

"Good folk," neighbors used to say, always adding, "they work hard for their living." For a half-century they'd labored, stuck together, raised children, gone to church, read their Bibles and prayed. Even when they lost their only son and hail wiped out one year's crop and drought the next, they'd never doubted God, nor His goodness and mercy.

Then I again heard an auctioneer's voice. But this one belonged to the Master Auctioneer. "Now here's a real rarity these days. An old-fashioned faith that lasts through thick and thin. What will you bid for such a treasure? No, I don't accept cash, check or credit card. Only complete devotion to Me."

Father, the most valuable possession of all is You, and all You ask of me in return is my complete devotion.   —ISABEL WOLSELEY

3

Let us consider how to stir up one another to love and good works . . . encouraging one another. . . .

—HEBREWS 10:24–25 (RSV)

I was tired. Bone weary. For six weeks, my schedule had been relentless. In the middle of it all I had been faced with one tragedy after another: the accidental death of a young woman in our church; the loss of a close friend to heart disease; the breakup of a loved one's marriage. I was beginning to feel like Job.

One Wednesday night at prayer meeting, the strain must have showed on my face. After the service, Tom Parrish walked up to me and put his hand on my shoulder. I knew he had something important to say. Tom is eighty years old. A survivor of Pearl Harbor, he has been a lawyer, a pastor and a university administrator. He is a man of wisdom and experience. I have learned to listen to him.

"Scott," Tom began, "let me tell you a story about something that happened to me in high school. I was strong and lean back then, and very fast. I ran the mile on the track team, but I was having problems. I always led the pack through the first three-and-a-half laps, but on the homestretch I was getting beat. One day after I lost by a whisker, my track coach pulled me over and said a single sentence that changed my life: 'Always remember that the other man is just as tired as you are.'

"Now, Scott, you haven't said it, but I can tell it: You're tired. But this is the moment when you must not give in. Just remember that others have gone through what you're going through, and they didn't lose the race. And they were as tired as you are. Keep your chin up and keep running."

There are times when all of us need to collapse and rest. There are other times when we need to tighten our jaw and "keep on keeping on." And sometimes the encouragement of a friend can make all the difference between winning or losing the race.

Dear Father, may I continue to run the race that is before me. And may I give encouragement to other runners along the way.

—SCOTT WALKER

4

T
H
U

Ye shall seek me, and find me, when ye shall search for me with all your heart. —JEREMIAH 29:13

"Would you pray for me? I'm being kicked out of my apartment and I need a new place to live."

"Our daughter had an emergency appendectomy. Pray for her speedy recovery."

"I'm taking the bar exam for the second time next week—please pray for me to pass."

One of the hazards with going public as a praying person is that people will ask you to pray for them. In a week's time I find myself flooded with prayer requests, not to mention the ongoing needs I keep posted on my computer: a friend suffering from Lou Gehrig's disease; a couple going through marital trouble; a friend struggling with substance abuse. Sometimes, I am embarrassed to admit, I get fed up. *I don't have time to pray for all these people!* I think.

Dutifully, unenthusiastically, I go to my praying place and go through my mental list. "God, please remember . . ." And this is when an amazing thing happens. Slowly, I begin to understand why it's important for me to say these intercessions. I need to be here praying. I need this quiet time alone with God. It's as though all those obligations to other people are calling me back to myself. To be attentive, understanding, compassionate, caring. In fact, I wonder if this isn't just God's way to pull me back to prayer. After all, He's the one behind each request.

So when I feel overwhelmed by prayer requests, a warning bell goes off. *Too busy, Rick? It's time to get praying.*

God, on this National Day of Prayer, please remember the needs of

_____. —RICK HAMLIN
(LIST NAMES)

5

F
R
I

And he said to her, "Daughter, your faith has made you well; go in peace, healed of your disease."
—MARK 5:34 (TLB)

Buzz, buzz, buzz . . . hum, hum, hum. The sound could be the background for relaxation tapes of the living earth. But this *buzz-hum* is the sound of three IV poles, lined up next to my eighteen-year-old son Andrew's hospital bed, pumping fluids into his arm. This young man is supposed to be careening through his last month of high school—writing that last essay for English class, bragging about how many hits he got in softball, getting the brakes fixed on his motorcycle. Instead, Crohn's disease eats at his intestines.

For the first three days I'm calm and serene. I read something by Sam J. Ervin, Jr., that says faith is an inner spiritual strength that enables us to face the storms of life with hope and serenity . . . and I'm proud of my inner spiritual strength.

By the end of day four, my son is cranky. Four days without solid food, punctuated with pain and constant intrusions into his personal space, have left him with no social skills. He complains about everything, declares that he's sick of visitors and phone calls, and in the end he reduces me to tears. I'm not such a pillar of strength after all.

That night I whimper to Pastor Tom, "What's wrong with me? I'm losing it. Doesn't my faith guarantee serenity?"

"Nonsense," he says. "You need to get out of here. Take care of yourself for a while. I'll stay."

I leave, afraid that if I don't I'll burst into loud shaking sobs. I head for my friend Betsy's house, where we walk, talk and finish off the visit with cold drinks, brownies and hugs.

Back in my son's room, I settle into the chair next to the IV pumps. *Buzz, buzz, buzz . . . hum, hum, hum.* As I listen, I understand that faith flows like medicine through an IV, sure and steady. Sometimes it buzzes. Sometimes it hums. For now the humming lulls me to sleep.

Lord, I can't always be a pillar of strength. But I know You are and that You're there for me every single day. Thank You.

—PATRICIA LORENZ

A PLACE OF MY OWN

6
S
A
T

By long forbearing is a prince persuaded, and a soft tongue breaketh the bone. —PROVERBS 25:15

There is a portrait in my apartment that always makes me think of Mrs. Boyd, my landlady when I was at the University of California. A short, dumpy woman with a big nose and a pair of brown eyes like a mad gypsy, she was, well, different. I lived in a two-room den, which was semiattached to her quarters. "Happy House" (her name for it) was high up on Panoramic Way with the great San Francisco Bay below, but for this delightful residence there were certain things expected of me. At first I thought they were too much. I had to endure (secretly, of course) her listening in to my conversations (how, I don't know); she called me "Colonel Varner" (her idea of making me more respectable); and, among other madnesses, she expected me to invite her for tea each day.

Somehow, though, I persevered. She had no friends, would trudge up the hill with day-old bread for herself and the raccoons she fed, and her pleasure was going to San Francisco and sitting for an afternoon in the lobby of the Francis Drake Hotel. The Bible says, "a soft tongue breaketh the bone" (Proverbs 25:15). In time, my tongue grew softer.

She knew I loved racehorses, and it happened that at tea one day she asked how much a horse cost. I stammered, knowing it could be any amount, but finally came out with, "A plater—an ordinary horse—down there at Golden Gate Fields could be had for, say, five thousand dollars."

Four years passed, and I was living in New York when a letter came from a lawyer. Mrs. Boyd had died of cancer. She had left a will, written in green ink, that left five thousand dollars to me and a thousand to a woman who worked in her doctor's office. The remainder of her estate of one hundred thousand dollars went to the state of California—no relation could be found.

So that is how I came to have a five-thousand-dollar portrait of my favorite thoroughbred, War Admiral.

Help me always to think twice, Lord, before casting a stone.

—VAN VARNER

7

S
U
N

We then that are strong ought to bear the infirmities of the weak, and not to please ourselves.

—ROMANS 15:1

The service had already begun when Linda wheeled Eva into her customary spot beside the front pew. Eva, already elderly when I arrived in Lander, Wyoming, twenty-one years ago, now worshiped from a wheelchair, dependent on hearing aids and an oxygen tube. Her frail arms rested on foam wedges. With only her face-splitting grin and crackling laugh undiminished, Eva depended totally on her caregivers.

And Linda's care showed. For several years she had faithfully driven Eva and her wheelchair to church every Sunday in a van equipped with a hydraulic lift. Not only did she dress Eva warmly and muffle her in blankets and lap robes, Linda also groomed Eva and helped her look attractive—perhaps with a velvet ribbon, a new hairdo or a scarf. Today, the extra minutes had really been worth it. Eva looked resplendent and very loved. A puffy scarlet bow clasped her cloud of luminous white hair. Red earrings hung daintily from her ears, and nail polish gleamed on her fingertips. From time to time, Eva inclined her head to look at her decorated hand, grinned, then focused once again on the pastor.

I don't know whether Eva understood what the pastor said that morning about Jesus being with us. I do know that as long as Linda cherishes and fusses over Eva, He is as close as the first pew.

Heavenly Father, help me to remember that every task is important when done for the love of You.   —GAIL THORELL SCHILLING

8 | M
O
N

O Lord, open thou my lips: and my mouth shall show forth thy praise. —PSALM 51:15

Let me start by saying that Teddy, our four-year-old Welsh terrier, is an excellent watchdog. He watches over us, the house, the yard, his food bowl and nonfamily people who come through the front door. The last he eyes like a hawk. The problem is getting him to relax once guests enter and not stalk them as if they're trying to pocket the silver.

When I described his distrust of strangers to another owner of a territorial terrier, she directed me to a nationally famous dog handler and trainer, Greg Strong, in Maryland. "He can straighten your dog out in a couple of weeks," she advised.

So, to make a long story short, we entrusted Teddy to Greg for two weeks, and returned to see the results, which were impressive indeed. Teddy heeded his handler's every command with soldierly obedience.

"Now comes the hard part. Teaching you," Greg said, smiling. But he wasn't kidding. For an hour and a half, Shirley and I rehearsed, and to make sure we didn't forget our lessons, the trainer gave us a crib sheet of instructions to take home. The gist of his methods is simple:

- Make your commands clear and concise: *Heel, stay, wait, down, come.*
- Give your commands in an authoritative voice.
- Insist that every command be obeyed (and give a jerk on his leash if the dog doesn't respond immediately).
- Most importantly, praise, praise, praise your pet when he succeeds.

"Praise is the magic wand," concluded Greg. "The more you praise him, the more he will try to please you."

"Something like raising kids," I rejoined. Greg nodded, and we drove off the wiser.

And Teddy? He's still a diligent watchdog, but a more congenial host when visitors arrive—as long as Shirley and I don't forget our lessons.

Help us remember, Lord,
No matter who or what we're raising—
All creatures great and small need praising.

—FRED BAUER

9 T
U
E *If any of you lack wisdom, let him ask of God, that giveth to all men liberally. . . .* —JAMES 1:5

I sat beside Mother's grave, reluctant to begin the long drive back home. I was saddened and shaken by my daughter's impending—and totally unexpected—divorce. Amy Jo herself was heartbroken, in need of my support. What could I say? Mother would have had the right words. She always had the right words. "Oh, Mother," I sobbed. "I need your wisdom!"

The wind moved through the cornfield adjacent to the cemetery. Overhead a crow cawed. Then, through my grief and despair, I seemed to hear my mother's voice. "Well," she said in her playful, matter-of-fact way, "you have the same Source for it I did!"

I touched the headstone, knowing it was true. And I had something else, too: Mother's love and prayers. They had enveloped me all my life, and I knew that, even now, they would comfort me.

I returned to my car and headed toward home. I flicked off the radio and began, "Dear God, I need wisdom. . . ." Four hours later, when I pulled into my own driveway, I was feeling much better, much wiser. I had a few words of comfort for Amy Jo. And a lot of hugs.

Remind me, Father, to turn to You for divine guidance and insight.
—MARY LOU CARNEY

10 W
E
D *Listen to your father, who gave you life. . . .* —PROVERBS 23:22 (NIV)

When Dad was getting Mom settled back home after her stroke, I was unsure of how best to assist them. I went nervously to work, clearing the living room of excess furniture to accommodate Mom's wheelchair. I was quite alarmed when Dad said, "We're picking up a new puppy on Monday."

The last thing he needs is a new puppy, I thought, *chewing up every bag in the garage and getting underfoot when Dad is backing the wheelchair through the front door.*

Dad read the look on my face and said meekly, "I've already promised the owner I'd take her."

I immediately added a new task to my list: Go to the junk store and buy a playpen to corral a four-footed, yelping cyclone. I didn't find a playpen, and I was upset that I hadn't been able to save Dad from the nuisance of a new, untrained puppy.

The next week when I telephoned Mom, she told me that they'd named the puppy Princess. It had been terribly frustrating trying to communicate with Mom over the phone, but suddenly there was one subject on which Mom could always manage to make sense: Princess and her antics. And the next time I drove up to visit, Mom was sitting in the yard with Princess on her lap. We sat and watched as Princess bounded over the blooming purple thrift and caught a butterfly. I was astounded when Mom laughed out loud, something she hadn't done in years.

I leaned over and gave Princess a pat on her sandy, curly head, thinking I'd learned my first lesson in parenting my parents: I'm sometimes wrong about what's good for them. Just as I do with my own children, I need to trust them—and trust God that they can make good decisions without my dictating what I think is best.

Lord, give me the grace to support the people I love in making their own choices and decisions.　　　　　　　　　　—KAREN BARBER

11 | T
H *Sons are a heritage from the Lord, children a reward*
U *from him.*　　　　　　　—PSALM 127:3 (NIV)

There were six families on the boat as it pulled out of the harbor on Hilton Head Island, South Carolina, awhile back. As we talked about the boat's many features, I noticed my ten-year-old son Ryan sitting alone in the back of the boat, looking out at the water. Worried that he was feeling left out, I went back to talk to him.

"Isn't this boat something, Ryan? It's just like a house. It has a bedroom, a living room, a kitchen, and it's all air-conditioned."

"Dad," he said, "it is amazing!"

"I'm glad you think so, son," I said. "But why aren't you up exploring it, or visiting with some of the other children? Are you feeling okay?"

Ryan leaned back in his seat. "Dad, I feel great just sitting here. Every few minutes the scenery changes. I can watch the people on the beach building sand castles, and the sunset on the water is so beautiful."

I sat down next to Ryan and looked out at the sunset. It *was* beautiful, an explosion of pinks and purples against the horizon. I'd been so impressed with the big, expensive boat that I hadn't taken the time to see the view right in front of me.

As I watched the harbor receding behind us, I said a thanksgiving prayer to God for a chance to be close to His creation, for friends in His church who were willing to share their bounty with us and, most of all, for Ryan and the joy of spending precious time with him.

Thank You, Lord, for the opportunity to see the wonder of Your world through my children's eyes.   —DOLPHUS WEARY

12 | F R I   *Those who walk in pride he is able to humble.*
                        —DANIEL 4:37 (NIV)

Every Little League season, my son Ross gets out his baseball books and reads the best stories to me. One of our favorites is told by two-time All Star Nate Colbert, who, as a San Diego Padres rookie in 1969, hit a big home run in the first inning of a game against the Atlanta Braves. His next time up at bat, the huge ovation he heard from the crowd brought tears to his eyes. To compose himself, he walked to the on-deck circle where his teammate Cito Gaston was waiting to bat.

"Cito, can you believe how great those fans are, cheering and clapping for me like that. I feel so proud," Colbert said.

Gaston shook his head and said, "Look at the scoreboard."

Colbert looked up. In five-foot-high letters the scoreboard read: MAN HAS JUST WALKED ON THE MOON.

Gaston laughed and said, "I just hope you can hit as big as your head!"

A funny story, but one that makes me think about the times I've grabbed the credit for a job well-done and forgotten to give credit to God. Still, as Colbert found out, God has wonderful ways of reminding and humbling me. When I asked a friend I particularly wanted to impress if she'd seen the brief mention of a project I'd worked on in the newspaper, she said, "Oh, we were out of town over the weekend. I guess we missed it." As I deflated, I knew I'd heard God's gentle but clear reminder that I'm not the big deal I sometimes think I am. In fact, I'm nothing without Him.

Remind me that it is Your greatness, Lord, that makes all things possible. —GINA BRIDGEMAN

13 | S A T

I called upon the Lord in distress. . . .
—PSALM 118:5

It was a truly awful week. Monday at midnight I awoke with the start of a vicious stomach flu. I was so sick that Andrew took two days off from work to care for the kids. Then at 4:00 A.M. on Wednesday, John came down with the bug. Still very weak, I nursed a clingy, cranky and very sick little boy while trying to entertain a stir-crazy three-year-old girl. John's fever broke late Friday afternoon, but it was a mere six hours later that Elizabeth awoke screaming, "My tummy is dizzy!"

Terribly sleep-deprived, weary and housebound, in the middle of it all I accidentally threw out my keys. And we had to cancel the long-awaited get-together with friends that we'd scheduled for the coming weekend.

On Saturday I took John to the playground while Andrew tended Elizabeth. I normally love playing with my kids, but that day I just couldn't do it. I'd been patient for what felt like forever, I'd withstood sickroom whines for days, I'd reached my limits and passed them many times. I wanted some distance. I sat on a bench and watched numbly as John meandered around, looking for a playmate or something to do.

A little boy came over to John and started blowing bubbles. Relieved of the need to entertain my son, I thought back over the week. I'd certainly prayed a lot: for strength, for perseverance, for patience, for my kids to feel better. I had never thought of the trials of motherhood as a blessing; my idea of a blessing is a sunny day with cheerful and well-behaved children. But what would I call a week filled with twice as much prayer as usual?

Perhaps an invitation to a closer walk with God.

Father, remind me that sometimes my greatest blessing is a knowledge of my limitations and of my need for You. —JULIA ATTAWAY

146 • MAY 2000

14

S
U
N

Her children rise up and call her blessed. . . .
—PROVERBS 31:28 (RSV)

Half of what I think I know about mothers comes from having one. The other half comes from being married to one. In fact, I probably know more about my mother from being married to my sons' mother for twenty-two years. Here are the key things I've learned:

- Mothers are the people who take Jesus at His word when He says to forgive each other "seventy times seven."
- Mothers are the ones who still believe in you when everyone else begins to doubt.
- Never get between a mother and her cubs. Even if you are the father, you lose.
- The best gift you can give your children is to love their mother.
- A mother's prayers are more powerful than any force on earth or in heaven.
- A father may know best, but a mother cares best, and children will pick caring over knowing every time.
- We may pray to "Our Father," but the face of God we see, the hand of God we clutch and the heart of God we trust belong to our mothers.

Lord, thanks for giving us mothers so that we can see, hold and hear You more clearly.
—ERIC FELLMAN

15

M
O
N

Free yourself . . . like a bird from the snare of the fowler.
—PROVERBS 6:5 (NIV)

Today is "Fledgling Day," the day around the middle of May every year when Mama Thrush encourages her babies to fly. Since my computer table faces out the dining room window onto the deck, I can observe unseen. Small and brown with tilted tails flicking, the young thrushes flit and hop more than they fly. And are they curious! One has just landed in my gardening basket, alighting on the purple glove, hopping off onto my shears, head tipped as if to say, "Gee, this is neat stuff. Wonder what it's for?"

Another lands in "Nellie" (my citronella plant) and pecks at the dirt. Suddenly a call comes from Mama, and hop, flit! Up to the deck rail; farther up onto the yellow umbrella. Another clear Mama Thrush warble and off they go, fluttering out of sight, headed for the garage gutter and then the tree beyond.

In my fifties, a fledgling spirit of adventure is arising in me. I am growing more excited at the idea of discovery than I am afraid of the "what ifs." And always leading me on is the clarion call of the Lord: "Good for you! You've come this far! Come farther!"

Lord, it is a heady thing to launch out away from fear and into discovery. Thank You that underneath are Your everlasting arms!

—ROBERTA ROGERS

READER'S ROOM

"Looking back over 'My Healing Journey' for the past three months is inspiring as I realize how God has been with me in special ways. Our younger son put a computer together for me. Both sons are teaching me how to use it, a reversal. They opened up a whole new world for me with e-mail and Internet and word processing. I relish fellowship with family: husband, sons, daughter-in-law, step-granddaughter. We visited one son and were inspired going to church with him. I like the family times of shopping and eating together. A friend and I visited a church choir member who had lost her only sister in death. At a shower given by the choir, the expectant father opened presents for his unborn son. The choir sang for 'Unity in Community' at the local university. Black and white retired teachers stopped rehearsal for a meeting devotional to hug each other. Leading them to sing is a joy. Playing piano and singing for nursing home residents is rewarding. A resident's son surprised me with a beautiful voice coming over my shoulders. We could harmonize with heavenly harmony. Celebrating a birthday with a couple of friends was healing. Husband and I celebrated Valentine's Day at a Sweetheart Banquet. We took a couple of friends in their eighties. An old acquaintance came by on Saturday when I needed help with a water-logged pump. After a year, my gum was finally healthy so my front teeth bridge could be cemented."
—*Allene W. DeWeese, Florence, South Carolina*

16

T
U
E

Give thanks in all circumstances, for this is God's will
for you in Christ Jesus.
—I THESSALONIANS 5:18 (NIV)

One spring day a few years ago, I was driving a backcountry road in Lancaster County, Pennsylvania, where I grew up. As I passed an old brick farmhouse with a weathered barn behind it, I noticed that an estate auction was in progress, and I pulled over to the side of the road. *A house from a day when life was simpler and slower,* I thought from my perspective as a modern-day working and carpooling mother of four.

I walked across the wide lawn, dotted with forsythia and a milling crowd of bidders. Furniture was strewn over the shaded cement porch. "There's more inside," an eager assistant said. She told me that the owner had come to the house as a bride and had recently died at the age of ninety-three, the last of her family. *What was she like?* I wondered. *What was it like to be young in her day?*

I went into the house. Wide painted floorboards led to a large step-down kitchen with an old-fashioned double sink, cupboards with china knobs, dishes stacked to go. Boxes of canning jars leaned on a wringer washer hauled up from the dirt cellar. A creaky door opened to the worn backstairs. Springtime fragrance swept through the screen from the open window. So peaceful. My eyes followed the garden path leading to a vegetable patch behind the barn.

A stooped old Mennonite woman limped into the kitchen, prayer cap clamped on her iron-gray hair. Following my gaze, she said, "Don't get too nostalgic. Life was hard back then. Sunup-to-sundown labor with no modern gadgets. You young people should thank God for what you have." Then she stopped and laughed a joyous, head-to-toes laugh. "But, of course, my grandmother said the same to me. The important thing is to be grateful for where you are."

Thank You, Lord, for showing me that every age has hardships of its
own, and make me grateful for all You've given me. —SHARI SMYTH

17

W
E
D

Many believed in his name, when they saw the mir-
acles which he did.
—JOHN 2:23

All the wild animals I saw on our trip to Africa were awesome, but with the giraffes it was love at first sight. Their long necks and slightly quizzical expressions as they munched on the tops of trees enchanted me, as did their odd, sloping run. One hot afternoon, as I was watching a whole family group move quietly and elegantly into the shade of some trees, I said breathlessly to our guide Newton, who knew more about the animals than anyone I had ever met, "Those giraffes—they are miracles!"

Newton, whose varied career had included time in a Lutheran seminary, knew I wasn't just expressing ordinary enthusiasm. "Why do you call them miracles?" he asked gently.

I hesitated and answered him with another question: "Well, what exactly is a miracle?" As the words left my mouth, it occurred to me that this unexpected conversation ranked as a small miracle by itself— discussing the nature of miracles in the middle of the Serengeti National Park surrounded by zebras and giraffes going about their daily lives.

We quickly agreed that there was no one answer, or at least that God sends a different miracle for each person. Then, as the largest giraffe awkwardly spread its front legs in order to stretch down and drink from the water hole, I said to Newton, "These giraffes are a miracle for me. One I shall never forget." And with a smile, he nodded.

Lord, open my eyes to Your miracles—large and small—which are all around me.   —BRIGITTE WEEKS

18   T   *And we desire that each one of you show the same*
         H   *diligence so as to realize the full assurance of hope*
         U   *until the end.*   —HEBREWS 6:11 (NAS)

It was a hard winter. In November, I lost my job as an advertising copywriter. Soon, the co-op building where we lived informed us they were evicting us to sell our apartment. So this was the task before me: to find a job in an already tight job market and a place to live amid New York City's skyrocketing rents.

Oh, and did I mention my wife Nicole was pregnant?

The next six months were exasperating. I was turned away from every ad agency in the city and laughed away by every landlord. The amount of money we had to spend on rent wasn't close to what landlords were asking. And nobody was going to give a lease to an unemployed writer. With every passing day, the pressure of a dwindling savings account and an expanding family weighed more heavily on our minds. But we held fast to God's promises.

Then one day we were walking home with Julian, our three-year-old, and I finally hit my breaking point. I could stand a silent God no longer. "What is God doing?" I asked Nicole. "How long is He going to make us wait? We'll be homeless soon! We need answers right now!"

Just then Julian saw that we had passed the ice cream truck and weren't going back. He started to scream.

"Not now, Julian," I said. "You can't have ice cream before dinner." That didn't work. "Julian, please stop screaming. You'll get your ice cream, only not right now." More crying. Finally I said, "Julian, you're just going to have to wait!"

Nicole looked at me and I looked at her. "You know, Julian's doing exactly the same thing to us that we're doing to God," Nicole said. "God is saying, 'Wait,' and we're telling Him we want our ice cream and we want it now."

Lord, help me to have confidence in Your perfect timing.

—DAVE FRANCO

19 | F R I

If ye be willing and obedient, ye shall eat the good of the land. —ISAIAH 1:19

Our daughter eats healthy. Tofu, sprouts, kale with hefty portions of tempeh, all laced with an overload of garlic. My husband abhors garlic. He's strictly meat and mashed potatoes, and the only thing he wants an overload of is gravy. As for me, well, I'm into hot fudge sundaes.

Come mealtimes, our daughter is generally stirring up some pot of her favorite garlic brew when her dad comes charging into the kitchen, his nose crinkled in disgust while he flings wide every window and turns on the vent above the stove with an irritated, "I can't stand the smell!"

"Hey, garlic is good for you. Here, try some," our daughter grins while handing him a spoonful of garlic-seasoned tofu spaghetti.

"Over my dead body," he snorts.

Well, he soon found out that garlic is good for him, and it was over his "change your diet or you could be dead" body.

"Your blood pressure is way up, and the cholesterol is high, much too high," the doctor said on reviewing his annual checkup. "Cut out the red meat. Go for fish. Substitute tofu when you can, and eat lots of garlic."

John's nose still crinkles when he comes upon our daughter making a meal, but sheepishly he looks into the pot and says, "Have you made enough for me to have some, honey?"

"Sure, Dad."

They now have a culinary bond. Trouble is, now the smell of garlic is nearly driving me mad. But if I can't avoid them, I guess I'll have to join them.

Bless this healthy food to our bodies' use, dear Lord, and extend our days so we may better serve You.　　　　—FAY ANGUS

20 | S A T

He made thee to hear his voice. . . .
　　　　　　　　　　　—DEUTERONOMY 4:36

My wife Tib can identify a great many birds by their songs. She's worked hard to gain this skill, listening to recorded birdcalls, studying graphs of characteristic song patterns. In the field she is uncanny.

On a recent spring walk, she'd stop, listen, point. "A veery! Do you hear it?" "Listen, a yellow throat." "That was a song sparrow." Where I heard only a cacophony of warbles and trills, she distinguished wrens, catbirds, towhees, finches—a total of seventeen species.

Over the years, with her help, I have learned to identify a few birds by their calls. It's a valuable skill in the world of the Spirit, too. As the new millennium opens, I know I will hear a chorus of voices calling to me from every direction. Which will be God's, which other people's, which my own? The more I practice listening in prayer, the more I study His Word, the surer I can be of recognizing the cadences of His voice.

Father, help me train my ears.　　　　—JOHN SHERRILL

21 | S U N

It is a good thing to give thanks. . . . —PSALM 92:1

As a child, I silently disapproved of my mother's obsession with making me say "thank you." I *had* to say it, even if I wasn't really grateful. One Sunday afternoon Mother took me to visit an elderly neighbor who lived alone. His house was dark and smelled of moth-balls. The antique furniture was covered with dust. Mother made po-lite conversation while I squirmed on the velveteen sofa. The man got up to prepare refreshments. After a few minutes he came back with a crystal plate of broken cookies and glasses of sour lemonade. While he hobbled away to get napkins, I whispered to Mother, "The cook-ies are stale."

"You will still say thank you," Mother whispered back. I had to say it three times because he was hard of hearing. As we walked home, she explained that we were expressing gratitude for his efforts, even if we didn't like what he served.

Recently, my two daughters brought their six children over to cel-ebrate Mother's Day and my mother's eighty-ninth birthday. I was keenly aware that I didn't have anything really fun for the younger children to do—no elaborate toys or playground equipment. But a few days after their visit I received a note addressed to me in pencil, the handwriting nearly slanting off the envelope. My almost-eight-year-old grandson explained, "I wrote this in the car after we went to your house. We had the best time at your house and eating and swinging on your back porch. Thank you for having us! We all love you! Love, Luke."

Lord, teach me always to be grateful for the kindness people show me. Amen.

—MARION BOND WEST

22

M
O
N

Open thou mine eyes, that I may behold wondrous things. . . . —PSALM 119:18

My wife Barbara and I were traveling south on the Will Rogers Turnpike through Oklahoma on our way to the farm. There weren't many exits, so when we saw the welcome center and those familiar golden arches we pulled over for coffee and a chance to walk around for a few minutes.

As we went into the restaurant, I noticed a man taking a very large black hose from storage and hooking it up to an outside faucet. When we came out a few minutes later, the hose lay across the walk as the man watered the shrubs along the edge of the building. I slowed my pace a bit, and a small boy passed me, pulling his mother along by the hand. When he saw the hose moving slightly on the walk, he stopped abruptly and exclaimed, "Look out for the big black snake!" His mother jerked him over the hose and said, "That's not a snake. It's just a garden hose."

As they moved away, I felt a little sad. I remembered the long flights on which I had been the pilot of the porch swing and all the cattle I had rounded up on my faithful stick horse. I wondered if exercising the imagination was something we were expected to grow out of in the process of becoming adults. And I wondered if when Jesus talked of our need to have the faith of a little child, He meant holding on to the ability to imagine things that are not yet a reality and to entertain visions of a better world.

I hope, no matter how old I am when it happens, that if a child says to me, "The evening star whispered something wonderful in my ear," without missing a beat I'll ask him to tell me what the star said.

Dear God, help me always to live with a sense of wonder in all of life's experiences.   —KENNETH CHAFIN

23 | T u E

And where the Spirit of the Lord is, there is freedom.
—II CORINTHIANS 3:17 (RSV)

The mall parking garage was full to bursting. My brother Jay and I, excited but tired from a morning of shopping, were glad to escape the mall. The car inched toward the exit, four levels below. Jay paused to let another vehicle into the line.

When the exit was in sight, I cheered, and Jay laughed at my little victory dance. We handed the attendant our validated parking stub. He had a beautiful voice with a musical Jamaican lilt. With a big smile, he wished us a happy day. Jay waited patiently for an opening in traffic, then made a right turn onto Fourth Street.

Traffic on Fourth wasn't much better than in the garage. We crept along, trying to merge left, but just as Jay got his opening, a beat-up white van came careening through, the driver laying on his horn. Jay swerved back to the right. We narrowly missed being sideswiped. And thanks to Jay's evasive maneuver, we were back in the garage!

When the attendant's booth was finally in sight, I realized that we had been in the garage so long that we needed to pay the parking fee again! Between us, we didn't have enough cash to pay the flat rate without validation.

When we pulled through the booth, the attendant smiled and reached for our ticket. Jay explained, "We were forced into the garage to avoid an accident, sir. Can we just drive through?"

The attendant gave a gracious nod and said gently, "This is not a prison." He eyed the traffic outside and pushed the button to open the gate just as the intersection cleared. "You are free!"

What a precious and joyful thing to hear! I thought. And as easily as that, we were safely on our way home.

Praise to You, Father. By Your grace, I am free! —KJERSTIN EASTON

24 | W E D

To him who is able to do immeasurably more than all we ask or imagine . . . be glory in the church and in Christ Jesus throughout all generations. . . !
—EPHESIANS 3:20–21 (NIV)

"Mama, can I have a dog? Just a little old dog."

I had abandoned the corporate rat race so that I could spend more time with my children. Now I could do all the things moms do when they are blessed with time to spend with their children. But I cringed when my son Chase asked for a dog. Our budget was tight, and dogs, I thought, cost money. "Well, just pray and ask God," I told him.

Chase prayed simply, "Dear God, please give me a little old dog. Amen."

The next morning, as we stood on the porch, we saw a little white and brown dog coming toward our trailer across the fallow field. It was an old, sway-backed beagle. Before I could say anything, Chase ran and wrapped his arms around the dog. "Scott!" Chase named him spontaneously. My son seemed very pleased to receive what he had asked for. But the dog was not at all what I expected.

Grateful for table scraps, Scott never wandered from home. Old and wheezing, he ran just fast enough to keep up with Chase's four-year-old legs. As time passed, we all grew to love Scott. His big brown eyes said he loved us back.

Lord, help me to open my eyes to unexpected blessings.
—SHARON FOSTER

25

T
H
U

The race is not to the swift, Nor the battle to the strong, Nor bread to the wise. . . .
—ECCLESIASTES 9:11 (NKJV)

It's Honors Day at Central Christian College where I teach, and there's tension in the air. Students in the chapel audience are wondering, *Did I win any awards?* Cerebral types are reviewing their grade averages. Tall basketball players are sitting stooped, trying to look humble. The president of the student council is smiling.

When all the awards have been given, the master of ceremonies says, "And now, I would like Earl to come to the front to receive this beautiful plaque in recognition for his years of study at Central."

Earl is a single man of fifty whose disabilities prevent him from doing college work. He doesn't come to Central to earn a degree. He comes for a very old-fashioned reason: to learn. He has audited twenty-one classes, everything from Hebrew History to Eschatology to Marriage Counseling to Oral Communications.

There is a hush as Earl steps forward. His face is transformed as he holds up his plaque for all to see. No one has ever been happier to receive an award. The applause is thunderous. Not because Earl won the college game, but because he played. His award plaque reads, "For his *pursuit* of excellence."

I sit there thinking of my tendency to shy away from things I cannot do well, my preference for the familiar and the manageable. I can see that even though I am a teacher, I have a lot to learn from my students. And I make a mental note to try something a little bigger than myself in the future.

Thank You, Lord, for people like Earl, who show us that winning the race is not as important as deciding to start. —DANIEL SCHANTZ

26

F
R
I

I will delight in thy statutes; I will not forget thy word.
—PSALM 119:16 (RSV)

For my forty-sixth birthday last May, my girlfriend Beryl and I went in search of Point Roberts Bible Camp, where I spent my summers as a child with my father, who was the camp director.

Surprisingly, nothing much had changed. The old water pump was still as big and as high as I remembered. The lodge where I'd painted a dozen of those 1950s Bible-verse plaster plaques was the same. I found the spot where my dad and I had our picnics, eating pork and beans and stewed tomatoes right out of the can. The cabins were all still there, and I pointed to one tucked under the forest's skirt. "That was my father's," I told Beryl. We walked over. "And right here"—I pointed to the front step—"I set out one of my Bible-verse plaques to dry. Someone stepped on it and crushed it to smithereens. It broke my heart."

My birthday well spent, I dropped Beryl off and headed home. My mind lingered on the memory of that broken plaque. *How many of the verses that I memorized as a kid have I forgotten? Verses lost to me as surely as that plaque.*

A verse from my middle-school years popped into my mind: *"I will delight in thy statutes; I will not forget thy word."* Yet I *had* forgotten so much of God's Word.

I got home and e-mailed Beryl. "What do you think of rememorizing all those verses we learned as kids?"

"Great!" she e-mailed back.

Every month now, Beryl and I get together and recite what we're relearning. My childhood plaque may have been destroyed, but its words, I've discovered, can remain with me forever.

Dear Lord, thank You for the chance to revisit my past and for the forgotten treasures I find there. —BRENDA WILBEE

27 | S A T   *My cup runneth over.*   —PSALM 23:5

When my sister Keri was about to graduate from college, she made a request to Mom, Dad and me: "Instead of a graduation present, why don't the four of us go to the Grand Canyon?"

It sounded like a great thing to do, but I was very busy and didn't feel I could afford to take the time. As their departure date drew near, I was feeling a little sorry that I hadn't planned to go, but wasn't getting ahead in my career more important?

Finally, while I was driving the three of them to the airport, I gave way to what seemed a foolish impulse: "Hey Keri, you'd better get Mom and Dad to the Grand Canyon Airport on July thirtieth, 'cause

I'm flying in to join you!" The look on Keri's face made me glad I had finally loosened up.

The family waited for me to get there before taking their first look at the canyon. So together we walked out to the rim and stood frozen in wonder. Over dinner at the old El Tovar Hotel on the rim of the canyon, we couldn't stop marveling over the canyon's beauty. Adjectives like *magnificent, splendid* and *gorgeous* crowded our conversation.

Except for Keri. She was noticeably quiet.

"Well, Keri, you haven't said much. What do you think about the canyon?" my father asked.

"I . . . I . . . I just kept looking over the canyon and at you, Dad, and at Mom and at Brock, and I kept hearing the words, *My cup runneth over.*"

The smell of fresh-grilled mountain trout at our table was sweet, but sweeter still was just being there with my family. I could have stayed at home to make some more money, but for once I made the better choice and ended up with something money can't buy: the beauty of God's creation, the goodness of being with those you love. My own cup was truly running over with God's blessings.

Father, You prepare a table before me; my cup runs over. Thank You.

—BROCK KIDD

28 | S U N | *How will anyone know what tune is being played unless there is a distinction in the notes?*
—I CORINTHIANS 14:7 (NIV)

As a new Christian, I heard that consistency was one of the most important characteristics of the Christian life. And in my insecurity, I assumed that *consistency* in Christian living meant *uniformity*—that we were all supposed to act alike and respond in the same way all the time. When we prayed or witnessed, we should all use the same gestures and speak in the same formulas. I guess I had thought that God was recruiting a spiritual trumpet corps, each member sounding and looking and acting like one another. If we carefully watched the players around us, we'd see at what angle we were to hold our trumpets and when to pick them up and put them down.

But as I studied the New Testament further, I discovered that

Jesus didn't behave that way. He was constantly out of step with the authorities of His day, which kept Him in hot water and eventually led to His death.

I began to see that the church is not a trumpet corps, but an orchestra. We're not supposed to sound alike, because God has given us our own individual sounds. For years I'd been a piccolo trying to play in the tuba section, because some of the men I admire greatly play the spiritual deep notes. I'd never felt free and natural in my faith because I had always tried to be something I was not so that I could be a "child of God" just like all those tuba-playing children of God around me. Perhaps it's all right for me to have only a small part in God's orchestra. Maybe my only job is to keep an eye on the Conductor and be ready to play when He needs me.

Dear Lord, help me to be willing to play whatever part You have in store for me, large or small, and to be patient and keep my eyes on You while waiting for Your signal that it's time to play.

—KEITH MILLER

29 | M O N

As we have therefore opportunity, let us do good unto all. . . . —GALATIANS 6:10

Dr. Peter Contompasis was my physician from 1954 until his retirement in 1996. When I injured my back in 1984, he was at my bedside every evening. After he retired, our contact dwindled. We kept in touch through our annual exchange of Christmas cards, and I wrote to him when he underwent a successful double hip replacement in 1997. But I missed seeing him, and I wondered how he was doing.

Recently, I was in my new doctor's office, waiting for a routine examination. Suddenly, I heard someone saying, "Happy birthday!" I looked up, and there was Dr. Peter, looking years younger than when I had last seen him. I leaped to my feet, hugged him and wished *him* a happy birthday. We were both born on May 28.

"I've just got back from a cookout on Cape Cod," he said. "When I arrived, relatives from Virginia, New York and Vermont were there to celebrate my seventy-fifth. It was great!"

I listened with a tinge of sadness. *How is he coping with retirement?* I wondered. So I asked him.

"What I miss most are my patients," he said. "But medicine changes so fast, it's hard for an old fellow like me to keep up." He paused, then added, "I'm attending a seminar and then enrolling in a course at the university, and when I'm finished, I'll be able to teach here at the hospital two days a week. That will be nice."

Our conversation was interrupted by the sound of a car horn. "That's Betty," he said. We shook hands and he said, "Oscar, have a godly day!"

I watched with a warm feeling of contentment as Dr. Peter eased into his car. How was Dr. Peter coping with retirement? Very well, I'd say. And yes, it had been a godly day.

Healing Father, through Your servant Dr. Peter You teach me that I'm never too old to serve. Thank You.   —OSCAR GREENE

30

T
U
E

And Jacob set a pillar upon her grave: that is the pillar of Rachel's grave unto this day. —GENESIS 35:20

One of our 4-H Club service projects was cleaning Colusa Cemetery. Each May, kids and parents with rakes, hoes and mowers would spend a hard, hot afternoon getting the little country cemetery spruced up for Memorial Day. My children usually complained about the waste of time. Secretly, I felt the same way. No one had been buried there for twenty years; most families now had plots in Copeland, Kansas. Besides, Colusa was practically hidden by corn-fields. No one ever saw it.

Then I received a letter requesting a strange favor. "My grandfather, George Wolfe, is in poor health," the writer explained. "Years ago his parents were traveling through Kansas when their baby girl was born and died. Grandfather thinks his sister was buried at Copeland sometime between 1906 and 1910. Her name was Dora or Doris. Could you check?"

"I'll try," I wrote back. But when I looked at the Copeland Cemetery roll book, my heart sank. Copeland hadn't opened until 1921. That meant the child was in one of the dozens of township and family cemeteries in the area. Ivanhoe, Lockport and, of course, Colusa had been kept up, but little remained of many others. But I'd promised to look, so a week later I took my camera and started the search. To my amazement, I located the tiny granite headstone right away—in the northeast corner of Colusa Cemetery. The inscription was worn but legible:

DORIS—Infant daughter
of
W.M. & Leota Wolfe

Thanks to the work of generations of 4-H'ers, the weeds had been pulled from around the headstone and the grass neatly mowed. I sent Mr. Wolfe a picture of the grave he's never seen. His letter of thanks changed my attitude about cemetery cleanup and Memorial Day. Someone remembers, and Someone sees.

Father God, thank You for 4-H'ers, Scouts and all young people who work to preserve the memories and dignity of long-dead family, friends and even strangers. —PENNEY SCHWAB

⁓

31
W
E
D
A broken and contrite heart, O God, you will not despise. —PSALM 51:17 (NIV)

When I moved recently, I took great care to pad my fragile treasures for the journey. But despite my best intentions, when I unwrapped my collection of teapots and cups and saucers, one of my favorite cups was chipped and a teapot shattered.

I've been known to trash a treasure because of a hairline crack. Still, these pieces were too pretty to discard, even though I knew their imperfections would forever remind me of my humanness. But amazingly, with a tube of glue and some trailing silk ivy, my wounded-in-action treasures were stronger and prettier than ever. One day a friend remarked, "Wherever did you get that teapot, Roberta? The one with the ivy in its spout?"

When I told her what had happened and christened my teapot "Chip-pendale," my friend remarked, "That's like that new decorating look. 'Shabby Chic,' they call it. Seriously, the knocks and bangs of life are in—Why, you're supposed to put them on display!"

I couldn't help but think how, in my life, it isn't the broken pieces but my resistance to make something useful of them that's the problem. I remembered the time I fell on my face with my new patient-education project at work. God was waiting in the wings to teach me a lesson in teamwork and to show me how with a little help from Him and others, the program could be stronger. Even a thing of beauty.

Shabby Chic? It may be a new concept in the world of decorating, but come to think of it, it's always been God's specialty.

Loving Father, help me trust You to make peace out of my broken pieces. Amen. —ROBERTA MESSNER

My Renewal Journal

1 _____

2 _____

3 _____

4 _____

5 _____

6 _____

7 _____

8 _____

9 _____

10 _____

11 _____

12 _____

13 _____

MAY 2000

14 _____

15 _____

16 _____

17 _____

18 _____

19 _____

20 _____

21 _____

22 _____

23 _____

24 _____

25 _____

26 _____

27 _____

28 _____

29 _____

30 _____

31 _____

JUNE

And the city had no need of the sun, neither of the moon, to shine in it: for the glory of God did lighten it, and the Lamb is the light thereof.   —REVELATION 21:23

S	M	T	W	T	F	S
				1	2	3
4	5	6	7	8	9	10
11	12	13	14	15	16	17
18	19	20	21	22	23	24
25	26	27	28	29	30	

1

T	*Ye shall be witnesses unto me both in Jerusalem, and*
H	*in all Judaea, and in Samaria, and unto the uttermost*
U	*part of the earth.* —ACTS 1:8

One of my favorite paintings of Jesus doesn't even show His face. In fact, all you can see of Christ are His feet and the bottom of His robe at the top of the picture. Beneath Him in a semicircle are the disciples, gazing up in wonder as He ascends to heaven. My guess is they can see His face, or at least His beard, but the important thing is they can remember Him from the three remarkable years when He was in their midst.

Why do I like the painting so much? Because it comes closest to the view I have of our Lord. In all my struggles to understand who He was, I've never seen Him face to face. I would consider myself lucky to glimpse His feet. I try to do that by reading the Bible and hearing how He affected those around Him. (I'm particularly fond of the woman whose faith was so strong she expected to be healed by touching His robe.) But I also see Him in the faces of other believers—our neighbor Margaret, who works tirelessly at our church; my fellow Sunday school teacher Peter, who has unimaginable patience with fifth-graders. Like the disciples in that painting of the Ascension, they reflect the God Who has touched them.

When Jesus appeared to the disciples for the last time, He said to them, "Ye shall receive power, after that the Holy Ghost is come upon you: and ye shall be witnesses unto me both in Jerusalem, and in all Judaea, and in Samaria, and unto the uttermost part of the earth" (Acts 1:8). What a promise! What a challenge!

Let me be Your witness, Lord, in all I do and say. —RICK HAMLIN

2

F	
R	*Be of good courage, and he shall strengthen your*
I	*heart, all ye that hope in the Lord.* —PSALM 31:24

Our son Eric found a newborn calf that had been abandoned by its mother in a meadow near our cabin in the Colorado mountains. He brought it back to the cabin in his truck where Beth, our daughter-in-law, began massaging it to keep it warm and stimulated. She also tried to feed it with an improvised bottle, but the calf refused to drink. Meanwhile, I phoned the rancher who owned the grazing rights to that meadow. When the rancher arrived at last, having driven over forty miles of rough unpaved mountain roads, he forced a long tube down the calf's throat and poured a large bottle of special formula into its stomach. He predicted that the calf would live, and we later learned that it did. Meanwhile, he credited Beth with having saved the calf until he could get there by constantly massaging its body, which he said had kept it from giving up.

I've seen people strengthened by comfort and encouragement, too, even when their situations looked grave. Some of those people have actually healed in ways that were then called "miracles." And I know from experience how a kind word, a gentle touch and a prayer can lift the spirits and reduce pain.

Comfort. Encouragement. Prayer. Three ways to help friends in need. And animals, too!

Father, keep me open today to ways in which I may encourage those around me. —MADGE HARRAH

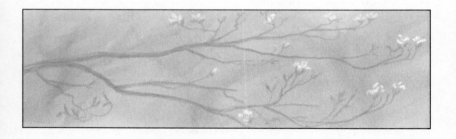

ALL THINGS NEW

3 | S Going Deeper
| A *Sing to the Lord a new song. . . .*
| T —PSALM 96:1 (RSV)

Saturday afternoons in June, I tune into the radio broadcasts from Lyric Opera of Chicago. That day the opera was Puccini's *La Boheme* with my favorite soprano, Mirella Freni, as the poor little seamstress Mimi.

I had seen Freni onstage in this role twice and had played her recording of the opera again and again. Yet over the radio that afternoon, she made the story of penniless young lovers and early death so fresh and poignant that as Mimi expired in that unheated garret, tears rolled down my cheeks.

How could she sing the very same lines time after time, I wondered, *without going stale?* During intermission, an interviewer asked her the same question.

"Miss Freni," he began, "you've sung in opera houses all over the world for forty-two years, the role of Mimi, in particular, many hundreds of times. How do you make it sound new each time?"

"But," the singer cried, her ebullient Italian accent underlining the words, "it *is* new each time!"

She herself was older—by a year, a month, a week—she reminded him. She had experienced more, felt more—"So I can go deeper." And always, when she did, there were new things to discover in the score, new beauties she had never grasped before. "With great music, you can always go deeper."

With great music, I thought, yes—and with all greatness. A great natural vista. A great book. A great Lord.

Help me go deeper today, Father, into the love that is always new.

—ELIZABETH SHERRILL

UNLOOKED-FOR BLESSINGS

Sometimes renewal catches us by surprise. Just when we think the day is at its darkest, God parts the clouds and dazzles us with His light. Over the next week, join Daily Guideposts *newcomer Marci Alborghetti as she tells us about the divine surprises that made a shower of blessings out of an encounter with her deepest fears.*

—THE EDITORS

4

S
U
N

The Gift of a Healing Relationship
We spend our years as a tale that is told.
—PSALM 90:9

I sat on the sand, watching the late afternoon sunlight on the lapping waves, the damp surgical bandage plastered against my back like a sweaty, unwelcome hand. The beach may have seemed a strange place to visit immediately after surgery. But for my mother and me, it was a place of comfort. We had driven to this bit of sand and ocean, in unspoken agreement, minutes after leaving the doctor. We sat wordless, considering his troubled observation that the mole he'd just removed from between my shoulder blades was "bizarre."

Not benign. Bizarre.

We watched the few young mothers remaining so late in the day as they gathered their children. My mother said softly, "Remember when . . ." and I smiled involuntarily. We were both reliving the many late summer days when she'd herded my sister and me and a friend or two toward the car, urging us first to duck under the much-too-cold shower and admonishing us against tracking sand into the car.

We were both remembering . . . and wondering if life would ever be that simple or joyful again. We'd grown apart in my adult years, lovingly distant, and this whole day together was as unusual as the circumstances that had prompted it. My mother had urged that I visit this doctor. Indeed, she'd all but demanded it, despite the fact that I was disconcertingly healthy and had almost no risk factors for the malignant melanoma that the doctor diagnosed a week later.

Sitting on that warm sand in our summer dresses just after Labor Day, I think we both knew that call would come. "It's a good day for the beach," my mother said, and she put her hand over mine.

Lord, help me always to discern Your opportunities for healing.
—MARCI ALBORGHETTI

5

M
O
N

The Gift of Flight
Oh, that I had wings like a dove! for then would I fly away. . . .
—PSALM 55:6

I know you're not supposed to run away from your problems. But I felt I was running from my life—or *for* my life—and that seemed to excuse the flight. In two short months my life had become something from which to flee. After finding malignant melanoma once and excising again to remove all the cancer, my surgeon told me that he would need to remove another suspicious-looking mole. And then there were the thirty or forty other sections of my skin that he would be "watching carefully" and might have to biopsy.

As soon as the second biopsy had been completed, I hit the road. I didn't even know if this biopsy had revealed another melanoma when I headed up the New England coast. I just knew I had to get away and, for me, that meant Ogunquit, a seaside community in southern Maine. My flight was thoughtless, instinctive, much like that of a deer fleeing from gunfire. I blindly fled to the one place, over the years, where I had experienced both joy and crisis . . . and dealt with both.

Except this time it didn't work. I felt none of the usual flooding warmth when I crossed the bridge between New Hampshire and Maine; I didn't stop in the village to see which restaurant had the most enticing menu; I barely heard the greetings of the friendly staff members at the inn where I stay; even the shimmering, sapphire-blue Atlantic just beyond the coastal cliffs, usually overwhelming in its vastness, did not move me.

For the first time, I felt beaten. If there was no healing for me in this place, there would be no healing anywhere.

That night, I opened the window of my third-floor garret and crawled onto the roof to rage silently at the stars. It was so cold and so clear that it seemed I could see every star in the universe, and the sliver moon merely made them glow more brightly. The dark ocean shuddered just below me in the light of the sky.

And the tears came. Not tears mourning all that I thought I'd lost, but tears of gratitude that I was sitting on this roof at this moment in this universe. Not tears because I had cancer, but tears because God had given me this to which to flee. And I could feel again.

Lord, let each of my flights bring me into Your embrace.

—MARCI ALBORGHETTI

6

T
U
E

The Gift of Sight
From the rising of the sun unto the going down of the same the Lord's name is to be praised.

—PSALM 113:3

It was a short route—ten minutes—but, as a teenager, I'd waste an hour's worth of gas circling it again and again before heading home after a date or work. It wasn't that I was particularly dazzled by the scenery in the town where I grew up; I just reveled in the private, soothing ride during which I blared music and daydreamed to my heart's content.

I tried not to consider the irony that, two decades later, I was soothing myself with the same drive. The surgeon's office was near my parents' home, and I'd grown accustomed to driving this familiar route after each appointment. Whether the news was good or bad, whether I'd had a surgery or not, I always ended up on the southern stretch of Main Street, swinging into the North Cove loop, over the causeway, circling along the beach and over the expanse of wetlands that led to my parents' home.

I never consciously decided to start this route again; it was more reflex than anything. Until one late afternoon. I'd begun my automatic drive after hearing that one of the two recent biopsies had been "clean," and one had shown traces of melanoma and would have to be re-excised.

And then I turned onto the causeway. The early winter sun was just sinking into the ocean, leaving horizontal streaks of pink, rose, fuchsia and, finally, indigo, before fading into the twilight sky. Vertical shards of deep violet embedded themselves into the wash of color. I pulled over and simply sat and watched. Commuters hurrying home blasted past me, considering me nothing more than an inconsiderate obstacle. I could almost sense their annoyance.

After all, I'd been very much like them: I'd lived in this town for many years and, even now that I was back, I was still so involved in my own inner world that I hadn't bothered to notice anything around me, much less this extraordinary sunset. I'm sure I'd lived through hundreds like it. I'd just never seen them.

Now, I knew enough to look.

Lord, thank You for Your glorious reminders to see.

—MARCI ALBORGHETTI

7 | W | **The Gift of Perspective**
  | E | *Behold, I will . . . reveal unto them the abundance of*
  | D | *peace and truth.*   —JEREMIAH 33:6

I am not, by even the kindest stretch of the imagination, a calm person. Maybe it's in my genes: In my family, selecting a restaurant could become a full-scale tragic opera. The result? I can be anxious, even frantic, about the smallest thing. At least, I could before cancer. Cancer has given me a different perspective. A different idea of time, perhaps, and how it should be spent.

Before cancer announced itself, I kept a constant vigil for potential problems, particularly at home. Since my house was the thing I depended upon most, I naturally expected it to be the thing that would stop working. Every fall when my heat clanged on, I was certain the noise was louder than last spring when it had clanged off. I constantly glanced upward at the skylights, not to enjoy their light and warmth, but to wonder when they would crack and let in the deluge of summer's downpours and winter's blizzards. I never opened my sliding glass door because it had a tendency to stick, and I just *knew* I'd never get it closed again.

Then came the morning, shortly after my second biopsy, when I awoke to see my ceiling marked with dark, wet splotches. The night's rainfall had been the roof's last stand, and my ceiling bore the scars of that lost battle. I lay in bed waiting for the inevitable stomach-dropping dread and terror to descend.

It didn't. I tiptoed cautiously downstairs to call the roofer, convinced that panic would overtake me. It didn't. In fact, I scheduled the repairs, barely blinking when the roofer said he couldn't get to my roof immediately; greeted him when the day finally came; left on errands while he worked; and returned to find the job completed and my bedroom a shambles—all with a decided sense of detachment.

Later, I related the whole story to a neighbor, telling him how surprised I was at my near-normal behavior. "Well," he replied, "I guess in the larger plan of your life now, a leaky roof just isn't a priority."

Lord, help me spend the time You've given me looking for joy and overlooking obstacles.
                                                          —MARCI ALBORGHETTI

8 | T H U | **The Gift of Surprise**
Grace did much more abound. —ROMANS 5:20

"I could die, you know," I blurted to my sister, not sure this would mean more than a blip on the screen of life for her. I hadn't even meant to say it; the words made me cringe. I sounded as if I wanted sympathy.

Perhaps I did. Although Lori and I had been very close as children, and I had happily played the role of older sister and protector, we'd chosen very different paths as adults and grown far apart. Married, she was a respected, beloved elementary-school teacher in the town where we'd been raised. She visited my parents just about every day. Decidedly unmarried, I was a writer living in a "difficult" neighborhood in a city far away from my hometown. If I phoned home once a week, it was cause for celebration. I spoke with Lori even less often, and I'd come to believe that I'd somehow let her down.

And then there was melanoma.

Suddenly, my sister and I were on the phone constantly; I soon discovered that I could share things with her that would only upset my parents. Hence, my unthinking declaration about dying. I wanted to take it back as soon as I'd said it. It sounded so pathetic, and how much would this sister, whom I thought could never love and respect me as she once had, be willing to tolerate?

There was a long pause before her voice resumed, "You won't die. You are like God's personal Internet, and He wants you here to keep touching and affecting people. He wants to keep reaching people through you."

I couldn't speak. It wasn't just her extraordinary statement, it was that she actually believed it! For more than a decade, I'd assumed she disapproved of my focus on work and people away from my family. Now she was telling me that she not only knew me, she was proud of me.

I don't know how I continued the conversation or what I said. I do know that cancer gave me back my sister . . . and the stunning knowledge that she'd never left.

Lord, thank You for unspeakably wonderful surprises . . . when we least expect them and most need them. —MARCI ALBORGHETTI

9

F The Gift of Agelessness
R *Ye shall hallow the fiftieth year . . . it shall be a*
I *jubilee. . . .* —LEVITICUS 25:10

Steve, a friend of mine, called to discuss the miseries of his fiftieth birthday, and as he talked, I found myself thinking how difficult aging is for my "poor, healthy" friends.

I spared Steve this unspoken comment as he described the emotions stirred up by his landmark birthday. He wondered where he would be if he'd chosen another career. Had he missed something important? Was he making enough money? How much was enough? Should he have had his own children? Was it too late for him and his wife?

Steve's not an insecure guy, but of all the "zero" birthdays, the fiftieth seems to hit men the hardest because it represents the point of no return. I've heard a number of men admit they dread this day and all the doubts it raises.

For women, it seems to be "the big four-oh" that triggers depression and worry. Many of my friends experienced minor crises on this birthday, and they had their own set of questions. "Why am I still single?" or "Why did I marry *this* man?" or "Why didn't my marriage last?" "Will I ever have a baby?" or "Why did I have kids?" "Is this the right career for me?" or "Did I sacrifice a real life to succeed at work?"

These days, I have a different perspective. Every day matters, and everything and anything I choose to do every day matters. Even if it's nothing.

Steve startled me out of my reverie, asking, "Are you dreading your fortieth birthday?"

I debated my answer. Surely, I could manage something gentle and slightly superficial. Instead, I treated Steve like the beloved friend he is and told the truth.

"That's one of the gifts of cancer. Every birthday—every day—is a cause for celebration."

Lord, help us celebrate—without regret or recrimination—every moment that comes with age. —MARCI ALBORGHETTI

10

S
A
T

The Gift of Awe
The earth is full of the goodness of the Lord.
—PSALM 33:5

I've always been "much too sensitive," as a high school teacher once labeled me. Before melanoma, that sensitivity had let me retreat from life. Granted, I was a writer working in a small city, but whenever I could barricade myself in my house with my computer, I did. So I surprised everyone by announcing that I'd spend the winter in sunny

KeyWest, Florida . . . right after a diagnosis of potentially fatal skin cancer!

In many ways, my cancer had opened my life, and Key West seemed a good place to keep the process going. I decided that what had started on a rooftop in frigid Maine would continue in the country's hottest city.

That winter was one massive, emotional blur of color, heat, tears, ocean and poignant joy. I wrote a lot. I walked more. I ate quantities of fresh fish. And toward the end of my stay, I had the most extraordinary experience of my life.

I'd been invited to a concert at one of the island's oldest homes. Roofless, it had a mammoth banyan tree growing up and out toward the visible, smoky night sky. Huge goldfish swam lazily in a reflecting pool surrounded by tropical plants on the ground floor. Each of the four floors had circular walkways facing this enclosed courtyard, and people mingled on walkways, elevated above the main space below.

I was on the third-floor walkway when the music began. Youngsters of every race and ethnicity had been moving silently among the guests, setting up extraordinary instruments: steel drums of many sizes and shapes. They began playing without any introduction, though I later learned that this diverse group of children had arrived fresh from performances at the White House and the Olympics.

The children pounded out their music with indescribable fervor; it throbbed through the still air until there was nothing but heart-stopping vibrancy, lavish flora, deep night and a thousand mingled scents. In that moment I felt the music join my soul to my body, and I knew that—in spite of sin and suffering and cancer—all these beautiful things were holy because they were created by God.

Lord, let me always be open to awe-inspiring "God-moments."

—MARCI ALBORGHETTI

11

**S
u
N**

But in fact God has arranged the parts in the body, every one of them, just as he wanted them to be.
—I CORINTHIANS 12:18 (NIV)

Almost anytime there's an activity at church, Dave is there, and he's usually among the first to arrive and the last to leave. Rain or shine or freezing cold, his bike is propped near the front door, the blue helmet hanging from the seat. If we've had a fresh snow he might be out shoveling the walks, but usually he's sitting in the back row, waiting and talking to himself.

Dave is probably in his thirties, but his face has a rugged, aged look. Sometimes he needs a haircut or hasn't shaved for several days, but he almost always has a big smile. Dave is developmentally disabled.

I first met Dave at the name-tag table. When I offered him a marking pen he handed it back, saying, "Maybe you could do it for me—it's 'Dave.'" Weeks later, I noticed in Sunday school class that he had his Bible open to some place in Genesis while the rest of us were discussing the Gospel of Matthew. It took me awhile to realize that Dave can't read or write.

Dave's presence adds a certain liveliness to our church gatherings. For example, Dave responds spontaneously almost anytime there's a pause in the service. Although they can be a bit unsettling to visiting speakers, Dave's interjections are sometimes surprisingly appropriate.

One Sunday morning, we were having a baptism as part of our worship. We all renewed our baptismal vows, reading from our service books in unison, not giving too much thought to the meaning of the words. Then Pastor John dipped his hand into the water, gently poured it on the child's head and welcomed her into the Body of Christ. "Amen," read the response in our books. But I thought our feelings were summed up much better in Dave's enthusiastic "Wow!"

On this Pentecost, loving Lord, may I grow in my appreciation of the diversity and beauty You bring together to make up Your Body, the Church.
                                                              —MARY JANE CLARK

12 | M Not that we are competent in ourselves to claim any-
      | O thing for ourselves, but our competence comes from
      | N God.   —II CORINTHIANS 3:5 (NIV)

With great anticipation, I paid for the bulging envelope of photographs and rushed to the privacy of my car to check them out. Our son Derek had gotten married the week before, and this packet contained photographs of the four-day family celebration. Not only would they chronicle the festivities, they would also show me the results of a resolution I made five months ago: that I would look better in these wedding pictures than I did in our Christmas pictures. Since January, I'd been on a diet. No desserts or bread or second helpings. Others had noticed a positive change in me, but these pictures would be the proof I needed. Nervously, I slid them out of the envelope, flipped through them and then let out a sigh of relief. I didn't look like the same puffy person I saw in the Christmas pictures.

When I got home, I taped several of the new pictures to the refrigerator door: Lynn and I hugging the nervous-looking groom after he escorted us down the aisle; all of us throwing streamers as the radiant bride and groom came out of the church; Lynn and I dancing at the reception.

These pictures are reminders of our great family celebration. But they also remind me that "I can do it!" I need to see that reminder, because now that the wedding is over, my resolve to continue eating better is more fragile and vulnerable. And if I am going to turn this short-term goal into a long-term lifestyle change, I need to remember to start each day with the same prayer I've been repeating for the last five months:

Father, at the beginning of this day, I recognize that I am totally dependent upon You for a moment-by-moment ability to overcome temptation, choice by choice. Please help me. —CAROL KUYKENDALL

13 | T u E | *The righteous will shine like the sun in the kingdom of their Father. . . .* —MATTHEW 13:43 (RSV)

The sunset was brilliant beyond description. Overhead, white clouds floated through the blue sky. As the sun reached the horizon, the red glow spread for miles in both directions. I stood enthralled. Only God could produce such beauty.

Some people radiate an indescribable glow, as beautiful as that sunset, that changes the atmosphere whenever they enter a room. They have a loving spirit that brings joy and disperses tension. I know several people who have this gift, and I'm sure you do, too. What's their secret? They have an awareness of God's presence in their own lives that lights up everything around them.

As you meditate during your quiet time today, ask God to "make His face to shine upon you" (Numbers 6:25), to let His light shine through you on all the people you meet. Ask Him to use you to help lighten a burden, relieve someone's loneliness, solve a problem or make God's ever-present Spirit real in someone's life. Your day will be happier—and more exciting.

Lord, help me to be filled with Your peace and show Your loving concern to the people around me. Amen. —RUTH STAFFORD PEALE

14 | W E D

We will rejoice in thy salvation, and in the name of our God will set up our banners. . . . —PSALM 20:5

My husband Bob hoisted our large American flag into the metal bracket designed to hold it on the front of our house. As he stepped back to see if it was hanging properly, the flag began to fall, and he lunged forward to catch it before it could touch the ground. The bracket had rusted and broken away from the house.

"How awful!" I groaned. "Flag Day and no way to display our flag!"

Bob took the flag into our garage. As I followed, he asked, "What about our Uncle Sam?"

From our collection of camping equipment, he pulled out a wooden statue of Uncle Sam carved in profile. He dusted it off and set it on the garage floor. Slightly scarred from many years of traveling with us and guarding our campsites, the little painted figure was still a sight to see. From the tip of his red-and-white striped top hat to the soles of his dark-blue shoes, he stood three feet tall. His white shirt sported a red bow tie and a dark blue vest. A light blue frock coat set off his long red-and-white striped pants. With a cheery smile on his familiar bearded face, he extended one foot in a big step and reached out his hand as if to greet the whole world. Bob anchored Uncle Sam to a wooden nail keg and secured a rod to his outstretched hand. To that, we fastened an American flag.

Uncle Sam has stood atop his nail keg on our front lawn, proudly displaying our red-white-and-blue banner, on every Flag Day since then.

Father, pour Your love on the people who live in this wonderful land. Help us to grow more united as we go into this new century.

—DRUE DUKE

15

Hath not my hand made all these things?
—ACTS 7:50

There is a spot I like to hike to in the Berkshire Hills of western Massachusetts called Bash Bish Falls. Over the west shoulder of Bash Bish Mountain forks a riot of white water that, cleaved by a granite promontory, sluices down in two twisting, tumbling midair streams to a deep, mossy pool a hundred feet or so below, producing the sound that has become its name.

I head for Bash Bish whenever I need a chance to get away and think. By the time I reach the trailhead above the falls, breathing hard, I've begun to feel peaceful, yet more alive to the world, my senses pricked by the air and sky and the water.

But not on this day. I come to Bash Bish feeling at odds with the world for no particular reason, just a little uncertain as to how I fit into it all. Forlorn, I crouch on a big, flat rock and stare down at the falls. I hear a rustle along the trail, and out pops a woman with a thick nest of once-red, now graying hair, making her way slowly but steadily with the assistance of a tall, crooked walking stick. She reaches the edge of my rock, stops and turns toward the falls. We are silent, except for our breathing, which is soon absorbed by the sound of the falls—*bash bish, bash bish.* We stay that way long enough for me to be aware of the sun sinking. Then the woman says, to no one in particular, "Well, if He can take care of all this, then He can surely take care of me." With that she's off, heading down the other side of the trail, first her head and then the crooked tip of her walking stick dropping slowly from sight.

I stay a bit longer on my rock before racing the sun down the mountain. I just want to get one last look at how I fit into it all.

Lord, You make a place for me in Your beautiful world. Surely You will not forget me.
—EDWARD GRINNAN

R E A D E R ' S   R O O M

"On Sunday evening, February 8, 1998, at 8:00, I was attending church service at my newly completed Fellowship Chapel at Blue Ribbon Downs Racetrack, Sallisaw, Oklahoma, when a lady came in saying, 'A barn's on fire, come help!' My mind was racing, 'Not again, oh, Lord, please not again.' I was there fourteen years ago when a barn burned, and I still remember it as if it were yesterday. Not a single horse could I save. But now I got four or five horses out before the smoke was too thick, and I could hear the electricity popping, and I knew I had to get out. I cried to God, 'Oh, Lord, I can't bear this anymore,' and He said, 'You don't have to. Put your eyes on me and I'll bear your pain.' I closed my eyes, and I saw Jesus on the sea of Galilee holding out his hand to Peter and Andrew, but then I saw me, and Him saying, 'Come follow me,' and the peace that passes all understanding flooded upon my heart and my mind like a river."   —*Lou Burlison, Sallisaw, Oklahoma*

16

F
R
I

O my Father, if it be possible, let this cup pass from me: nevertheless not as I will, but as thou wilt.
—MATTHEW 26:39

Three-year-old Elizabeth was limp in my arms as the cab swerved smoothly through traffic. I brushed back her bangs and kissed her forehead. It was clammy. She was going into shock.

"Honey, we're going to the hospital. The doctors will try to help you."

She did not respond, perhaps because her throat and tongue were so swollen that words were impossible. She'd eaten a bite of shrimp at dinner and was having a serious allergic reaction.

"The doctors will probably have to give you a shot to get medicine inside you." I was relieved to hear a moan of protest; it meant she hadn't passed out. "But that will only hurt a little bit for a little while."

Elizabeth mumbled something that sounded vaguely like, "Feel better?" I wondered what to say. I didn't know if she was going to feel better. My brother had nearly died of anaphylactic shock the year before, and I knew that timing could mean the difference between life and death. I would never lie to her, but I didn't want to scare her either. *Holy Ghost, be in my heart and on my lips.*

I wiped stray tears from my little girl's swollen face and kissed her again. Then, quietly, gently, I prayed aloud for Elizabeth and for the doctors who would treat her. But the harder and more essential prayer still remained: I had to pray for the grace to accept God's will, whatever it might be. Holding my precious girl in my arms, I did not know how anyone could say those words. *Holy Ghost, please help me.*

"Thy will be done, Lord." The prayer emerged from my heart as the cab pulled up to the emergency-room entrance. Whatever the outcome, Elizabeth would be okay. And after a shot of epinephrine and a dose of Benadryl, she was.

Lord Jesus, how little I grasp Your words, "Not as I will, but as thou wilt." Make them a part of who I am and how I live each day.

—JULIA ATTAWAY

17

S
A
T

And when he had opened the seventh seal, there was silence in heaven about the space of half an hour.
—REVELATION 8:1

The sun is not up yet when Matt and I arrive at Sugar Creek Lake. My son-in-law is taking me fishing in his new boat.

We stand beside the four-wheeler, transfixed by the morning silence. The lake is a sheet of glass. The rim of the earth is tinted rose and rises to meet a sky of navy and ivory, with a fingernail moon and a few mashed-potato clouds in the distant darkness. Slivers of silver glide over the water, dropping down to snatch at careless minnows. Mayflies dimple the surface of the lake like random raindrops falling from the fingertips of God. Rugged oak trees lean out over the water, as if longing to wade into the cool morning drink.

The only sound is the squeak of the pulley as Matt lowers the boat. It swishes softly across the sand and enters the water with musical gurgles. I catch a whiff of bananas, as Matt sets the sack lunch in the boat.

We are anxious to get started, but we are chained to this spot by its bewitching beauty. We speak in whispers, as if we were in a cathedral. I stare at the moon and think of the Creator. In the absolute silence I can hear myself swallow. "Only You could create this beauty, Lord. Thank You for it."

In a few minutes we will be streaking over the lake in a noisy machine, carving a jagged gash in this crystal plain. The lake will be a frothy sea of happiness for fishermen and swimmers. But for now, silence.

I need this quiet place, but I can't come to this lake every day. So each day I will find an excuse to step outside the office and look up at the sky and consider the great, quiet forces of the universe, like gravity and sunlight and God. It's a little slice of heaven that will make my day bearable.

Lord, if You don't mind, I would like just to sit and listen for a while.
—DANIEL SCHANTZ

18 | S u N | *A wise son heareth his father's instruction. . . .*
—PROVERBS 13:1

I've become like my dad. I don't just mean "I have kids." I mean I have become my father. Had you told me this twenty years ago, I would've laughed so hard I'd have spit up my soda. "No, no," my seventeen-year-old self would've told you, "I'll never be like my dad."

Well, I'm not just like my dad, I *am* my dad. The other night I caught my reflection in the kitchen window. I was sitting on the back porch, complaining about the body work I needed to do on the van. If you change the van from a Chrysler to a VW microbus, then it could be 1968, and I could be my old man. Often, like him, I'll fetch the morning paper still in my jammies. I spend weekends unshaven. I often eat my lunch at my desk, leftovers out of a plastic container. I'm rude to phone solicitors.

Where does it come from? At what point do young men trip into somewhat older men, becoming incarnations of their fathers? At what point do we trade our sedans for station wagons and minivans?

I have one guess. For me, it happened on a morning in May a few years back, when my oldest daughter was born. I was in the operating room when my wife delivered, and I was the first to hold Faith.

And I remember holding this crying, wrinkled baby, thinking, *I know they keep saying this is my kid, but surely there's a mistake. I've never met this person before. Believe me, I'd remember.*

And the first thing I said to my new daughter?

"Hello, Faith Margaret. I'm your dad. I love you."

Now where did that come from?

On this Father's Day, Lord, I thank You for the gifts You've given me through my father.   —MARK COLLINS

19

M
O   *"But you will chase your enemies and they will fall*
N   *before you. . . ."*   —LEVITICUS 26:7 (NAS)

When one of my thirty-something-year-old children asked me to pray about a particularly painful trial, I immediately did so. But when I didn't see much result, I wondered if my prayers were really making a difference. Was God really hearing me? Discouraged, I was about to give up the battle as I headed to the mailbox one hot morning in June. I'd written what I hoped was a letter of encouragement, but I wasn't certain that I should mail it.

As I stood hesitating at the mailbox, I heard a loud commotion overhead. I looked up, shading my eyes with my hand and squinting into the bright sun. An unbelievably tiny bird was screaming loudly as she chased a huge hawk. Again and again they circled in the sky above a small wooded area. Were the little bird's babies there? Relentlessly, the small bird pursued the enormous hawk, darting in front of him as if daring him to catch her. At last the hawk began to grow weary. Fascinated, I watched as the exhausted hawk flew slowly out of sight and the victorious little bird returned to her babies. I continued to stare up at the cloudless sky long after the battle was over and the birds were gone, and listened with my heart.

I thought I heard clearly: *You can't imagine how effective your prayers are. The enemy is growing weary.* "Yes!" I said out loud joyfully, and I dropped my letter into the mailbox. Even as I walked back to the house, I prayed for my child with new energy.

Father God, teach me to be a patient, persistent prayer warrior.

—MARION BOND WEST

20

T
U
E

But be ye doers of the word, and not hearers only. . . .
—JAMES 1:22

"Daddy, what planet are you?"

I squinted at four-year-old Elizabeth across the breakfast table, trying to think of an answer. Mornings have been very hard lately. With newborn Mary Frances in the house, sleep isn't easy to come by. John, at two, thinks his breakfast is excellent modeling material. And then there are Elizabeth's games.

Last year, it was dinosaurs. That meant pretending to be velociraptors looking for prey or maiasauras tending their eggs. The year before that, it was zoo animals, lined up on the living room steps for parties while we sang "Happy birthday, dear hippo." But this year, it's planets.

My powers of invention were wearing thin. "Neptune," I said.

"Oh, Daddy, you have to be an *inner* planet! I'm the outer planets!"

"Okay, I'll be Mars."

"Okay, Mars, I'm Jupiter!"

The game went on for another ten minutes. We changed planets three or four times. I had run out of inner planets and cycled back to Mars by the time breakfast was over.

If I'm often fatigued by Elizabeth's games, I'm always amazed at them. I can hear the wheels turning inside that little head, as her pretending sorts out and structures the things she's read about books or seen on videos. Elizabeth becomes the things she wants to know about; she feels them in her body as she holds up her hands like tyrannosaurus rex or twirls around like Saturn orbiting the sun, holding a scarf in front of her for rings.

I think something like that happens in the life of faith. When I kneel in prayer, reach out for the Bread and Cup, lift my arms in praise, offer my neighbor a shoulder to lean on or bear a sorrow for Jesus' sake, I'm giving the Spirit a chance to teach me what it really means to be a Christian. I've got to hear the preacher or read my Bible to get the Word into my head, but I've got to use everything God has given me if His Word is going to live in my heart.

Lord, thank You for the chance to act out my faith today.

—ANDREW ATTAWAY

21 | W
     | E   *He orders his angels to protect you wherever you go.*
     | D   —PSALM 91:11 (TLB)

"Stop, lady—don't do it, you'll never make it!" The man screeched his camper onto the shoulder of the fast lane, perilously close to my car, jumped out and rushed toward me waving his arms.

It was my first flat tire. It caused my car to careen out of control on the freeway and had me so terrified that all I could do was pray a frantic "Help!" Fortunately it was mid-afternoon, before the crush of rush-hour traffic. I had waited for a long gap between oncoming cars and was just about to run across four lanes to the call box on the right shoulder when the man grabbed my arm and pulled me back.

"I'm pretty fast," I told him, "I think I can make it. I need to phone—"

"Listen, lady, on the freeway no one's ever fast enough to make it. A car close enough to see, and even a car not close enough to see, is a car close enough to hit you!"

"But what am I supposed to do?" I spluttered. "I have to get to a meeting."

"No meeting is worth your life. If you have a flat, or stall, and can't somehow bump your car over to the right lane, just stay in the car. Someone with a cell phone will call the highway patrol and get you help. You're lucky I came along. Here, I'll change your tire for you."

My eyes filled with tears of relief and gratitude. "Thank you, thank you so much." I paused, then smiled. "You know, your coming along wasn't just luck; I prayed for help."

He raised his eyebrows and grinned. Then, sweating with effort, he changed my tire. I handed him a twenty-dollar bill. "You saved my life. Please, the least I can do is buy you lunch."

He wiped his forehead with his shirt. "No way, lady. Just pass on a favor whenever you can. Help someone else in need."

Thank You for earth angels, Lord, the ordinary people You use to answer our prayers.   —FAY ANGUS

22
T
H
U

He that refraineth his lips is wise.
—PROVERBS 10:19

During 1935, photos appeared in our local paper of a young athlete reading the Bible. Scripture verses appeared under some of the photos. The athlete was twenty-one-year-old Joseph Louis Barrows, called Joe Louis to conceal his identity from his mother, who disapproved of boxing. This young man excited boxing fans as no one had since Jack Dempsey. His effect on me was different. I carried the burden of feeling that anything done by a man of color reflected on me.

I felt good about Joe Louis as he won bout after bout. I felt even better when his handlers said, "We are out to prove he can win the heavyweight championship and still remain a gentleman."

By 1936, Joe Louis, in the minds of many, was the uncrowned heavyweight champ. All he had to do was defeat Max Schmeling, and a match with champion Jim Braddock would be next. But at Yankee Stadium in New York, Max Schmeling knocked out Joe Louis in the twelfth round. I remember my father turning off the radio and saying, "That's what happens when you become overconfident!"

I was crushed. Joe Louis went on to win the championship in 1937. But his lone defeat still troubled me. Was Max Schmeling the better boxer? In a 1938 rematch, Louis defeated Schmeling in two minutes and four seconds of the first round. I had my answer.

I was elated by my hero's success, but even more, I was impressed by his comportment. In the two years between his defeat by Schmeling and his victory, Joe Louis had said little. He made no excuses, nor did he utter any disparaging remarks about Max Schmeling. Joe Louis showed me that a great athlete can lose and still remain a gentleman. As I prepared to face life's obstacles, I could do the same.

Father, in every action, let me be a mirror of Your love and understanding.
—OSCAR GREENE

23
F
R
I

"Your sacrifices do not please me."
—JEREMIAH 6:20 (NIV)

I'd always thought of myself as a "people pleaser." And I'd always thought that was a positive thing—until I overheard a comment that let me know I shouldn't be patting myself on the back.

My two friends hadn't meant to be hurtful; it was just that I was a little late and had stopped to buy our local newspaper so we could decide what movie to see together. As I got to the door, I heard Marie say, "It's really hard to choose a movie when Linda's around."

I stopped walking abruptly, my fingers clenching the paper. They couldn't mean *me!* Why, I went out of my way to be agreeable! "It doesn't matter to me" or "Anything you want is fine" were among my favorite phrases. I just wanted to be nice. Surely, Jan would correct Marie's statement. But Jan didn't. "*Mmm.* She makes us do all the work of choosing. It's as if she's not doing her share!"

"And then, do you remember that time we saw *Elizabeth?* After we left the theater, she mentioned that she'd seen it already but hadn't wanted to tell us because we seemed eager to see it."

I did remember that! Here I thought I was being so thoughtful, but obviously they were annoyed with me. I was taking the easy way out, letting my unwillingness to make a decision masquerade as being easygoing.

I unfolded the newspaper and took a moment to glance over the movie listings. I didn't know what we would finally see, but I did know that I would put my opinion right in the middle of the table, with the rest of them.

God, don't let me take the easy way out by saying, "I don't care" or "Whatever you want" when my opinion is called for today. Help me to do my part in the decision-making. —LINDA NEUKRUG

24 | S A T

Neither do I condemn thee: go, and sin no more.
—JOHN 8:11

The spiritual theme of my life in this past year has been grace, simply unmerited favor. Either I received something wonderful I didn't deserve, or I didn't receive something negative that I did deserve. Sometime in the last year I saw a TV show that summed up my experience very well. The main character was identified as the minister of "The Church of the Second Chance." All were welcome in his church, but especially those in need of a second chance. The minister proclaimed that Jesus, along with being divine, holy, a wonderful teacher and loving friend, was "Lord of the Second Chance."

I've been reminded of second chances lately because I'm trying to learn to play golf. Some of my friends, those not committed to the purity of the game, offer me a "mulligan" once or twice a round. If I hit a very poor first shot, I can ignore it and hit a second ball in an attempt to improve the result.

It seems to me that Jesus was in the habit of giving out mulligans for life. There was the woman caught in sin, Peter at the lake, Mary in the garden, Zaccheus up a tree and a host of others. Like you and me, when we forget to love those close to us or be kind to people in need or forgive ourselves for past regrets.

So, if you need it today, take a mulligan from Jesus.

Lord, thank You for the "do overs" You give in life. Help me to need fewer and fewer of them. —ERIC FELLMAN

25 | S U N | *Ask in faith without any doubting, for the one who doubts is like the surf of the sea, driven and tossed by the wind.* —JAMES 1:6 (NAS)

Recently, our church faced a major decision. As our deacons contemplated our options, we all grew leery of financial cost and emotional strain. But we had delayed the decision long enough. It was time to vote yes or no.

As we sat in tense silence, our Deacon Chairman Dick Jackson walked to the microphone. In a quiet voice he said, "I have always wished I could have been present with Moses when Pharaoh trapped the Israelites against the Red Sea. I'm willing to bet you that the Red Sea never parted until Moses stuck his foot in the water. The waters won't part until your feet get wet."

All of us shook our heads and chuckled. We knew what Dick meant: It was time to step off the shore and put our feet in the water. God wouldn't act until we moved forth in faith.

When I'm facing a new challenge or transition in life, I want to have all the answers and be fully prepared before I move. But the fact is, the life of faith doesn't work that way. Often God won't help us until we commit ourselves to a decision.

A week before our wedding, Beth and I combined our checking accounts and discovered that between us we had a net worth of one hundred and ten dollars. This was not enough money for a few dates, much less the start of a marriage. But the time was upon us, and we had made our commitment. We put our feet in the water. And for us, as for Moses, the Red Sea parted, and we walked on dry ground. Never did we go hungry or lack our basic needs. We learned that when we act in faith, God is with us.

Dear God, give me the courage to live out my commitments.

—SCOTT WALKER

26 MON

"Do not be frightened or dismayed, for the Lord your God is with you wherever you go."
—JOSHUA 1:9 (NLT)

Driving by my old grammar school one windy summer day, my thoughts focused on my daughter Misty and her husband Indelethio. They were moving to New York City to pursue their dreams of dancing and acting professionally, and I was worried. They had no jobs waiting for them and had rented an apartment sight unseen. "Lord, give me peace about their decision," I prayed.

I noticed that the front doors of the school were open, so I pulled over and walked inside. The smell of chalk, paste and crayons reawakened pleasant childhood memories. I walked down the hall, listening to the wooden floors creak beneath me as they had some thirty-six years before. I opened the door to my first-grade classroom and walked in. Not much had changed: The desks were still in long rows, the group of tiny chairs still clustered in the back for reading time.

The one thing missing from the room was our wishing well. Our teacher Mrs. Brock had made one out of cardboard and painted it to look like gray stone. Often we were allowed to sit alone at the well and write a wish on a slip of paper. Mrs. Brock taught us that a wish is a tiny dream, and when you add a prayer, it gives your wish its wings to fly to heaven. I found a piece of paper and wrote my wish: *For my daughter and her husband to have a glorious life living out their dreams in New York City.* I added a prayer for their safety.

At that moment a gust of wind blew through the open windows. My slip of paper wafted through the air and floated out of the window. My tiny dream, on its wings of prayer, was on its way to heaven.

Eternal God, I place my loved ones in Your everlasting arms.

—MELODY BONNETTE

27
T
u
E

He looked up, and said, I see men as trees, walking.
—MARK 8:24

Sometimes it takes a personal experience to bring a Bible passage vividly to life for you. Do you remember the healing of the blind man that St. Mark tells about? I've always been fascinated by that one because Jesus found it necessary to touch the man's eyes *twice* before his vision was restored.

Last year, in two very successful operations, the cloudy lenses in my own eyes were replaced by clear artificial ones. The results were remarkable. Not only could I see distant objects distinctly, but colors were much more vivid, and most spectacular of all was the combination of colors that we call white. Before the operation, the cataracts had made it look a muddy yellow. Now it gleamed brilliantly, and I wondered how the man healed by Jesus felt when he saw it for the first time: the marvelous, uplifting *whiteness* of white.

No, I didn't wonder, really. I knew. What he felt was joy and gratitude beyond words, and these things shine through his story even after two thousand years.

Father, thank You for the rainbow colors that surround us, and for the radiance that happens when they are blended into white.

—ARTHUR GORDON

28
W
E
D

We know that the whole creation has been groaning as in the pains of childbirth right up to the present time. —ROMANS 8:22 (NIV)

After a summer storm, I went walking with my little black dog Leah. We picked our way down the steep hill of Merry Log Road, turned left past open fields and the usually placid river, now rampaging and muddy. Gardens were soggy, and the air smelled freshly washed. We walked into the little town of Kingston Springs, Tennessee, past the police station, the log cabin library. I felt exhilarated by the storm.

I stopped cold at a low cement wall. In a crevice lay a robin's egg, hurled from its nest by the storm. I picked up the blue egg and looked through a window-like hole in the shell. Inside was a perfect hatchling, tiny head with beak and eyes on a long neck curled around its body and legs in a transparent sac. It looked as if it were sleeping.

A lonely sadness filled me. I kept moving, but my exhilaration was gone. Leah felt it, too, her tail lowered, her toenails clicking a dreary rhythm on the sidewalk.

We walked up the hilly road, shiny and wet with rain. *If only we lived in a world where all creatures were protected and cared for, where all babies grew up healthy and happy.* Around the elbow of the road, where the sky seemed to dip into a yard, an elderly man was staking flowers broken by the storm. Gently his fingers worked to tie them up so they would grow again.

Father, You sent Jesus to weep with us and redeem us. Thank You for the rainbow of hope that follows every storm.   —SHARI SMYTH

29

T
H
U

Words from the mouth of a wise man are gracious. . . .
—ECCLESIASTES 10:12 (NAS)

I had looked forward to upgrading my computer, and spent considerable time and effort reading up on the latest technology. The day finally came when I sat down in front of my large, new monitor, and instead of plain black printing lining a white screen, colorful graphics introduced me to a new adventure—or so I thought.

Within hours I felt frustrated, discouraged, sorry I had even made the change. At my age, switching from the familiar to the foreign was just so overwhelming.

"Perhaps a manual would help," my husband Leo suggested.

Arriving at the computer store, I sought the advice of the nearest clerk. "Sorry, but your program is so new we have no manuals available for it yet."

As I stood in the aisle pondering my dilemma, I heard a man's gentle voice saying, "Excuse me, madam, but I just overheard your problem. Maybe I can help."

As I poured out all my frustrations, he patted me on the shoulder. "I teach computer to dozens of young people, and sooner or later they all experience the same thing. You are just encountering a sharp learning curve. Here, this book will help."

There have been many times since then that I have stopped to thank God for the kind encouragement of that stranger. This morning, as I struggle with another new aspect of computer technology, just knowing that I am "encountering a sharp learning curve" is certainly preferable to letting frustrations "push me around the bend"!

Thank You, Lord, for placing a certain person in a strategic place at a crucial point. And may I in turn be an encouragement to someone else when he or she most needs it.   —ALMA BARKMAN

30 | F R I

He who makes haste with his feet misses his way.
—PROVERBS 19:2 (RSV)

When I first heard the saying, "Instant gratification takes too long," I thought it had been written by someone who knew me. Patience was not a virtue I knew how to cultivate. Then I ran the Colorado River through the Grand Canyon for the first time.

One of the interesting things about a thirteen-day river trip is that you spend a lot of time on the raft, drifting with the current. Our head boatman Phil would gather us at the rafts every morning and say, "I'll tell you what we're going to do today: We're going to go down the river a ways." Someone might ask what hikes we'd be doing or what rapids we'd be running, and Phil would answer, "Oh, we'll do some stuff like that. Let's see what develops."

The first few days it drove me crazy. I wanted to know what was going to happen, and I wanted it up front. Phil said that planning wasn't worth a lot, because the river might be slow today. The current varied with the release from Glen Canyon Dam upstream. Sometimes it was a lot of water, and we'd go faster. Sometimes it was very little water, and we couldn't get as far. "But we'll always be going downriver," he assured me. "You can depend on that."

By the end of the first week, I wasn't so bothered by it anymore. By the tenth day of the trip, I understood that the river was just like life. There's a current, and it has its own pace. I can't make it go faster than it does. I have to look at each day as getting me a little farther downriver, and whatever challenges it presents, I will accept and, I hope, enjoy.

Lord, help me to welcome each day as a gift from Your hands.
—RHODA BLECKER

My Renewal Journal

1 _____

2 _____

3 _____

4 _____

5 _____

6 _____

7 _____

8 _____

9 _____

10 _____

11 _____

12 _____

13 _____

14 _____

15 _____

16 _____

17 _____

18 _____

19 _____

20 _____

21 _____

22 _____

23 _____

24 _____

25 _____

26 _____

27 _____

28 _____

29 _____

30 _____

JULY

And he shewed me a pure river of water of life, clear as crystal, proceeding out of the throne of God and of the Lamb.

—REVELATION 22:1

S	M	T	W	T	F	S
						1
2	3	4	5	6	7	8
9	10	11	12	13	14	15
16	17	18	19	20	21	22
23	24	25	26	27	28	29
30	31					

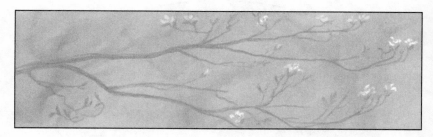

ALL THINGS NEW

1 S **Expecting Adventure**
A *His mercies never come to an end; they are new every*
T *morning. . . .*   —LAMENTATIONS 3:22-23 (RSV)

The daylilies are in bloom along our road this month, lifting their orange trumpets in joyous profusion. More than a blaze of color, for me they carry a message.

It was my friend Margaret Henrichsen who taught me to read it. Margaret was a widow in her sixties who stopped by our two-room apartment when I was a young mother. "There's no place to put things," I said, apologizing for the clutter. Baby bottles and children's toys competed for space with boxes of keepsakes—menus, travel souvenirs, theater programs, mementos of high school and college.

Margaret looked around for a place to set her coffee cup. "Tib," she said gently, "when you hold on to all these things, is it, perhaps, because you're afraid there won't be other exciting times?"

She paused while truth made its slow progress from the ear to the heart. "Your life won't always be diapers and piles of ironing, you know. There'll be other trips, other adventures. You don't have to hoard the high spots. There will always be new ones."

She thought of it, she said, as the "Daylily Principle." "God never made a more glorious flower," she explained. "Yet each one, in all its perfection, lasts only a single day. God doesn't have to preserve it just because it's beautiful. He makes another one just as beautiful in its place."

Four decades have passed since Margaret's visit, and the adventure and variety she promised have come in abundance. I still keep reminders of special times—for a while. And when I need to let them go, I remember the daylilies and look forward to the new beauties that will unfold tomorrow.

What new adventure, Father, will come my way today?
—ELIZABETH SHERRILL

2 | S U N | *To him that overcometh will I grant to sit with me in my throne. . . .* —REVELATION 3:21

"Claude is a great big old brat!" I lashed out in my mother's hearing while slamming the door. (I could get away with banging the screen door, but no one ever banged our walnut door, with its antlered stag-at-dawn etched in its oval glass face.)

Claude was at our farm for a family reunion. He'd made the older cousins laugh at me because I'd believed it when he said, "I put a hair from your horse's tail into your rain barrel. Tonight it'll turn into a snake and come bite you."

Mom glanced out where, at that moment, Claude was digging dead grasshoppers from our Model A's radiator grill. She nodded agreement. "Mark my words, that boy will be the death of his mother yet. But she won't give up on him, poor soul. She's praying he'll turn out all right. I hope he does, but he's got a long ways to go."

Well, Claude lived in another part of the state, and back then you didn't travel much, unpaved roads being what they were. So years passed without my seeing—or even hearing about—him, which, after his horsehair-snake-making razzing, was just fine with me.

I was married and a mother when a startling letter came from Mom. "Your cousin Claude dropped in, introduced me to his wife and daughters. Nice-looking family. He's a college professor now, well-respected, too, I understand."

I glanced down at my small sons and said a quick, believing prayer:

Lord, if You've made a new Claude, I know I can trust You to make fine men out of two mischievous little boys. —ISABEL WOLSELEY

3
M
O
N

But eagerly desire the greater gifts. . . .
—I CORINTHIANS 12:31 (NIV)

I'll admit it: I was dreading my first camping trip. Shortly after Paul and I were married, he wanted to share with me his lifelong passion for outdoor living. But I had never gone camping and knew nothing about it. I knew what I liked, though, and that was a warm, soft bed, a clean bathroom, fresh water at the twist of my wrist and a fully stocked refrigerator. I couldn't imagine giving up all that, even for a weekend.

"Why do people do this?" I asked as we packed the truck, deciding what would fit and what would stay behind. "Do you really enjoy doing without all the comforts of home just to live in the woods for a couple of days?"

Paul smiled as though he'd heard the question many times. "I wish you wouldn't think of camping as 'doing without.' I like to think of all the things we'll be 'doing with,'" he said.

"Such as?"

"Such as fresh air, millions of stars and all that quiet. Lots of good stuff, you'll see."

He was right. I had been focusing so hard on what I thought I'd miss, I hadn't even thought about what I might gain. That first trip wasn't easy for me. But once I was relaxing in northern Arizona's cool pines, nothing important seemed to be missing and I discovered many new joys. Now, relaxing under a night sky awash in stars, sleeping in the cool air, waking to a birdsong chorus outside my tent, and spending uninterrupted time with my husband and children are all things I look forward to "doing with" as I anticipate our next camping trip.

I've found the same thought works in other areas of my life, too. When I trust God, He surprises me with countless joys, and I discover how many riches I'm "doing with" each day of my life.

Lord, teach me to understand that in Your great generosity, You give me all I truly need.
—GINA BRIDGEMAN

4

T
U
E

It was your own eyes that saw all these great things the Lord has done. —DEUTERONOMY 11:7 (NIV)

Several years ago when my husband Harry and I were in Kenya on a work assignment, we arranged to spend a day with Ndwati, a Tanzanian friend studying in Nairobi. Driving out to meet him, we discussed ways we might spend our time together. "Hey, it's the Fourth of July! We could go to the U.S. Embassy celebration." Ndwati was eager to go, even after our warnings that it might be a rather dramatic cross-cultural experience for him.

We ate hamburgers and hot dogs with all the fixings, potato chips (called "crisps" in Kenya), brownies and Ndwati's favorite—ice cream cones. There were relay races, volleyball games, popcorn vendors, face-painting booths and long lines at the international phone company tables offering free two-minute calls to the United States.

Trying to see it all through Ndwati's eyes, we were surprised and embarrassed by some of the things we noticed: not-quite-sober adults talking much too loudly; children talking back to their parents; plates of half-eaten food in the trash bins—and almost everything we ate had been flown in from the States for the party. We felt embarrassed about the excess and waste, and critical of some of our fellow citizens' values.

On the way home we discussed it all with Ndwati. He agreed with us about the materialism and consumerism on display that day. But he also reminded us of many things we had taken for granted. We've had a democracy for more than two hundred years while the "emerging democracies" of East Africa have been independent for a bit more than three decades, and multiparty elections are a relatively recent development. In other places in Africa, there are no elections at all. In many countries people still aren't free to express dissenting opinions or ask probing questions of their government or worship as they please.

Sometimes it takes a fresh pair of eyes to see the beauty in a familiar landscape. Looking at our country through Ndwati's eyes helped us remember that while there's always room for improvement, there's also always reason for gratitude.

God our Father, may we celebrate our heritage with both thankfulness and thoughtfulness.
—MARY JANE CLARK

A PLACE OF MY OWN

5 | W
       | E   *He cometh forth like a flower, and is cut down. . . .*
       | D   —JOB 14:2

I could hardly believe it. A flower, a single bloom of impatiens, pure white, no more than three inches high, growing on the street in front of my apartment house. I came upon it when Shep and I returned from our morning walk. We stopped in amazement. There it was, hugging the curbside, with no noticeable reason for its being, no birthing dirt, just cement and stone. And what an unlikely spot for it, since the corner of Eighty-first Street and Central Park West is inordinately busy, with traffic emerging from the park and buses rolling up to their appointed stop.

"Carlos," I cried out to our doorman, "look at this!" He came and was just as excited as I was.

"It's unbelievable," he said, shaking his head. "Beautiful."

We chatted awhile, trying to figure what we should do to protect it, and just then a crosstown M79 bus rolled up, its wheels ending our dilemma.

What minuscule womb that I could not see lay hidden in the pavement? What seed could find its way there? What courage it took to struggle up to birth, and then what matchless beauty that was so fleeting.

I went into the building knowing I had received a godsend.

I am grateful, Lord, for that one exquisite moment. —VAN VARNER

6

T
H
U

"And the truth will set you free." —JOHN 8:32 (NIV)

Looking back, I'm not sure just how it happened, although I suppose I was a little embarrassed that I was taking the remainder of my steak dinner to my homebound mother. Dining at the neighborhood steak house, I had found myself stuffed after the salad bar, so when the steak and baked potato arrived, with a little loaf of that delicious homemade bread, I asked for a "to-go" carton.

"Honey, you haven't eaten hardly anything," an elderly man dining alone hollered my way. An entire section of diners glanced at me.

"Oh, I thought I'd take this steak home to my dog," I answered quickly, almost apologizing, then chagrined that I had lied.

The next thing I knew, the man hobbled over to my table and dumped the scraps off his plate onto the pristine steak dinner in my foil carton. "More for the pooch," he explained with a grin.

Mom and I both got a laugh out of that steak dinner she *didn't* get, and my dog Spanky was one happy pup. And I had learned a lesson I needed to learn: Always tell the truth. It will set you free in more ways than you can imagine.

Dear Lord, thank You for Your gentle reminders of the way I should live.
—ROBERTA MESSNER

7

F
R
I

Thou hast filled me with wrinkles. —JOB 16:8

I had enthusiastically embarked on a new assignment, only to fill my trash can with crumpled paper. By the time I left home to visit a sick friend I was ready to trash the whole project. As I entered her foyer, I noticed a huge, colorful object shaped something like a large paper lantern hanging from the ceiling. "What on earth is that?" I asked.

"It's my *gambatte*," she told me. She went on to explain that the object had been mailed to her by a Japanese exchange student she had hosted. The hanging was made of a thousand paper cranes, each the size of a half-dollar, which had been patiently hand-folded by the student's family out of squares of brilliantly colored paper. The cranes had been strung in streamers, and the streamers had been hung together like a cascading haystack.

After I finished admiring the *gambatte*, my friend showed me the letter that had accompanied it. The student explained that each crane had been made with a wish for healing. He added the Japanese characters for *gambatte* and after them wrote in English, "Go for it!"

My friend's son, who knew a bit of Japanese, added, "Of course, I wouldn't say *gambatte* to just anyone. It literally means 'to fight it out.'"

As I drove home, I prayed for some *gambatte*—the daily, hourly discipline of slugging it out until I got my current assignment right. At home, I hummed as I dumped the trash can to make room for a new batch of crumpled papers. After all, sometimes the most astonishing works are created one tedious crease and wrinkle at a time.

Lord, help me persevere until I make something useful and new out of these old wrinkles.   —KAREN BARBER

8 S *And when she had finished giving him a drink, she*
     A *said, "I will draw water for your camels also, until*
     T *they have finished drinking."*
                                    —GENESIS 24:19 (NKJV)

To be waited on hand and foot is one of the finest feelings I know. Maybe that's why I miss the corner gas station of the forties and fifties.

When my father would pull into the station, a *ding ding* would send the manager and his assistant running out to serve us.

"How are you doing today? Shall I fill that up, Ed?"

While the manager pumped the gas, his assistant scrubbed the windshield with pink paper towels that made a musical *squeak, squeak.* He also cleaned the side and back windows, the taillights and the headlights. While we got out to stretch, he checked all the tire pressures, then popped the hood. He checked the oil, coolant, battery, fan belts and air filter, and studied the engine for anything broken or leaking.

"You're down about a quart, Ed. That's seven dollars. I'll get your change."

There were few extras at the corner station: a gum ball dispenser and a pop cooler, which was not a machine, but a metal box filled with ice water and blocks of ice. Buried under the water were local brands in real glass bottles that felt like silken marble on my lips, far different from sucking fizz from an aluminum can.

The charm of the old station was the way it made you feel special, as if you were a celebrity in a limousine. Today's convenience castle sells everything from wiper blades to fried chicken, but no one knows your name or checks your oil.

Making people feel important is an old practice that I need to revive. When I go into my classroom, or barbecue for my friends, or lead my small group, I need to help people realize just how wonderful they really are.

"Let me turn on some more lights for you."

"Can I get you something more to drink?"

"Is it warm enough for you in here?"

Lord, show me how to give good service with a smile.

—DANIEL SCHANTZ

9

S
U
N

O God, you are my God, earnestly I seek you; my soul thirsts for you, my body longs for you, in a dry and weary land where there is no water.

—PSALM 63:1 (NIV)

During our travels last year we spent one marvelous week in Thessaloniki, Greece. My husband Alex's colleague Stelios Massen showed us many sights, including ancient Roman ruins and a monastery built on the site where St. Paul preached to the Thessalonians.

One day as we strolled around a courtyard outside the ancient church of St. Panteleimon, we came upon a circular stone enclosure that looked like the remains of a well. Professor Massen commented, "Yes, it is common to find wells here, right in the middle of the city. You only have to dig down twenty or thirty meters and there will be water. There may not be water right away," he added, "but if you wait, soon the water will come."

As we stood by the stones, hearing the noises of the city around us, I thought of my struggles with prayer. Lately my words had seemed to bounce back to me. I would finish praying and feel I had accomplished nothing. But as I looked at the trickle of water at the bottom of the well, I felt encouraged. The rest of the day, as we ate in a busy Greek *taverna* with waiters shouting orders, crossed streets pounding with traffic and wandered among ruins, I looked down and thought, *Just a few meters underneath, fresh water is flowing.*

Just beneath the surface, under the coarse rubble of my earthly life, the living waters of God's Spirit flow. I have only to persevere, prayerfully dig a bit deeper and expectantly wait.

Dear God, please help me find Your living presence flowing again.
—MARY BROWN

10 | M O N | *O Lord, our Lord, how majestic is your name in all the earth! You have set your glory above the heavens.*
—PSALM 8:1 (NIV)

Our son Peter was blessed to have had a great mentor. Lt. Gen. David McCloud, U.S. Air Force, was a test pilot moonlighting as a civilian flight instructor when they met. As McCloud rose through the ranks to his third star, he never forgot to encourage our son toward the excellence he saw in him.

Then came the black Monday in July 1998, when I had to call Pete and tell him the general had been killed in a plane crash in Alaska. Peter came home for the ceremony at Arlington National Cemetery. He brought me back the program. Near the front was a poem Dave McCloud had written to one of his children. It told of his love for what he was doing for his country. In the back was a poem by another general, expressing tremendous affection for his fallen friend. I took the program with me when I went to a neighbor's recently.

"Generals writing poetry?" She gave me a startled look.

I nodded. "And on page two, there's a poem by another poet-general. See, here it is. 'The Lord is my Shepherd, I shall not want. . . .'"

Lord, help me grow beyond my preconceptions and see what's unique about each person through Your eyes of love. —ROBERTA ROGERS

11 | T U E | *God is not one who likes things to be disorderly and upset. . . .* —I CORINTHIANS 14:33 (TLB)

It was 8:45 A.M., the beginning of another hectic day during my first summer as director of a church-related social service agency. Linda, a nine-year-old from the neighborhood, sat across my desk and watched as I shuffled through stacks of files and piles of papers left over from the day before. I needed to complete and mail a report by noon, but I couldn't even find the forms. Five minutes of frantic searching unearthed them from under the dictionary, but by then I'd lost my pen. "I think I'm losing my mind, too!" I muttered.

Linda solemnly surveyed the scene, then replied, "If you cleaned up the mess, I believe you might find it."

Clean up the mess. I stopped, took a deep breath, then spent the next twenty minutes filing, sorting and throwing away things. Once the clutter was gone, I zoomed through the report. Linda and I even had time for a cola on our way to the post office.

Linda's advice was a sanity-saver. Fourteen years later, her words continue to influence my work habits. That same old desk still gets littered with parts of projects and notes about calls during the day, but every night—no matter how late I finish or how tired I am—I put everything in its place and write out the next day's plans. Every morning I know what tasks must be accomplished and exactly where to find the materials I need.

Father, thank You for good advice to guide my life and work.

—PENNEY SCHWAB

12 | W E D | *If there is any excellence, if there is anything worthy of praise, think about these things.*
—PHILIPPIANS 4:8 (RSV)

This past November, we found ourselves with no income, soon to be kicked out of our apartment and expecting a second child. As time went on and I was unable to find work, and therefore unable to afford an apartment, we were actually facing the unthinkable prospect of not having any place to live. It was all we could do to fend off panic.

With the eviction date just days away, we found ourselves calling out to God with all the urgency of shell-shocked soldiers in a foxhole. Our rescue came with two simple rings of the telephone. First an advertising agency offered me a job (for far more than I was expecting), and then we found out that the family that was first in line for an apartment we could afford had found another place to live. We'd be a little more crowded than we had been, but we rushed to take the apartment. Suddenly, an income and a place to live! You'd think I would be praising God, right?

Well, as we were moving in, it became increasingly clear that not only was our new apartment smaller than our old one, it was significantly smaller. We simply were not going to fit without a lot of cramming. To add to our frustration, the walls weren't painted, fixtures didn't work, and the noise from the street below was deafening.

Late that night, I got out of bed and went into the darkened living room to sulk. After a while, my wife Nicole came out and saw me sitting in the shadow of a stack of boxes. "What's the matter?" she said.

"What's the matter? We're never going to fit, that's what's the matter!" I snapped.

She looked at me for a moment without saying a word. And as she did, I felt myself shrink under the weight of her hurt eyes. How ugly, how pathetic I was. Just days before, I was telling God that I'd live in a cave if need be. Now, in just a few hours, I had completely forgotten how desperate we'd been and how merciful His provisions.

Lord, forgive my ungrateful heart and help me to see clearly Your gracious gifts.
—DAVE FRANCO

13

T
H
U

I will lie down in peace and sleep . . . O Lord, you will keep me safe. —PSALM 4:8 (TLB)

The constant *chirrup* was driving us crazy, especially at night when in the hush of darkness it was louder than ever and seemed to be coming from every corner of our bedroom. "That darn critter! I'm gonna catch it if it's the last thing I do." My husband was at his wit's end. We had spent sleepless nights with flashlights trying to trace the sound. He had crawled under the house by day to see if some animal was nesting there.

"This is it. If I don't catch it tonight, in the morning I'm calling the exterminators!" He was adamant, and although I winced at the cost of exterminators, I didn't blame him: Our rest had been disturbed for too many nights. He went around with a rolled up newspaper as we played a game of "Hot or Cold."

"Cold," I said as he moved away from where I thought the sounds were coming from. "Warm, warmer," and then, "Hot!" as we tried locating the spot.

"You got it!" I said. "Right where you are."

John stopped, motionless in the middle of the room. He looked down and lifted the rug. Nothing there. Then he looked up. He was standing right under our smoke alarm. He chuckled, then doubled over in laughter. "We've been worried sick over nothing! We've been stalking a smoke alarm that is sounding off the need for a new battery!" With a twist of his wrist he disconnected it, and took it to the kitchen to change the battery. That night we slept soundly.

We tend to worry, fret and stew over problems that, when they're wrestled down, usually have a pretty simple solution. Now John and I remind each other: *Chirrup, chirrup, chirrup!*

Help me to remember, Lord, that problems are really just solutions in disguise.　　　　　　　　　　　　　　　　　　　　　—FAY ANGUS

14
**F
R
I**

They came every one from his own place . . . to mourn with him and to comfort him.　—JOB 2:11

When I was a kid, my Aunt Arlene, my mother's sister, was the one who introduced me to church. Eventually my mother and father and sister and brother followed, and as a result of Aunt Arlene's efforts, the lives of everyone in my family took a much different route. That's why Aunt Arlene has always had a special place in my heart, and why I was devastated to learn of her grandson Garret's death in an auto accident. He was just sixteen.

Though the tragedy was an enormous test for the family, the strength of their Christ-centered faith was amazing. *How can they be so resolute, so firm, so unshakable in their faith?* I wondered.

Sometime later, I had a conversation with Garret's parents, Gene and Linda Lockhart, and got my answer. "God is good," Gene said simply. "We don't always understand the *why* of events, but we trust the *Who.*"

Linda credited the presence of church friends and of Garret's high school friends, who lifted their spirits with their memories of him. But it was the people who had lost loved ones who seemed the most understanding, she said. "I recall one very thoughtful note from a couple who had lost a teenage daughter. While many friends tried to identify with our grief, those parents could truly say, 'We know how you feel.'"

Sometimes we struggle with our sufferings and for the life of us can see no earthly reason for them. But later, sometimes years later, they serve a meaningful purpose. When someone else hurts as we did, we are able to sympathize with them because of our shared experience. That's how God uses our sufferings to minister to others. And rather than breaking us, the soul-searing fires we go through serve to strengthen us, so we can be conveyers of His grace and conduits of His love.

> *Teach us, God, when others are reeling,*
> *How to express the love we're feeling.* —FRED BAUER

15 S A T   *God is able to make all grace abound to you, that always having all sufficiency in everything, you may have an abundance for every good deed.*
—II CORINTHIANS 9:8 (NAS)

I've probably hosted fifteen or more garage sales in the past twenty years. It's work, hard work: clean out the garage; set up tables; unpack the boxes of junk; price everything; make signs; post them; put an ad in the paper. Then comes the real work. By midday you're so hot, tired and cranky from arguing price with every customer who thinks haggling is a national pastime that you're ready to close up shop in favor of a cool bath.

Those days are over for me. In the summer of 1997 I discovered a new kind of garage sale. One morning I simply went through my house and garage, threw everything I wanted to get rid of onto some tables set up out by the street and made a huge sign that simply said FREE.

Then I went to work in the house. Every so often I'd look out the front door to see if any of my junk collection was disappearing. By 2:00 P.M., two-thirds of it was gone. By the end of the day, the only things left were one shoe that had no mate, two well-used purses and an old metal garbage can with a hole in the bottom.

I enjoyed that sale so much that I've done it every year since and will continue to do so until I pare down my fifty years' worth of collections to the point where I can move to a smaller home some day and not suffer shock when I try to cram a gallon's worth of stuff into a quart jar.

Just think, if everybody had "free sales," parents of older children could share the baby clothes and toddler toys with young couples who really need the stuff. Older couples could get rid of the items they've enjoyed for thirty years without a hassle. New homeowners could have the rakes and lawn equipment not needed by those moving to condos.

What all do you have that you can give joyfully to others?

Lord, thank You for the grace not to miss any of my treasures once they're gone and for the joy that comes from sharing.

—PATRICIA LORENZ

R E A D E R ' S   R O O M

"My main healing is emotional. I feel I'm gradually being healed of an inferiority complex concerning the computer. The path to my healing was I Corinthians 12, which deals with each of us having been given special gifts. I now realize God made me with the ability to be outgoing with strangers, prisoners and mentally challenged people. The twist in this healing is that now that I'm feeling good about myself I'm getting better at the computer." —*Phyllis Rian, Hibbing, Minnesota*

16

S
U
N

And he shall be unto thee a restorer of thy life, and a nourisher of thine old age. . . . —RUTH 4:15

I remember the Sunday in church when I first realized my father was getting old. He and Mother were visiting us, and we'd taken them to our Episcopal church, where they didn't feel at home. There was a crowd and we had to sit up front, and Dad wasn't prepared when the collection plate was passed. His uncertain hands trembled as he reached in embarrassment for his pocketbook—an old-fashioned snap pouch—and struggled to get it open and find some coins for the offering.

I took Dad's hands in mine. His hands had always been so strong, hands of authority and conviction. Wagging, playful hands, kind hands fixing things, hands you could depend on. I could feel Dad's discomfort and wondered what to do.

But when the service was over, the minister came down the steps to Dad and embraced him. It turned out that he and Dad had been boyhood friends and had often chased each other through the countryside. They shared their memories, and soon both of them were laughing.

The inroads of age are inevitable, whether or not they show themselves in our hands. But our friends—and our memories—can help us keep our spirits young.

Father, when I'm weary and need refreshment, renew me with friendship and laughter.
—MARJORIE HOLMES

17 | M O N | *Be ye kind one to another, tenderhearted, forgiving one another, even as God for Christ's sake hath forgiven you.* —EPHESIANS 4:32

"Did you see that car?"

"Yes, thanks, I saw it."

"You need to turn right at the signal."

"Okay, okay. I remember that."

"This is really the longer way—it would be shorter to take the highway."

"The highway is so crowded right now—I figured we'd have better luck this way."

I'm a terrible backseat driver. I think that's why my wife lets me drive if we're together in the car. She can't bear listening to my suggestions. But I should let you know that she's a backseat driver, too. Over the years I've become well acquainted with my errors: I go too fast. I cut it too close at yellow lights. I don't brake soon enough. I pay no attention to where I'm going.

Is there any resolution to this problem? Yes, I suppose so. You see, sometimes she's right.

"Do you see that car up there?" she asks. Suddenly, I slow down. Dare I tell her? Should I admit to the truth?

"Thanks. I didn't really see it."

See, she's thinking. *You're right,* I'm thinking.

"It's a good thing to be warned," I say.

"Okay," she says.

That's what marriage is like. Admitting when you're wrong. Not acting too smug when you're right. And forgiving each other for all those times in between.

Lord, make me a kind and loving spouse. —RICK HAMLIN

18 T By wisdom a house is built, and through under-
u standing it is established. . . .
E —PROVERBS 24:3 (NIV)

My husband Gene kept insisting that I "simply had to do something" about my mother's house. Mother, on the other hand, insisted that nothing be done—"Just leave it be," she said. She'd come to live with us almost four years before, when it was discovered that her cancer had reappeared. Even though she was nearly ninety, she still talked of going back to her home in Elberton, Georgia. I honored her wishes by keeping the house as she'd left it.

One day I got a call from a new physician in Elberton who wanted to rent Mother's house. I told him it wasn't available but, undaunted, he asked to meet with Gene and me. We drove to Elberton to tell him no in person.

We sat in Mother's living room on an unbelievably hot July day. Looking out the window, I saw our would-be renter approaching the front porch: fiftyish, trim, wearing a white short-sleeved shirt with no tie and smiling confidently. Once inside, he relaxed in an ancient rocker and said matter-of-factly, "I really want to live here. I'll only be in town a few days a week."

I told him sternly that it was out of the question. "There's not even room for your clothes. The closets are chock-full of Mother's things. All her stuff is here. Come, let me show you."

The doctor continued rocking. "I don't need to see the house, thank you. I just want to live here. I'll hang my clothes on the back of a door and live in a corner. I'll take really good care of the house."

Feeling ridiculous, I phoned Mother. She listened carefully, asking only one question: "What's his name?"

"George Parker," I said.

"Let him move in," Mother said. "That's a good name. I loved my

Uncle Parker, and George was Gene's dad's name. They were fine men."

Mother's new tenant recently wrote her, "Your charming little house seems happy to have someone in it. Your camellias are blooming. Everything's fine here."

Father God, help me know when it's time to let go of the things I've been holding on to. Amen. —MARION BOND WEST

19 | W E D

But Aaron and Moses persisted. . . .
—EXODUS 5:3 (NLT)

For more than a year now, I have been working as a consultant and giving all my extra time as a volunteer with a ministry in Washington, D.C. Recently, I had to sort through several potential projects requiring varying amounts of time and energy. One involved going to Africa for several days. I couldn't decide on the best combination of tasks for the next several weeks, so I did the logical thing—I went canoeing with a friend.

We live inside the D.C. Beltway, and the upper Potomac, just an hour away, is a beautiful river. We decided to float down a part of the river we had not navigated before. This was not exactly a mistake, but did provide for an interesting day that lasted hours longer than we'd planned.

The first few miles were peaceful and beautiful. Then the river took a turn and divided into several channels around big rocks and a couple of islands. We couldn't see very far ahead and had to go by feel. First one channel and then another became too shallow or too steep. We back-paddled, tried again, then carried the canoe over rocks and small islands. At one point I got out into the river and dragged us over a quarter mile of shallow gravel. Finally, when we were tired and no end was in sight, we lifted the canoe out of the river, carried it up a steep bank, and floated it down a restored portion of the Chesapeake and Ohio Canal to our destination. But we had had more fun than frustration and headed home filled with stories of the adventures we had experienced.

That evening I went over my work options again. I decided that I would choose a path and, if it didn't work out, simply back up, climb over the rocks, drag through the shallows and keep going. Accepting uncertainty at the beginning makes it a lot easier to get started.

I'll let you know if I get to Africa.

Lord, I am trusting in You to help with these choices, and for the strength to get around the obstacles ahead. —ERIC FELLMAN

20 THu

Rest in the Lord, and wait patiently for him: fret not thyself. . . . —PSALM 37:7

I'll let you in on a secret: These devotionals are a blessing to write, but they're also a challenge, and around deadline, I begin to worry about getting them done on time. One of my due dates is coming up, so this morning I turned on my computer and sat down to do some final editing. But instead of my familiar pieces, I got pages of gobbledygook, like this: Trusting God xxyz Normal Default Paragraph Font Le&&Re&&.

I panicked!

I only know the bare minimum about computers, so I immediately called our computer hotline and waited on the phone for almost an hour. *(All of our service representatives are busy at the moment, but your call will be answered in the order it was received.)* Then I called a friend who knows computers. She wasn't home. Then I called some people in the Yellow Pages. They never called back.

I tried the hotline again and finally got a diagnosis of the problem: My computer had contracted a macro virus. I remembered all the horror stories I'd heard of people losing everything on their computers because of viruses, and I wanted to cry. I'll spare you the details of the rest of that agonizingly long and frustrating day, but by 9:00 P.M., the problem was fixed, and I was able to open my files once again.

The damage? I'd lost only one devotional. But in the midst of worrying and waiting, I'd lost something else: the opportunity to practice my trust in God's promise that He will be sufficient in all circumstances.

Father, things rarely turn out as badly as I fear. Forgive me for my panic. —CAROL KUYKENDALL

21 | F
      R   *Perfect love casteth out fear: because fear hath*
      I   *torment. . . .*   —I JOHN 4:18

My fear of flying is a family joke. I've studied the statistics a million times, and I truly do know that I am more at risk in the bathtub than in an airplane. But just the same, I go cold at the thought of taking off and, once in the air, make a solemn vow never, ever to enter a plane again. And I don't—until I want to go somewhere exciting!

This summer evening everything was set to be nonthreatening. The flight from Miami to Quito, Ecuador, was fairly short; the weather was serene; my three grown-up children were along to be encouraging; and the youngest, Daniel, adopted from Ecuador many years before, was excited to be going to his birth country. That helped to neutralize my nerves. My seat was, as I had requested, near the front of the cabin and on the aisle. I just felt safer there. All the children were seated together almost at the back of the plane. We flew into the dark and I pretended to read.

"Ladies and gentlemen," boomed the captain's voice over the public address system, "due to a malfunction in this plane's hydraulic equipment, we are forced to return to Miami. Flight attendants will be coming through the cabin to demonstrate emergency evacuation procedures."

So, this was it. I knew I should have stayed on the ground. I felt so scared that I could barely swallow. Seat belts were tightened, emergency exits were identified, brace positions were demonstrated. No one left his seat. The lack of chatter was remarkable.

"Mom," said a quiet voice just behind me. Daniel had crept forward from his seat at the back and looked very shaken. "You want to take my seat and go sit with the guys?" he whispered. "I'll be all right here by myself."

I gulped. My son, my often feckless youngest, was taking the initiative to behave in a thoughtful and selfless manner. He had put his fear behind him to help me with mine. "It's okay, dear," I said. "I can manage. But thank you more than I can say. Go sit down quickly, or the flight attendant will be after you." He went back to his seat between his brother and sister and took my helpless panic with him.

We laughed about it all when we had landed safely.

Thank You, Lord, for sending help through those we love and knowing just how to comfort the frightened.   —BRIGITTE WEEKS

22 | S A T

And the Lord shall guide thee continually. . . .
—ISAIAH 58:11

To be truthful, though I've fished for bass, crappie, brim and catfish all my life, fly-fishing has long been something of an enigma to me. So several years back, I decided to study the techniques and practice the moves until I became an expert. Fortunately, one of my fraternity brothers, Rob Hoskins, took up the sport about the same time I did. Rob and I spent many an afternoon in the backyard of the Sigma Chi house at the University of Tennessee practicing our casting, and soon we were ready to try out our newfound skills.

Our first experience was on the Hiawasee River, about an hour's drive from Chattanooga. Through two solid days of fishing, we didn't catch a single fish. Over the next few years, we fished until our technique was practically flawless and our casting was nothing short of beautiful, but our initial problem didn't go away.

"Brock," Rob began one Saturday evening as we drove home after an all-day outing, "I've got to be honest with you. I'm getting sick and tired of not catching any fish. This is ridiculous!"

"Tell me about it, man!" I said. "We've got to be doing something wrong."

A few days later, Rob called me with a suggestion. "Brock, we need help with this fishing thing. Let's hire a guide and see what happens."

"What can some guide give us that we don't already have?" I asked.

"Oh, I don't know . . . maybe a fish."

Two Saturdays later, right before sunrise, we met Chris Nischan at the Caney Fork River. From the second we pulled up our waders, Chris was fantastic. He patiently gave us pointers on everything from picking the right fly to presenting it to the fish. Both Rob and I caught our limit that day and learned a good lesson besides. As it turned out, our casting was fine and our techniques were well-tuned. All we needed was a little guidance from a real pro.

God, You're the pro. As hard as I might try, I know I'll never be the best I can be without Your guidance. —BROCK KIDD

23

S
U
N

"Is not this the fast that I choose: to loose the bonds of wickedness, to undo the thongs of the yoke, to let the oppressed go free, and to break every yoke? Is it not to share your bread with the hungry. . . ?"
—ISAIAH 58:6–7 (RSV)

After my divorce, my three growing children and I lived off the food bank. Blake, being the youngest, was the one who spent the most time waiting in line with me and wondering what we might get. "People weren't very generous this week, were they, Mum?" he'd say. Or, "Wow, Mummy! Ravioli!"

Always we were given whatever bread we needed, and that was Blake's job, to trundle up to the car beside me with that bread. I counted on the bread, but troubled by my inability to provide for myself, I promised God I'd pay back every loaf Blake carted home.

When Blake went off to kindergarten, I stood in line by myself. The years passed. Still I was at the food bank. *Will I ever be able to pay this back?*

Finally, when the children were in high school, we had enough to eat—though never enough to pay back the food bank. "When? How?" I'd pray to God without answer.

This summer, Blake—having graduated from high school and getting ready to study at Wheaton College—was chosen by World Vision to go to Kenya to learn firsthand about famine relief. The Scripture used at his commissioning was Isaiah 58. I'd only started to read the passage when, out of nowhere, came the tears. And I was swept back to that food bank line, and to my enormous debt and vow before God.

Through my tears, I suddenly saw God's answer: Blake had taken on my debt! "God has called me to serve those around me," he said, "and I see no better way than to learn how to help."

I no longer fret about paying back the food bank. I give, instead, the child who helped me cart home free bread and ravioli.

Dear Lord, let me learn how I may help my community feed the hungry, house the homeless, clothe the naked and heal the sick. Amen.
—BRENDA WILBEE

24
M
O
N

On that day I swore to them that I would bring them out of Egypt into a land I had searched out for them, a land flowing with milk and honey, the most beautiful of all lands.
—EZEKIEL 20:6 (NIV)

The rural landscape in North Carolina was very beautiful. My family, moving in slower country rhythms, took time to notice. In the fall, my daughter Lanea and my son Chase ran and tumbled through breathtaking leaves. Gold, green, brown and crimson foliage showed against autumn skies decorated with curling wisps of smoke that trailed into nothingness. Early mornings were quiet except for an occasional hunter.

In spring there was planting. Activity was everywhere. Fields were cleared, turned, readied for seeds. Rain, heat and the smell of new earth hung heavy in the air. Plows and graders moved over the roads while people enjoyed their seasonal prosperity. Up early in the morning and home late at night, they seemed invigorated by the work they performed.

Their joy continued into summer. Hands darkened by the sun held blueberries almost the size of grapes, full to bursting, ready for market. Later in the summer, the same hands, now even darker, brought in the rest of the harvest.

And at night, no matter what the season, my children and I sat under midnight-blue canopies sprinkled with stars brighter than any stars we had seen in the city.

Lord, wherever I am, help me to appreciate the beauty Your hand has made.
—SHARON FOSTER

25
T
U
E

For as he thinketh in his heart, so is he. . . .
—PROVERBS 23:7

Before I was married, I was a newspaper reporter in Lancaster, Pennsylvania. My beat was called "general assignment," which meant anything that fell between the cracks. One July day, the second week into a scorching heat wave, I walked wilting into the office, sank into my cool, air-conditioned space and prayed to be given obituaries to write, which meant working on the phone. Instead, the city desk editor trained his beetle-black brows on me and said, "I'd like you to do a street piece on how people cope with the heat."

Fixing a smile on my face, I punched the elevator button for the first floor, and then made my way outside into the furnace. Pencil poised above notebook, I started stopping people, introducing myself and asking the stupid question, "How do you cope with the heat?"

People's answers were predictable: "Drink lots of water." "Stay in the air conditioning." "Take a cold bath." "Take a hot bath." "Sit next to a fan." "Find some shade."

I pounded the scorched, nearly empty streets—down West King, right on Duke—until I found a skinny, leathery man on a ladder, painting and whistling. "How do you beat this heat, sir?" I asked.

Laying his paintbrush across the can, he mopped his brow, came down the ladder and said, "Well, first of all, I accept it and remember it will end. Then I think cool thoughts—about swimming in the creek or the blizzard we had last winter. I imagine myself walking in that blizzard and feel the snow on my neck." He grinned, tapping his head. "It's just like the good Lord to give us an escape hatch. Try it. It works."

I did, and it does. I also used it as the lead for my story. It made the front page.

Lord, thank You for the wisdom to accept trials, and for the imagination to rise above them. —SHARI SMYTH

26 | W E D

For this reason a man will leave his father and mother and be united to his wife. . . . —GENESIS 2:24 (NIV)

My mother was an intelligent, capable, strong and loving person. But whenever she came to see my wife and me in the early days of our marriage, she subtly tried to run things. "Oh, Keith," she'd say as soon as she was through the front door, "you look so *thin*! I'll have to fatten you up!" My wife was furious at what she felt was a criticism of her cooking. But she felt helpless. After all, my mother was a sweet woman, recently widowed. I was caught in the middle, and I felt I had to do something.

I went to see Mother. After the two of us finished dinner, I told her what I had come to talk to her about and how hard it was for me. Finally I said, "You've always been a wonderful mother, but I'm married now, and you can't be first in my life anymore." She looked at me, stunned. "Mother," I went on, "you told me the Bible said something about leaving your father and mother and clinging to your wife. We want you to visit us often, but you're not in charge of the kitchen or the running of the house, and I'm going to stand by my wife if you try to control her."

Mother just looked at me in disbelief. I told her that I loved her very much, but that what I was doing just had to be right. I told her again that I loved her, and then I just sat there. Finally, I left.

Two weeks later, Mother called to tell us that she had taken a position as a hostess in a sorority house. She put aside her grief over Dad's death and spent the rest of her life loving and helping young women. She had needed to make her break, too. And I was finally able to relate to her as an adult—at least most of the time.

Dear Lord, thank You for the miracles that happen when I risk acting on Your Word.   —KEITH MILLER

27 | T H U

He is . . . a man of sorrows, and acquainted with grief. . . .   —ISAIAH 53:3

I'm in the process of moving from Nebraska, where I've lived virtually all my life, to Colorado Springs. I've been looking forward to the move for several months with great anticipation. It will mean being closer to the man I love so our relationship can grow, the opening of many new opportunities unavailable to me in Kearney, making new friends and responding to a heart-level call to new ways of using what talents I've been given. It will truly be a time of new beginnings, and I am alive with hope.

Yet there's a sadness braided into the joy. This is my last week here, so I've been deeply aware of the fact that I'm doing many things for the last time. Yesterday I spent the afternoon with my dear friend and soul sister Mona. As always, we enjoyed a good lunch together, some laughter, deep sharing, quiet moments, talk of dreams, problems, hopes and fears. And as the sky turned orange and the candles she'd lit began to flicker low, we shared our tears. We'll keep in touch, of course, but we both know things will never be quite the same again.

Like all of us, I've had my share of losses, and what they've taught me is this: My capacity to love holds hands with my capacity to cry. When I look back on my life, I find that it was in my sadness that I felt most intimate with God, like the one whom Isaiah called "a man of sorrows and acquainted with grief." There's something sacred about sorrow, about loss, about the fact that joy is always braided with a certain quiet sadness. I think it's there to remind us of our true home, which is and always has been within the heart of God. It's a home from which we can never be separated.

Thank You, Beloved Comforter, for the warmth of the home we share.
—MARILYN MORGAN HELLEBERG

28
F
R
I
Pride ends in a fall. . . . —PROVERBS 29:23 (TLB)

There wasn't a ripple on the lake as I slipped down to the dock just before 6:00 A.M. I started to put the blueberry pail in the rowboat, then saw the canoe. I stopped to listen . . . not a sound from the cabin, everyone still asleep.

I hadn't gone out in the heavy old canoe since I'd tipped it over on a previous visit, to the amusement of the entire extended family who assemble here in this Catskill mountain retreat on summer weekends. Here was my chance to get in some secret practice. I'd gather berries along the opposite shore and be the breakfast hero.

Noiselessly, smoothly, I paddled across the lake. Half an hour later the pail was full. I was about to head back when I spotted one last perfect berry high in the bush. I reached up, leaned forward . . . and in dreadful slow motion felt the canoe slide out from under me.

I sat down in two feet of water, the capsized canoe beside me, blueberries bobbing away in the early morning sunshine. Slipping, sloshing, muttering, I managed to get the canoe upright, climb soggily in and bail out enough water to paddle home.

And now what? The canoe still had six inches of telltale water in the bottom. It would take forever to bail it all out. Of course, I could go inside and take my ribbing. But if I could just manage to lift the canoe onto the dock and empty out the evidence . . . I grabbed the gunnel and pulled. The canoe didn't budge. I gave a mighty heave. And winced.

One chiropractor, two orthopedists, three physical therapists and six months later, I am at last able to get out of a chair without pain. How much easier to have learned from Scripture this same lesson about the painful price of pride.

Lord, help me to laugh at myself.
—JOHN SHERRILL

29 | S A T

Hope we have as an anchor of the soul. . . .
—HEBREWS 6:19

We had been at the farm for eight weeks, and there hadn't been a drop of rain. The wildflowers, which had been so beautiful earlier, began to dry up. The pastures turned brown, and the farmers had to sell their calves early and feared they might need to start feeding hay to their cows in the middle of summer. Cracks were opening in the ground. People with flower beds or vegetable gardens had to water every day just to keep their plants alive. To add insult to injury, a tiny spider built a web in our rain gauge. The whole scene was depressing as we watched the sky for signs of relief.

Then one night, when we had almost given up, a fast-moving front hit with high winds, hail and rain that came down in sheets. Within minutes, puddles formed in low places in the field, and the car ruts turned into creeks. At dark the rain slackened a bit and then settled into a steady, all-night rain. By morning it had rained three inches and everything had that bright, washed look. Blades of grass sparkled as the sun hit them. There were already hints of green. It picked up everyone's spirits, and I felt that even the birds reflected it in their songs.

The following morning I looked out into the yard, and there were dozens of flowers blooming where only yesterday there had been dried-up grass. Each one had a white star-shaped blossom at the top of a slender stem. I got out the wildflower book and found that they were called rain lilies. The tiny bulb lies dormant in the earth during a drought and then bounds up and blooms when conditions are right. It was, to me, a symbol of the hope that lies just beneath the surface, which can burst forth, surprising us in some of the most discouraging of circumstances.

Dear God, let me be sensitive to the messages of hope that You send to me in all You have made.
—KENNETH CHAFIN

30 | S U N

Return unto thy country, and to thy kindred, and I will deal well with thee.
—GENESIS 32:9

For months my sister, brother and I, who were all living in different parts of the country, planned my father's eightieth birthday celebration. We called back and forth, discussing food and arrangements. We decided to invite everyone from church, all his friends and all the neighbors, along with our family. At last the day arrived. My sister and I stood at the door, excited by the prospect of seeing people we hadn't seen for years. "Do you think we'll recognize everyone?" I asked.

"It's been more than thirty years," she replied. "People change."

Just then a tall man with a warm smile appeared. He and his wife shook our hands. "Do you remember me?" he asked. "I drove your school bus." For a moment I didn't recognize him. "I ran over your dog," he said. "I've always felt so bad about it."

The look of sadness on his face plunged me into the past. I remembered that rainy morning and how I had grieved for our dog. But I had put all that behind me, while he still carried the burden after all these years.

"It must have been a terrible thing for you," I said. "But what I really remember is the way you waited for us on those mornings we were late. And I remember how you always greeted us with a big smile when we got on the bus. Hitting our dog wasn't your fault. We shouldn't have let her follow the bus. We should have kept her in the yard."

I hugged him, and he smiled. "It's good to be back home again," I said.

Lord, thank You for opening the doors that help us move on.

—SUSAN SCHEFFLEIN

31 | M O N | *I will forgive their iniquity, and I will remember their sin no more.* —JEREMIAH 31:34

When it comes to keeping secrets, I am supremely trustworthy. Why? Because I forget everything, including secrets.

My memory is shot. Gone. Blank. In the course of thirty-some years (I can't remember my exact age), I've forgotten the Alamo, the Maine, 1977, simple math, the Gettysburg Address, my address and my wife's wedding dress (I was supposed to pick it up from the cleaners in 1983). I have no idea where my car is parked, or whether it's gym day for my five-year-old. She needs to wear tennis shoes on gym day, but some mornings I just slap on the tennies even if she's wearing a dress, just to cover my bases.

My name is Mark, and I am mnemonically deficient. Despite these troubles, there is some good news. Three things, actually.

First, a bad memory makes for great friendship. Instead of a photographic memory, I have the memory of a photographer's assistant: I can airbrush away the mistakes, the parts of the picture that are better left unseen. My brother recently (and bravely) apologized to me for some long-ago slight. I assured him that the matter was forgotten—and I couldn't have been more sincere.

Second, I'm much more appreciative of the wonder around us. While those who can remember today's forecast bring their umbrellas, I'm free of such accoutrements. Maybe I'm a little wet, too, but a quick walk in a stiff rain can be bracing.

And third . . . well, I can't remember what it is, but I'll bet it had something to do with spontaneity. I once went camping in the middle of the week, blissfully unaware that I was also missing a momentous meeting at work. But guess what? Life went on. I apologized profusely, yet I regretted nothing. Oh sure, maybe I had forgotten to take a few things to the campsite—a lantern would've been nice, and some tent stakes, but I had a good time nonetheless. I also forgot all about petty problems at work.

I may go back to that campground some time. It was . . . north of here, I think. I had a map around here somewhere.

Lord, no matter how forgetful I get, let me always remember that You are my Savior.   —MARK COLLINS

My Renewal Journal

1 _____

2 _____

3 _____

4 _____

5 _____

6 _____

7 _____

8 _____

9 _____

10 _____

11 _____

12 _____

J U L Y   2 0 0 0

13 _____

14 _____

15 _____

16 _____

17 _____

18 _____

19 _____

20 _____

21 _____

22 _____

23 _____

24 _____

25 _____

26 _____

27 _____

28 _____

29 _____

30 _____

31 _____

AUGUST

In the midst of the street of it, and on either side of the river, was there the tree of life ... and the leaves of the tree were for the healing of the nations.

—REVELATION 22:2

S	M	T	W	T	F	S
		1	2	3	4	5
6	7	8	9	10	11	12
13	14	15	16	17	18	19
20	21	22	23	24	25	26
27	28	29	30	31		

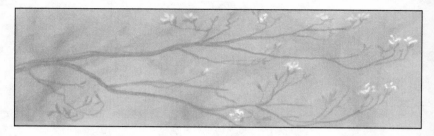

ALL THINGS NEW

1

T **Reading the Bible**
U *Behold, the former things are come to pass, and new*
E *things do I declare. . . .*   —ISAIAH 42:9

No matter how early I was up, I would find her in her reading chair, her big Dutch Bible open on her knees. I was staying with Corrie ten Boom in Holland, researching the story of her heroic rescue of Jews under the Nazis. Whatever else was on the schedule, she began each day "seeing what the Bible says."

Eager to start work, I would grow impatient. "Corrie," I blurted one morning as thirty minutes, forty-five minutes, an hour went by, "you must *know* what the Bible says!" Hadn't she told me how all through her childhood her father had read a chapter of Scripture to the family each day? How since then she had read the Bible through again and again? Studied it, marked it, memorized long passages?

"Yes," she agreed, "I know what the words say for always. But I don't know what they say *today*." The Scriptures' message is new each day, she said, because each day is new. For her, reading the Bible was like opening the morning newspaper. "I wonder sometimes how the ink can be dry on the page."

Since that time thirty years ago I, too, have read the Bible each morning. And I have found what every Bible reader knows: The more often you turn to it, the more immediately it speaks. The lectionary reading yesterday, as I waited for the results of a cardiac stress test, spoke to lingering anxiety about my heart history. *I will praise thee,* I read in Psalm 138: *with my whole heart.* How, I wondered, could the ink be dry?

Father, what will the Bible say today?   —ELIZABETH SHERRILL

2

W
E
D

The dream comes through much effort. . . .
—ECCLESIASTES 5:3 (NAS)

As my husband Leo and I strolled along, admiring some of the million bedding plants of over seven hundred varieties that bloom in the world-famous Butchart Gardens on Vancouver Island, I recalled reading about how it had all begun. If the Butchart household was anything like our own, I imagined Jenny Butchart back in 1904 saying to her husband, "Robert, I have the most wonderful idea! You know that ugly old abandoned quarry on our property? Let's turn it into a sunken garden!"

"You mean you want to bring in tons of topsoil by horse and cart to line the bottom of that old quarry? And grow flowers in it? Woman, what's got into you?" Whereupon Robert probably stomped off to his Portland cement factory.

But Jenny was not to be deterred. Little by little, under her personal supervision, the grounds took shape, and soon thousands of visitors were coming to see her garden. Eventually, Robert was so impressed by his wife's remarkable achievement that he added his collection of ornamental birds to Jenny's blooms. Then came the Japanese garden and the Italian garden and the rose garden and the . . .

I mentioned to Leo that ugly patch of ground just outside our own back door.

"But it's hard as rocks," he protested. "And you want a flower bed there?"

"We'll bring in some topsoil," I countered.

"I can already guess who's going to be the workhorse carting it in," he said, grinning wryly.

One thing led to another, and now every summer we enjoy a colorful display of annuals right outside our back door. Leo is so impressed by my green thumb, he's even added a path and a little windmill and a trellis and . . . well, you get the picture.

Father God, whether I am dealing with seeds or souls, give me vision for the hard places and send new growth, that the resulting beauty may glorify You and motivate others.   —ALMA BARKMAN

3

T
H
U

The body is one, and hath many members. . . .
—I CORINTHIANS 12:12

I was making rounds on the medical unit where I worked as a nurse when one of my patients remarked, "I'm sure glad you're back. While you were off, that Darla took care of me, if you could call it that. She's the nearest thing to no nurse I've ever had."

The truth was, Darla was a superb nurse. But sometimes her no-nonsense approach to patient care seemed like indifference. I had seen her behind the scenes, waking a doctor in the middle of the night because a patient "just didn't look right and if he were my father, I'd want a nurse to do the same"; staying after her shift to complete her charting because she had gotten behind helping me with a complicated dressing; drilling a new nurse on medications to ensure patient safety. There was no greater patient advocate than Darla.

But my patient's compliment rang in my ears, and I was tempted to let the whole thing pass. Nurses don't get many warm fuzzies as it is, and I wasn't one to look a gift horse in the mouth. But I caught myself, and asked God to help me help my patient to understand Darla better. "Thanks for the compliment," I said, "but I have to tell you that Darla is really one fine nurse. If I were ever sick, she's the nurse I'd want taking care of me."

Several days later, on Darla's shift, that very patient suffered a cardiac arrest. When I later visited him in the cardiac care unit, he told me, "I sure am glad you set me straight on that Darla. She was with me when my heart stopped."

I cringed at the thought of what might have happened had I failed to give Darla a deserved pat on the back. What terror it would surely be to think you were dying and in the hands of an incompetent or uncaring nurse! And I asked the Lord to help me never to pass up the chance to ease the way for a co-worker.

Heavenly Father, at work and in life, help me always to see and share the best in others.
—ROBERTA MESSNER

4

When I became a man, I put away childish things.

—I CORINTHIANS 13:11

A few summers ago my son Reggie had an opportunity to work as an intern for an insurance company based in Jackson, Mississippi. He accepted the job with a great deal of pride. Then one day Reggie phoned me at my office. "Dad," he asked, "can we have lunch together today?" I quickly agreed.

As we sat and talked in the restaurant, Reggie, who is normally ebullient, said in a solemn voice, "I'm way over my head at the insurance agency, Dad." I asked him what he meant, and he said, "All that stuff you and Mom told me to study at college would really come in handy now. I was satisfied with just getting by. I wasted too much of my time at school, and it's coming back to haunt me." He paused. "The most difficult thing is my language. I don't really know how to talk to the people at work. I'm scared."

I had no simple answer for Reggie, nothing to say that would make up for years of "just getting by." In the quiet that followed Reggie's confession, I said, "Son, facing up to where you really are can be a great beginning. But if you're going to meet this new challenge, you're going to have to make an effort. You're going to have to read more, get to the office early so you can get a head start on your work, and spend time talking to your colleagues. Most of all, you have to remember that you're no longer a child, and you'll have to put away the childish things, the bad study habits you had in school. If you have faith, God is able to take away your fear. But the hard work is up to you."

Lord, help me to release my worries for my children to You. Help them to trust You as they look to the future. —DOLPHUS WEARY

5

Pride goeth . . . before a fall. —PROVERBS 16:18

There was no television when I was growing up and little for a farm kid to do on long, drawn-out summer days. One hot afternoon, I remembered a movie I'd recently attended—a Western starring Tom Mix, dressed in dazzling white, mounted on his spirited horse Tony.

"I'll be a movie star, too!" I told Mom and Dad. Trixie, my

Shetland pony, was a far cry from sleek steeds on the screen, but already I visualized myself on her back in brightly bannered arenas with cheering crowds and deafening applause.

Before long, every animal on the property headed for cover when they saw me with a rope, so a fence post became my lassoing target. By month's end, even my parents were impressed. But I had yet to lasso the post while thundering past on my trusty steed. Trixie was too lazy to thunder. She wouldn't even hurry—except to her feed trough. *I can solve that,* I thought. *I'll put a bucket of feed way on the other side of the post.* I was so confident of success that I invited Dad, Mom and several cousins to my premier performance.

Trixie's ears hit high alert when she spotted the bucket. With bucket in sight and startled by my unusually loud command, Trixie finally thundered. My audience cheered. My rope twirled. Success! Neatly and picture-perfectly, the lasso looped over the target, and I cinched it by yanking the rope's loose end.

A superb performance, but only a split second of fame. I'd not noticed Tom Mix kept the other end of his lasso over Tony's saddle horn; I rode bareback. Shetland and I dashed at top speed; the post was stationary. Trixie—still thundering and eyeballing the bucket—zipped from beneath me, leaving me flailing and somersaulting, spraying loose hay as I hit the ground. Covered with straw, I tottered and stood. Pride left as my audience laughed.

That happened six and a half decades ago, and I've fallen—figuratively at least—almost daily ever since. Friends admit that they do, too. So did King Solomon, the richest, wisest man in history. He's the one who wrote about pride going before a fall.

Come to think of it, he probably fell a lot harder and farther than off a Shetland pony's back.

When I get discouraged about my failures, Father, Your Word tells me to forget the past and look ahead instead. —ISABEL WOLSELEY

6
S
U
N

I will feed my flock . . . saith the Lord God.
—EZEKIEL 34:15

One Sunday afternoon our whole family drove the twenty-five miles to Byers, Texas, to our country place where we once lived full-time. My husband Joe still has some cows and calves there, and we went to help him feed them. Usually he drives in to feed them in his red pickup, honking his horn to let them know that he is there. Their heads jerk up, and they begin trotting after him—the fat mothers in a slow-motion gallop, the babies kicking up their heels and running with their tails flying behind them. Today, however, we came in my car, and the cows didn't seem interested when Joe honked my different-sounding horn. So Joe stuck his head out the window to call them: "Wooo . . . wooo . . . wooo"—a cattle call they recognized immediately.

They trotted across the golden brown grass, heading for the barn, where they'd get sweet grain and a scratch behind the ears. We beat them to the barn, and as they neared, Joe called again. They answered back with their own bawling calls. As they lined up at the feeding trough, the girls stroked them, and we listened to their loud munching of the hay and grain.

I marveled that, no matter how far these cattle wander, they still listen for the sound of their master. And when they hear his voice, they know it is time to come home.

Father, help me to listen for Your voice in all times and all places, and to answer when You call. —MARJORIE PARKER

7 | M
    | O *They surrounded me like bees . . . For in the name of*
    | N *the Lord I will destroy them.* —PSALM 118:12 (NKJV)

Lord, it's late, but I can't sleep. I'm on vacation, but I lie here in the motel, my brain buzzing as if it were full of angry bees: fears and guilts, resentments and temptations.

I was short with my wife today. I know she was hurt, even though she denied it.

I'm just tired, Lord. All this driving. Forgive me.

You know, I can't believe I ate a one-pound box of cheese crackers all by myself. All that sodium and grease! How can a grown man be so juvenile?

And, no, I haven't forgotten that I was driving too fast out there. The deer that leaped in front of me was a good reminder, and I'll be more careful tomorrow.

I'm sorry I stared at those two women in the gift shop. The one was so beautiful that I was flabbergasted by her perfection, a visual feast, which only You could create. And the other was an old woman so disfigured by disease that my heart ached for her. Life is just not fair, is it?

Speaking of fair, my new contract increases my workload, but I haven't had a raise in three years. I suppose I'm being petty. Am I still up to teaching, after thirty years of it? I know, I'm supposed to be on vacation, but the summer goes like the wind. That new young teacher is so full of zip that I feel Jurassic. Give me strength to go back and serve.

I'm sorry to bother You with all these piddly problems, Lord, but this is my life. I don't have planets to keep in orbit or a thousand suns to stoke. Just lots of little things I need to unload before I burst. I hope You can take these bees and make some honey.

Lord, if You'll give me a new day tomorrow, I'll see if I can't do a better job with it.

My, I suddenly feel so sleepy. Good night, God. —DANIEL SCHANTZ

8 | T U E

Support the weak, be patient toward all. . . .
—I THESSALONIANS 5:14

In 1970, I volunteered as a Play Lady at Boston Children's Hospital. Most often I read stories, drew cartoons or helped with crafts that could be done in bed. Sometimes I would play quiet games to calm an overly excited child who had thrown his slippers across the ward as he awaited a tonsillectomy. At other times, I would use puppets to cheer up a teary child who'd been confined to her bed for weeks or months, or just stop to admire a child's get-well cards. My repertoire varied, but I could always find something to share with the children.

One sultry summer evening, I walked into the last room on my list and found a toddler prone in his crib in the twilight. His head was wrapped in bandages, and an IV tube was dripping fluids into his leg. He didn't raise his head to look at me when I spoke to him. I sang a couple of lullabies. No response.

Oh, well, I thought, *there's not much I can do here. I may as well go home.*

I stroked the child's tiny forearm, gave his little hand a gentle squeeze good-bye—and then froze. The little guy seemed to be squeezing back.

I tried squeezing in a pattern: *squeeze, squeeze, pause.* Sure enough, he squeezed back: *squeeze, squeeze, pause.* I tried another pattern: *squeeze, pause, squeeze, pause.* Again the little boy, who couldn't even turn his head, mimicked me. We continued our game for many minutes, without words, without eye contact.

When I finally left for the night, I felt ashamed that I had nearly given up on a tiny being who had needs that could not be spoken, and grateful to God for using one so helpless to teach me a lesson in love.

Father of all, keep me alert to the needs of those around me, spoken or unspoken.
—GAIL THORELL SCHILLING

9 WED

I have learned to be content. . . .
—PHILIPPIANS 4:11 (NIV)

When Paul and I moved into our brand-new condominium a decade or so ago, I was envious of one of the things that most of our neighbors had: a washer and dryer.

As I carried our dirty laundry in a big, blue plastic wash basket, I fantasized about the day when I would have a clothes dryer. It seemed like such a small thing to want. I began to linger over the glossy pages of lifestyle magazines, comparing different appliance brands. And when I went into a neighbor's house for coffee, I asked to use the bathroom only so I could try to check out her washer and dryer. When I couldn't find them, I steered the conversation around to laundry. "I hate having to go to that Wash-O-Rama," I said, hoping to discover that my neighbor was a kindred soul.

She grinned. "I used to feel the same way," she admitted, "but now I feel so lucky. I have a solar dryer now!"

A solar dryer! I was really impressed—and jealous. Until she led me out to her tiny backyard that was just like mine and showed me her rope clothesline and clothespins. I gazed at her dumbly for a moment, and then we both burst out laughing.

Our conversation took a serious turn, though, when she said, "Linda, I discovered a long time ago that I have the power to make the best or the worst of every situation in my life. You have a beautiful, although small, new condo. I know, because mine is identical. So why not enjoy what you do have, rather than dwell on what you don't?"

Her words made good common sense. Ten years later I finally have a modern clothes dryer. But do you know what? I hardly ever use it. My wise neighbor moved away many years ago, but my faithful "solar dryer" has served me well for ten years!

God, today help me to appreciate what I have and enjoy the blessings You have given me. —LINDA NEUKRUG

10

T
H
U

Tell it to your children, and let your children tell it to their children, and their children to the next generation. —JOEL 1:3 (NIV)

Randy Todd and I were born in the same hospital in South Carolina, spent our early years in the same county and attended the same university. But strangely, we never met each other until I moved to Waco, Texas, five years ago. Now far removed from our old stomping grounds, we have become good friends.

Randy loves to fly-fish. Central Texas is not known for its great fly-fishing, so every chance he gets, Randy is on his way to Colorado or Montana or Virginia in search of one more great river to explore and fish.

Recently, Randy's eighty-four-year-old father decided to join his son on a fly-fishing expedition. Fly-fishing was a new experience for Randy's dad. He was much more adept using a cane pole or a shrimp net to fish the tidal creeks of the South Carolina Low Country. But he was game for new adventure. Several days after he returned from his fishing foray, I saw Randy and asked how the trip had gone. Randy grinned and said, "Well, we didn't catch many fish, but we sure caught a lot of good memories."

A few months later, I received an invitation to deliver some lectures at the Baptist seminary in the Philippines where my father had taught. Located in the mountainous city of Baguio, this place above all places is home for me. I was delighted to accept the invitation and anxious to go. As I made my plane reservations, I thought about my mother. She had not been able to return to the Philippines since Dad's death thirty-three years ago. Now seventy-six years old, she had given up hope of ever revisiting this place of fond memories. So on impulse, I bought her a ticket as well and gave it to her last year for Christmas.

Mom and I shared two of the best weeks of our lives together on this journey. It was great for mother and son to relive the past, heal old wounds and marvel together at the goodness of God. We caught a lot of memories.

Nothing bonds the generations better than spending time together. I won't catch fish if I don't go fishing. And I seldom catch memories by chance.

Father, help me to make time now for the things that will make fond memories for me and my loved ones.   —SCOTT WALKER

11

F
R   *Whatsoever ye do, do it heartily. . . .*
I   —COLOSSIANS 3:23

A couple of summers ago, my then-eight-year-old son Ross decided he wanted to learn how to play tennis. It was August in Arizona, already 103 degrees at nine o'clock in the morning, but Ross was anxious to start, so we signed him up for a class. When I picked him up after the first lesson, he looked a bit melted but not defeated.

"How did it go?" I asked, as he enjoyed the blasting cool of the air conditioner.

"Okay. I hit a bunch of balls over the fence, but that was all right."

The next day Ross reported that he had hit the teacher with the ball. "He didn't seem to mind too much, though," he said with an impish smile. In spite of the heat and the slow going, Ross remained enthusiastic. But when I picked him up one morning of the second week, he was downcast.

"What happened today?" I asked.

"My ball accidentally hit a girl on the leg, and she wasn't very nice about it."

"What did she say?"

"She told the whole class, 'He's so bad, he shouldn't even be here!'"

I felt my stomach turn, hurting for him. "How did that make you feel?" I asked.

Ross didn't hesitate. "I don't care. I want to learn how to play tennis."

He did learn, well enough to play with friends and have fun. What I learned that summer was this: Some people will always tell me "You can't do" something or "You shouldn't even try." But as long as God has given me ability and desire, I owe it to Him to try to live up to my potential. Maybe God is leading me toward some hidden talent I'm meant to explore. I won't know unless I rise above the nay-sayers and the setbacks and give it a shot. If I can do that, then, like Ross on the tennis court, I will have succeeded, regardless of what anyone says.

Lord, strengthen me to take the risks You've set before me, and let me hear Your voice above any other. —GINA BRIDGEMAN

12

S
A
T

With this news, strengthen those who have tired hands, and encourage those who have weak knees.
—ISAIAH 35:3 (NLT)

It pains me to admit this, but my body no longer can achieve what my mind remembers. Take me on a five-mile hike today and I will ache in muscles I didn't know I had tomorrow. Nowhere is this more evident than when I go skiing. Now, instead of racing to the mountain and hustling from the car to be first in the lift line, I need thirty minutes of stretching and at least two liters of water for hydration before even the gentle slopes cease to pose the threat of a bruised tailbone or wrenched shoulder.

Observing how my over-forty body takes longer and longer to adjust, I've started paying attention to both preventive and curative measures. Two ibuprofen tablets before taking the lift can do wonders for the rest of the day. I've also noticed how attitude and expectations can override physical aches and pains. For instance, when my oldest son calls and says, "Dad, why don't you drive up to school and we'll go skiing on the weekend," my joy at being with him makes me forget the soreness that will likely result.

Spiritual aches and pains seem to accumulate with age, too. More years mean more relationships have suffered strains and more sorrows have passed through my life and the lives of those I love. In my twenties, I rarely knew anyone whose father had died. Last month two friends buried their dads. While ibuprofen does nothing for the hurts in our hearts, sharing the stories of our mutual spiritual journeys brings the good news of God's faithfulness into focus. And that news "strengthens tired hands" and "encourages weak knees."

Try this remedy next time doubts or fears get you down: Ask someone to tell you what God is doing in his or her life. Let the warmth of the message revive you.

Lord, thank You for always leaving us with traces of Your loving hand that can warm our fearful hearts. —ERIC FELLMAN

READER'S ROOM

"In January 1994, my beloved husband of nearly fifty-two years died after a ten-year fight against cancer. Despite my six children, fifteen grandchildren and nineteen (and counting) great-grands, I was living in a void. This year, however, I am really looking forward to marking my eightieth, because my outlook has changed. On Christmas 1997, God and a couple of grandchildren gave me a companion—a six-week-old kitten. With her to watch I began to laugh again; I had "someone" to touch and to talk to. Now she is an adult cat, and she has me well-trained. I understand clearly that it is her house, but that I may live here so long as she may do as she pleases. Since she joined me, God has opened new channels through which I may serve Him; I have increased my Bible study and prayer times, and life is interesting again. I praise the Lord for His graciousness and healing."   —*Kathryn M. Link, La Harpe, Illinois*

13 | S U N | *For the eyes of the Lord run to and fro throughout the whole earth. . . .*   —II CHRONICLES 16:9

From my street in Manhattan I have a clear view of the Empire State Building. I love living beneath the once-tallest building in the world. Several other skyscrapers now surpass it but to me it stills *looks* like the tallest building. It has that attitude. The colored floodlights illuminating its pinnacle change frequently. During Christmas it's red and green; on the Fourth of July, red, white and blue; if the Yankees win the pennant, the lights go proudly to blue and white, the team's colors. Then there are the nights when the whole upper part is wrapped in cottony clouds.

Not long ago I noticed something curious. Tiny explosions of light were emanating from near the top of the Empire State Building, almost like urban fireflies. I'd never noticed them before. "Those are camera flashes," my wife Julee explained, "from people on the observation deck."

I had to laugh. The effective distance of a flash is only a few feet, certainly nowhere near enough to capture the sprawling panorama of the five boroughs and beyond, a vista that people from around the world come to behold. Back home when they develop their film it will be mostly black.

I suppose that should bother me a little bit, all that wasted flashing. It doesn't. I like knowing that there are people up there looking down at me, trying to take my picture. I like feeling part of a larger whole, a web of life that is too vast, too deep and too textured to capture in the mere flash of a camera. It is a wondrous pattern that only the eye of God can take in all at once.

That's why, on a clear night, I always look up and check for that fusillade of camera flashes, just for the reminder of how much our lives on earth are connected in little ways that are part of a larger pattern that God has laid out. "Look," I say to Julee, "there go the fireflies."

I will always seek reminders, Lord, of my place in Your world.

—EDWARD GRINNAN

14 | M O N | *Surely goodness and mercy shall follow me all the days of my life. . . .* —PSALM 23:6

When I was a child, my world was a few miles wide—the distance to school, church and friends' homes. But it seemed enormous and sometimes scary. I walked to first grade with my friend Estella, who wore a St. Christopher's medal around her neck. He was the patron saint of travel, she explained to her Protestant friend as we waited for a green light at North Queen Street. "Every time I go out my door, I say a prayer," she said. "Our priest says God protects us in ways we'll never know."

"Well, we have angels," I said, quoting my Sunday school teacher. Together we made an ecumenical decision that God had us covered. When a car careened around a corner one day, missing us by inches, it confirmed our faith.

Then my world enlarged to high school and beyond. Though I still had a strong faith, my childish need for protection was lost in sophistication and self-confidence. I could cross the street—or the country—by myself. And I did—to Glacier National Park in Montana for a summer job with many other college students. The 1964 season opened with torrential rains and floods that shut us off from the outside world. At first it was a lark to us young people. Then the normally placid stream beside Lake MacDonald Lodge rose with terrifying suddenness to a raging river, crashing through the lodge's walls. Huddling in one end of the dining hall, we watched the water fold steel and wood as if they were paper.

Finally, we escaped to our dorm on high ground. Sitting on her bunk shaking and soaked, my new friend Joni opened her hand to show me a St. Christopher's medal. I closed trembling fingers around it, suddenly childishly aware again of how small I am, and how big God is—whether I'm crossing the street, the country or just stepping out of my door.

Lord, thank You for Your constant protection, often in ways we don't even know.
—SHARI SMYTH

15

T
U
E

Call unto me, and I will answer. . . .
—JEREMIAH 33:3

I remember that the first time I visited Spain, I found both the country and the people delightful, and one of the most charming things was the way the telephone operators in hotels responded when you picked up the receiver to make a call. They said *"Digame,"* pronounced *dee-gah-may,* which simply means "speak to me" or "tell me" what it is you want, and I will try to be of service to you if I can.

I've always thought that *Digame* would make an effective little prayer if you just added the word *Dios* to it. "Tell me, Lord, what it is You want me to do."

Then listen closely.

And finally, obey!

Lord, teach me how to listen for Your still, small voice.
—ARTHUR GORDON

16

W
E
D

"Your strength will equal your days."
—DEUTERONOMY 33:25 (NIV)

When my seven-year-old great-niece Danielle was diagnosed with juvenile diabetes, we were all worried. What would happen if her body couldn't tolerate the insulin? Would she ever have a normal life?

One night I was talking to Danielle's mother, and I confessed that my fears seemed to grow larger every day. "I know what you mean," she said. "But Danielle has really helped me with that same problem." She confided that she, too, was constantly worried about the future, about the progression of the disease. Until she listened to Danielle's prayers.

Every day, twice a day, Danielle must test herself and give herself an insulin shot. Before each shot, Danielle prayed aloud, "Jesus, help me through this shot." That was it. Every time. "Jesus, help me through *this* shot."

Danielle is doing fine these days, with her diabetes under control. And the future doesn't seem quite so scary, because I know that Jesus will be there to help. One shot at a time. Always.

Thank You, Father, for giving us what we need, when we need it. Forgive me for borrowing tomorrow's trouble; teach me the comfort of trust.   —MARY LOU CARNEY

A PLACE OF MY OWN

17 | T H U *Use hospitality one to another without grudging.*
—I PETER 4:9

"You live alone?" came the question.

"Well, yes, that is, kind of," was my reply.

The New York apartment was supposed to be mine alone, but somehow it wasn't. There was Shep, my Belgian sheepdog, who would be affronted at being overlooked. And that was just the be-ginning, for the couch in my den became threadbare from use. My godson David was the first to name the place the Varner Hotel. His sister Valerie used to visit alone, but then came her husband Jim and one, two, three children who spread out into the living room. There was Edward from London; Ty, just out of college; and Joe, recuper-ating from surgery. There was my brother Ham and an assortment of nieces and nephews and their offspring. (I recall this day an evening of Eric crying while his parents were at the theater.) Lala from Paris; Daniel from Baltimore, Maryland; and for the Christmas holiday, Eddie from Santa Fe, New Mexico—the list goes on.

"You are a glutton for punishment," said a concerned friend. "You are Conrad Hilton."

"Why stop there?" I said. "Why not choose someone like Abraham in the Bible, entertaining angels, or Lydia, who was hostess to Paul and Silas?"

"You know what I mean," she replied. Of course I did. But what she did not know is that I enjoyed these guests. They kept me from living alone.

So, anybody out there interested in checking into the Varner Hotel? You'll get breakfast, maybe, but there is one thing I will not do. There will be absolutely no foot washing.

Lord, I am grateful for friends who come to live with me—even for a little while.
                                                          —VAN VARNER

18 | F R I | *My grace is sufficient for thee: for my strength is made perfect in weakness. . . .* —II CORINTHIANS 12:9

"Elizabeth, if I hear one more complaint, we're turning around and going home." My voice had that iron edge that unmistakably marked me as a mother.

Elizabeth couldn't resist. Out came the whine, and around we turned. I knew there was going to be a scene. We'd been headed to an outdoor dance festival, and Elizabeth had been looking forward to it. So had I. But I knew better than to attempt a trip on the sub-way with two small children when one of them was in an ornery mood. And this had not been the first incident of the day.

The scream of protest came, followed by the tears and the too-late promises of good behavior. She'd had a lot of tantrums lately, and though she'd been making some progress, I was weary of them. Besides, it was hot and I was six months pregnant. The mental and physical energy needed to deal with these fits was exhausting me.

Elizabeth threw herself down on the sidewalk and began her tantrum in earnest. When she blows, she puts a lot into it, and she's got the tenacity of a pit bull. I am not Super Mom: I don't always handle her fits calmly, and at night I worry and wonder what I should be doing differently. Yet, somehow, this time I handled the tantrum with complete calm. It was clear to me that even with pedestrians gaping at us, this was a moment of grace. God was giving me the chance to see something. I thought, *If only I can channel some of that stubbornness into good things, Elizabeth is going to grow up to be a strong woman. But how do I do that?*

As Elizabeth paused to take a deep breath for another screech, I smiled. *With prayer and patience. God gave us His own Son to show us the way.*

Jesus, You conquered death through weakness. Take my weaknesses and perfect them in Your strength.
                                                                —JULIA ATTAWAY

19 | S A T | *For thou, even thou only, knowest the hearts of all the children of men.* —I KINGS 8:39

"I'll never get another dog," my friend Deborah said when her beloved dog died. "The loss is too painful." A lot of people feel that way when they lose a pet. Nevertheless, when you love animals, it's hard to live without them, and Deborah just wasn't smiling anymore.

Then one day she called and said, "Guess what? I'm a foster parent to a puppy!" She sounded like her old joyful self.

"What does that mean?" I asked.

She explained that she met a woman who was part of a group that attempted to find new homes for dogs whose original owners couldn't keep them. One of the dogs was a boxer puppy who had been given to a shelter by its breeder because he couldn't sell it. The puppy had a deformed leg. "I'm just keeping her until they find a permanent home," Deborah said. "But she's adorable!" I sort of knew what was coming.

A month later Deborah adopted the puppy. "I couldn't give her up," she said. She named the dog Sweetpea. She was considering surgery for the dog's leg, but her veterinarian said it might not be necessary unless she was concerned about Sweetpea's looks.

"I love her looks!" Deborah told me. "She's the most beautiful thing in the world."

When I saw her with Sweetpea, I agreed. They were perfect for each other: the dog who needed love, and the woman who had so much to give. And I don't think it was a coincidence that brought them together. I think God had something to do with it.

How blessed I am to have a Father Who knows my needs even when I can't put them into words. Amen. —PHYLLIS HOBE

---

20 | S U N   *He will be our Peace. . . .* —MICAH 5:5 (TLB)

After ambling through an ancient monastery in the hills overlooking Thessaloniki, we drove back into the city. Driving in a Greek city is stressful, to say the least—cars cutting in front of each other, horns blaring, streets suddenly blocked by parked vehicles. The peace of the hills vanished, and I felt slapped in the face by the tension of modern life.

As our host, Stelios Massen, maneuvered the car through an extremely crowded part of the city, he said, "There's one more church I want to show you today." He spotted a small gap between parked cars and explained, "This is the closest we can drive. We'll have to walk a few blocks." We watched with amazement as he maneuvered his car into the tiny spot. Then we threaded our way down narrow streets between blocks of high-rise apartment buildings, turned a corner and glimpsed a round, brown brick church.

"This is the Church of the Apostles," Stelios announced.

We entered the darkened church, illumined only by flickering candles and oil lamps, and heard chanting of the evening Vesper service. The quietness of the church, the beauty of the icons and the chanting of the prayers brought tears to my eyes. I lingered as long as possible, reluctant to leave the peace and go out into the city.

As we left and headed back to our car, I stopped to look back on the church one more time. The domed brick circle with a sliver of green garden around it, surrounded by the tall buildings, within the modern city, seemed to be a visible reminder that Christ was within me, too. My dwellings may look different now, two thousand years after His coming, but He is eternally the same, in us and among us. My life, too, could be built around Christ and His church.

Lord, You are with me as certainly as You were with the apostles, giving meaning and peace to my life. —MARY BROWN

21 | M O N *Pray without ceasing.* —I THESSALONIANS 5:17

My older brother was typically matter-of-fact in his manner, even if the news he had was not. "The biopsy came back. I have cancer," he told me over the phone from Detroit. On balance, he continued, there was more good news than bad. Doctors caught it early—the most important thing—and there was an encouraging prognosis with surgery and follow-up treatment. Yet there was that one dreadful word, *cancer*. Still, I did not make the mistake of telling my brother I would pray for him.

Later, though, I talked with my sister-in-law, who told me that my brother's graciousness was being sorely tested. "With all these people saying they're going to pray for him, well you can imagine!" she laughed. I laughed, too, picturing the look on his face, that skeptical scowl I knew so well.

My brother, a hard-nosed lawyer, has never put much stock in prayer or religion. Miracles he places in the same category as fairy tales. Telling him you're going to pray for him is like serving steak to a vegetarian. It doesn't go over very well. Yet, I wonder, does the person prayed for really have any say in the matter? I don't think you can be sued over praying for someone. And I don't believe that God pays any less attention to prayers said for agnostics or even atheists. Besides, praying is a two-way street. The person may not want them, but doesn't the pray-er have rights? We have no choice but to pray! After all, praying is believing.

My brother's news stunned and frightened me. I must admit, though, that I am pleased to think of all these people praying for him, the old skeptic. So if you feel like saying a prayer, say one for my brother. But don't tell him.

Dear God, watch over all Your children, believers and nonbelievers alike.   —EDWARD GRINNAN

---

22 | T
U
E | *I will seek that which was lost, and bring again that which was driven away. . . .*   —EZEKIEL 34:16

When I was about nine, my mother and I spent several days at Jacksonville Beach in Florida. I was ecstatic; it was only the second time I'd ever seen the ocean. When Mother said it was time to head home, I begged to stay on the beach while she checked out of the motel. She agreed to let me stay and asked the lifeguard to look after me. She would be gone for only about twenty minutes, and I could see the motel from the beach.

I'd only been on the beach for a few minutes when we were surprised by a sudden dark storm. The sun disappeared, and so did everyone on the beach, including the lifeguard who was supposed to be watching me. The waves on the sea looked sky-high, the wind blew sand into my eyes, and the cold rain hurt my skin. It seemed like the end of the world. I cut my foot on a piece of broken glass, and I wondered if I'd bleed to death as I tried to find the motel in the driving rain. I started to run as fast as I could—in the wrong direction. Looking frantically over my shoulder, I thought I saw someone else on the deserted beach. *Yes!* It was my mother. I ran straight into her arms, secure and overjoyed at having been found.

There have been times in my adult life when things have seemed dark and emotional storms have threatened to swallow me up. Like that lost little girl on the beach, I've felt abandoned, confused and scared. But the Good Shepherd has come looking for me—just for me—and I've run with joy into His warm embrace. *Found!*

Salvation remains an old, old story, Father, and yet it becomes brand-new every time you rescue a lost soul. Amen.

—MARION BOND WEST

23
W
E
D

Whoso findeth a wife findeth a good thing....
—PROVERBS 18:22

Business people who travel a lot have always amazed me. They can be on the road for weeks at a time and survive. I, on the other hand, begin to chomp at the bit and grow restless for my own pillow and bed after three or four days. It is a double bed that I have shared with Shirley for forty-six years. Today is our anniversary.

Shirl and I will, of course, observe this marriage milestone with a little celebration, and our four kids will make a fuss over us, and the folks in our little church will give us a hand. And, if things go true to form, some young couple will ask us how we've stayed together all these years. I will answer them as I have in the past.

Before marrying, try my personally proven bicycle-built-for-two test. The procedure, I tell the fellas, is to put the prospective bride on a tandem and attempt to peddle up a steep hill. If she peddles all the way to the top, marry her before the sun goes down. If she quits en route or fails to contribute her fair share to the climb, consider a different mate—or a different bike!

King David's wish, as related in the Twenty-third Psalm, was "to live in the house of the Lord forever." He sounds like a world-weary traveler to me, one who wants to spend eternity at home in his own bed. If so, he reflects my sentiments exactly. I would only add the rest of the verse, suitably modified to read, "Shirley, goodness and mercy shall follow me all the days of my life."

> *Thank You, Lord, for a helpmate sublime*
> *To peddle with me up every climb.*   —FRED BAUER

24
T
H
U

I will never leave thee....   —HEBREWS 13:5

I don't like to travel alone, but sometimes my job requires it. A few weeks ago I had to fly to Nashville, Tennessee, for a conference.

"We had a tornado near here this morning," my taxi driver said over her shoulder as she drove me into the city. "Radio said we might get a couple more."

As I'm from Colorado, I don't have much experience with tornadoes. But I shuddered when she pointed out my high-rise hotel in the Nashville skyline. "That's about the last place I'd want to be in a tornado," I told her.

After checking into my room on the fourteenth floor and unpacking, I glanced out the window and gasped at the swirling dark clouds. Suddenly, I saw explosions of light on rooftops all around, and then large pieces of debris flying by my window: twisted pieces of metal, an air-conditioning unit, huge tree branches. The windows rattled, and then the whole building started swaying.

Dear God! This is a tornado! What shall I do?

Just then a man's voice came over the public address system in the hall. "This is an emergency. Find a stairwell and go down to the basement of the hotel immediately."

In my stocking feet, I ran down the hall and joined a growing throng clomping down the cement stairs all the way to a basement loading-dock area. Everyone around me seemed to be with someone else: a young couple holding hands; a group of people attending a conference together; two women speaking Spanish. Feeling alone, I sat down in a corner, hugged my knees and began talking to God.

Three hours later, we finally got the "all clear" signal and emerged to find downtown Nashville devastated by damage. Amazingly, there were no major injuries, and the hotel building was intact. I returned to my room alone.

That night, after making all the phone calls home and rearranging plans for the conference, I turned out the light and said this prayer:

Thank You, God, that when I'm all alone, I'm most clearly aware that You are with me.   —CAROL KUYKENDALL

25 F R I   *Have two goals: wisdom—that is, knowing and doing right—and common sense. . . .*

—PROVERBS 3:21 (TLB)

Lately I have been deluged with several dilemmas I'm just not wise enough to handle. First, there's our persimmon tree. Several years ago, overnight our beautiful crop of ripe persimmons was stolen. The next year the Department of Agriculture decided to hang a medfly trap in our tree and we put up a notice: DO NOT PICK OR EAT FRUIT. THIS TREE IS BEING MEDFLY TESTED. Not a single persimmon was swiped. Trouble is, after the season the trap was removed and our tree was taken off the medfly testing list. We still have the sign. Do we put it up to deter the thieves, or let them plunder?

Then there is our neighbor's tall sprinkler that flips water over his grove of camellia bushes. Unbeknownst to him, that sprinkler never turns completely off. The deer love the leak in that sprinkler, and I love watching them come and drink (this year with two little fawns). If I tell him, it will save him much on his water bill, but the deer will go thirsty.

My husband is ruthless in his decisions: Don't put up the sign; tell the neighbor. With him, it's either right or wrong. But I frequently see a bit of wrong in what seems to be right and a bit of right in what seems to be wrong. Dilemmas.

We put up the sign after I changed IS BEING MEDFLY TESTED to the now acceptably accurate MEDFLY TESTED. And, thanks be to God, He looked after the sprinkler decision for us: The neighbors installed a beautiful fountain that keeps the deer well watered, and then fixed the leak.

I'm not into tossing coins to make up my mind, but I am into prayer. How good it is to know that we can run to the Lord for help in our dilemmas. He uses our common sense to solve most of them, and if we prayerfully wait on Him, He guides us through the tough ones.

All wise and loving God, give me Your guidance to sift through and sort out the many dilemmas that confuse me.   —FAY ANGUS

26

S
A
T

The ear of the wise seeketh knowledge.
               —PROVERBS 18:15

In a used bookstore recently, I came across a history of U.S. submarines in World War II. I pulled out the book, glanced at the dusty cover, then put it back on the shelf. I'm not really a World War II buff.

As I wandered down the next shelf, replete with novels that were more to my liking, I remembered a regret my mother once expressed: "I wish I had asked my mother more about her life. I guess I was too busy."

A little alarm went off in my head. *Too busy?* You see, my father was in the submarine service in World War II, and he was always giving us dinner-table glimpses of it when I was growing up. "I tried not to forget my manners, even aboard the submarine," he might say. Or, "I think I'm overly sensitive to smells because of those years underwater." Or, "We took to whispering when they were dropping depth charges around us." When I saw that book, I realized that in my adulthood I had never asked Dad about his experience. I only had these scattered bits.

I retraced my steps to the dusty history of the submarine service and bought the book. Looking through the index, I found three pages about Dad's sub, the *Parche*. He'd gone through some gripping experiences that I never knew about. They must have colored the whole of his life. I promised myself to ask him about them.

For now I was glad to have this reminder: Don't be too busy to hear what your loved ones are saying.

Help me, God, listen to those closest to me.   —RICK HAMLIN

27 | S U N   *. . . A still small voice.*   —I KINGS 19:12

Night falls as my husband David drives down the narrow road that runs over the lake and through the pine woods to our family cabin in north Alabama. Sitting beside him, I look out the window into the darkness. "Better slow down," I say. "A little fox might dart out in front of the car."

"I don't think that will happen," David answers as he slows almost to a crawl. "The fox tends to be very—"

Before David's sentence is complete, a young fox leaps out of the dark brush and runs across our path just inches from what would have been sure death a moment earlier.

"Wow! What a coincidence," David says. "I've never seen that happen before. If you hadn't said 'slow down' . . ."

"Funny," I answer, amazed, "I didn't even think before I spoke. What I said about the fox, it came into my mouth out of nowhere."

Later, David says, "All your life, you hear people say, 'trust your instincts.' Something told you to say 'slow down,' and you trusted it. I believe that's one way God is involved in our everyday lives. He speaks to our inner selves, and it's up to us to listen."

I smile at David. "God on a lonely road, looking out for one little fox. Imagine, God using my voice to keep His creature safe."

Father, help me to hear Your "still small voice" and be a doer of Your work.   —PAM KIDD

28

M
O
N

I pray that your hearts will be flooded with light so that you can see something of the future he has called you to share. . . . —EPHESIANS 1:18 (TLB)

I took a walk on the beach this morning. As I scuffled along in the sand, roaring waves crashed so loudly it made me wonder how many decibels of sound they create. Lake Michigan is so mighty that it looks, sounds and feels like the ocean. I winked at the handsome lifeguard on duty, my seventeen-year-old son Andrew, who smiled but only said a few words because lifeguards aren't supposed to talk with beach patrons.

In my heavy running shoes I plowed through the sand, thinking about life. Three of my friends are in turmoil. One was advised to see a surgeon immediately after a bad mammogram. Another, who is being promoted to captain for the local airline, was just told his partner had failed the exam and was fired. Another friend just separated from his wife and moved three hours away, leaving their seven-year-old without his father on a regular basis. I'm also in turmoil, knowing this is Andrew's last school year before he leaves home for college. I'm already feeling the empty nest and aching.

As the noisy waves crashed on the sand and soaked my shoes, I was reminded of the gift of hope. With hope I can be eternally optimistic. When I get sick, I have hope that I'll get better. When I lose a job, the gift of hope buoys me through the hunt for the next one. When I'm separated from a loved one, the gift of hope keeps me moving forward, one step at a time, toward a new life.

Like the waves at my feet the gift of hope returns again and again to carry me like a boat on the water to safer territory. Hope is the cushion that keeps me sane when the waves crash down upon me. What a marvelous treasure, this gift of hope!

Lord, thank You for the gift of hope that carries me through the rough times and spurs me on to the action of problem-solving. And, Lord, thank You for the freedom my empty nest will bring.

—PATRICIA LORENZ

29

T
u
E

I have loved thee with an everlasting love. . . .
—JEREMIAH 31:3

Last summer, while recuperating from a critical hospital stay, I developed an urge to plant perennials in the flower bed. What I'd been through had made me feel so fragile that I wanted to plant something that would keep coming back. Physically, it didn't make sense because the least exertion tired me. But I decided to do it even if it took all summer.

I gathered everything I would need—garden fork, peat moss, plant starter, seeds and plants—plus a lawn chair so I could rest when I got tired. The hardest part was preparing the soil. I would turn over two or three forkfuls, break it up, take out the weeds and grass, and then sit in my chair and rest for a while. It was a very slow process.

At the nursery, along with Shasta daisies, oriental poppies and other plants, I had found some purple coneflowers like the ones in my mother's yard. In addition, I planted some hollyhock seeds I'd been given on my seventieth birthday. I grew up loving hollyhocks, which I associated with all the places we'd lived when I was a child.

Since it was late in the summer when I put them out, I didn't expect much the first year. But the purple coneflowers put out a bloom or two, and the hollyhocks made lots of leaves. The next spring they all came back, and by midsummer they had rewarded my labor with a profusion of flowers that attracted butterflies, bumblebees, hummingbirds—and me. The purple coneflowers had spread, and one day I counted eighty-eight blossoms. The hollyhocks had large pink double blossoms that covered stalks that were eight feet tall.

Each time I look at the flowers, they remind me of the persistence of the life that God has created and His love that continues to sustain me during the winters of my life.

Lord, thank You for the love that never abandons me.

—KENNETH CHAFIN

30
W
E
D

I have shown you kindness, that ye will also show kindness. . . . —JOSHUA 2:12

Several years ago our daughter Meghan, very distressed, phoned us to say she had lost Woo, her gray chow puppy, en route from Albuquerque, New Mexico, to our cabin in southern Colorado. When I drove up to the cabin the next day, I hung "lost dog" posters in restaurants, stores and gas stations along the way. Two weeks later, back in Albuquerque, Meghan got a long-distance call from a couple saying they had found Woo, matted, starving and footsore, resolutely headed down the road toward home. She had walked more than seventy miles from the place where Meghan had lost her.

The couple had seen Woo beside the road and recognized her from the description they had read on a poster in a restaurant earlier that day. They picked up Woo and took her to a motel in a nearby town, interrupting their cross-country trip to do so. They got the restaurant's number from directory assistance and called to ask for Meghan's phone number off the poster. They gave Woo water and dog food, which they bought at a nearby store, and petted her while waiting for her to be reclaimed, sacrificing a day of their journey.

Talk about Good Samaritans! Their unselfishness has become the measuring stick for me when I'm tempted to pass by someone in need because I don't want to interrupt my busy schedule. And if I start to forget, there's always Woo, now grown into a big gentle bear, to remind me.

Lord, today I will take the time to help someone who is hurting or struggling. —MADGE HARRAH

31
T
H
U

Inasmuch as ye have done it unto one of the least of these my brethren, ye have done it unto me. —MATTHEW 25:40

My friend John recently took his three-year-old son Joey to a Frontier Days parade. The street was crowded, but they found the perfect viewing spot—almost. "Their" corner was also occupied by a scruffy, bearded young man. So while Joey watched the procession of marching bands and prancing horses and floats, John watched the man. *Was he homeless? Would he ask for a handout or a place to stay?* John didn't relax until the man shouldered his way past them and melted into the crowd.

After the last cowboy rode into the sunset, Joey turned and asked, "Daddy, who was that man?"

John was about to say, "Oh, just some bum," when Joey added, softly, "Daddy, do you think that man was Jesus?"

"I'd always considered myself a mature, caring Christian," John told me later, "but Joey brought me face to face with a private sin: my judgmental attitude toward people who aren't like me. It's hard work, but I'm trying to follow Joey's example and look for Jesus in everyone I meet."

John's willingness to look for Jesus in other people may be the reason it's so easy to see Jesus in John. It *is* hard work, but I'm trying to follow John's example . . . and Joey's. Maybe someone will catch a glimpse of Jesus in me and continue the parade.

Precious Lord, change my way of seeing so that I can see You in everyone I meet.
—PENNEY SCHWAB

My Renewal Journal

1 _____

2 _____

3 _____

4 _____

5 _____

6 _____

7 _____

8 _____

9 _____

10 _____

11 _____

12 _____

13 _____

14 _____

15 _____

16 _____

17 _____

18 _____

19 _____

20 _____

21 _____

22 _____

23 _____

24 _____

25 _____

26 _____

27 _____

28 _____

29 _____

30 _____

31 _____

SEPTEMBER

I am Alpha and Omega, the beginning and the end, the

first and the last.   —REVELATION 22:13

S	M	T	W	T	F	S
					1	2
3	4	5	6	7	8	9
10	11	12	13	14	15	16
17	18	19	20	21	22	23
24	25	26	27	28	29	30

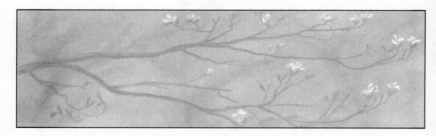

ALL THINGS NEW

1

F **Building on the Past**
R *Think not that I am come to destroy the law, or the*
I *prophets: I am not come to destroy, but to fulfil.*
—MATTHEW 5:17

We drove to the lakeside cabin, speculating on how much the re-modeled porch bedroom would change things. Any alteration in the one-hundred-year-old place was suspect. Five generations had come here, and we had come to cherish even its inconveniences.

The old porch bedroom, though, really had needed work. It was so small you couldn't walk around the bed, its warped walls let in the winter wind, and the rain drumming so soothingly on the roof seeped through to drip on sleepers beneath. My brother-in-law and his sons had worked on the renovations all summer. "You'll love it, Aunt Tib," my nephew Steve assured me as I walked up from the dock. "We've totally redone it."

And so they had. It was two feet wider on each side; I would be able to get into bed without crawling over a sleeping husband. New walls and ceiling concealed fiberglass insulation; new pine planking silenced creaks in the floor. Bigger, snugger, brighter, the new room was in every way better.

But what was this large indentation in the ceiling? Four square feet of the new Sheetrock had been cut away, exposing a rectangle of bare wood. "What's that for?" I asked.

Steve looked at me as though I'd failed to grasp the utterly obvi-ous. "Why," he said, "so you can still hear the rain on the roof."

A new room . . . retaining what we loved about the old. I thought about this new millennium with its haste to discard the old. And about God's newness, built on the firm foundation of the past. I remembered that the New Testament, far from replacing the Old Testament, grows from, affirms and completes it. And I thought how glad I was that when God makes new, He, too, preserves the sound of the rain.

Teach me to ask, Father, not "Is it new?" but "Is it of You?"

—ELIZABETH SHERRILL

2 | S A T | *But for that very reason I was shown mercy so that in me . . . Christ Jesus might display his unlimited patience. . . .* —I TIMOTHY 1:16 (NIV)

We were visiting our friend Peter Willard and his wife Jean at Chop Point, their camp and school in Bath, Maine. Our son Jon had gone to camp there for years and loved it. But it was only when my husband Whitney accepted a position on the board that we began to hear of the kids whose lives had been turned around. The amazing thing was Peter's tenacity. Belligerent, hurting kids came year after year and didn't seem to change at all, despite patient, loving attention. But years later, there would be letters from these same children, testifying to a conversion that began at Chop Point.

Now, sitting in their two-hundred-year-old farmhouse, with rain pouring outside, I asked Peter a question that had long troubled me: "Have you ever given up on anyone?"

He shifted in his chair and said softly, "One person. My brother. He was an alcoholic. He wanted nothing to do with God. My mother prayed for him every day. She died without seeing an ounce of change, but she believed it would come. I didn't. Three years ago, at age sixty, my brother suddenly gave his life to God and stopped drinking. Now he drives a truck with a Bible on the seat next to him, and tells everyone he meets about Jesus."

Peter got up and poked the dying fire. "My brother's conversion was sudden. But you know, it was working in him all those years through my mother's prayers, like the sparks under these ashes, waiting for God to fan it into flame."

Peter ambled back to his chair. "And God is never in a hurry," he added. "He waits and waits until the time is right."

Lord, help me to pray with patience and perseverance.

—SHARI SMYTH

3

S
U
N

But of that day and hour knoweth no man, no, not the angels of heaven, but my Father only.
—MATTHEW 24:36

Last year I decided to start researching my family history. I guess that now that I have children, I feel obligated to be able to tell them something about who their forebears were and what their lives were like. It used to be that genealogy work meant poking through musty courthouses and spending hours bent over microfilm readers. It still does, but in our high-tech age, it also means visiting the many genealogy sites on the Internet and joining family history e-mail lists.

One afternoon, as I was surfing the Net, I found a letter, posted to an e-mail list by a distant cousin of mine, about my Great-Great-Great Grandfather Joseph Attaway. In November 1833, a spectacular meteor shower set the sky ablaze all over the eastern United States. My great-great-great-grandfather, the letter reports:

> . . . had an ungodly son-in-law who lived a mile away. . . . When he saw the elements on fire he supposed that the end of time on this earth was at hand, and . . . took his family and ran to the home of the good, old man and awoke him, begging him to pray for him. [Great-Great-Great-Grandfather Attaway] opened the door and the good old man thought, himself, that the final time had come, but he was not afraid. He stepped to the door and exclaimed, "Come, Lord Jesus. I am ready!"

One day, I know, Jesus is coming to take me home. He may come for me alone, in the stillness of the night, when my allotted days on earth are over, or He may come "from heaven with a shout" (I Thessalonians 4:16), so that every eye shall see Him. However He comes, I hope to be able to say, "I am ready"—and to meet Great-Great-Great Grandpa on that other shore.

Lord, help me to live every day so that I'll always be ready to meet You.
—ANDREW ATTAWAY

4

M
O
N

"I know you by name. . . ." —EXODUS 33:12 (NIV)

I stepped into battalion headquarters south of Rome and looked at the old Underwood I'd be using for the next six weeks. Someone had found out that I could type and taken me off the front lines for this temporary duty. Now the lieutenant in charge was handing me a sheaf of papers. "Your job, soldier, is to type these requisitions." He walked away.

At first I was grateful for a break from dust, mud and forced marches, but within a week I began to hate the new assignment. In my unit on the front I'd been a person at least; here I was a cog with a name tag that the lieutenant never bothered to look at. It was just "soldier" this, "soldier" that.

Then one day a colonel visited the office. I was typing requests for things like K-rations and powdered milk, and the colonel must have caught me yawning. He glanced at my name tag.

"Not very exciting, is it, Sherrill?" he said. That's all. I kept typing. The job remained as routine as ever, but those few words lifted my spirits. Someone had looked at me as an individual, noted what I was doing, called me by name.

Ever since then, I've gone out of my way to speak to people doing repetitive work—scanning bar codes at a checkout counter, collecting tolls on a highway, pumping gasoline. I call them by name if I can spot it, otherwise I say something about the job itself. "Do you like bar codes better than keying in?" "Do you ever find a rare coin here at the toll booth?"

Labor Day. When I was a young soldier, a stranger took the trouble to call me by name. Today I try to pass on his kindness.

Father, You know us each by name. Let me never treat a child of Yours as an automaton.
—JOHN SHERRILL

5 | T
U   *I will bring the blind by a way that they knew*
E   *not. . . .*   —ISAIAH 42:16

When I graduated from high school in 1970, some friends gave me a white leather-bound Bible with my name embossed on the cover. Although I had been raised in the church, I had little interest in Bible study; God was an abstract figure to me, elusive and unpredictable. But the letters of my name in gold looked elegant against the white leather, and I was proud to own the Bible.

The years passed, and I married and began to raise children. Now and then I'd notice the Bible on my bedside table and look at my name stamped across the cover: OLIVIA SUE PITMAN. It seemed to say that I had staked a claim to the wisdom and the promises on the Bible's pages, but in my heart I knew I had not.

Then my youngest son started kindergarten. I went through a rough adjustment period, missing Jeff and worrying that he'd be lonely and homesick. One day I casually picked up the Bible from the bedside table and opened it. My gaze fell on Deuteronomy 31:8: "And the Lord, he it is that doth go before thee; he will be with thee, he will not fail thee, neither forsake thee: fear not, neither be dismayed."

I rushed to find a pen to underline this Scripture and to record the occasion and the date, September 5, 1979. Because that's when the words on the pages of that pretty white Bible suddenly came alive for me. And for the first time, my name, written across the cover in letters of gold, seemed really to belong there.

Thank You, Father, for reaching out to me through Your Word.

—LIBBIE ADAMS

6
W
E
D

In the fear of the Lord is strong confidence: and His children shall have a place of refuge.
—PROVERBS 14:26

Last fall, the dreaded "empty nest" syndrome happened to Joy and me: All our kids were off at college. Suddenly, the house was deathly quiet, and it took five or six days to fill the dishwasher. Bathrooms stayed clean, and the gas tank in our car stayed filled. In a word, we hated it!

Now, however, as the second fall rolls around and they are off again, we have found a solution for every parent who mourns the loss of animated table conversation and empty refrigerators: a personal 800 number.

The 800 number means the kids can call home toll-free and, believe me, those kids will call. If I am lucky, once in a while I will answer the phone and they'll talk to me for 37.5 seconds before asking, "So, Pop, is Mom there?" Mind you, you'll have to pay the bill for long discussions of the latest injustice from the academic dean or the most recent ultimatums from girlfriends. Be prepared to pace the floor, waiting for the call they promised to make but forgot, telling you they had arrived safely after a weekend trip home. Forget peaceful quiet nights as the phone rings at 2:30 A.M. with questions like, "Mom, what's this rash on my arm?" However, all this is worth it, even after you pay the bill, because you have kept the thing you wanted most: a close relationship.

As the years fly by, and the miles increase, staying in touch with those you love becomes more and more important. So, whom should you call today? It won't bring them home for supper, but it will bring them into your heart.

Father, remind me today to do what it takes to stay in touch with those I love.   —ERIC FELLMAN

7 | T H U   *Behold the beauty of the Lord. . . .*   —PSALM 27:4

After a sometimes strenuous, sometimes peaceful day of "floating the Buffalo"—paddling a canoe down the Buffalo River in Arkansas—my cousin and I had a leisurely dinner at a quiet, little restaurant overlooking the river, which was cradled in the arms of the richly green Ozark Mountains. Several times during the day, I'd been upset with myself for forgetting to bring my camera. Everything was so beautiful, and I wanted to preserve these memories in pictures.

That evening, we went for a stroll on a little trail that wound among the tall trees. The night was alive with the summer song of cicadas and the magical glow of fireflies, and then, through the trees, we caught a glimpse of a scene that was enough to take an artist's breath away. Framed by overhanging branches and sloping hillsides, the full moon was reflected over the flowing river. Again, I wished for my camera. Then my cousin said, "We don't need a camera. We can memorize it." So we stood in silence for several minutes, breathing it all in, memorizing the beauty of it.

As we continued our walk, I realized that the essence of it was imprinted on my heart. Even now, two months later, I can call it up, along with the sound of the cicadas, the glint of the fireflies, the joy and peacefulness of the whole experience. No snapshot could have captured all of that!

How often do I take time to delight in the beauty of God's creation? How many times do I grab my camera instead of taking a few moments to be still and let the beauty of the moment seep into the deep places of my soul?

Loving Creator, let me not rush through life without taking time to feed my soul upon the beauty You have created.

—MARILYN MORGAN HELLEBERG

8 | F R I | *For the message of the cross is foolishness to those who are perishing, but to us who are being saved it is the power of God.* —I CORINTHIANS 1:18 (NIV)

It's the last day of the season for our local pool. I take my two older kids down for the last swim of the summer. Faith and Hope swim off to play with friends, and I sit on the edge of the water.

I'm thinking that today, in 1994, a few miles from my house, USAir Flight 427 made its approach to the Greater Pittsburgh International Airport, then fell out of the sky. There were no survivors. There was no apparent cause. One hundred and thirty-two people died, one hundred thirty-two fathers, mothers, sons and daughters, each with truncated versions of their brilliant lives.

Death is generic. Even this mysterious, violent demise happens every day. Highways and alcohol chew up a couple of hundred people per weekend, and who blinks? So why did I have trouble sleeping for a few nights after the crash, watching the news far past midnight? What was I hoping for? An answer?

Now, as I sit on the edge of the pool, I watch all these people, the white skin and black skin and old skin and young skin, troll and splash and dive and swim. There's a joy here, perhaps pressured by the setting sun, pressured by the knowledge of this, the last day before the coming chill. With darkness approaching, the kids—young and old—keep playing, loose and boisterous in the buoyant water.

In the bathhouse, rinsing the chlorine from my faded trunks, I think, *Sometimes God offers no explanations, just the opportunity to wonder—the purity, the ineffable, crystalline beauty of life itself.* In an instant it could end. What would we think, in the final moments of our abrupt lives, of those who told us to work more, to give up our time to anyone but our God, ourselves, our loved ones? Would we remember the fun we had, playing and splashing in the water, playing with our parents, playing with our kids, playing in the shadows of the fading light?

Lord of life and death, when my mind grapples with questions it can't answer, help my heart to remember Your Cross.   —MARK COLLINS

⌘

9 | S A T *God resisteth the proud, but giveth grace unto the humble.*   —JAMES 4:6

My father and I were fishing together on Weiss Lake near Leesburg, Alabama. Dad and I are devout bass fishermen. None of this live-bait business where you sit and watch a bobber; we are artificial-lure guys who depend on our skill with a plug to catch the big one.

We were aboard *Thunder*, a small, glass-bottomed fiberglass boat with an even smaller outboard motor. I noticed a fancy new bass boat several hundred yards away. "Hey, Dad, look at those two women fishing over there. Probably crappie fishing with minnows." Dad just shook his head wisely.

About an hour went by, and we weren't having much luck. All of a sudden my reel screamed as line was quickly pulled out of it. "Whoa, Dad, I think I've got a big one!" I yelled. As I leaned my rod against the fish, I noticed the ladies in the other boat looking over at us. I was proud that I was showing them what I was made of. "The net, Dad!" I yelled. "Get the net under him!" Finally, I boated the bass. It was magnificent, at least seven pounds.

As we prepared to return to the dock, we heard a low roar. The two fisher-ladies were coming over to eyeball my trophy. They cruised next to *Thunder*, and one of them stood up. "We couldn't help notice that y'all were keeping your fish, and we thought you might want ours." Before we could answer, the other lady reached into the well of the boat and pulled out the biggest bass I've ever seen. It was a good two pounds heavier than the one I had caught.

To be honest, I don't remember exactly what happened after that. I don't remember the ladies roaring away down the lake, or my father letting both of the fish go. But I'll always remember the day when my macho prejudices evaporated forever in the disappearing wake of two superior fishermen—or rather, fisherwomen.

Father, keep my haughty spirit at bay and set me free to enjoy the successes of others.
—BROCK KIDD

10

S
U
N

Wise men store up knowledge. . . .
—PROVERBS 10:14 (NIV)

"We don't think we'll be able to make it," Derek's ninety-two-year-old grandfather told us as we made plans to travel from Colorado to Seattle, Washington, for our son's wedding. "We don't travel as well as we used to, you know."

Papa has always been a special person in Derek's life, often offering his opinion with the kind of tough and tender honesty that comes from years of experience. We felt sad about the hole their absence would create, especially at the rehearsal dinner. So the week before the wedding, my husband Lynn and I took them out to lunch.

"Do you have a message you'd like us to deliver to the bride and groom at the rehearsal dinner?" I asked as we sat across from them in a booth at their favorite restaurant.

Papa looked over his menu at Eva, his bride of sixty-five years, and thought for only the briefest moment. "You always hear that a successful marriage is a fifty-fifty proposition," he said, "but that formula is wrong. They'll both have to give ninety percent most of the time, and then things will come out just about right."

After lunch, over pie and ice cream, he added another bit of advice. "Tell them not to let little things grow into big things."

Later, as they settled into the car and helped adjust each other's seat belts, Papa said, "There's one last thing. Tell them that in addition to loving each other, be sure they like each other."

A week later, as Lynn delivered those messages at the close of the rehearsal dinner, Derek wiped his eyes as he listened. I think he knows, as we know, that his beloved Papa won't always be around. But in his absence, we can always carry his wise words of wisdom in our hearts and pass them on to others.

Father, thank You for grandparents whose wise words help to guide our paths.
—CAROL KUYKENDALL

11 | M
O   *"There is only One who is good. . . ."*
N   —MATTHEW 19:17 (NIV)

Evan, our five-year-old neighbor, started kindergarten last September. He was brave and happy for the first few days, but then he began crying before school, saying he didn't want to go back.

"What's wrong?" his mother Jerri asked.

"I don't want to get my color card changed!" Evan wailed.

Years before, my own children's classes used the same system: Each child begins the day with a green card. If the child misbehaves, it is changed to yellow. Another offense, and the card is changed to red, meaning punishment.

"Evan, you're a good boy," his mother said. "Why are you afraid of getting your color card changed?"

"Because I can't be *that* good!" he sobbed.

Evan came to our house for a cookie, and our teenage daughters talked it over with him. They still remembered the sadness of their occasional color-card change. "But you know what?" Sarah told him. "Our teacher still liked us. Our friends still liked us. Our parents loved us. It was okay."

Evan went home feeling a little better, but it was only after the classroom gerbil Kanga got *his* color card changed for nibbling a book that Evan finally understood.

I know how Evan felt. I want to be good, but so often I can't be *that* good. Thankfully, though, I don't have to be afraid. Because Jesus paid for my sins, my card with God is always green. Yours is, too!

Father, thank You for taking my fears—and sins—with Jesus to the Cross.   —MARJORIE PARKER

12 | T
U   *This is my comfort in my affliction. . . .*
E   —PSALM 119:50

I have been retired for nineteen years, but I still have nightmares about technical problems at work that were resolved twenty-five years ago. Often I wake up weary and troubled. Sometimes I wake up to find myself out of bed and on my feet. Then my wife Ruby's soft voice reassures me with, "Everything's all right, Oscar. Come to bed."

I was too ashamed of my nightmares to mention them to anyone.

Then I received a letter from my former manager, Norrie, who is also retired. "I think back to the days at work, and it seems a lifetime ago," Norrie wrote. "Yet my most frequent dreams are nightmares about problem situations at work." Norrie, too? He had always seemed so confident and self-assured.

Recently, I met Bob, another retired co-worker of mine, at the Medford Council of Churches Lenten service. Over coffee, he said, "You know, I've been retired as a machine operator for three years and I still have these crazy dreams. Some nights I dream my foreman has handed me a rush job, but I can't find the blueprints or the planning sheets. When I do find them, I can't find the tools I need. After finding the tools, I can't find the machine I'm to work on. I wake up tired and shaking."

I was relieved to know that I wasn't alone in my problem. And do you know, after sharing with Norrie and Bob, I haven't had a single nightmare!

Gracious Lord, Your healing comes in many forms. Help me to replace denial with hope and trust. —OSCAR GREENE

13
W
E
D

Giving thanks always for all things unto God and the Father in the name of our Lord Jesus Christ.
—EPHESIANS 5:20

"But I don't have anything to say," I used to tell my mother.

"Just sit there for a moment," she responded. "You'll think of something." The "or else" was left unsaid, but we all knew what it was. If we kids didn't finish our thank-you notes in the week after Christmas or after a birthday, we didn't get to go out and play. We sat at our desks, pen in mouth, gazing longingly out the window until we could think of something to put down.

After all these years, I have to admit, Mom's method worked. I learned to write thank-you notes. After a dinner party, after receiving a gift, after being a guest in someone's house, I take out a sheet of paper or a postcard, and pen a few lines of appreciation. The sooner the better.

Only recently I realized there was another purpose to Mom's teaching. It came when you had to write a note to your great-aunt in distant Maine who sent you a woolen cap that was pretty ugly and virtually useless in sunny California. Mom never accepted the too hasty, "Thanks for the hat. I've always wanted one just like it." You had to say something personal and heartfelt.

So as I was wondering what to say about a dinner party, I recalled the good friends, fine conversation and the beautiful bouquet of irises at the table. It's just what I tell my children (the lesson is being passed on): You can be thankful for many, many, many things. Sit there and think about it.

Today, I thank You, Lord, for _____. —RICK HAMLIN
(FILL IN BLANK)

14

T
H
U

And I, if I be lifted up from the earth, will draw all men unto me. —JOHN 12:32

Two-year-old John was up early this morning, and since it wasn't too hot, we made muffins. We haven't made them all summer, since without air conditioning we try not to use the oven from June to September. John was quite excited, both by our project and by the opportunity to have Mommy to himself. He immediately launched into a monologue that had obviously been brewing for some time.

"Mommy, Jesus died on cross. Put nails in hands and feet. Hurt Jesus very, very much. Jesus love John. Jesus love Elizabeth?"

"Yes, John," I answered, "Jesus loves Elizabeth. He loves everybody. We have to look for Jesus in the heart of everyone we meet."

"Baby come out and Jesus come to our house. Jesus love baby, too?"

"Yes, Jesus will love our new baby."

"Muffin very, very good."

"Thank you," I said. "I'm glad you appreciate it."

"I no 'Preciate! I John!" Then: "Mommy, Jesus died had toenails."

I had to think hard about that one. Oh—the nails in His feet! Toenails! Trying not to choke on my muffin, I wondered at the way my son's brain works. When did I stop thinking like a child? For that matter, when did I last get up thinking about how Jesus died for us? Do I spend *my* free time pondering how much He loves me?

Jesus, let me reflect on Your passion with the intensity of a child.
—JULIA ATTAWAY

15

F
R
I

I thought it good to show the signs and wonders that the high God hath wrought toward me.
—DANIEL 4:2

One of my favorite pastimes when I'm driving around town is to read the message boards outside churches. I shuttle my kids to and from school to piano lessons, dancing and Little League, so I have some favorite signs along my routes that I always watch for. Sometimes the message is welcoming: COME HOME. ALL IS FORGIVEN. Sometimes it's inspiring: THE WAY TO GET AHEAD IS TO GET STARTED. Often the message is humorous: WE ARE OPEN BETWEEN EASTER AND CHRISTMAS.

One afternoon, in the middle of a particularly rushed and stressful day, I passed one of the signs, and a question suddenly occurred to me: What does the sign outside *my* door say today? I remembered that morning. The sign my children saw might have read, SHE'S CRANKY TODAY, STEER CLEAR. Not a very welcoming message. To the other moms I hurriedly passed by at Maria's school in the afternoon the sign said, SORRY, TOO BUSY FOR YOU TODAY. TRY AGAIN TOMORROW. There was no inspiration or laughter there either.

A church with signs like those wouldn't attract many members. Yet I'd never thought much about how my relationships with my family, friends and acquaintances are affected when the message I send out is less than welcoming and seriously lacking in joy. So I'm working on my personal message board every day now, and it's a challenge, especially on those less-than-great days. But at least I'm trying to post a message out front that says, YOU ARE WELCOME ANYTIME. I don't always succeed, but I'm sure it's an effort that pleases God. How do I know? Just the other day I drove by a church with this message: IF YOU'RE LOOKING FOR A SIGN FROM GOD, THIS IS IT!

Heavenly Father, Your signs of love are all around me. Show me how to reflect that love in the signs I show others, and may they see You in me.
—GINA BRIDGEMAN

16

S
A
T

Since we live by the Spirit, let us keep in step with the Spirit.
—GALATIANS 5:25 (NIV)

At a wedding reception a few weeks ago, I met a woman who was looking for advice about the local churches. "I really want to find the right one," she said, listing the ones she'd visited. I barely listened, desperately trying to make a top-ten list of the churches in the area. I ended up saying, "You'll know the right one when you find it," and then hurried off, quite embarrassed that I couldn't be of much help.

When I got home that evening, I sat down with a piece of paper and asked myself some serious questions about how I could better help people who asked for my advice. *Can you solve their problems, Karen?* No. *Can you be as insightful immediately as you might be if you had a long time to think things through?* No. *What can you offer someone who's in need of a listening ear?* Three simple words came to my mind: Listen, Encourage, Thank. To make them easier to remember, I wrote down their first letters: L-E-T.

Several days later, a clerk at a photo shop started talking to me about his problems with his teenage son. I called my little acronym to mind: I really listened. I told him that God loved him and cared about his problem. Then I thanked him for sharing it with me. As he thanked me for helping him, even though I hadn't offered a word of advice, I discovered another meaning for my acronym: *Let* the Holy Spirit work in my encounters with others. I've found that when I do, He lets me become a better helper.

Lord, today help me to give out more encouragement than hasty advice. —KAREN BARBER

17 | S U N | *Other seeds fell into good soil and brought forth grain, growing up and increasing. . . .* —MARK 4:8 (RSV)

Perhaps it was my bow tie that gave me away that morning, but somehow the young Asian man laboring over a notebook at my gym's juice bar decided I was the right stranger to look over the paper he was composing. I had just emerged from the locker room, still perspiring from the sauna and having abandoned all hope of symmetrically knotting my bow tie (a recent impulse gift from my wife Julee). I must have *looked* like an editor. Hurried as I was, his appeal was difficult to dismiss: "Please, sir, just for a minute you look, okay?" Okay.

His written English surpassed his spoken, and I gathered that his paper was in response to an essay question for some sort of citizenship class. Yet it wasn't so much the words as the ideas that caught me. Americans, he opined, should care more about family and less about material things, like cars and product logos. He thought we had too few children because we wanted more money and "lazy time" (I presumed he meant leisure and corrected it). He also noted with considerable displeasure that Hollywood gives an inaccurate depiction of life in this country.

Neighborhoods, he lamented, should be like family "where no one is afraid and everyone helps. All must take responsibility." The tone was more earnest than critical, and ended on a hopeful note, "America is the best place to grow."

I made a few suggestions I hoped were helpful, he was polite and grateful, we shook hands, and I was on my way.

We Americans occasionally give immigrants a rough time, maybe because many of us come from immigrants who had a rough time. I think maybe secretly we worry that newcomers might outdo us natives at being American. But that's good—it's the kind of thing that makes all of us grow.

On this Citizenship Day, thank You, Lord, for a chance to see my country with fresh new eyes—and to grow a little, too.

—EDWARD GRINNAN

R E A D E R ' S   R O O M

"My name is Michael Callahan. I am 46 years old. I am married with two daughters. On August 20, 1992, God saved me. I am an alcoholic. Today I can see God in my life. I am back with my family. My older daughter Monica, 24, is in the Army and doing very well. Catherine, 20, is a sophomore at Cornell University. They are back in my life, and they love me (I know this because they tell me so). Even my wife Doreen, after all I put her through, loves me. The change in my life has been nothing short of miraculous. I went from a drunken garbage man whose hobbies were hate and anger to a sober, God-centered man who enjoys writing poetry and living the gift of life God has given me. And this change occurred when I prayed for death and God's healing touch gave me life."

—*Michael Callahan, Uniondale, New York*

18

M
O
N

"Real life is not measured by how much we own."
—LUKE 12:15 (NLT)

The weather reports did not look good. Hurricane Georges, packing winds up to 110 miles per hour, was expected to hit New Orleans in twenty-four hours. We live twenty-five miles north of the city. When a mandatory evacuation was ordered, we knew we had to move quickly.

I had lived through Hurricanes Betsy and Camille and had haunting memories of destroyed homes, uprooted trees and weeks without electricity. I rushed to the grocery for the usual items that I knew would be out of stock soon: batteries, water, bread and peanut butter. My husband Roy nailed heavy sheets of plywood over the windows. We brought the large ferns and palms inside. I took down the wind sock and the bird feeder. Roy stowed the patio furniture inside the toolshed.

"Melody, it's time to go," Roy said.

I hesitated. However irrational it seemed, I wanted to stay and protect my possessions against the storm. I looked at the living room one last time. I saw the new olive green sofa we bought right before our Christmas party last year, the mosaic tile table given to me by my children on my birthday, the Jazz Fest art print signed by Peter Max. "This may all be gone when we come back," I said to Roy. "How do I leave?"

I stopped in the doorway and prayed, "Lord, protect these things so dear to me. But what I need to ask most of all is that You give me the courage to let it all go."

Later that night, at a friend's home in another town, I stood on the porch, watching the treetops caught up in a maddening swirl of strong wind gusts. I was at peace. Somewhere between leaving my home and arriving here, I had let go of my possessions, and of the fear of losing them. The Lord was indeed answering my prayers. He had protected the things most dear to me. My friends and my family and I were safe from the storm.

Father, when I forget what my real treasures are, thank You for reminding me. Amen.
—MELODY BONNETTE

19

T
U
E

Have fervent charity among yourselves. . . .

—I PETER 4:8

When I was a young man on my first job as a newspaper reporter, I was required to write obituaries, one of the lowliest assignments a writer can get. But I found people's life stories fascinating, because they were full of art-of-living lessons. To this day I read obituaries with appreciation.

One of my recent favorites was the obituary of Gladys Holm of Evanston, Illinois. On the surface she seemed a rather ordinary woman. Oh, she liked bright red suits, drove a red Cadillac, and was generous to friends and relatives, but she lived in a tiny apartment and remained single all her life. Born on a farm in Wisconsin to immigrant parents, she moved to Chicago at age eighteen and went to work for a small hospital supply company, serving the firm's founder as a secretary.

When the business went public, Gladys was given stock options and was named to the executive committee. The company grew and eventually was absorbed by a larger one, and Gladys retired. But she didn't sit down; she continued doing volunteer work at Children's Memorial Hospital where she had, over the years, become a fixture.

Known as the "Teddy Bear Lady," she brought smiles to hundreds of sick children by giving them stuffed animals. If hospital bills were a problem for a family, she quietly contributed from what was thought to be her meager pension and savings. Her job never paid more than fifteen thousand dollars a year. That's why friends were amazed when she died at age eighty-six and left fifteen million dollars to the hospital for medical research. Her stock had grown manyfold, and there was only one place she wanted it to go: to children.

As a tribute to Gladys, the hospital held a memorial service a few weeks after her death. When the guests arrived, they found at each chair something that made them smile: one of her trademark teddy bears.

And that's why I read obituaries.

Teach us, Lord,
It's not how much we have or how long we live,
But how well we serve and how much—of ourselves—we give.

—FRED BAUER

20
| W |
| E |
| D |

Likewise, teach the older women to be reverent in the way they live. . . . Then they can train the younger women. . . . —TITUS 2:3–4 (NIV)

Not long after my little family arrived in North Carolina, we met Mother Davis. She was the mother of seven children and grand-mother to many more. As a mature woman of faith, she was honored with the responsibility of mothering the younger people in her church, particularly the young women.

I often watched her sweeping up the leaves in her yard. Though her back was stooped and her eighty-year-old hands gnarled from years of washing other people's clothes to help feed her family, Mother Davis's mouth was full of praise for God. And praise for the trees He had given her, trees that produced an abundant harvest of apples, pears and pecans.

Every Wednesday when I could, I met her in her small screened "prayer house." The voice that rose from her—sometimes alone, sometimes accompanied by two or three others—filled the air around the little shack. "God is a good God. Yes, He is!" she sang in a voice more baritone than alto. I was a city girl, and for me, hymn singing was something done in church, not outside in the open. My own prayers were said silently indoors, not out loud to an open sky. But pray out loud Mother Davis did, effectively, boldly and fervently, right up until the very end.

Mother Davis taught me the beauty of praising in season and out of season. From her I learned the power and beauty of faithful, in-dividual worship. Because she was living prayer and praise.

Lord, help me to pass the wisdom of prayer and praise to a new generation. —SHARON FOSTER

21
| T |
| H |
| U |

Thou hast put off my sackcloth, and girded me with gladness. —PSALM 30:11

Sometimes it seems like tough things come in bunches. All at once last year, my best friend had a heart attack, and the complications following open-heart surgery landed her in intensive care for more than five weeks. At the same time, the job I'd depended on for in-come for the past eighteen months came to an end. I was thrown into what my husband Keith calls "bag lady syndrome" as all my fears of poverty and homelessness came to the fore. Then the synagogue we had belonged to for ten years fired our rabbi. I felt that I was losing my job, my religious community and my best friend all at the same time.

I battled the depression. I kept telling myself, "God will provide," but I had a hard time believing that everything was going to turn out all right. I had trouble sleeping and once I fell asleep, I hated to get up for a new day in which something else awful might happen. I would huddle down in the covers, pulling them up around my ears when the radio alarm turned on, using them as a barrier against whatever bad things the world might have to offer.

One morning I was trying to stay huddled, but my cat Tau had other ideas. He wanted me to pay attention to him, and he kept pushing his cold nose under the covers and purring so loudly that I couldn't hear the radio. "Get up," he was saying. "Pet me now. That's enough moping. I'm here, and I want you to come out from under those covers and play with me."

I wanted Tau to go away, but he didn't, and eventually I gave in, sat up and petted him. The Bible teaches that God creates the world anew each day, but I'd forgotten that until Tau reminded me of it.

My best friend got out of ICU the next day. And I got up with energy and played with my cat.

Lord, when I'm weary of my world, show me the ways that You make it new.
—RHODA BLECKER

22 | F R I | *Remove sorrow from thy heart, and put away evil from thy flesh: for childhood and youth are vanity.*
—ECCLESIASTES 11:10

Approaching ninety, Norris is not my oldest friend, but a few years ago Lyme disease made him seem the oldest. He struggled back, but his gait was a slow shamble and his hearing was seriously affected. He likened his life to the "evil years" of Ecclesiastes 12, and though one would think a recitation of everything found there, from trembling limbs to deafness, would cause despair, on the contrary, he was quite cheerful in accepting God's judgment.

"I'm old," he'd say. "Come on, you don't get away from that."

He was practically housebound, and those things he had enjoyed before—travel, dinners out with friends, Sunday church—were a great effort. I was riding on a bus one day when it stopped and the driver came back and lowered a platform, which a man in a wheelchair used to come aboard. *How about a wheelchair for Norris?* I said to myself. *Why not?*

The "why not" was Norris's fault. Evidently I wasn't the first friend to suggest a wheelchair. "Bosh!" he shouted it down. "I may be ancient, but I won't be seen as an invalid!"

Several months passed, when who should arrive for a birthday party at my apartment but Norris—pushed in a wheelchair by his loyal friend Frank. He was just back from, and excited about, a trip to St. Petersburg and other points on the Baltic, but I wanted to know about his change of mind.

"Oh, that," he said, as though it were old news. "I simply reread that chapter in Ecclesiastes." He took a mouthful of birthday cake. "Vanity of vanities, all is vanity."

Lord, help me to be free of false pride.   —VAN VARNER

---

23 S "His mouth is full of sweetness. And he is wholly de-
        A sirable. This is my beloved. . . ."
        T   —SONG OF SOLOMON 5:16 (NAS)

Here's how my quiet times have been lately: I get on the subway with my Bible. I read a chapter. I try to pray. I get off at my stop and go to work. Pretty passionless stuff.

Recently, my wife and I went to the wedding of a couple who attend our Bible study. Craig is a handsome gentleman, thoughtful and kind. Judy is a lovely young woman, quiet and restrained. They're both wary about displaying their feelings. The only way we knew they were dating was that they seemed to arrive at the Bible study at the same time. Otherwise, there were no visual indicators, not even hand-holding.

It wasn't until the wedding reception that we could see how Craig and Judy really felt about each other. They walked to the middle of the dance floor as the music began to play. With her small arms firmly around him, Judy looked up at Craig with extraordinary intensity. It was as if the lights had been switched on and she was seeing her beloved for the first time. Craig seemed to move a little tentatively, as if he could feel the weight of being watched by the more than two hundred wedding guests. But not Judy. For her, there was only Craig. And by the song's end, there wasn't a dry eye in the room.

As I stood there, I felt a strong dose of conviction about my quiet times. Quiet times are not just about reading the Bible and praying. Those things are the means, not the ends. Through them, I can gaze at my Beloved, and see the glory and grace in His eyes.

Lord, may I live this day in love with You. —DAVE FRANCO

24 | S U N | *Now when the queen of Sheba heard of the fame of Solomon she came to Jerusalem to test him with hard questions. . . .* —II CHRONICLES 9:1 (RSV)

Walking home from work one drizzly Friday night, I noticed the sermon text posted in front of a church I passed every day: "Unanswered questions are less dangerous than unquestioned answers." I had never attended that particular church, but I felt as if I had so many unanswered questions that I ought to be questioning my few and tentative answers. Perhaps I would add that eleven o'clock service to my already overscheduled Sunday. The church was, after all, only a fifteen-minute walk from home.

But it looked rather prim when I peeked in. Would I feel comfortable going to morning prayer in sneakers? No way. I should wear some kind of dress shoes. But then my feet would hurt by the time I got there, and carrying another pair of shoes would be a nuisance—

Wait a minute. *Could I really decide whether or not to attend a church service where I might learn something important based on what shoes I wear?* Now there was an answer that needed to be questioned!

On Sunday, the sneakers stayed on, and I reached the church in time to hear the organist launch into a Bach fugue. I looked around at the congregation as they sat enjoying the music. Then I looked down at my feet and smiled sheepishly at the obvious answer to my earlier question: No one there had gone to church that day to look at my shoes.

Lord, let me not be so busy looking down that I miss the simple answers to simple questions. —BRIGITTE WEEKS

25
**M
O
N**

Now faith is the substance of things hoped for, the evidence of things not seen. —HEBREWS 11:1

I didn't know much about the Internet, but what I had heard about it had convinced me it was an instrument of the devil. It took an experience of my good friend Bettye Weatherford to make me realize how wrong I was.

Bettye has a disease called mastocytosis, a disorder of the mast cells, which are part of the body's system of self-defense. It is not a widespread or well-known illness. In fact, when Bettye was diagnosed in 1986, she was told that hers was only the five hundredth documented case in the world. It is a complicated and painful disease, and Bettye needs to be hospitalized four weeks out of every five. In addition, the rarity of her condition had made her feel isolated and alone.

Then Bettye's son Bob discovered the Mastocytosis Society on the Internet (www.mast.gil.com.au). The society publishes *The Mastocytosis Chronicles,* written by and for mastocytosis patients. When Bob asked for information, he received hundreds of replies from patients, their families and friends, some from as far away as Australia.

"Through them," Bettye says, "and the newsletter, which I receive regularly, I've gained information not just for myself, but for my doctors also. And now I have hope and faith that the ongoing research will eventually find a cure for this disease."

As for me, my eyes have been opened to the ability of the Internet to provide vast amounts of good, useful data, as well as access to caring people who can help turn a bad situation around to good.

Lord of the present and the future, increase my faith so that I may accept the blessings You have waiting for me, whether I first understand them or not. —DRUE DUKE

Editor's note: We would love to have you visit the Guideposts Web Site at www.guideposts.org.

26
**T
u
E**

In all things at all times, having all that you need, you will abound in every good work. —II CORINTHIANS 9:8 (NIV)

This morning as we leave our house to walk to the office, a cluster of small boys waits expectantly outside our gate. Their clothes are ragged and dirty, and their shiny tomato tins identify them as boys who are being raised by local religious leaders called *marabouts*. Sent into the streets to beg, each boy turns over his daily takings to the *marabout*, facing a beating if it isn't enough—*Oliver Twist* in Senegal. So what shall I do with these small boys? Toss in a few coins? If they're not stolen by the bigger boys, they'll go to support a system I don't think is right.

Despite our years of living in East Africa and this three-month assignment in West Africa, I know I will never get used to sights like the mother camped on the street corner with her four small children; the young man who goes about on all fours because of a spinal defect; the more fortunate ones in makeshift wheelchairs fashioned from old bicycle parts. There are many beggars here in Dakar, as there were in Nairobi—as there are in every big city in the world. We struggle with how to help them. Sometimes we give them coins, or buy an extra loaf of bread or some bananas to share.

In a few weeks we will be going home. I've never seen beggars out on the streets in Durango, Colorado. But what about all the hurting people who long for a listening, sympathetic ear, those discouraged ones who need the nourishment of loving words, the disabled who could use help with shopping or a ride to the doctor, the elderly and the shut-ins who sit waiting for the doorbell or the phone to ring? They are begging for my attention, even if they are silent and out of sight.

Give me Your eyes to see the needs around me, loving Lord Jesus, and Your compassion and courage to help meet them.

—MARY JANE CLARK

27 | W E D | *The Lord hath given me my petition which I asked of him.* —I SAMUEL 1:27

Back in the late seventies, I decided that writing my first book was the hardest thing I'd ever done. I stuck with it because I believed God wanted me to finish it. I complained to Him often that the task was simply too difficult. But finally—like childbirth—it was over. When I sensed that God wanted me to write a second book, I told Him no. I didn't have the time, the energy or the know-how. And all my time was taken up by my four children.

I continued to write articles, but everything I wrote during that three-year period was rejected. *Maybe my writing career is over,* I thought. But I carefully put each rejected story in a box that had held a ream of paper.

One day I saw that the box was more than half full. Feeling pretty sorry for myself, I thumbed through the stories while I hummed a gospel song I liked—"No Turning Back." For some reason I wrote the title of the song on top of the box.

Suddenly, I gasped out loud as I saw what God had been doing. *The book's written, Marion. This was the way I planned for you to write it all along. I was only waiting for you to say yes.*

Lord, You have so many ways of doing marvelous things that I've never dreamed of. Whatever they are, yes, yes, yes. Amen.

—MARION BOND WEST

---

28 | T
H
u | *Be devoted to one another in brotherly love. Honor one another above yourselves.*
—ROMANS 12:10 (NIV)

One afternoon, my friend Paulette was reminiscing about the days when her two college-age sons Adam and Chad were small. Remembering how I used to bicker with my older brother, I asked her how she kept the peace.

"It wasn't easy," she said. "They were about six and seven when I decided something had to change."

Paulette had the children buckled safely in the backseat and was trying to think about her next errand.

"Mom, he made a face at me!"

"Did not!"

"Oh, is it just always that ugly?"

"Mom! Mom!"

"He started it! He made a face!"

Taking a deep breath, Paulette pulled over to the side of the road and turned around. She summoned her sternest face and said, "That's it! Since you must compete with one another, we'll have a new game. You"—pointing to Adam—"are the oldest. So you get to go first." Chad stuck his tongue out at Adam, who returned the gesture. "Now, say the nicest thing you can think of to your brother. Give him a compliment. And I mean business!"

Scowling, Adam said, "Well, the last time you hit me, it almost hurt." That wasn't exactly what Paulette had in mind, but it made Chad smile proudly.

"And now it's your turn," she prompted her youngest.

He put a finger to his forehead and scrunched up his face in thought. "You're very tall," he said.

"Oh, yeah? I can do better than that. You made a very big tower with our blocks this morning. It was almost as big as mine."

"That's only because you hogged all the blocks," the youngest screeched.

"Wait—that wasn't a compliment! You have to play by the rules!"

"Oh, then I'll say you're very good at taking all the blocks first."

Soon each boy was trying to outdo the other, paying compliment after compliment.

"It was just as noisy in that car as before," Paulette told me, "but it was a different kind of din, somehow, and I didn't mind it at all."

Father, when I'm in the mood for an argument, help me find something nice to say instead. —KJERSTIN EASTON

29 | FRI

To every thing there is a season, and a time to every purpose under the heaven. —ECCLESIASTES 3:1

It was only a Timex with a frayed, black leather band and a stubborn second hand. But to my patient, scheduled for major surgery that morning, it was his most prized possession, and he wanted his daughter to look after it while he was in the operating room. "Nurse, is she here yet?" he asked a half dozen times after I gave him his preoperative bath at 7:00 A.M. And each time I had to tell him no.

I was almost as anxious for Patty to arrive as Joe was. The two of them, Joe had confided, had just begun to resolve years of misunderstanding. But there was still another reason. This was no ordinary surgery: Joe was to have a large cancerous tumor removed from his jaw, and I knew he'd never look the same again.

As they wheeled Joe away to the operating room, he relinquished his beloved watch to my safekeeping. Forty-five minutes later, I spotted Patty making a mad dash off the elevator. "Did I make it on time?" she asked breathlessly. "I got held up by a train." Then she cried, "Daddy's watch!" as I pressed it into her palm. "Could you take me to him? Please? For *just* a second?"

I made special arrangements for Patty to speak to her dad in the surgery holding area. Patty returned, now at peace, the tattered old Timex on her wrist. It would be their last good-bye; Joe died from unexpected complications during his surgery. An old Timex. A new beginning. And God's impeccable timing.

Lord, I commit my time to Your guiding hand. —ROBERTA MESSNER

&

30 | S A T | *Trust in the Lord with all thine heart; and lean not unto thine own understanding.* —PROVERBS 3:5

This fall I find myself in disagreement with my employer, and I feel I can't compromise on the issue anymore. But what to do?

I'm currently memorizing the Epistle of James. Chapter 1, verse 5 begins: "If any of you lacks wisdom, let him ask God, who gives to all men generously." I understood the asking part, but not the answering. Just how would God answer this one? Still, my part of making this decision was to pray for wisdom, so I did.

The next day I received a letter from my mother expressing her worry about my job situation. While she supported my stand in the matter, she cautioned me to ponder things slowly and with great care. I figured Mum's letter was part of God's answer. I took the day off to paint the house and to think.

Paintbrush in hand, I realized Mum was particularly concerned about my breaking my employment contract. So I put away my paintbrush, pulled out my contract and read it very carefully. I was amazed. For there, in the last paragraph, was my answer! In the event of a dispute between us, we were to submit our differences for mediation.

But what if they get mad at me? I wondered. "Let him ask in faith, with no doubting."

I knew I had to trust God's answer. I'm not sure what will happen now. But I do know this: Having someone else settle the matter makes the most sense. I also know that I'd never have thought to do it by myself. I had to ask for wisdom and then trust God to find *His* way to answer.

Dear Lord, whenever I need direction, lead me always to look to You, and help me to accept Your guidance resolutely. —BRENDA WILBEE

My Renewal Journal

1 _____

2 _____

3 _____

4 _____

5 _____

6 _____

7 _____

8 _____

9 _____

S E P T E M B E R   2 0 0 0

10 _____

11 _____

12 _____

13 _____

14 _____

15 _____

16 _____

17 _____

18 _____

19 _____

20 _____

21 _____

22 _____

23 _____

24 _____

25 _____

26 _____

27 _____

28 _____

29 _____

30 _____

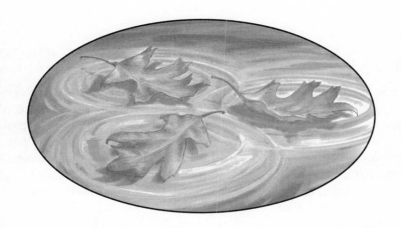

OCTOBER

And let him that is athirst come. And whosoever will, let him take the water of life freely. —REVELATION 22:17

S	M	T	W	T	F	S
1	2	3	4	5	6	7
8	9	10	11	12	13	14
15	16	17	18	19	20	21
22	23	24	25	26	27	28
29	30	31				

1

S
U
N

That . . . he might gather together in one all things in Christ. . . . —EPHESIANS 1:10

At South Main Baptist Church in Houston, Texas, all the ethnic congregations come together several times each year for a service of worship and communion. Each time it happens, I find myself reveling in the diversity of the group—Anglo-Americans, Cambodians, Hispanics from many different Central and South American countries, Koreans, Chinese and Japanese. It seems that the whole world has gathered at the Lord's table, and the sense of joy and God's presence is overwhelming.

In the midst of these services, I sometimes recall how much I had dreaded communion Sunday in the small rural church of my youth, because the primary emphasis was on who *couldn't* participate— church polity excluded those who weren't members of our church. Mrs. Croman and her children were all members, but Mr. Croman, in deference to his aging Methodist mother, had not officially joined, though he was there with the family every time the doors opened. So during the service, Mr. Croman sat outside on the church steps, where he was joined by Clyde Mullins, who boycotted the communion in protest.

In sharp contrast, the focus in Houston is on inclusion, reaching out to all God's children. And when the people hold hands and sing, "We are one in the bond of love," it feels joyfully like Pentecost. My heart tells me that this is what World Communion Sunday is meant to be.

Dear Lord, help me to celebrate the whole family of God on this day.
—KENNETH CHAFIN

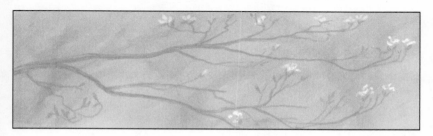

ALL THINGS NEW

<table>
<tr><td rowspan="3" style="font-size:2em">2</td><td>M</td><td>**Catching the Light**</td></tr>
<tr><td>O</td><td>*Be ye transformed by the renewing of your mind. . . .*</td></tr>
<tr><td>N</td><td style="text-align:right">—ROMANS 12:2</td></tr>
</table>

It caught the lamplight last night, a strand of shiny plastic Easter grass on the back of the sofa. I stared at it, baffled and bemused. How many times since Easter has this room been vacuumed? How many times have I picked up lengths of the elusive stuff that the vacuum missed? How often have I looked at that very spot and failed to see this one?

It's the same phenomenon each year. Weeks, months after I put away the Easter baskets, stray green wisps of artificial grass keep showing up. For years it was a battle, me vs. Easter grass. Tired of endlessly stooping for it, I'd comb through a rug on hands and knees. "Now I *know* I've got it all." And days later it would twinkle at me from that very rug.

It was perhaps ten years ago that a casual comment by my husband turned warfare into a treasure hunt. "Look!" he said one chilly fall evening, pulling a piece of the grass from the sleeve of his sweater. "Easter in October!"

Easter any time of year! Any time unexpected life puts in its surprise appearance: a phone call on a lonely day; a thoughtful driver in a traffic snarl; a misunderstanding set right. What if each time some overlooked strand of Easter grass popped up from nowhere, I was prompted to look for some sign of new life?

Renewal is everywhere, I have found, when I look for it. I no longer need these escapees from an Easter basket to remind me that resurrection has no season. I just have to catch God's light upon an event. And there, in the very place I've looked without seeing, I catch Him at work making all things new.

Thank You for the Easter grass of life, Father, that reminds me to stop and look. —ELIZABETH SHERRILL

3

T
U
E

Walk worthy of the vocation wherewith ye are called.
—EPHESIANS 4:1

Each morning after my cup of tea and a little breakfast I walk down one flight of steps, through the family room, down a short hall into my office and, *zip-zap,* I'm at work. Total commuting time: twenty-one seconds.

My daughter Jeanne, a freelance artist in New York, has a different kind of commute. Down forty-nine clanking steel warehouse steps where she lives in Brooklyn, walk two blocks to the bridge, climb sixty-two steps to the sidewalk across the bridge, walk the quarter-mile across the bridge, down two flights of steps on the other side, walk three blocks, down two flights of stairs into the subway station, ride for ten minutes, get off, walk up one flight of stairs, get on another subway, ride for fifteen minutes, get off, walk two blocks in an underground tunnel, up one flight of stairs and emerge into the heart of midtown Manhattan. Then walk anywhere from a few blocks to over a mile to wherever it is she's supposed to be that day.

After making the commute with her for a few days during a visit, I watched Jeanne at work, painting scenery for an off-Broadway production one evening. She was positively radiant as she mixed paints and told me about the production. I learned by watching her create something beautiful that she absolutely loves what she does and that the commute is worth every step, every minute.

The joy Jeanne feels at work taught me that whether you get to work the hard way or the easy way doesn't matter. What matters is that you love what you're doing when you get there.

Jesus, help me always to do work I love and am proud of, so that my journey to get there, whether it takes twenty seconds or an hour, is worth the effort. —PATRICIA LORENZ

4

Each one of you also must love his wife as he loves himself. . . .   —EPHESIANS 5:33 (NIV)

When Andrea and I were first married, our relationship was beautiful. We could tell each other anything, it seemed. We enjoyed being together all the time. We promised ourselves that we would always work hard to keep things that way.

But one day several years later, everything seemed about to fall apart. We could hardly talk about the changes without becoming angry and afraid. Without saying it out loud, we knew that our conscious feelings of love had definitely subsided. Since we both went to church and prayed regularly, we couldn't imagine how it had happened.

When we married, Andrea was marketing director for a large music company. She is a very competent manager, and she seemed to enjoy getting my office and vocational life organized. But as the years passed, she wanted to try her hand at her own business. As she got more and more involved in it, she had less and less time to help me. I felt like a deserted little boy inside, and I couldn't get nearly as much work done as I had before. When Andrea saw me floundering, she felt guilty.

The thing that saved us was our spiritual discipline of prayer and our commitment to share our feelings honestly with each other, even if it was scary to do so. I finally told Andrea that I was having feelings of being deserted. She expressed her fear of not being able to try her vocational wings. We discussed how we could rearrange the way we approached our two jobs and hire the help we needed to move ahead. And to our surprise, our feelings of love and caring for each other came back.

To me, this conversation was one of God's miracles. As we both listened and honestly expressed our understanding of the other's feelings, we suddenly knew that with God's help we could work out a way that we could both do the work we felt He was calling us to do.

Dear Lord, thank You for teaching me that marriage is a community in which both partners can realize their dreams.   —KEITH MILLER

5

T
H
U

Do not be conceited. —ROMANS 12:16 (NIV)

I've prayed to God to help keep me from showing off, but I still fight the tendency. Someone next to me on the bus was doing a crossword puzzle and couldn't fill in a word, and I had to bite my lip to keep from butting in. More importantly, when my co-worker Julie told me about her problems, it was very difficult for me just to listen and not tell her to cancel the wedding if her fiancé treated her that way! While I debated slapping some adhesive tape over my mouth, I remembered something that happened when I was just fourteen and made pocket money by baby-sitting.

I thought it would be an easy job watching blond twin girls, age four, while they viewed cartoons on television. But when a cartoon stork appeared, carrying a plump pink baby to a chimney, one of the girls asked, "Linda, is that really how a baby comes into the house? Does a stork bring it?"

I opened my mouth and began to say, "No, the mommy—" when I stopped abruptly, realizing this was *not* the kind of thing a baby-sitter should be talking about with a preschooler. So I said firmly, "When your mommy comes home, you can ask her."

Her sister whispered, "How do babies get here?" and the girl who'd asked me whispered back, "She said we have to ask Mommy. She doesn't know."

I still remember how, even though I chuckled to myself, I bristled at the idea that they thought there was something I didn't know! Apparently, I'm still bristling. And, apparently, I still have work to do in this area. So on the bus I closed my mouth, did not barge in and say that I knew an eight-letter word for *chickpea (garbanzo)*. And I heard Julie say that she was going to call her pastor and ask for some pre-marital counseling—which was an even better idea than the "solution" I had for her.

God, today help me mind my own business and allow people to work things out at their own pace and Yours, not mine.

—LINDA NEUKRUG

6

To him that is afflicted pity should be shown from his friend. . . .
—JOB 6:14

Turning from the X-ray, the country vet said gently, "It would be kindest to put her to sleep." I nodded dumbly. Snowflake, my daughter Trina's eighteen-month-old kitty, had been struck by a car near our new home. Her spine was severed; nothing could be done.

"What will you do with her body?" I asked.

"Well, you see . . ." he paused, embarrassed, "I'm afraid we just take them to the landfill."

Shock and grief left me speechless. *No! Not for Trina's dream-come-true kitten, who had snuggled in a red stocking on Christmas morning! Not for the compliant creature whom Trina had dressed in doll clothes and tucked into a cradle, where she dozed contentedly. No way! Even a cat deserves a dignified end.*

"I'll bury her myself," I announced. But where? We now lived in a rented home and no longer owned land. In desperation, I phoned my animal-lover friend Marianne.

"Oh, Gail, how sad! You bring her right out here. I have just the place," she assured me with her customary warmth and decisiveness.

When I arrived at her ranch on Windy Ridge about five miles outside of town, Marianne was ready with shovels and more sympathy. She led me to a bluff overlooking Wyoming's Lander Valley and the snow-capped Wind River Mountains. "Skipper is buried here," she said quietly. "We'll put Snowflake right beside him."

As we dug in the stony soil, Marianne reminisced about the faithful old Labrador she had laid to rest several years before. Once we were done, she plucked several yellow chrysanthemums from her garden, arranged them on the mound, then gave me a quick hug before I drove home.

Even in grief, I found a blessing. I still mourn for Snowflake, but I rejoice that God has given me a friend so full of compassion.

Lord, thank You for blessing me with friends who share my sorrow.
—GAIL THORELL SCHILLING

7

S
A
T

My dear children, I write this to you so that you will not sin. But if anybody does sin, we have one who speaks to the Father in our defense—Jesus Christ, the Righteous One. —I JOHN 2:1 (NIV)

My wife Rosie stood in the yard gazing at the concrete driveway and looking up at the tall pine trees that stood there. She said to me, "Dolphus, I just swept a bagful of pinecone pieces off the driveway yesterday, and here are more today." I looked at her and saw the frustration on her face as she stared at the fragments of pinecone under the tree and then up at the squirrel who was having a good time eating the nuts in the pinecones and letting the pieces fall to the ground.

"Dolphus," Rosie went on, "do you think God sometimes looks at us the way I'm looking at this squirrel? I imagine He must grieve at the messes we make when we're just looking out for ourselves and paying no mind to Him.

"But the amazing thing is, instead of casting them away, He gently picks up the pieces of our broken lives and makes us whole again."

The fragments keep falling, day after day, and we keep on sweeping them up. Although we still get angry at that squirrel sometimes, we've come to see it as a great reminder of the patience of our loving Father and His restorative power.

Lord, thank You for making new creatures from the fragments of broken lives. —DOLPHUS WEARY

8

S
U
N

Give unto the Lord the glory due unto his name: bring an offering, and come before him: worship the Lord in the beauty of holiness. —I CHRONICLES 16:29

There was a time when I attended church and the worship service unfolded around me like magic. The altar was bedecked with flowers, hymns were sung, psalms recited, the sermon preached, prayers said, and I left feeling uplifted by the devotion of my fellow worshipers. Then I became a member. The next thing I knew I was recruited for choir rehearsal on Tuesday nights and the soup kitchen on Saturday mornings and on alternate Wednesday evenings could I work with the teens?

But as I became more involved with the church, something happened to worship. I gazed on it and listened to it with a more critical eye. *Choir sounds a bit out of tune on the anthem. Don't the flowers seem skimpy for this time of year? Why can't someone fix that buzzing mike?* And when I saw the congregation, I not only recognized tireless volunteers and people of unflagging faith, but I was aware of tensions in their lives. *Celia is still on the prayer list. Where's Paul's wife? Are they having marital problems? I need to apologize to Hugh for what I said to him at Thursday's meeting.* Sometimes I wished for the undistracted Sundays of former days.

A friend of mine put me straight. "You were a bystander back then. Now you're a participant."

"Is that a good thing?"

"Of course. Worship is not a performance. It's a service. You come to it with all your doubts, critical thoughts and hesitations. Then with other Christians, you ask God's forgiveness, pray for His blessings and praise Him. It's a participatory art."

"Amen," I said.

I praise You, Lord, for the blessings of my church and its congregation.
—RICK HAMLIN

9

| M |
| O |
| N |

O Lord . . . we are the clay, and thou our potter; and we are all the work of thy hand. —ISAIAH 64:8

"This is *work*," I told myself one warm October afternoon while readying the yard for winter, so I stopped, stalked into the house and phoned the local library. "May I speak to one of your researchers?" A woman came on the line and I asked, "How many leaves does a tree have?"

After several seconds of startled silence, she gasped, "Why do you need to know that?"

"I've been *raking* them, that's why."

Two hours later she returned my call. "Depending on the kind and size of tree, it's fifty to one hundred thousand."

Our ten trees are huge. Let me see—ten times a hundred thousand . . . no wonder my back hurts!

My husband found me collapsed on the couch when he came home expecting dinner on the table. "I've raked a *million* leaves today. I'm too tired to cook. I'll just heat up leftovers." Roland disliked leftovers (this I knew), so he suggested we eat out instead (this I hoped).

Later in the twilight, we marveled at the vibrant colors of the leaves resting in neat piles on the lawn. "God made no two alike," Roland mused. "I'm already looking forward to next spring when He'll replace these fallen ones with new ones. None of them will be alike either." Then he squeezed my hand and grinned—letting me know he'd recognized my ruse—before adding, "And God will never make anyone else just like you."

Father, thank You for making each of us unique, never to be repeated.
—ISABEL WOLSELEY

10

T
U
E

And the Lord said, "Simon, Simon! Indeed, Satan has asked for you, that he may sift you as wheat. But I have prayed for you, that your faith should not fail. . . . —LUKE 22:31-32 (NKJV)

One of my favorite boyhood toys was a sand sifter. It was just a kind of pie pan with a wire-screen bottom in it. I could sit for hours in the driveway, sifting gravel and dirt, making miniature mountains of powdery dust. As the sand filtered through the screen, it often left behind little treasures: an ancient square nail, an iridescent beetle, a pretty quartz pebble—sometimes even an Indian Head penny or a bright agate marble.

Now, in middle age, I myself am being sifted, and it's not so much fun. The college where I teach is undergoing a revolution of change, and the sifting has uncovered some traits I didn't know I had: resentment, mixed motives, sloppy work habits. I have to let these fall through the screen.

On the other hand, I have been surprised at the treasures this sifting process has developed in me. I have discovered hidden courage to speak up in faculty meetings. "I think that's a dangerous direction to go in," I hear myself say, and others agree with me. I have even found strength to attempt new things, such as computer tasks.

I don't suppose anyone really escapes this sifting, shaking process. Marriages go through it. Churches are stirred. Friendships are filtered. The trick is for me to submit to the Sifter and look for the beauty and opportunity the process brings out. Simon Peter survived his sifting to become the chief of the Apostles. With God cheering for me, I, too, can survive.

Lord, I yield myself to You in faith that You are doing what is best for me.
—DANIEL SCHANTZ

11

W
E
D

But the steadfast love of the Lord is from everlasting to everlasting. . . .   —PSALM 103:17 (RSV)

A few years ago I remember returning to the site of my boyhood home, which had been torn down to make room for a new road that ran right through the spot once occupied by our front porch. It gave me a strange feeling to stand there watching cars cross the place where, as a young man, I had once sat and talked with my mother and dad long into the summer nights about my hopes, dreams and ambitions. My father is gone, too, so that added to the transience I felt.

How quickly things can change, places disappear, circumstances blur, friendships dissolve, loved ones pass on. And though we sometimes act as if we are only watching the passing parade, we are all marchers in the procession.

All of this came to mind recently when I learned that the people to whom we sold our house plan to tear it down and put up something much more elaborate. The large, wooded, acre-and-a-half lot lends itself to expansion. But I wonder when I come back someday what my reaction will be to seeing a different house on the property where Shirley and I lived for nearly three decades and raised our four kids. As I did when I visited my childhood homestead, I'll probably be looking for stone and tree landmarks to help me remember what it was like.

There is something in all of us that resists change, but change is one of life's constants. It's guaranteed. The Psalmist speaks darkly, but accurately, about the human condition: "As for man, his days are like grass; he flourishes like a flower of the field; for the wind passes over it, and it is gone, and its place knows it no more" (Psalm 103:15–16, RSV). That would leave me very depressed were it not for the twelve powerful words that follow: "But the steadfast love of the Lord is from everlasting to everlasting." That's something that doesn't change.

> *Instead of past-loving, sunset clingers,*
> *Transform us, Lord, into sunrise singers.*

—FRED BAUER

12

T
H
U

You are a letter from Christ delivered by us, written not with ink but with the Spirit of the living God....
—II CORINTHIANS 3:3 (RSV)

Throughout the more than fifty years since Norman Vincent Peale and I started the Guideposts ministries, I've received many, many wonderful letters from our readers.

Some, like this fifteen-year-old girl, write to share insights that all of us should take to heart: "Christmas is not a time of year to be expecting high-priced gifts, but is our Lord's birthday. We should celebrate by thanking Him for everything in our lives and helping those who are less fortunate than ourselves."

Others, like this businessman, share the beautiful examples of their own devoted lives: "When I arrive at my office on Wall Street, I shut my door, sit quietly at my desk and offer a simple prayer. 'Dear God, please be with me and help me make right decisions all day.' "

And still others, like this homemaker, provide heartening testimonies of the ways they serve God in their daily lives: "I am so fortunate to have wonderful friends and many opportunities to help people who are lonely or depressed. God is good."

It's letters like these that brighten my day and make coming to the office a joy. Never underestimate the power of a letter to inspire, to comfort and to encourage. Why not take some time today to share your story of faith with a friend or loved one?

Lord, thank You for the opportunities we're given to share the message of faith with one another every day. Amen.

—RUTH STAFFORD PEALE

13

F
R
I

He sent them out two by two.... —Mark 6:7 (NIV)

Having moved from a rural to an urban setting a year ago, our family is still getting used to some aspects of city life. One of them is the "HOV," or "High Occupancy Vehicle," designation on highways around Washington, D.C. In fact, the interstate nearest us, I-66, is "HOV-2," meaning you can't drive on it at all during certain hours without at least two people in the car. It seems the pollution problem has caused the government to reach back to a principle of Jesus, one articulated by Robert Fulgum as, "When you go out into the world, hold hands."

One of the wonderful results of all the transitions we faced last year was that we were forced to reach out and to rely on others. How do you find a new dentist or learn the quickest shortcuts across town unless you ask others? After years of following the John Wayne theory of rugged individualism, I was suddenly faced with the reality of reliance.

Whether it's driving on I-66 or flying to Asia, I now ask, "Who will go with me?" Sometimes it's not possible to find a companion, but when it is, the work is halved, the results are doubled, and the enthusiasm is multiplied.

Do you have a journey coming up? Whether it is across town, across the globe or into some uncharted emotional territory, find someone to go with you. It can make all the difference.

Lord, give me companions for the journeys of my life, so that, like the disciples You sent out so long ago, we can return rejoicing.

—ERIC FELLMAN

14

S
A
T

"If you had faith even as small as a tiny mustard seed you could say to this mountain, 'Move!' and it would go far away. Nothing would be impossible."

—MATTHEW 17:20 (TLB)

Every fall, our Southern California desert community of Twenty-nine Palms celebrates its annual weed festival. Yup, you read it right . . . a weed festival. For most of us, weeds are just nuisances that we pull out of our gardens. But in Twenty-nine Palms, weeds are prized. They are scavenged from the rocky, dry terrain, carefully sorted and turned into exquisite art.

Driving through the windy Cajon Pass en route to the desert, I've often outraced tumbleweeds bouncing along the highway beside me. How delighted I am to find them at the weed festival as porch-front decorations, strung with fairy lights or one round ball stacked on another then garnished with angel wings.

Weeds are merely misplaced plants, growing where we'd rather not have them. Their Latin botanical names give them a classical dignity: *Taraxacum officinate* (dandelion); *Ambrosia trifida* (ragweed); *Asciepias syriaca* (milkweed). Their endurance is spectacular: Some of their seeds can remain dormant in the ground for as long as forty years before the right conditions get them growing again. Their productivity is mind-boggling: A single pigweed can yield as many as two hundred thousand seeds.

Seasonally, our California hills are turned golden with flowering mustard grass (*Brassica hirta*), a weed I often yank from between the bushes on our boulevard. Yet Jesus used the lowly mustard seed, the tiniest of all, to show us the spiritual power of even a glimmering of faith.

I have a new respect for weeds, and I'm having a lot of fun arranging them. My only problem is that now my husband has a good excuse not to weed the lawn. "Pshaw!" he'll say. "You want me to pull up *Digitaria sanguinalis?*" And I'll let you look up that one in the dictionary.

Lord, open my eyes to see the special beauty in the things I take for granted and so often overlook. —FAY ANGUS

15 | S U N *And he said unto her, For this saying go thy way. . .*
—MARK 7:29

When you reread those marvelous stories about Jesus, do you ever wish you could have been there in person, an eyewitness able to hear the words spoken and see the expressions on people's faces? I do, especially in those stories where the telling seems sparse or almost too brief.

One such story is the account St. Mark gives of the Greek woman who comes to Jesus for help because her daughter is desperately ill. The Lord's first reaction is almost a rebuke. He knows that the woman is not a Jew, and He tells her that His Jewish listeners must come first: "But Jesus said unto her, Let the children first be filled" (Mark 7:27).

It must have been unthinkable for a woman, especially a foreigner, to question or challenge a rabbi or teacher. But this woman's mother-love makes her brave. "Yes, Lord," she says, "yet the dogs under the table eat of the children's crumbs" (Mark 7:28).

There must have been a stunned silence for a moment. But then, although St. Mark doesn't say so, I like to think that Jesus smiled.

Impressed by both her courage and her quickness with words, He re-assures her: "For this saying go thy way." And her daughter is cured.

Is it possible that this episode played a small part in the expansion of the church's mission to include the whole world? If so, we can all be grateful to that unknown woman, "a Greek, a Syrophenician by nation" (Mark 7:26), whose love and devotion saved her own child.

Lord, give us the faith and the courage to ask Your help when we need it.   —ARTHUR GORDON

GRANDMOTHER REMEMBERS

Stepping boldly into the future doesn't mean forgetting our past. In fact, the more good things we bring with us from where we've been, the better our future will be. This week, Mary Lou Carney shares the precious legacy her mother left for Mary Lou's own children. There'll be smiles all around, and perhaps a tear or two, as we listen to a grandmother's memories of one-room schoolhouses, traveling preachers and orange Christmas cakes.   —THE EDITORS

16

M
O
N

Day 1: The "Grandmother Remembers" Book
Write it on a tablet for them . . . that for the days to come it may be an everlasting witness.
                                                        —ISAIAH 30:8 (NIV)

"Look, a garage sale!" My daughter Amy Jo pointed to a brightly painted sign. I kept my foot on the accelerator. I had a dozen errands yet to run, and a garage sale was definitely not on my to-do list.

But when we finally came upon it, even I was impressed with the line of cars stopped to shop for bargains. We parked and got out. Tables covered the yard, laden with old records, baby clothes, even a lava lamp. In the middle of one table was an oversized, spiral-bound book. Amy Jo reached for it. "Look," she said, waving the book over her head, "it's a 'Grandma Remembers' book! Can we get it?"

I thought about Mother. Although she loved to write, her eyesight was failing. And after her stroke a few years ago, she simply wasn't as sharp as she had once been. Still, she had stories to tell and memories to share. And at seventy-four, I wasn't sure just how much longer she could share them in person.

"Come on," Amy Jo pleaded. "It's only a dollar, and I know Grandma will love doing it!"

So we bought it. Little did we know just how valuable that book would become to us. For Mother spent the last year of her life pouring out her past, leaving a legacy in longhand. A legacy laced with God's wisdom. A legacy I want to share with you this week.

For memories preserved, I thank you, Lord.   —MARY LOU CARNEY

17   Day 2: Grandmother Remembers . . . Home

T
U
E

And I will provide a place for my people . . . so that they can have a home of their own. . . .
—II SAMUEL 7:10 (NIV)

I came into this world on May 17, 1921, in Pittsburgh, Kentucky. I was born at home and given the name Sarah Nancy, after my grandmother. My father called me "Nance"—and I hated that with a passion!

We lived in the Depression, but no one felt sorry for himself. Everyone was in the same position, so it wasn't bad at all. We had no radio, no electricity, no inside water or toilets. But we loved our home! At night we'd go to a neighbor's house or they'd come to ours, and the kids would play for a while. Then we'd gather on the porch to sing and pray and go home to bed. There were no modern conveniences, but the work was done early, and the nights were free to visit, talk and play.

Today I live in a nice, cozy little house, with way more comforts than I had growing up. I have been in this place twenty-three years, ever since my husband died, and I am happy here. My home is in a lazy little town, mostly older people now that the school is gone. The grocery store is gone, too. There are three churches here, though. And lots of nice people. I expect to go to heaven from this very place!

Thank You, Lord, for home. Help me to make it a refuge for all those I love. And thank You for my heavenly home where You—and Mother—wait to greet me. —MARY LOU CARNEY

18

W   **Day 3: Grandmother Remembers . . .**
E   **School**
D   *I devoted myself to study. . . .*
—ECCLESIASTES 1:13 (NIV)

I started school at age six. The first year I made three grades, although I never left the room, since all eight grades were taught right there. My brother and I walked to school and home, about a mile and a half each way along the road to town. I studied hard and loved my teachers. I always cried when vacation came in the summer. My friends thought I was silly.

I remember a long library table in our hall at home, and I kept my books there and sat to study. Schoolwork came before play. That was a good idea! At school we had spelling bees, and I especially remember when I was in the seventh grade and my brother was in the eighth. In the spelling contest, everyone was down but Brother and me. The teacher said "misspell" and my brother spelled it just the way it sounded: with one *s*. I said "m-i-s-s-p-e-l-l" and won a book of poetry. I was so happy!

My sister worked in town for the couple who ran the movie theatre. She'd come to school at noon and bring my brother and me a sack of popcorn or peanuts. Boy, did everyone like us! One day the teacher took my peanuts and ate them during class. I cried all over my geography book.

What a privilege it is to learn, Lord! Thank You for curiosity and intelligence. Remind me that small acts of kindness—or meanness— make lasting memories. —MARY LOU CARNEY

19

T
H
U

Day 4: Grandmother Remembers . . . Church

. . . Members together of one body, and sharers together in the promise in Christ Jesus.

—EPHESIANS 3:6 (NIV)

As I was growing up, we were very active in church and did a lot of walking to and from there. The minister who held revivals always stayed at our house. I remember Mother frying chicken often then. Sometimes that minister would stay for two whole weeks. I always thought it had something to do with Mother's chicken.

I went to Sunday school and church one morning, and that's where I met the man who would become your grandpa. When I saw him, my heart did double beats. I told the girl sitting next to me, "He's mine!" I didn't know she was his sister!

I have attended church my whole life. I've gone to several different types and learned this important fact: Names and denominations aren't really important as long as there is service to only one God and love for everyone.

How grateful I am, Lord, for the faith of our fathers—and mothers! Forgive me for building barriers where none should exist. Make us all one in Your love.   —MARY LOU CARNEY

20

F
R
I

Day 5: Grandmother Remembers . . . Answered Prayer

Whatever you ask for in prayer, believe that you have received it, and it will be yours. —MARK 11:24 (NIV)

When your mother, Mary Lou, was small, she was sick a lot and, motherlike, I was always afraid she would die. I prayed for her every day! Once my mother bought her the nicest stroller to prove to herself—and to me—that Mary Lou would live.

We were very poor as we grew up, and after we were married, it wasn't much better. So I would put toys (and other things we needed) in lay-away at the dime store and pay them out a little at a time. Well, Mary Lou was sick, and I was afraid she would die, but of course I didn't tell her that. I did ask her if there was anything she wanted, and she said, "Yes, I'd like to have a walking doll."

She didn't know I had one in lay-away. I can't remember where I got the rest of the money I owed on that doll, but I said, "I'll be right back." I hurried uptown and brought the doll home, so happy I was crying. I remember several people I met commenting on how lovely that doll was. I hurried home and gave it to Mary Lou. She was so excited!

I can still cry today when I think of that incident more than thirty years ago. As you know, your mother didn't die. She lived to be healthy and strong. And that walking doll is the very one that sits on the mantel in the living room of your mother's house today.

For granting a mother's request, and the yearning of a sick child, thank You, God! Increase my faith through answered prayers of the far— and near—past. —MARY LOU CARNEY

Editor's note: A month from today, Monday, November 20, 2000, we'll be observing our seventh annual Guideposts Family Day of Prayer. We'd like to include you in our praying family. Please send your prayer requests to Guideposts Prayer Fellowship, PO Box 8001, Pawling, NY 12564. If you can, enclose a picture with your letter.

21

S
A
T

Day 6: Grandmother Remembers . . . Christmas
Every good and perfect gift is from above, coming down from the Father of the heavenly lights. . . .
—JAMES 1:17 (NIV)

Christmas was always a joyful time—Mother made sure of that! We had fruit and food and some small gift and were satisfied. We didn't miss all the fancy stuff, for we never had it. My sister Rinda worked in Ohio and came home on Christmas. She always brought my brother and me gifts.

Every year we went to the Baptist church where there was a huge Christmas tree and Santa. I remember one night I sat with these girls, and we saw this beautiful doll

310 • OCTOBER 2000

on the tree. We decided to see who got it when Santa took it down. Well, he took it down and said, "Little Miss Nancy."

I jumped up, yelling, "Here I am, Mr. Ponder!" I didn't even say "Santa Claus." Till today I don't know how I knew that was Mr. Ponder, our neighbor across the road. I always knew the dolls were from Rinda, but I still liked to pretend.

That was my last doll. The next year, I got gloves—and cried.

Every Christmas for a long time now I have baked orange cakes. The recipe is an old one. My cousin gave it to me. We use it at Christmas to give as gifts. When your mother, Mary Lou, was younger, she sold the cakes door-to-door to give us money for Christmas presents. God has always helped provide my needs.

At Christmas and always, Father, I look to You for every good and perfect gift. Help me create memories sprinkled with love and seasoned with generosity.
                                                    —MARY LOU CARNEY

22 | SUN | Day 7: Grandmother Remembers . . . Her Mother

Precious in the sight of the Lord is the death of his saints.
                                            —PSALM 116:15 (NIV)

My mother was the best person who ever lived. I never heard her yell or raise her voice in anger to anyone. She was the most patient person I ever knew. She worked so hard doing laundry on the board and tub and ironing with flat irons. My father was ill a lot with asthma, and he didn't work much. Mother kept things going at home. She never complained. She was honest and sincere, a good Christian who never had an enemy that we knew of. The best friend ever!

My mother had a heart condition in her later years and died a peaceful death in my arms one Saturday morning when she was eighty-eight years old.

I love poetry, and I have written some through the years. One I especially like is about the space in our house after Mother died.

There's an empty room at our house
And a vacant chair by the door.
Someone used to love that room,
But she doesn't live here anymore.

We shared many things together—
Laughter, tears, and problems sore.
God allowed her to stay a long, long time,
But she doesn't live here anymore.

In her new home with Christ above
And saints on heaven's shore,
My mother waits to greet me there . . .
But she doesn't live here anymore.

*When I yearn for Mother and Grandmother and all my lost loved ones,
God, remind me that nothing is truly lost if You know where it is.
Thank You for the hope of heaven and the certainty of Your love.*

—MARY LOU CARNEY

READER'S ROOM

"My healing journey for this year has only begun, I believe. My dad was diagnosed with stomach cancer in February. My parents were told that they should contact a hospice, and the phone and e-mail lines started burning up with plans for all my sisters and brothers to come home to say good-bye. Within a week, the doctor told him that it was a slow-growing cancer and that he and my mom would probably celebrate their 50th wedding anniversary in 2001. We never even had a chance to grieve his impending death before life resumed as usual. My dad signed up for 11 bowling tournaments (bowling is his hobby and passion), and when his doctor suggested surgery to remove a tumor, he insisted that it wouldn't be until bowling season is over in mid-May. I haven't seen any outward signs that his life has changed because of his brush with mortality. I talk to God about all this, but He isn't giving me answers. I trust Him anyway; He doesn't have to explain things to me."   —*Martha A. Suter, South Bend, Indiana*

23

M
O
N

Who hath ears to hear, let him hear.
—MATTHEW 13:9

My husband was performing in a musical at a local college, and I decided to attend. "You can read while you wait," he said. "The doors will open in about twenty minutes."

Finding a comfortable spot, I propped my purse by my feet and took out a paperback. My reading was interrupted by the two girls sitting next to me.

"Oh, he's just so totally real. Like, really, he's like too much, you know? It's like, like, awesome."

Her friend responded, "Yes, really cool. I know what you mean. Like, how wild. Like, too much. You know, like, I mean really. It's like, really way out."

Is this the way college students converse with each other? I wondered. *They need a course in communication.* I promised myself never to use the word *like* again.

At last the doors opened, and I went inside to claim my seat. After settling in and making myself comfortable, I reached for my purse. With a sinking feeling, I realized it wasn't there. I got up and ran out to the lobby. No purse. It was gone! Without much hope, I went to ask at the reception desk, though I thought my purse must be halfway across campus by now.

"Did anyone turn in a purse?" I asked.

"Yes," the young man replied. "The two girls sitting next to you found it after you left." He handed it to me.

"The girls?" I queried. "The ones sitting next to me?"

Those lovely girls. Those, like, totally awesome girls.

O Lord, teach me to listen for the sweet sounds of totally real communication.
—SUSAN SCHEFFLEIN

24

T
U
E

And the work of righteousness will be peace. . . .
—ISAIAH 32:17 (NAS)

In 1961, Dag Hammarskjold, secretary general of the United Nations, was killed in a plane crash. He was on his way to negotiate a cease-fire in what was then Rhodesia. As his family and friends gathered his personal effects in his apartment, they found his spiritual diary, later published as *Markings*. A friend gave me a copy of *Markings* when I was in college, and it soon became one of my favorite books. I was particularly moved by these words, which Hammarskjold had written just days before his death:

> I don't know Who—or what—put the question. I don't know when it was put. I don't even remember answering. But at some moment I did answer *Yes* to Someone—or Something—and from that hour I was certain that existence is meaningful and that, therefore, my life, in self-surrender, had a goal.

These thoughts helped me, an impressionable young man, to see that my own life needed to be focused on a goal greater than myself.

Dag Hammarskjold was a quiet and reserved man. Never one to wear his religion on his sleeve, he was nonetheless a man of profound faith and commitment to peace. On United Nations Day, I am thankful for men and women like Dag Hammarskjold who give their lives for world peace. And I commit myself to pray for the success of their efforts throughout our world.

Father, let there be peace on earth.   —SCOTT WALKER

25 | W E D

Consider him . . . so that you may not grow weary or fainthearted.   —HEBREWS 12:3 (RSV)

It's getting toward that time of year when Andrew has to spend more hours of the day at work. In another two months, he will need to work on Saturdays, too. This happens every year in late fall and through the winter; I think of it as my single-motherhood season. But the rest of the year Andrew arrives home for dinner promptly at 6:30 P.M., so I can't complain.

What's hard for me is the anxiety Andrew carries around with him as he nears his annual deadline. He doesn't grumble or argue or kick his way through the house. No, he simply retreats. He reads books. He doesn't talk. That gets frustrating, especially after I've had a long day filled with children. I remind myself that silence is a pretty innocuous way to handle stress. And the lack of communication wouldn't be so hard if it weren't that I have a husband who genuinely wants to talk to me the rest of the time.

This year promises to be a bit harder than years past, for our third child is due at the beginning of November. I will be more exhausted than usual, probably frazzled and wanting to vent at the end of the day. Andrew will arrive home more likely to find a crying baby and a household in disarray than peace and respite. How will we ever handle it?

We can look ahead dreading the stress and strain. Or we can admit that God knows Andrew's schedule and yet chose this time to give us a new baby. We can trust that He is giving us an opportunity to learn something about how to rely on Him, grow closer to Him, sanctify our lives through the practice of patience and humility. We can pray a bit more . . . which will allow us less time for complaining.

Lord Jesus, You were tired when You reached Calvary. When I grow weary, help me to pick up my cross and follow You.

—JULIA ATTAWAY

26 | T H U

Now I want you to know, brothers, that what has happened to me has really served to advance the gospel. —PHILIPPIANS 1:12 (NIV)

By and large, modern information technology has my blessings. Anything that enhances our ability to communicate is probably good. But there are times when nothing beats the human touch.

I had received word that a friend of mine was recovering from a minor accident in a hospital upstate, so I called the area code I believed the hospital to be in and got the number—without ever talking to a human being, of course. Very quick, very efficient. But when I dialed the number and a real-life human voice answered that sounded decidedly unofficial and unhospital-like, I knew I'd made a mistake. "Sorry," I muttered and hung up. I'd forgotten the number by that point so I had to call information again, this time jotting down what the calm, computerized voice said. I redialed. Same voice. "I'm so sorry, I've dialed the wrong number," I said, flustered, and hung up.

I redialed information and chose the automatic dial option to connect me directly with the right number. I wasn't taking any chances. Again the woman's voice. I was just going to hang up without saying anything when the woman shouted, "Wait! Are you trying to call the hospital?"

"Yes, I am," I admitted sheepishly. "I keep dialing the wrong number."

"No, you're dialing correctly. It's the number that's wrong. For some reason, information is giving out my number as the hospital's. If you hold a second, I've got the right one written down."

She was back in a flash with the number, and I said something about all of us being at the mercy of computers. "Don't blame the phone company's computers," my new friend laughed. "They just do what people tell them." She was right. But I couldn't help feeling thankful that I had gotten the right wrong number.

Help me to see, Lord, Your perfect hand in all things, even a wrong number. —EDWARD GRINNAN

27 F R I *Carry each other's burdens, and in this way you will fulfill the law of Christ.* —GALATIANS 6:2 (NIV)

"Sometimes that person just irritates me!" I complained to my friend Kathy as we power-walked our way through the neighborhood early one crisp autumn morning. Kathy is a prayer partner and kindred spirit friend who understands me even when I don't understand myself. On this morning, we had set aside an hour to walk and talk, but I was doing most of the talking. Or complaining.

"Every time I see this person, I remember all the ways she has hurt me in the past," I said. "So those irritations come popping back up to the surface."

Kathy let me vent my feelings, then she cupped her hand and held it out in front of me. "Now put those irritations here, and let me carry them for you this week."

Intrigued, I did just that. I pretended to take the words right out of my mouth and heart and deposited them in the palm of her hand. She clenched her fingers around this imaginary lump of feelings and said, "Now you are free from the burden of these feelings because I am carrying them for you. If you want them back next week, you can have them."

For the whole week, I pictured Kathy carrying the burden of my irritations. Do you think I was ready to ask for them back at the end of the week? No way. But out of that experience grew a friendship ritual that Kathy and I now share. If one of us mentions a pain or struggle or irritation, the other thrusts out an open hand with the invitation, "Put it here." And the burden-carrier tucks it in her pocket.

Thank You, Lord, for a friend who listens and then lightens the load by carrying my burdens. —CAROL KUYKENDALL

28 | S A T

My times are in your hands. . . .
—PSALM 31:15 (NIV)

My day was overloaded. I was on deadline for two projects, and I was excited and nervous about getting them into final shape. But the bottom of the coffee can glared at me, and there was only white dust in the bottom of the flour canister. Clearly, a trip to the grocery store was mandatory. Worst of all, in doing some last-minute research on the Internet for one of my projects, I ran into a problem telling time. Different Web sites listed time in different ways.

"Bill, help! What is GMT? What is Zulu Time? How do I know what time it is here?"

"GMT is Greenwich Mean Time. It's the actual time in Greenwich, England, written in Zulu Time. Zulu Time gives every hour of the day its own number. For example, 2:00 A.M. is 0200, but 2:00 P.M. is 1400 (12 noon plus two hours). To find out what time it is here in Maryland, figure out the hour in England, and, since it is Daylight Savings Time at the moment, subtract four hours. So if the screen says 2215 GMT, then it is 2215 Zulu Time in Greenwich, which means 10:15 P.M. there. Subtract four hours. It's 6:15 P.M. here. Got it?"

Well, not really. And my day was still fragmented into all my tasks clambering to be done. Then Psalm 31:15 popped into my head. I saw it in a new way: My own personal time was really part of GET—"God's Eternal Time." And He knew where I was in it. All I had to do was pause and wait prayerfully. Slowly, the chores of the day formed themselves into a doable list. And in all the spaces between, there was time for me to turn and smile and thank Him.

Lord, help me remember my times are in Your hand, hour by hour, day by day, from my imperfect now until Your perfect forever.
—ROBERTA ROGERS

29 | S
      | U
      | N

For we are God's workmanship. . . .
—EPHESIANS 2:10 (NIV)

My children don't merely wrap presents—they elaborately disguise them. "But, Mom," my daughter Elizabeth exclaimed in consternation as I began to put paper around a cassette tape for my husband Alex's birthday, "he'll know what it is before he opens it!" She put the cassette in a small box within layers of boxes. Later she and Mark were thrilled when Dad didn't know what his gifts were until he finally found the core of each package.

Today at church, I found myself looking fondly at Patricia and thought, *Why, she's like those disguised birthday gifts.* When we first came to this church, I stared at her tiny, thin frame, her humped back and protruding spine. How frail and disabled she seemed. But after the service she welcomed us with a firm handshake and a kind smile. Since then, I've noticed how important this small slip of a lady is to the parish. Her love seems boundless as she welcomes newcomers like us and also cares for her homebound mother and many elderly parishioners.

It was Patricia who introduced us to Johnny, a young man with braids sticking out all over his head and several earrings in each ear. During breakfast after the service, Johnny told us how he had been an atheist until he experienced God's love a few years ago. The children listened wide-eyed as he described his journey from darkness to light. Recently Elizabeth had been expressing some faith questions and doubts. Johnny provided many answers I had been unable to give. Another gift to us, and uniquely disguised!

This morning at church, a young man came in with the most unusual hairdo—bleached blond, with black circles stamped all over his head. Mark whispered, "Look, Mom, he has yellow hair with black polka dots!"

What a weird— I started to think, but caught myself. *I wonder what gift he has to give us?*

Father, help me find the precious gift underneath each person's special wrapping!
—MARY BROWN

30

M
O
N

I have given to all able men ability, that they may make all that I have commanded you.

—EXODUS 31:6 (RSV)

In early 1954, I was a class A machinist at an aircraft-engine plant. I had been upgraded from the production to the development division, where I machined parts for new engine designs. I loved the challenge and the responsibility—and the attention, too.

By October, things had changed. Contracts had dwindled, and senior workers from other divisions where work was slow were "bumped" into our division. One day my foreman said, "Oscar, I hate to lose you, but you are being replaced. I'm certain personnel has a job for you!"

They had; I went from being a class A machinist to sweeping the floors, a nine-step downgrade and a sixty-six percent reduction in pay. I agonized before accepting the job, but I felt I really didn't have a choice. As I worked, I found the duty relaxing, and I made up my mind to do my best and to do it enthusiastically. I even requested an extra-long broom so I could reach those long-untouched crevices. And I liked my foreman, Art Sullivan, who did the best he could to make me feel appreciated with a kind word or a pat on the arm. My co-workers said they had never seen the area so immaculate.

Twelve weeks later I returned to my machinist's job rested and relaxed. Promotions came, and in 1968 I was interviewed for a technical writing position, the one I really wanted. When I walked into the publications office, the interviewer smiled. "Welcome!" he said. "You have a friend here, your old boss Art Sullivan. If you accept this job, he'll be your new team leader. Can you start on Monday?"

I left the office and walked out into the sun. What had begun as misfortune had, all those years later, become good fortune. And all because of a common task done in an uncommon way.

Oh, Lord, teach me to be patient, and that doing my best work will bring its rewards, all in Your own good time.

—OSCAR GREENE

31
| T |
| u | *With thanksgiving let your requests be made known* |
| E | *to God.* —PHILIPPIANS 4:6 (NAS) |

Just prior to the last election here in Canada, the doorbell rang and in popped our neighbor Peggy. After introducing herself as the official enumerator for this district, she began to write down the details of our household on the official form.

Having completed that little duty, she pulled out a receipt book from the shopping bag she carried and reintroduced herself as the local canvasser for a well-known charity. "Would you care to donate?"

"Why, of course," I replied.

She accepted the money I handed her, tucked it away into another corner of her shopping bag and wrote out my receipt.

"Oh, by the way, I'm also the new Brownie leader. Would you by chance have any eggshells to spare?"

"Eggshells? Whatever for?"

"Oh, the kids in the pack are doing mosaics using broken eggshells and they could do with a few more."

It just so happened that I was in the process of baking a cake, so I rinsed the eggshells, dried them off and felt glad to know they would be of use.

Expressing the hope that nobody on the street would take exception to her wearing three hats at once, Peggy picked up her shopping bag and was off to the next house to "enumerate, canvass or scrounge. Today they can have their pick," she said, with a grin.

I thought of her today during prayer time. My prayer concerns had wandered literally all over the map, from our home to the church to another country and back again. Not only that, but I had interceded as a mother, given thanks as a sister and made requests as a wife. How would God ever be able to sort things out?

And then I smiled as I remembered that God doesn't mind if I come to His door wearing one hat at a time or a dozen on alternate days. Instead, He simply says, "The one who comes to Me I will certainly not cast out" (John 6:37, NAS).

God, it's so good to drop in on You with my requests, knowing that You will respond to them according to Your divine will.

—ALMA BARKMAN

My Renewal Journal

1 _____

2 _____

3 _____

4 _____

5 _____

6 _____

7 _____

8 _____

9 _____

10 _____

OCTOBER 2000

11 _____

12 _____

13 _____

14 _____

15 _____

16 _____

17 _____

18 _____

19 _____

20 _____

21 _____

22 _____

23 _____

24 _____

25 _____

26 _____

27 _____

28 _____

29 _____

30 _____

31 _____

November

And there shall be no night there; and they need no candle, neither light of the sun; for the Lord God giveth them light. . . .

—REVELATION 22:5

S	M	T	W	T	F	S
			1	2	3	4
5	6	7	8	9	10	11
12	13	14	15	16	17	18
19	20	21	22	23	24	25
26	27	28	29	30		

1

W
E
D

And I give unto them eternal life; and they shall never perish. . . . —JOHN 10:28

As part of my hobby of genealogical research, I visit a lot of cemeteries, seeking information to make a connection to the past. But sometimes the stone monuments and statues only accentuate the distance I feel between myself and the grandparents and great-grandparents I never knew. The solitude seems to belie the once-full lives of those now at rest.

While visiting a lovely cemetery one afternoon, I was thinking about these things when a flash of movement caught my eye. *Did I see a jackrabbit scampering among the headstones?* Walking on, I spied a huge hawk circling above and noticed the varied musical accompaniment of birdsong and whistles. Later, when talking to a cemetery worker, I learned that several rabbits call the place home, as well as many birds who nest safely within the crypt flower vases. Even a few foxes regularly visit this urban oasis.

God's message seemed clear: Even in death, new life prevails. Filling this cemetery with life was a reassuring reminder that death was not God's final word. The distance I had felt began to melt away. And in the days that followed, I understood more that each life that came before me continued in some small way. I watched my son throw a baseball left-handed, like my grandfather Ed; I thought of my brother Steve, the only one of us tall enough to have stood eye-to-eye with our Papa John; my husband Paul said that his grandma seemed to be right beside him and our daughter Maria when they baked Grandma's favorite snickerdoodle cookies from her recipe. A part of them or of something they loved goes on, keeping their spirits as alive as the busy animals I watched that afternoon. God makes all things new, yet thankfully never leaves the old completely behind.

On this All Saints' Day, I thank You, Lord, for Your gifts of eternal life and love. —GINA BRIDGEMAN

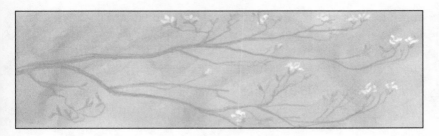

ALL THINGS NEW

2 | T | **Learning from Loss**
      | H | *But they that wait upon the Lord shall renew their*
      | U | *strength. . . .* —ISAIAH 40:31

At first it was only an occasional twinge, but as the heel spur grew, I could put no weight on my right foot at all. Costly orthotic inserts for my shoes didn't help; cortisone shots made no difference. The doctor prescribed a cane, then crutches.

It was at the peak of my frustration that a letter came from my friend Jean Nardozzi. Jean and I had been prayer partners for many years, so when I wrote her about my problem, I expected her to reply that she would pray for healing.

Nothing of the kind! "I pray," the letter announced, "that this episode will bring new insights and be rich in teaching from the Holy Spirit."

Insight? Teaching? I wanted my foot to be fixed! At last, though, since I was doing a lot of enforced sitting anyway, I halfheartedly echoed Jean's prayer, all but challenging God to bring something good from my predicament.

Well . . . new empathy, certainly, for all those who cannot walk. New admiration, too, for cane- and crutch-users. How much skill is involved! How clumsily I handled them.

Day after day, as I asked, "What will You teach me next?" the list of discoveries grew. And when, as heel spurs do, mine mended, what delight I took in every pain-free step! Walking . . . first the left foot, then the right . . . balance, coordination, freedom . . . what a complex and wondrous endowment! What joy it still gives me every day!

As always, God had taken loss, temporary and small in this case, and brought from it something better, longer-lasting, new.

Father, remind me to ask when setbacks come, "What new good are You preparing now?"
                                                        —ELIZABETH SHERRILL

3 | F
    R   *In all things showing thyself a pattern of good*
    I   *works. . . .*
                                                        —TITUS 2:7

Boxes of envelopes and letters, several thousand in all, were stacked on every chair and table in our den. I had just lugged them home from the printer and planned to make a family activity out of stuffing and stamping the envelopes. The letters had been written by Mabel McDole, a respected educator in a nearby town, on behalf of a good friend who was running for public office. Our job was to get out the mailing to all the voters in the community.

Two days later, as we neared the end of this arduous project, the return address on the envelope I was stamping caught my eye for the first time. *Surely not,* I thought to myself. Dashing for my notes, I tore through the pages—*Mable McDole.*

"Oh, my gosh!" My wail echoed through the house and brought my husband David in on a run. "You'll never believe what I've done," I moaned. "I misspelled Mrs. McDole's name when I placed the order with the printer. Her name is M-A-B-E-L—not M-A-B-L-E. I'll have to go and have all this stuff reprinted. I can't send these letters with Mrs. McDole's name misspelled."

"Calm down, Pam," David said. "The first thing you need to do is call Mrs. McDole and tell her what's happened."

Well, I wasn't exactly wild about admitting my stupidity, but I gathered my courage and dialed her number. "Mrs. McDole," I began, "you're never going to believe what I've done . . ."

Mrs. McDole laughed. "Why, honey," she said, "people make mistakes and that doesn't matter a bit! The letter isn't about me, anyway. It's about getting a good man elected to an important office. Get it in the mail, and don't think twice about the way my name's spelled."

I knew Mrs. McDole was revered by many for her good works. Now I saw a beautiful pattern emerging. By incorporating virtues like kindness and forgiveness into all she did, from teaching English to serving her community, she was teaching important lessons in living. And I was feeling mighty lucky to count myself her student.

Father, Your best saints show me patterns that make life good. Help me be a fast learner. —PAM KIDD

4

S
A
T

O Absalom, my son, my son! —II SAMUEL 18:33

I have felt the need to take pictures lately. Not photographs, but mental pictures of the moments when my son still shows the affection he did during his first three years. Because, little by little, I can feel it slipping away.

Frequently now, he doesn't run to see me when I come home. When he gets hurt, it's his mother he runs to for kisses; mine don't feel quite right anymore. When I tell him that I love him, he doesn't say, "I love you, too" as he used to. Often he'll endure my hugs with his arms at his side. I must be careful not to hug him too long, but I know I still do. I just can't help myself.

So at night, when he's asleep, I'll go into his room and whisper in his ear, "Daddy loves Julian," hoping to give his heart what he'll no longer accept from my arms and lips. And maybe I can shoo away those nasty crocodiles that have crept into his dreams lately.

But now, alas, he is realizing he is a boy. And now the separation is beginning. I must admit, it hurts a little. Actually, it hurts a lot.

And so, whenever he lets me, I sit down with my arm around my son and think about how good I still have it. But I'll keep taking those mental pictures while I can.

Lord, as my little ones grow up and away, help me to give them the space they need. And keep my memories of them ever fresh in my heart. —DAVE FRANCO

5

S
U
N

The patient in spirit is better than the proud in spirit.
—ECCLESIASTES 7:8

After thirty years as a college teacher, I was thinking of quitting, when my wife handed me a clipping: "Here, read this." It was a tribute to John Wilson, a minister from Springfield, Ohio, where I was born in 1942. The article listed his contributions: sixty-five years in the ministry, with thirty-six of those also spent teaching in a nearby Christian college. There were 4,350 people added to the church during his term, and several other churches were started by his members. Four million dollars were given to missions, and seventy young men became "Timothies" of the church and entered the ministry. One of them was my father, Edward.

"Johnny," as we have always called him, is a small, elegant man, with permanently smiling eyes and the innocent voice of a little boy. He's as unobtrusive as a bellhop in a fine hotel. When you talk to him, you feel as if he loves you, which he does, and you are sorry when he leaves. Day after day and year after year, Johnny went door to door, talking to people about their relationship with God. Patiently he sat through interminable board meetings. He married and buried; he wrestled daily with God in prayer.

So what is his secret?

He didn't quit.

In a world impressed by speed, Johnny is a reminder that the tortoise can still beat the hare in the long haul. Whether I am building a church or a family, a community or a career, the critical ingredient is patience.

Steady as she goes.

Father, when I am ready to give up, don't let me. Hold me to my task till it's done.
—DANIEL SCHANTZ

6

M
O
N

Thou, Lord, hast helped me, and comforted me.
—PSALM 86:17

When I was growing up, my mother's mending basket, laden with torn socks from a husband and seven children, waited by the green chair under a lamp in the living room. In the evenings she would sit there, sock pulled over a darning egg, and skillfully repair the holes with soft thread. When she was finished, the sock had a new heel or toe that was stronger than the original.

After I got married, Mother gave me a darning egg and thread to mend Whitney's socks. I tried, but the holes bunched into knots. I didn't have Mother's skill, so I threw away the old socks and bought new ones. But I kept the darning egg, a wooden contraption with a handle. It reminds me of the holes—the losses—in my life that nothing but God can fill.

Our triplets, Whitney, Jr., Patrick and Douglas, were born prematurely in 1970. One after the other, at different times and from different causes, they died. Staring into that awful hole of loss drove me to God. As I sat in His presence, I felt, slowly, threads of comfort weaving through my pain, tugging at me to accept what I could not understand. The pain has never entirely gone away. But I've come through it patched with God's strength and woven with the certain hope that my loss is temporary: My three boys are safe and loved on the other shore.

Comforter, in Jesus, our loss—God's loss—is turned to gain. Thank You for consoling me. —SHARI SMYTH

---

7 T u E

And Paul . . . received all that came in unto him, Preaching the kingdom of God . . . with all confidence. . . .
—ACTS 28:30-31

I am always interested in elections, and this one was no exception. I felt that there was one fine candidate who needed help, and a small check produced a call from his headquarters: "Would you be interested in working for him?" I hadn't volunteered since my school days, but I was retired, so why not?

I couldn't go out and represent the candidate or even telephone people (the result of my stroke), so I stuffed and licked envelopes, compiled lists of potential voters, and colored maps as instructed with red, yellow and blue crayons (I never found out the meaning of the colors).

On Election Day I was up early, voted and then went over to the office. I was dispatched with a bundle of literature under my arm to Broadway and 72nd Street. This is a major intersection, and it caught everybody—men and women of every race and class.

How many times have I glorified New Yorkers for their friendliness? Forget it. Beside an occasional woman who said she had voted already or little boys being dragged away by their mothers, no one even looked at me. And my hands were freezing. As I stood there forlornly, I realized that I was selling something, and the resistance was severe. It made me think of Paul. Paul was selling Jesus. It was that simple, but the selling was complex.

I dragged myself home, took down the Bible and turned to Acts. What a salesman Paul was! Witnessing was as natural to him as breathing. So absorbed did I get, I almost forgot about the election returns. I switched on the TV. My man had won, but I was not so jubilant. I thought of myself on the corner feeling sorry for myself. Next time, however, I will be different. Next time, with a smile on my face, I will give out those pamphlets with a passion that would have made Paul proud of me.

Oh, yes, Lord, I'll do my best for my Candidate in mind and heart— and never fail to vote. —VAN VARNER

8
W
E
D
When you are tempted, he will also provide a way out so that you can stand up under it.
—I CORINTHIANS 10:13 (NIV)

By the time my friend Rick Thomas was twelve years old, he already had a name in north Florida as a boy who could tame wild horses. But one old mare very nearly defeated him. She was gentle enough in the corral, but when Rick took her out into the palmettos he could not control her.

There was a stand of pines a short way off that Rick always avoided because low, dead branches stuck out like spears. The first day Rick took the mare out, she galloped straight for these pines. "Whoa!" Rick shouted. "Whoa!" The horse raced ahead. Rick pulled on the reins as hard as he could, but the mare plunged into the trees. Ducking, shouting, Rick was barely able to stay in the saddle. Branches ripped his pants, cut his face, whipped his shoulders until at last the mare came to the far edge of the woods and stopped.

Next day, the same thing. Was there a way to deal with the horse's strange compulsion? Night after night Rick pored over his training manuals, until at last he found what he was looking for. "If a horse is running away from you and you cannot rein it in, turn its head."

It was worth a try. Next day Rick saddled the mare and once again set out cross-country. Sure enough, as soon as she spotted the pines, she sped toward them. But this time, instead of trying to stop the charging animal with his twelve-year-old strength, the boy pulled hard to the right. At first the horse kept dashing forward, but then, slowly, her head swung to the right. Bit by bit her pace faltered until she was walking docilely.

The technique had worked, but *why?* The answer was as simple as it was effective: When the runaway's head turned, she could no longer see the mysteriously alluring grove. Distraction. That had been the key.

Shortly after this experience, Rick Thomas heard God calling him into the priesthood where he would follow the celibate life. Strong drives, of course, would lure him toward areas he elected to avoid. But Rick has the memory of a day in the palmettos to help him. Never, he has learned, try to control wild horses with your own strength. Instead, turn your head.

Father, many kinds of temptation assault the soul. The next time one comes along that I cannot handle, give me something else to focus on.
                                                          —JOHN SHERRILL

9 | T
      H   *"He will yet fill your mouth with laughter and your*
      U   *lips with shouts of joy."*   —JOB 8:21 (NIV)

It had been a really hard day at work when a storm slamming into Los Angeles took out the power to our office building. Not only did the outage kill our electric typewriters and word processors, it also took out our phones and our heat.

There were all sorts of groans and complaints and cries of "We're never going to make the deadlines now!" We all came out of our offices into the large-windowed reception area and sat around complaining.

Then our departmental assistant, a bright young woman who had recently seen *The Sound of Music* for the first time, told us what a great song she thought "My Favorite Things" was, and suggested we make a list of the things that make us feel better when we are sad. After a little while, the complaining tailed off in the face of her enthusiasm, and we got into the spirit of the game.

Some of the suggestions were: sleeping for at least twelve hours; walking through a field of knee-high wildflowers; drinking chicken noodle soup from a mug; buying lots of pairs of new shoes; wearing a big old floppy sweater; having a dog with a cold nose lick your face; playing old wartime songs from the forties for hours. By the time the power came back on, we found that we were in a great mood and eager to get back to work.

Sometimes, I think, what we need most when we're pressured is a little laughter and a few of our most outlandish favorite things.

Lord, when I'm feeling low, bless me with laughing friends.

—RHODA BLECKER

10
**F
R
I**

Sorrow is better than laughter, For when a face is sad a heart may be happy.   —ECCLESIASTES 7:3 (NAS)

It had been raining; the streets were slick and glistening. As I walked with Beau, my golden retriever, who delighted in potholes filled with water, I saw three boys on bicycles spinning "wheelies" on the glassy asphalt surface. Suddenly, one of the boys lost control of his bike and crashed, scraping the side of his leg and banging his elbow. As I rushed over to help, he hopped up quickly. With tears of pain shining in his eyes, he forced himself to laugh and exclaimed, "Boy, that sure felt good!" Then he straightened his handlebars, hopped back on his bike and was off with his friends.

For a moment I stood there and thought about the irony of his pain-filled words. Then I remembered that just the week before, I had tripped on a crack in the sidewalk while running, taking a pretty nasty tumble. Instantly I, too, was up, frantically looking around to see if anyone had seen me. Only when I was assured that I was alone did I stop to assess the damage my fall had done to my hands and knees.

Young or old, it seems that few of us are comfortable expressing our pain. With tears streaming down our faces, it's easier to look the world in the eye and say, "That sure felt good!" But I have confided my pains and struggles to my two or three closest friends—and that's what has made us close.

When life flies out of control and we bruise our shins or bust our britches, it's important to be able to forget about our embarrassment and allow a friend to help take away the pain.

Father, when I'm tempted to "put a good face" on painful things, help me to admit my need for healing—especially to You.

—SCOTT WALKER

11

S
A
T

Ask God for anything in line with the Holy Spirit's wishes. Plead with him, reminding him of your needs, and keep praying earnestly for all Christians everywhere. —EPHESIANS 6:18 (TLB)

Have you ever experienced a fear of flying? When I fly, I sometimes feel a little nervous during those first thirty seconds of takeoff. But then I remember an experience my dad had during World War II and I suddenly become calm and thankful that I'm in a huge modern jet.

Imagine flying alone in a tiny, single-engine P-39 over the South Pacific during wartime in 1943. Suddenly, you see enemy planes just ahead and below you. A military intelligence magazine wrote about my dad's experience: "Lieutenant Kobbeman closed to one hundred fifty yards before opening fire. The tracers hit the enemy plane but the Japanese pilot bailed out at ten thousand feet."

Then, from above and to the left, Dad's plane was hit by the enemy. "One was a direct hit in the tail section, which knocked off half the rudder and half the elevator. The left side of the horizontal stabilizer was also damaged. One shell hit the left wing, blowing out the landing light. Six shells struck the right wing. One hit the gas bay nearest the fuselage. Shrapnel entered the cockpit—injuring Lieutenant Kobbeman in the right foot and cutting the oxygen tube. Three 20-millimeter shells exploded inside the wing and blew a hole two feet in diameter. One shell hit the door of the cockpit and the radio was shot out by shells or shrapnel. Lieutenant Kobbeman dived into clouds below and lost the enemy plane. Despite all this damage he was able to land safely."

"Weren't you terrified flying that tiny damaged plane over the ocean?" I asked Dad after I read the account. He said he just remembers flying one mile after another, knowing God was his copilot, and that one good wing and a very lengthy prayer got him back to land safely.

If prayer can do that for a young pilot whose plane is barely limping along over the ocean with enemy planes circling around, think what it can do for us on a day-to-day basis, whether we're flying a jumbo jet or driving a car to work.

Heavenly Father, be with everyone traveling today, on land and in air, from sea to shining sea.   —PATRICIA LORENZ

12
S
U
N

For by one Spirit are we all baptized into one body. . . . For the body is not one member, but many.
—I CORINTHIANS 12:13–14

Yesterday, on Long Island, I attended the baptism or christening or infant dedication—different Christian denominations have different traditions—of my niece Caroline Kay and her husband James Kuvaja's first baby. Because I helped name Caroline and her twin sister Catherine, I listened with special interest as their mother, the Reverend Joy Bauer Bulla, baptized her beautiful, sleeping granddaughter, Kierra Rae.

How utterly fascinated we are with given names; they follow us all the days of our lives. One of the first questions we ask of someone we meet is his or her name. When Jacob wrestled with the angel in Genesis, he asked, "Tell me what your name is." The angel, you recall, didn't oblige, but did bestow a blessing on Jacob—and a new name, Israel.

When a baby like Kierra Rae is christened in a Christian sacrament with her very own name, we acknowledge God's wonderful gift of life and His blessing on her parents and on all who hold her dear.

Thank You, God, for babies tender,
A reminder of their loving Sender.   —FRED BAUER

13
M
O
N

Remember the former things of old. . . .
—ISAIAH 46:9

I was fourteen that fall back in 1967, and determined to hit the business world with a bang in my afterschool job selling cosmetics. The latest excitement was that the district manager would be attending our November sales meeting. He would be awarding a fifty-dollar savings bond to the rep whose satchel best displayed the new Christmas merchandise.

I covered an old, woven picnic basket with a scrap of red velveteen and rummaged through my closet for anything else that might do the trick. I threw my childhood to the winds as I grabbed my Barbie doll from its pristine box and displayed its head atop a bottle of cologne. Mother paused at my bedroom door and told me one of those things they learn in "Mom School": "You better hold on to that doll, honey. She's liable to be worth something someday."

As it turned out, Mother was right. An original Barbie in mint condition, just like mine, recently brought more than five thousand dollars at auction. That's what I sacrificed for a fleeting moment of fame and a long-gone savings bond.

A lot of things have changed since 1967. Barbie has her own Web site now. But one thing hasn't changed. And that's my need for guidance lest, lured by the present, I forget the past, foolishly sacrificing my future.

O God, our help in ages past, be with me as I face the changes and challenges of today. —ROBERTA MESSNER

14 | T U E

Now there are diversities of gifts, but the same Spirit.
—I CORINTHIANS 12:4

I've been a writer for fifteen years. Lately I've added a new job: helping my five-year-old daughter form her first written words.

Faith has trouble with certain letters; she confuses *d* and *b*, *p* and *q*. And she writes right to left, Hebrew style. Her preschool teachers assure me it's a phase, a trait common among lefties. So I sit across from my southpaw daughter at the kitchen table and we draw letters together, her left hand mirroring the movements of my right.

"No, sweetie, the hump goes the other way."

"Like that?"

"There you go. Nice job!"

I teach writing in a formal way, too, as a college composition instructor. Once again, I watch younger renditions of myself struggle with the strange song of writing. They even look like I did twenty years ago, albeit with baseball caps turned backward. Sometimes I write in the margins of their essays, "There you go. Nice job!"

My friend Amy once told me, "I'd give anything to be a writer like you." I wasn't honored but floored: Amy can play "Amazing Grace" on the bagpipes so well that even atheists cry. What would I give for her talent? Why would she ever want to trade? What joy could she get out of *d* versus *b*, *p* versus *q*?

There are diversities of gifts, St. Paul says, "given to every man to profit withal" (I Corinthians 12:7). I am a somber soldier of my gift. Whatever talent I have seems neither an aptitude nor a burden, but part of who I am, as immutable as my height. Faith—my mirror image—wants to be a ballerina. "You go, girl!" I tell her. Who can tell where she'll land, *en pointe* or otherwise? Let her dance. One day she'll find where her talents lead. Maybe to college, sitting in a freshman comp section. Maybe to parenthood —make that *q*arenthoo*b*).

Whatever. The key is hearing the song, enjoying the letters of the lyric, dancing with whatever talent there is.

"There you go," I'll say to her. "Nice job!"

Lord, help me use the gifts I've been given for Your glory and my neighbor's good. —MARK COLLINS

15 | W E D | *. . .To be a joyful mother of children. . . .*
—PSALM 113:9

"Mom, the doctor says I have to get my tonsils out," Lindsay told me in a long-distance call from San Diego, California, to Boulder, Colorado. "Could you come and take care of me?"

Her request zoomed right to my heart, because Lindsay and I had been hitting some bumps in our relationship lately. *Growing pains,* I'd decided, as I kept trying to learn how to be the mom of an adult daughter.

"Of course, I'll come," I answered without hesitation. "When?"

We worked out the details, and a few weeks later, I flew to California to move into her small apartment and her life for a week. The doctor warned us that a tonsillectomy is painful for a young adult. "But you can't heal without some pain," he said. He was right. From the moment she came out of surgery, Lindsay needed lots of TLC. So I held ice packs to her swollen face, filled her prescriptions, made gelatin and bowls of mashed potatoes, cleaned her apartment, and simply sat by her bed to encourage her while she endured the pain.

"Thanks for coming, Mom," she told me one afternoon. "Sometimes a girl just needs her mother."

"Sometimes a mom just needs to be needed," I told her.

By the time I left a couple of days later, Lindsay was much stronger. And we both knew that something more than her throat had healed during that week.

Father, when relationships experience growing pains, show me how to be part of the healing process. —CAROL KUYKENDALL

READER'S ROOM

"My husband and I are one of countless couples who have experienced the challenges of infertility. As we prayed for guidance, the fork in the road pointed strongly toward pursuing adoption. In October 1997, we were chosen by a teenage birthmother whose baby was due in March 1998. Problems arose and the baby died. In January 1998, we were chosen by another birth-mother; she was also due in March 1998. On March 9 the baby died. This latest loss left us with many questions, but two things were still evident: First, the same God was on the throne during our times of disappointment as when we were anticipating joy. Secondly, God had never abandoned us before, and He wasn't likely to do so when we needed Him the very most. So, we dusted ourselves off, put down our load of self-pity and started again. Five months old now, Abbey is the joy of our lives. After all of the waiting and wondering, we now know that she is the little girl who was meant to be our daughter."

—*Sue Cassel, Auburn, Indiana*

16
T H u

Buy the truth, and sell it not. . . .
—PROVERBS 23:23

The morning couldn't have been busier when Mr. Bookman came into my office. "Brock, have you noticed that the market's down today?" I heard him say in his rapid-fire voice, which tends to get raspy and short when he's worried. And believe me, I know, because Mr. Bookman doesn't hesitate to drop by when the first hint of a troubled thought floats through his head.

"Now, Mr. Bookman," I answered, "you remember what we talked about when you came in last week. You don't lose money when the stock market falls unless you sell your stock. And there's really no need for you to sell unless you want to take a loss." Satisfied, Mr. Bookman stayed long enough for a cup of coffee. He smiled as he said good-bye.

As a financial consultant, I keep very close tabs on the stock market. While it's fascinating, it can be unnerving at times. From day to day, nobody on earth, no matter how wise or well-educated, can predict what the market is going to do. Even the nation's top analysts miss the mark on a regular basis. But still, I felt comfortable reassuring Mr. Bookman when he fretted about this down-day because statistics show that history is on his side: Over the past seventy-five years, the market's been up a lot more than it's been down.

Which reminded me that when I'm down in life, when I'm ready to sell out, throw in the towel and simply give up, I can count on God's promise that, in the final analysis, all things work together for good. That's a truth I'll never consider selling.

Father, I hold tight to Your truth and trust You to work in my life.
—BROCK KIDD

17

F
R
I

He held fast to the Lord; he did not depart from following him. . . . —II KINGS 18:6 (RSV)

"So, what do you think?"

Andrew and I were on a bus coming home from an open house at a public school here in New York City. Elizabeth is now four, and we are assessing options for kindergarten. We're assuming we will homeschool, but prudence dictates that we evaluate all the choices available to us before making a final decision.

"Academically, it's great." This is a big concern, for Elizabeth is a precocious learner. She is a strong reader, and most kindergarten programs aren't equipped to handle students like her. "I liked the principal, and there were lots of books in the classrooms. Foreign languages, computer lab, art—they have good resources."

We talked for a while about what we did and didn't like. After a while, Andrew said, "I think we should apply. We have nothing to lose."

Somehow I wasn't sure if that was true. It's an elite school, and if Elizabeth gets in, we might want to send her without considering other factors. "Okay, but on one condition," I replied, "We have to make a commitment to pray about it together, or fast, or do something to ask for guidance. What's this school's biggest advantage?"

"The academics—and we both value academics so highly."

"Yes. So we can be easily persuaded by that alone."

Andrew paused. "You're right."

We sat in silence for a few minutes, thinking. Our decision must be based on what is best for Elizabeth intellectually *and* spiritually. For learning will be useless if it doesn't help her use her God-given gifts in His service.

Heavenly Father, remind me that wise decisions are always guided by what will bring us closer to You.   —JULIA ATTAWAY

18

S
A
T

Justice—do you rulers know the meaning of the word?
Do you judge the people fairly? —PSALM 58:1 (NLT)

As Thanksgiving approached, I was having more misgivings than thanksgivings when it came to our boys. One had a girlfriend I didn't think suited him, another had chosen a college I wasn't sure would be best for him, and the third one's hairstyle seemed to indicate rebellion.

I was wondering how to sort all of this out when Joy asked me to help her transplant a miniature maple tree. We accomplished the task, but a week later all the leaves fell off, and the tree appeared to have died. Alarmed, Joy called the nursery and asked what she could do. "It's probably not dead," the gardener told her. "It's just lost its leaves because of replanting. Go out and scrape beneath the surface of the bark with your fingernail and see if the branches are still green." Sure enough, the branches were bright green beneath the surface, full of life ready to burst out next spring.

I wondered whether things worked that way with sons, too. So while the boys were home, I determined to ignore outside appearances and scratch beneath the surface to see what was there. This led to a significant reduction in nagging and a great increase in listening. It was heartening to learn that the girlfriend relationship was more mature than mine had ever been at that age. The struggle with college was really about direction in life, so talking about that was more satisfying than arguing about academic standing and tuition costs. Most striking was the neatly groomed hair that appeared on the third day of our holiday together. "C'mon Dad, I was just trying to get a rise out of you. I can't believe it didn't work."

Sure wish I'd discovered this gardener's method of parenting sooner.

Lord, help me to remember to keep looking for the real person under the bark.
—ERIC FELLMAN

19 | S U N

Then opened he their understanding, that they might understand the scriptures. —LUKE 24:45

There weren't many books in the house where I grew up. There were sets of Charles Dickens and Mark Twain, a medical encyclopedia, a few popular novels from the 1940s, and a copy of *The Pilgrim's Progress*. And there was Great-Grandpa Attaway's Bible. The leather was wearing off the front and back covers, the binding was loose, and the gilded J. B. ATTAWAY on the front cover was faded. But it was Dad's most prized possession.

When I was old enough to read, my parents gave me a big book of Bible stories, full of colorful illustrations of Joseph's coat, David slaying Goliath and Jesus preaching His Sermon on the Mount. And whenever I asked, Dad would let me look through Great-Grandpa's Bible. But the columns of dark type with their *thees* and *thous* seemed mysterious and forbidding.

Then, a few years later, my mother took me to see the newly released film *The Ten Commandments*. I was so excited that as soon as I got home I asked Dad to let me look at the Bible. With a dictionary beside me, I made my way slowly through the first few chapters of the Book of Exodus. Now the big picture book was no longer enough; I wanted to know the whole story, *thees* and *thous* included.

I'd like to say that my childhood encounter with the Scriptures changed my life, but it didn't—at least not then. What it did do was give me a love for the stories in that battered old book, and for the beautiful language in which King James's translators retold them. And in His own good time, the Spirit gave me eyes to read those stories not just as exciting tales, but as the answers to my heart's deepest questions.

Now our house is full of books, and we have six or seven different translations of the Scriptures. But Great-Grandpa's Bible still has the place of honor in our home, and in my heart.

Lord, on this National Bible Sunday, open my eyes to see You in Your Word. —ANDREW ATTAWAY

20 | M O N

"You will see neither wind nor rain, yet this valley will be filled with water, and you, your cattle and your other animals will drink." —II KINGS 3:17 (NIV)

You might think it's depressing to listen to prayer requests in a conference room, as we do every Monday at Guideposts. In just this one morning, I heard from a prisoner who asked us to remember the children he hadn't seen in years, we prayed for a four-year-old with an inoperable brain tumor, and I read a letter from a middle-aged man startled to learn that his wife was asking for a divorce after thirty years of marriage. Closing my eyes, I listened to my colleagues read heartrending requests tinged with loneliness and despair. Cancer, obesity, financial distress, substance abuse. How could forty-five minutes of hearing such problems be inspiring?

This morning I think I heard the answer in a letter from a would-be scholar in Addis Ababa, Ethiopia. He desperately needs money to attend the university there—one hundred dollars in U.S. currency. He's prayed for it, and he asks us to pray for it. In fact, he has already enrolled in the school, sure that his prayers will be answered. He quotes the biblical passage above in support of his faith and adds, "Thus I am planning to start or to be registered in the university next September." What an extraordinary faith!

It's glimpses of such faith that make our Monday morning prayer fellowship inspiring to me. My own fragile faith is supported; my own problems fade into the background. I like the way the Ethiopian man put it as he signed his name: "Yours in His grip." Over and over again, when people are in the midst of the most dispiriting situations, when I hear of my own colleagues' concerns and worries, I'm glad to be reminded that we are all in God's grip.

Keep me, God, in Your grip.   —RICK HAMLIN

Editor's note: Today is Guideposts Family Day of Prayer. Please join us as we come before the Lord for all the needs of our Guideposts family.

21 | TUE
And I will show you a still more excellent way.
—I CORINTHIANS 12:31 (RSV)

I didn't find motherhood to be exactly what I'd expected. It was much more difficult. One rainy, gloomy day, when my twin toddler sons seemed to be destroying everything in their path and depression stalked me without mercy, I gathered up my nerve and phoned a counselor.

I liked her at once—she had four children of her own. After a few visits, she asked me to bring my husband Jerry along for one of the sessions. He came, all smiles, as happy and relaxed as if we were going to a football game. Right away, he and the counselor were talking and laughing while I sat stiffly in my chair watching the rain hit the window.

When I went to our next meeting, she asked me a question. "Do you remember when you two left my office last week and encountered the low tree branch that hung way down over the sidewalk?" I nodded. "Well, what I saw from my office was a clear picture of your approach to life. Jerry simply stepped down from the sidewalk and circumvented the obstacle easily and quickly. No big deal. You plowed right through the wet limb. You got your hair caught in it and actually had to do battle with it. Jerry rescued you. Even so, you got pretty wet."

Her face showed genuine compassion; only her eyes held a slight hint of restrained laughter. She looked at me as if to say, *You are just plain stubborn, Marion. Always wanting your way. Sometimes it's okay to do things an easier way.*

Back home that afternoon, I discovered that supper didn't *have* to be at six on the dot. Jon and Jeremy didn't *have* to wear matching clothes all the time. I didn't *have* to pick up toys twenty times a day; life went on if I only did it twice. I could learn to focus on the beauty of my children rather than the inevitable crumbs on the floor.

Father, show me Your more excellent ways and help me to yield to them.   —MARION BOND WEST

A PLACE OF MY OWN

22 | W E D | *Let us come before his presence with thanksgiving, and make a joyful noise unto him with psalms.*
—PSALM 95:2

For twenty-five years I've lived in this apartment in the middle of New York City, three rooms, second floor, home. Before I took the quarters, I remember taking my dog Clay to look it over, and the nearness of Central Park clinched it for him. For me, there was the convenience of bus and subway right outside. I didn't know it at the time, but I was delighted—and the kids I knew were even more so—when the night before Thanksgiving the street below my windows was chockablock with balloons for the Macy's parade.

Ah, Thanksgiving eve. It seems the best of times to me. It is cool to cold, and there is something in the air, a lilt, which the children sense, and their parents recognize all over again. It's a time for true pleasure, no burdens of gift-giving, no work tomorrow, and the crowds that gather beneath my windows are in a happy mood. No wonder that my godchildren and their friends have come again and again. Little wonder that *their* children come now.

"Uncle Van, here are the turkey pies, as promised," says David.

"Pizzas from me," says Valerie. And that is just the beginning of food and drink at what has come to be the "Varner Open House." For hours the door opens and closes with friends arriving or leaving or coming back to the warmth. For hours we gape and gasp as Barney takes shape, or Kermit the Frog, or some creature of Dr. Seuss. Finally the kids are up past their bedtime, and their parents, too, and gradually they drift away, until I'm alone. I look down at the quiet, unformed parade, waiting for sunrise when pandemonium will reign again.

"Thanks," I say out loud, "thanks for Thanksgiving."

Lord, this is only one of the things I am thankful for.

—VAN VARNER

23 | T H U

You will be enriched in every way for great generosity, which through us will produce thanksgiving to God.
—II CORINTHIANS 9:11 (RSV)

Holiday dinners are festive events at the nursing home where my father lives. Family members come from miles around to share a special meal with their loved ones, and the dining room is filled with happy conversations. But not this Thanksgiving. The flu season had been especially severe, and many relatives who ordinarily would have visited were sick at home. Some of the residents had flu symptoms, too, and they were served in their rooms.

In the dining room there were only twelve of us, some residents, some family, and we gathered at one big table so we wouldn't feel lonely. Steve Moyer, the chef, had prepared a wonderful turkey dinner and helped to serve it because some of his staff were out with the flu. He did his best to cheer us up and we tried to smile, but it was a sad occasion. Most of us were remembering other Thanksgivings in happier times, when our loved ones were well and at home with us. We were finding it hard to give thanks to God.

Then we heard music coming from the far end of the room. A woman was sitting at the piano, playing "How Great Thou Art," and with each note our hearts and spirits began to lift. The piano was in need of tuning, but the woman played so beautifully that it didn't matter. We gathered around the piano to sing hymns of praise and thanksgiving.

The woman was a retired music teacher named Dorothy Goda, who lived up the street from the nursing home. She had heard that the flu epidemic was keeping relatives away, and she wondered how she might cheer up the residents. "I thought perhaps some music would help," she told us.

It certainly did. As we enjoyed the gift of Dorothy's music, we learned that a good way for us to thank God for our blessings is to share them with others, as she had done with us. And some of those others may be just down the street.

I thank You, Lord, for Your constant love, Your greatest gift. Amen.
—PHYLLIS HOBE

24 | F R I

"Do not worry about your life. . . ."
—MATTHEW 6:25 (NIV)

After we moved to rural North Carolina, my toddler son Chase and I spent many wonderful days in our trailer reading and coloring. As Thanksgiving approached, we danced outside, spinning and falling into piles of multicolored leaves. In the afternoons we picked up my eleven-year-old daughter Lanea at the school bus stop. Chase and I questioned her about her day and talked about our preparations for the coming holiday. We spent our evenings together talking, reading, singing and praying—learning to be grateful for simple things.

Our family grew stronger every day. When Thanksgiving arrived, our budget was tight, and turkey and the trimmings were out of the question. So we made our meal of beans, rice and cheese, and feasted on our love for one another and the richness we found in one another's company. We learned that happiness isn't a matter of a big house, fine clothing or lots of possessions. Abiding joy is a matter of our relationships—with God and with one another. That Thanksgiving in our trailer in the woods has become the model for all our holidays since.

Lord, thank You for the joy we have today and for Your promise of provision for tomorrow.
—SHARON FOSTER

25
S
A
T

Jesus was troubled in spirit. . . . —JOHN 13:21 (NIV)

A few years ago, I picked up a curious old metal frame at the thrift store. It was a bit rusty and full of cobwebs, but with a touch of fresh gold paint, it made an interesting piece. I was about to discard the picture that had come in it when, impulsively, I put it back under the newly cleaned glass. It was a picture of Christ seated at a table, His hands folded on the tablecloth. Something about the expression on His face intrigued me. There was none of the peaceful, otherworldly serenity I had seen in other portraits of Jesus. In this picture, His brow was furrowed, His mouth drawn into a taut line, and His eyes looked directly out toward the viewer. I named the picture *The Troubled Christ* and propped it up on my desk.

The next day when I sat down in my chair opposite the picture, I had an odd sensation as I peered across the desktop. It felt like I was seated at the table opposite Him. He looked as if He had something very serious He wanted to discuss with me. I could almost imagine Him saying, "I'm worried about you. You're letting your priorities get mixed up. You're hanging on to some old sins we need to deal with." As I sat uncomfortably looking at the picture, I decided on a new name for it: *The Troubling Christ.*

I looked at the peaceful pictures of Christ that decorated my office, and then looked back at the paper picture I hadn't meant to keep. It was the one I needed most. It's still on my desk today, troubling me when I need to be troubled.

Lord, help me meditate deeply on what might be troubling You about the way I'm living my life.
—KAREN BARBER

26
S
U
N

"My door was always open to the traveler. . . ."
—JOB 31:32 (NIV)

I grew up in a small town in Michigan's Upper Peninsula, part of a large family—six kids—with cousins and grandparents nearby. We were far from any city, but our parents felt it was important to make us aware of a bigger world out there, and one of the ways they did that was by inviting guests. Anybody who came through town was fair game, but visiting preachers and speakers at church were always invited to our home, and missionaries from exotic places were special favorites.

One Sunday morning, my dad uncharacteristically took off in his pickup truck as the rest of the family walked across the street to church. He had read in the county newspaper about a young couple who were moving to their new ranch in Oregon and would be traveling through our area—on horseback! Somehow he figured out their route and drove around until he found them. When we arrived home, the visitors and Dad were getting acquainted, and the horses were happily grazing on the lawn. There was always plenty of pot roast, so we mashed a few more potatoes and set the table while our guests enjoyed the luxury of hot showers.

Over the years I've heard friends remark that my parents' hospitality influenced their lives in significant ways. I have no idea what kind of influence our family may have had on that young couple, but it was certainly fun for us to hear of their adventures and imagine the journey ahead of them. And I know from years of experience that bringing the world to my doorstep can be a mutually beneficial arrangement.

Help me, Lord Jesus, to open up to others, and to be generous with my life.
                                                   —MARY JANE CLARK

27 M O N *Let us therefore come boldly unto the throne of grace, that we may obtain mercy, and find grace to help in time of need.* —HEBREWS 4:16

When my daughter Emily was four years old, I took her to a large department store. Just inside the front door was a scale, the kind you stand on, drop a penny in the slot and a little card scoots out with your weight printed on it. Emily was fascinated with the scale and asked me to weigh her on it. She hopped up on the platform, I dropped in a coin, and Emily grabbed the card as it popped out.

Emily was happily clutching the card as we headed down the aisle to attend to the shopping. I was studying the list I'd made and looking at the merchandise on display, assuming that Emily was following me. I was in the middle of the store when I realized she was nowhere in sight. Anxiety turned to panic as I dashed up and down the aisles looking for her. Two clerks joined in the search, but I didn't find Emily until I headed toward the front of the store. There she sat on the platform of the scale. She saw me and ran to hug me around the knees.

"I couldn't find you," she said, "and I got scared. Then I remembered the door we came in. I knew you wouldn't go home without me. You love me, and you'd never leave me alone."

Lord, when I've strayed and can't find my way, let me remember where I can always meet You—on my knees.   —DRUE DUKE

---

28 | T U E   *And I saw a new heaven and a new earth. . . .*
                                      —REVELATION 21:1

A lot of wonderful changes have happened over the course of the twentieth century. Here are a few of them, in no particular order.

- *Light.* We've gone from most of us finding our way with candles and gas lamps to the miracle of electricity almost everywhere.
- *Heat.* We've gone from chopping wood and carrying cobs or coal to heat the stoves or furnace in a house (or even Mother's flatirons) to turning a dial on the wall to control the temperature.
- *Refrigeration.* We've gone from ice boxes and long hot hours of canning food to electric refrigerators and frozen foods.
- *Laundry.* We've gone from scrubbing clothes on a washboard or in a hand-driven wooden machine to electric washer-dryers.
- *Writing.* We've gone from pencils, pen and ink to typewriters, computers, fax machines and instant e-mail around the world.
- *Transportation.* We've gone from railroads, the horse and buggy or a wobbly Tin Lizzie to fast automobiles and airplanes—and even rockets to outer space!

I'm glad I've been on planet Earth long enough to witness and profit by these improvements. If only they made people happier, more decent and honest, more loving and kind. But, alas, technology has failed to solve our problems. Emotionally, we are still as primitive and susceptible to pain and evil as all the generations of people in all the centuries before us.

No better, no worse. As for the future: Humans are tough, inventive creatures. Someday our grandchildren's children will be asking, "You mean there was really a time when you had to depend on *computers* and *airplanes* and had never been to Mars?"

Father, the wonders of this present time can't compare with what You have in store for us. Help me to face the future with hope and good cheer. —MARJORIE HOLMES

29

W
E
D

Submit yourselves therefore to God. . . .
—JAMES 4:7

I haven't missed a day of work in three years . . . until today. I'm laid up in my apartment fighting off a fever. Nothing serious, but my co-workers insisted I stay home. I can't blame them for not wanting to catch what I have.

Usually, when I feel something coming on, I work a little harder or push myself a little further, as if I could outrun it. I get this from my mother, who thought the best thing to do if you were getting sick was to scrub the kitchen floor or shovel snow off the driveway. Today we'd call it denial, no doubt. Personally, I see nothing wrong with a healthy dose of denial occasionally. There is, after all, a fine line between denial and positive thinking.

This time, though, there is no denying it. I am sick. Chills, fever, body aches. My wife Julee's at rehearsal all day, but she rented me a stack of videos, got the daily papers and put some soup on the stove. She went out the door admonishing me, "Now relax and let yourself get better."

Relax? How can I relax if I just sit here and do nothing? I have responsibilities at work. I'm missing a meeting. I was supposed to call so-and-so first thing this morning. Everyone is counting on me—

Outside I hear the scrape of metal on pavement. My super Ricardo is clearing some light overnight snow from the sidewalk. A couple of taxi horns beep impatiently. A dog leashed to a parking meter woofs at a policeman writing a ticket. Overhead a jet plane follows the Hudson River north on its flight pattern into LaGuardia.

Funny how the world seems to be getting along without me. Is everyone really counting on me so heavily? Or do I mistake self-centeredness for responsibility, ego for conscience?

I pass the rest of the day reading and watching movies and . . . *relaxing*. I have discovered that the biggest part of getting better is letting go and being sick.

What a challenge it is, Lord, for me to let You take over.

—EDWARD GRINNAN

30 | T H U

Be brave, stouthearted and courageous. . . .

—PSALM 27:14 (TLB)

I've lost my "Undaunted" button and I miss it dreadfully. For years it swung from the tip of the curtain on the window beside our bed: a bulldog image of Winston Churchill, scowling and holding his fingers in the V for Victory sign, with the war-time slogan, "Undaunted!" Somehow it helped get me up each morning and face the challenge of each new day.

For me, Churchill is a constant source of encouragement. He was well into his eighties when a young schoolboy asked him, "Sir, what is the greatest thing you have done in your life?" The great man could have opened up a portfolio of accomplishments: the blood, sweat and tears of the Battle of Britain; his oratory, wit and literary genius. But without hesitation, Churchill said the greatest thing he had done in his life was to survive, because to survive is to begin again. We think of all the accolades of his life; we forget the times he stood up to speak in Parliament and was heckled and booed down, and the times he was voted *out* of office. Undaunted, he began again and again.

Even now, in what I call the third trimester of my life, I continue to face many new beginnings. One of the most challenging has been my husband's retirement. I love a symphony of silence, where thought has the uninterrupted freedom to strum its own tune; now I have suddenly found an intrusive presence in my quiet. We've had to talk things through and adjust our routines to make this new beginning work. He goes lawn bowling three times a week; he's sensitive to my need for creative space and doesn't take offense when I say, "It's not that I don't want to be with you, but I don't want to be with you right now!"

As we come into the excitement of the turn of a century, for whatever new beginning may be around the corner, I'm holding on to Churchill's slogan, "Undaunted!" (Now if only I could find that war-time button!)

Give me courage for each new day, Lord, so that I may bravely face whatever challenges are before me.   —FAY ANGUS

My Renewal Journal

1 _____

2 _____

3 _____

4 _____

5 _____

6 _____

7 _____

8 _____

9 _____

10 _____

11 _____

12 _____

13 _____

14 _____

15 _____

16 _____

17 _____

18 _____

19 _____

20 _____

21 _____

22 _____

23 _____

24 _____

25 _____

26 _____

27 _____

28 _____

29 _____

30 _____

DECEMBER

Behold, the tabernacle of God is with men, and he will dwell with them, and they shall be his people, and God himself shall be with them, and be their God.

—REVELATION 21:3

S	M	T	W	T	F	S
					1	2
3	4	5	6	7	8	9
10	11	12	13	14	15	16
17	18	19	20	21	22	23
24	25	26	27	28	29	30
31						

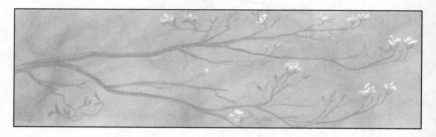

ALL THINGS NEW

1 F **Retaining Wonder**
R *And the evening and the morning were the first day.*
I   —GENESIS 1:5

My grandmother was a grown woman before she saw her first automobile. That seemed remarkable to me as a child, but what seems more so to me now is that in the six decades that followed that first astonished encounter, she never got over the marvel of the internal combustion engine. "So quiet!" she would exclaim when she was in her eighties. "So fast! Just a little pressure on the pedal and off we go!"

My father kept a sense of wonder, too. For him it was oranges. I would come into the kitchen and see him holding one, unopened, in his hand. He would stroke the textured skin, sniff the tangy rind: "Marvelous!"

At Christmastime, as the pile of presents grew beneath our tree, he liked to tell about the year when he was nine and drew from his stocking his sole gift—a single orange. "It was the first one I ever had, and I've never forgotten the thrill." By the time I myself was nine, Daddy was buying oranges by the bagful; there was always a bowl of them on the kitchen table. Yet to him they remained an ever-new delight.

As I remember Grandmother and Daddy, I reflect that with everything that touches our lives, there had to be a very first time. Our first pair of shoes. Our first snowfall. The first time we read a book all by ourselves. What if the thrill of first discovery stayed with us? What if we added a new one each day? What if every day we drew a never-before-tasted orange from the toe of our Christmas stocking?

Father of first-things, thank You for Your presence through this first year of a new millennium. Give me grace in the years ahead always to see Your world with newly opened eyes. —ELIZABETH SHERRILL

A CHRISTMAS FOR THE HEART

It's time to start getting ready for Christmas! No matter how many times we've heard the carols, no matter how many presents we've wrapped or cards we've signed, there's no exhausting the meaning and the message of this most joyous season. And although holiday preparations can sometimes get us down, Marilyn Morgan Helleberg has the remedy: the old but ever-new magic of "A Christmas for the Heart." She'll help you prepare to welcome the Christ Child in a new birth of faith and love. —THE EDITORS

2 | S A T

For unto us a child is born. . . . —ISAIAH 9:6

Tomorrow is the first Sunday of Advent, and as I sit here pondering the miraculous event of Jesus' birth two thousand years ago, an image flashes across my mind. It's a picture of me as a small girl (maybe three or four) with Shirley Temple curls, a red velvet dress, long white stockings and black patent-leather shoes. The strains of "Silent Night" and the scent of fresh pine fill the candlelit church. And there, in the center of the sanctuary platform, is a live manger scene! Mary in her hooded blue gown and Joseph with his graying beard are bending over a crib of straw. And, oh—I can still feel the wonder of it!— Baby Jesus, His little arms and legs flailing, is cooing happily in His manger as a live lamb looks on. In my child's heart, I am truly *present* at the scene of Jesus' birth!

Where has that childlike sense of Christmas wonder gone? Would it be possible to recover it, even at my age? At various times in my life, I've turned to the Christmas story for insight and guidance. Could I find Christ's living presence there today?

I open my Bible to Isaiah 9:6. Suddenly, I hear something in those familiar words I've never heard before. When Isaiah prophesied the birth of the Prince of Peace, he said, "Unto us a child *is* born." Could it be that Isaiah speaks of an event that is both historical and also eternal and ongoing? Though Jesus was born two thousand years ago, Isaiah suggests to me that His birth is also an event that occurs in the life of each one of us.

As we complete the first year of this new century, I invite you to look with me at some familiar scenes from the Christmas story: Gabriel's announcement to Mary; the angel's reassurance to Joseph; the gifts of the wise men; the birth of Jesus; and the angels' appearance to the shepherds. Let us seek, in each of these centuries-old events, that dimension of timelessness that can reawaken our childlike sense of wonder.

Blessed Jesus, the time draws near to celebrate Your birth in a new century. Open my heart that I may cradle You in newness deep within my soul.
—MARILYN MORGAN HELLEBERG

3 | SUN A CHRISTMAS FOR THE HEART
First Sunday in Advent
And Mary said . . . be it unto me according to thy word. . . . —LUKE 1:38

It was a sleepless night in 1955, and I lay awake with a deep and insistent longing for a child. Married just over a year, we were living in a tiny attic apartment we could barely afford. We'd decided to wait until we had some financial security before starting our family. Yet this longing felt insatiable. Unable to sleep, I got up, went to my prayer chair, opened my Bible to Luke 1 and reread the familiar story of Gabriel's announcement to Mary.

I pictured a small, open-windowed hut in Nazareth filled with a bright, unearthly light, and I overheard Mary's response to the archangel: "How shall this be?" I felt her doubt in my bones because I, too, was convinced of the impossibility of having a child at this time. Gabriel spoke again. "The Holy Ghost shall come upon thee, and the power of the Highest shall overshadow thee. . . . For with God nothing shall be impossible." A puzzled look stole over the smooth young face. A breathless silence hung in the air. Then Mary lowered her head and, with a serene smile, responded: "Be it unto me according to thy word." To my own amazement and totally beyond reason, I found myself answering with her. *Be it unto me according to Thy word.*

On Christmas Eve, as we gathered with our extended family to open gifts, I was overjoyed to receive a layette, a dozen diapers and a rattle, in anticipation of our first child who was due to be born six months later. Those gifts were precious, but I knew in my heart that the dearest gift was the one I held within me.

My child-bearing years are long past, but I still carry a Holy Child within me. It is the Christ Child. I can sense His presence there whenever I touch my heart and whisper His name.

O Child of Light, pierce the dark within that I may know Your presence. Amen. —MARILYN MORGAN HELLEBERG

4 | M O N

Walk circumspectly, not as fools, but as wise, Redeeming the time. . . . —EPHESIANS 5:15-16

Many years ago, as a rookie teacher with a young family, I was feeling pulled in every direction and finding it hard to get things done. So when a mentor of mine, Elton Trueblood, professor of philosophy of religion at Earlham College, and I were together for a meal I asked him, "With your heavy teaching load, how do you find time for all the other important things in life?"

He smiled, reached inside his coat pocket for his date book, held it up and said, "The secret is in keeping my calendar full." I thought mine was already too full. When he sensed that I hadn't gotten his point, he continued, "A long time ago I discovered that other people would decide how I used my time unless I decided to keep my appointment book full with the things that were important to me."

Ever since that day, I've tried to use what he taught me. I sit down and plan the things I *want* to do, whether it's getting together with friends, attending the wedding of a relative, camping with my daughter, driving to see my mother, helping my wife Barbara with a project, working on a poem or taking a class. And as I write it into my date book, I think of Dr. Trueblood, who first taught me how productive a full calendar can be, especially if you plan it yourself.

Father, give me wisdom in deciding the things to which I give my time and energy. —KENNETH CHAFIN

5

T
U
E

Finally . . . whatever is pure, whatever is lovely, whatever is admirable. . .think about such things.
—PHILIPPIANS 4:8 (NIV)

After the sea itself, the things I loved best about Topsail Island, North Carolina, were the live-oak and sea-pine groves on the intracoastal side of the narrow island. Gnarled and windswept, they were a canopy of tangled, deep, cicada-filled green.

But in September 1996, Hurricane Fran devastated Topsail. Tornadoes blew homes away, and tidal surge inundated the entire island. Not a house was left untouched. And the saltwater killed all the groves.

When my husband Bill and I visited the island that December, the beach road was still filled with backhoes scooping up sand and debris. Yet when we returned the following fall, to our delight, every house had a new roof and most were rebuilt. The smell of fresh pinewood decking mingled with the salty air. But the groves remained split open, gray, ugly with bits of pink insulation and junk caught in their bare branches—a reminder of the death a hurricane can deal. Although here and there a green shoot poked up, the messy dead masses depressed me.

During my last morning walk on the beach, an older woman stopped to chat. We talked about Fran and the devastation and the remarkable recovery in one year. "Oh, yes!" she smiled. "We thought it would be years, and here, in only one, the island is almost fully restored. And the groves. I was so worried. And then spring came, and here and there the green sprouted up! I was so happy!"

Where I had seen only the dead gray, she had instead focused on the green, the living hope of restoration and renewal.

Lord, enable me to focus on the good, the pure, the hopeful. And please, in Your perfect time, make new the groves of sea pine and live oak on Topsail Island. —ROBERTA ROGERS

6

W
E
D

Let the wise listen and add to their learning, and let the discerning get guidance. —PROVERBS 1:5 (NIV)

When I was helping Mrs. Menina, a woman from Uzbekistan in the former Soviet Union, get ready for her citizenship test, I was often reminded of how much I didn't know about our country. I found myself boning up on such topics as the length of a senator's term (six years) and the vice presidents under Abraham Lincoln (Hannibal Hamlin and Andrew Johnson), so I wouldn't look foolish when I quizzed her.

When I gave this tiny woman—almost seventy years old and in the United States for only a few years—a practice test, the results were humbling. She got one hundred percent, while I got only ninety-four! I was so embarrassed that I almost stopped showing up on Wednesday nights. "You don't need me anymore," I told her. "You have outshone your teacher."

She shook her head. "Now I must teach *you*."

Frankly, I was puzzled. What could this lady from Tashkent teach me?

Russian.

"We will start with the alphabet. And I will make you *piroshki* [meat turnovers], and *golubtsi* [stuffed cabbage]. You will come back next Wednesday, and I will teach you."

So I stayed. And stayed. Two years later, I am still going to her house on Wednesday nights. And while she is far better at English than I am at Russian, I learned that I can learn from everyone who crosses my path in life. And I also have learned to make a pretty decent *piroshki.*

God, everyone You created has something of value to teach me. Today, let me learn from everyone I meet.
                                                                —LINDA NEUKRUG

7 | T
  | H   *They have more than heart could wish.*
  | U   —PSALM 73:7

It suddenly occurred to me that I am not going to live long enough to see all my dreams come true in this life. Oddly enough, it doesn't bother me. I've already had more than my share of life's sweets, and I take pleasure in seeing others accomplish what I cannot.

I always wanted to have a fix-it shop. My brother Tom in Kalamazoo, Michigan, fixes power tools for surgeons. I enjoy hearing about his work.

"I would love to make a commercial," I say to myself, every time I see a humorous one on TV. My brother Mark in Tampa, Florida, makes commercials for a living.

I love to work with wood, but have no time for it. My brother Bob in Lowell, Indiana, designs and builds fine furniture, and has a waiting list of orders.

My sister Linda Joy is the single, free spirit that appeals to my restless bones and gypsy heart.

And my most persistent dream is to live on a small farm, like the one on which my sister Gloria lives near South Bend, Indiana.

Perhaps my daughters will write the great American novel that I won't, and maybe my grandchildren will travel to Australia, where I would like to go.

Increasingly, I find more joy in helping others reach their dreams than I do in having my own dreams come true. When one of my students says, "I would like to become a teacher," something comes alive in me, because I train teachers for a living. My dream is to fulfill his dream.

I have a friend who told me once that "some people are good at saying prayers. Others are good at answering prayers." It's the same with dreams, I think.

All of us will leave this earth with an unfinished canvas, but no matter. If I can contribute a few strokes of the brush to the masterpiece, then my life has been worthwhile.

Lord, You scattered the joys of life among us. Together we can make our way to heaven, where all our dreams will come to pass.

—DANIEL SCHANTZ

8

F
R
I

For he will command his angels concerning you to guard you in all your ways. —PSALM 91:11 (NIV)

Like any mother, I had always worried about my daughter's safety. But after Amy Jo's divorce, I seemed to worry even more. How vulnerable she seemed—especially when she elected to take a class that meant she would have a late train ride home from Chicago two nights a week. I was especially worried about her getting safely to the train station. Her class was held in an area many blocks from the station, and I shivered to think of my petite, blond girl walking alone on the dark city streets.

I was driving home from Bible school on one of Amy Jo's class nights, trying not to think about all the things that could happen, when I seemed to hear a voice commanding: *Pray for a guardian angel!* I knew it was God encouraging me to trust Him, so I did. "Please, God, send a guardian angel to walk to the train station with Amy Jo tonight." I felt a deep peace as I turned into my driveway.

Next morning, I couldn't wait to talk to Amy Jo. "Any trouble getting to the train station?" were the first words out of my mouth when she came downstairs for breakfast.

She broke into a wide smile. "Nope! I had a guardian angel!" Amy Jo went on to describe how, on impulse, she'd paused at the door of the classroom and asked if anyone might be planning to catch a train.

"Yo, that would be me!" one of the biggest men in the class said. And he walked with Amy Jo all the way to the door of her train.

Thank You, Father, for divine protection in all its varied forms. Help me to trust my children to Your care whether they're newborn or full-grown.
                                                    —MARY LOU CARNEY

9

S
A   *Give therefore thy servant an understanding*
T   *heart. . . .*   —I KINGS 3:9

My wife's voice was soft, but her words were firm. "Oscar, don't be so exacting. Learn to accept and appreciate what people do. You were remembered. What more do you want?"

Ruby was responding to my annual complaints about the Christmas cards we receive. "Why don't they include their return address? It's only once a year, so why don't they say something personal? They can't mean the same brief greeting for everybody!"

What I was trying to say in my clumsy way was this: The Christmas season is short, and so is the life of a Christmas card. So why not be sure our Christmas greetings communicate? Why not use our cards as an opportunity to encourage and renew?

"All right, Oscar," Ruby said. "Why don't you try to help instead of complain? How about sharing your suggestions?"

Ruby was right, so here they are:

• Include a personal message with each card, no more than ten words.
• Share a joyful experience. Say, "Remember the time—"

- Thank each person for some small act of kindness they have forgotten they did. They will be delighted!
- Be sincere and let your thoughts come from the heart.

Shortly after our discussion, I attended a talk by Rabbi Yosef Wosk. "Sharing," he said, "is like lighting a candle. Nothing is lost even though one small candle lights a thousand others."

Dear Lord, help me to use my Christmas cards to light candles of love in my loved ones' hearts. —OSCAR GREENE

10

S
u
N

A CHRISTMAS FOR THE HEART
Second Sunday in Advent

The angel of the Lord appeared unto him [Joseph] in a dream. . . . —MATTHEW 1:20

It was a December night in 1979, and the rest of the family was asleep. I was sitting alone in the living room by the light of the Christmas tree, wrestling with a life-changing decision. Should I continue teaching college English, writing only in moments stolen from my too-busy schedule? Or should I pay attention to this strong inner leading to give up my teaching position so I could write full-time? I was torn because I truly enjoyed teaching, and we'd come to count on my income. Yet I had this heart-level sense of being called to write a book on Christian meditation. Again, I turned to the Christmas story to seek an answer to my dilemma.

This time I visited a carpenter in Nazareth who had just learned that his betrothed was expecting a child. I found Joseph kneeling by his rough-hewn workbench. And I overheard his prayer: "Father, should I send Mary someplace where she can have the baby privately? It would save her—and me—from being disgraced. Yet she tells me this child is Yours! Forgive me, Father, but that's a hard thing for me to believe. Please, Lord, I need Your guidance." I stood in silence as Joseph waited in prayer. Finally, with a long sigh he wiped his damp forehead and went to bed without a clear answer.

I blinked my eyes, and it was morning now. The sun was streaming through the window above the mat where Joseph lay sleeping. He rubbed his eyes, opened them and rose again to his knees. "Thank You, Father, for sending Your angel into my dream. Finally, I can *trust* that the Child in Mary's womb truly is conceived of the Holy Ghost. I will take my beloved Mary for my wife. Thank You, Father! Amen."

Joseph, man of great faith, you've shown me that receiving guidance is a matter of *trusting inner leadings.* God spoke to you in dreams. He sometimes speaks to me that way, too. Or else His guidance comes through something I read in the Scriptures, or in a chance remark by a friend. But it only happens when I ask.

I followed Joseph's lead that December night, gave my decision to God and went to bed. And, yes, a dream confirmed my heart's leadings. I have never regretted my decision to become a full-time writer.

Shine on my path, Light of God, as I walk forward in this new century.
—MARILYN MORGAN HELLEBERG

---

11 | M
O | *"For I, the Lord, am your healer."*
N | —EXODUS 15:26 (NAS)

When our beloved Red Dog was hit by a car, the bone in her right rear leg was shattered. She required surgery and confinement for three months. The most difficult part of Red Dog's recovery was her adjustment to the four steel pins that protruded from the six-inch steel bar the vet had placed inside her leg. To prevent her from pulling the pins out with her teeth, she had to wear an awkward but effective device called an E collar, a funnel-shaped plastic contraption that fitted around her neck.

Red Dog hated the collar as much as she hated the pins and the bar. I removed the collar when she ate and for brief trips outside when I could watch her closely. She loved these times of freedom and always held perfectly still so I could take off the collar. When the time came for it to go back on, her eyes pleaded silently, *Please don't make me do this again.* "Come on, girl, it's part of your healing," I'd explain.

And she would obediently stick out her neck and stand still as I replaced the dreaded collar.

One day while I was fastening the collar, I was certain God was showing me something: *You know the collar brings healing. Red Dog only knows it brings torment. Nevertheless, she trusts you—totally!*

I sat quietly, stroking Red Dog's head. "Oh, Father," I prayed, "are the very things I desperately want removed from my life the things You're using to restore me to wholeness? My terror of public speaking—You've had me doing it almost twenty-five years, and it's not so scary now. My fear of getting lost on the highway—I'm learning to stop and ask directions. What else, Lord? Show me."

Father, help me not to resist Your marvelous ways of healing.

—MARION BOND WEST

12

T
U
E

"If he lays the foundation and is not able to finish it, everyone who sees it will ridicule him. . . . "

—LUKE 14:29 (NIV)

In January I made a very firm and prayerful decision to cut back on my work schedule, particularly on my out-of-town commitments. A few months later, I prayed about my schedule for December. It was a little full—two conferences and a visit to Mexico—but it definitely seemed doable.

But a week ago last Monday, when we came home from a visit to relatives in Missouri, I discovered that a huge rainstorm had hit Austin, Texas, while we were gone. Water had come in through two skylights, ruining wallpaper and the plaster ceiling of our guest room, soaking carpets, flowing into the attic, through the attic floor and into the garage below, depositing plaster on cars, cabinets and the garage floor. A much smaller but similar scenario had played itself out in the kitchen. And all this happened just days before some friends were scheduled to arrive for a long-planned first visit with us. By the time we got home, all the roofers and repair people were already busy, and we couldn't get anyone even to look at the damage until after our friends' visit was scheduled to be over.

I won't bore you with the rest of the unplanned events of that week. But I was not the calm and sweet Christian I had planned to be. I had planned for a delightful end of the year, and suddenly, overnight, I was feeling frantic and overwhelmed. I could almost hear my mother's voice saying for the millionth time, "Keith, I think your eyes were bigger than your stomach."

But as I prayed, I finally remembered that as a Christian I have been given tools to deal with the chaos. So I made a few phone calls, confessed I had put too many things on my plate and asked our friends to reschedule their visit. I managed to schedule repairs, prepare my talks—and we just got back from a delightful trip to Mexico.

Dear Lord, thank You for teaching me that no matter how carefully I plan, I had better leave room for unplanned things. Amen.

—KEITH MILLER

13 | W E D

"Do not dwell on the past. See, I am doing a new thing! . . ." —ISAIAH 43:18-19 (NIV)

Earlier this evening I stepped onto our patio to plug in our outside Christmas lights. I almost didn't string them up this year because our three children are all grown and our oldest, who is newly married, may not even come home for Christmas. *Maybe I need to grow up, too, and accept life the way it is in this new season,* I told myself. The thought magnified a growing emptiness inside me.

Crackle! Pop! Pop! The prongs of the plug sparked in my hand as I plugged in the lights. They flickered on and then went off—for good.

"What's wrong with those dratted lights?" I asked my husband Lynn as I went inside.

"Probably blew a fuse," he said, opening the kitchen junk drawer and pulling out a little plastic bag filled with teeny cylinder-shaped things. "Maybe I can fix it."

I followed him outside and watched in amazement as he pulled apart the runner plug, removed a tiny cylinder just like the ones in the bag and inserted a new one.

He plugged the lights back in, and *voila!* They flashed on perfectly.

"Those little plugs have replaceable fuses?" I asked incredulously as we walked back into the house. "How did I get to be fifty-two years old and never know that?"

"Probably because I take such good care of you," he said with a smile as he dropped the plastic bag back in the junk drawer. "But aren't you glad there are lots of things left for you to discover in life?"

Of course, a husband doesn't really expect an answer to a question like that, but I felt something flicker in that empty place inside me. Being grown up doesn't mean I'm done growing. And there is a whole world of exciting discoveries waiting for me in this new season of life.

Father, as long as I am on this earth, help me to keep growing and discovering the wonders all around me. —CAROL KUYKENDALL

14 | T H U | *By him were all things created, that are in heaven, and that are in earth, visible and invisible. . . .* —COLOSSIANS 1:16

There's a huge pothole in the red mud in front of us. It is filled with water. On the side of the road is an ancient truck with a broken axle. Our Jeep has been climbing painfully up the dirt road into the Tanzanian mountains. The whole family is thirsty and shaken up by the lurches and drops. I open my mouth to complain and then shut it again.

From out of nowhere, the voice of my late mother comes into my head. With her quiet, often slightly ironic smile, I hear her saying, "Count your blessings, my dear. Always count your blessings." Without hesitation, I begin to count:

One, I am visiting this breathtaking country with my grown-up children, who are traveling with their parents of their own free will.

Two, I live in a country of surfaced roads and indoor plumbing.

Three, a lifetime of other blessings has brought us here on this scorching December day.

Four, I had the kind of mother whose words of wisdom on all the important things in life have stayed with me after she herself has gone.

I don't kid myself that Mother would have enjoyed this kind of rough adventure travel. But how she would have loved to see the graceful Thompson's gazelles bounding across the road as if in slow motion, and the stately elephants lumbering along, seeming to say, "I have the right of way here. This is my country."

We maneuvered around the pothole and reached the top of the hill, and I was still counting my blessings. Looking up, I saw stretching out before me the unbelievable wonder of the Ngorongoro Crater, sanctuary to hundreds of varieties of animals and birds. Who can even begin to count the blessings of God's creation?

Keep me always aware, oh, Lord, of the uncountable blessings of Your creation. —BRIGITTE WEEKS

15

F
R
I

Our Lord Jesus Christ, himself, and God, even our Father, which hath loved us, and hath given us everlasting consolation and good hope through grace. . . .
—II THESSALONIANS 2:16

The luncheon was arranged in Victorian style: warm elegance with beautiful antiques decorating the speaker's platform; table centerpieces carefully crafted around bone china teapots; lace doilies with pastel cloth napkins. Each detail reflected the love and care of the women organizing the event.

I shared my Christian testimony and concluded with the reminder that there is no guarantee that life will not hurt. I left the audience with my favorite quotation from the playwright Eugene O'Neill: "We live by mending, and the grace of God is the glue."

Imagine my delight when I was presented with a charmingly wrapped package. "A small token of our thanks to you," they said. Imagine my horror when I dropped it! "Oh dear," I gasped, "I hope it wasn't breakable." Breakable it was, and . . . sure enough, I had broken the handle off the lovely English bone china teacup they had selected for me.

"It's a clean break. It could easily be mended." The women's ministries director's eyes were soft as she picked up the three pieces from the floor. "Not safe to hold and drink from perhaps, but you could put in a silk flower arrangement."

"You're so right," I smiled in relief. Then a thought came to me: "God is turning this accident into something very special. This will be my 'Grace of God' mended-life teacup—a sign of encouragement from all of you."

I give You the damaged pieces of my life, dear Lord, and I thank You for Your mending grace that makes me whole again. —FAY ANGUS

16

S
A
T

"But seek first his kingdom and his righteousness, and all these things will be given to you as well."
—MATTHEW 6:33 (NIV)

One Saturday in mid-December, I took a break from my weekend whirlwind of decorating, baking and mall shopping, and stopped at a local flea market. Before I knew it, I found myself digging through a box of old Christmas decorations. You name it, it was there: tattered felt stockings, a plastic gumdrop tree, chipped ornaments, a tangled garland of silver stars.

And then I spotted a treasure: an antique crèche, its chalk figures softly faded by time. The dealer must have caught the gleam in my eye. "You can have the whole thing for a dollar," she announced. "It's all there except Jesus."

All there except Jesus! I was still recovering from her comment when she struck up a conversation with another prospective buyer.

Just then an insistent voice spoke to my own heart. *You've missed me, too, this Christmas season. This morning I was there in the grocery store when that lady asked you which apples looked the best. She was lonely, Roberta, and she needed to talk about more than apples.*

My mind replayed the past few frenzied weeks. I had done more than people expected of me; I had even snared a blue ribbon at the Festival of Trees for a wreath I crafted. But that didn't seem to matter as I relived my impatience with the salesclerk for shorting me a yard of red velvet ribbon I needed to make the bow just so. In my endless preparations, there was a missing piece in my heart.

There were nine days left until Christmas. Still time to put first things first.

Christ Jesus, come into my heart today. To stay.

—ROBERTA MESSNER

R E A D E R ' S   R O O M

"The Lord has brought much healing and growth in the last 18 months. In 1995 I found out my husband had been unfaithful. He moved out in October 1996. When I realized he no longer wanted to work on the marriage because he was again with someone else, I accepted the fact that God had a better plan. Along the way, God sent many healing touches to help me get through. He led me to join a Bible study. He also led me to a terrific Christian counselor. He provided friends who supported, loved and prayed me through. Now I have a new life. I had become so wrapped up in my husband that I had lost myself, but God woke me up and made me a whole new person."

—*Kim Stahl, Peoria, Illinois*

17
S
U
N

A CHRISTMAS FOR THE HEART
Third Sunday in Advent
And when they had opened their treasures, they presented unto him gifts. . . .   —MATTHEW 2:11

The date is lost in my memory, but the moment is alive and flaming within me. My third-grade Sunday school class was having a birthday party for Jesus. I'd baked a chocolate cake and decorated it with a crèche of frosting and the words *Happy Birthday, Jesus!* I'd added eight candles to help my third-graders connect personally with this birthday Child. I turned off the light, pulled down the shade and lit the candles. A sudden hush of reverence settled over the group, and as my gaze moved from one child to the next I saw candle flames—and a newborn sense of holy awe—reflected in their wide eyes. It was a magic moment that touched even the aging heart of their teacher.

We sang "Happy Birthday," blew out the candles and turned on the lights. After eating cake and reading the Christmas story, we talked about the wise men and their treasures. That's when Jimmy asked, "How did the wise men know what Jesus wanted for Christmas when He hadn't even been born yet?"

How do you answer a teacher-stumping question? You change the subject by asking another question! "What would you give Jesus for a present, if you went to His birthday party?" I asked. Janet suggested a teddy bear, and Danny said he thought a dump truck would be nice. But Mary Lou, the youngest in the class, caused the class to laugh and tears to form behind her teacher's eyelids. "How about a flaming candle?" If I'd thought all day, I could not have found a better answer.

Many years have passed since that birthday party, but here I am again, thinking about the wise men's gifts even before Christmas has come. As I ponder what treasure I might have to offer, I still can't think of a better gift to bring the Christ Child in this year 2000 than a heart aflame with His divine fire.

Blessed Jesus, fire my heart with a childlike sense of wonder, and let that be the treasure I offer back to You on the day of Your birth—and always.   —MARILYN MORGAN HELLEBERG

18

M
O   *Neglect not the gift that is in thee. . . .*
N   —I TIMOTHY 4:14

One December, a few years ago, I decided to put together a memory book for my parents. I contacted friends and relatives and had each of them write down two memories: one for Mother and the other for Daddy. Then on Christmas Eve, our entire family gathered at my parents' farm for dinner and a gift exchange. After the last gift had been opened, I brought out the memory book and presented it to my sister Pam, who had volunteered to read each memory aloud so I could videotape our parents' reactions.

Today, that tape is one of my most treasured possessions, not so much because it preserves some interesting stories about my parents, but because it catches the amazement on their faces as they listened to what other people remembered about the two of them. They were deeply moved to learn all the ways in which they had touched the lives of so many others.

Since that night, I've tried to give some of that same joy to others. When someone does something that makes a difference to my life, large or small, I tell them. There is no finer gift I can give.

Lord, help me find the words to express my appreciation to those who mean so much to my life.   —LIBBIE ADAMS

19

T   *"For it will not be you speaking, but the Spirit of your*
U   *Father speaking through you."*
E   —MATTHEW 10:20 (NIV)

Our Sunday school class was gathering in the church parlor for a Christmas banquet. Crackling flames danced in the fireplace, greenery was on the mantel, the smell of hot apple cider filled the air, and laughter could be heard from every corner of the room.

I was anxious. I'd asked a friend—a nationally acclaimed pianist and composer—to come and play a short program of Christmas music. A rented grand piano was to have been delivered for the occasion, but something went awry and the piano never arrived. Now the only instrument in the parlor was a dusty old upright that hadn't been tuned for years. The keys were snaggle-toothed where ivory had been chipped away, and the pedals squeaked. I was thoroughly embarrassed.

When my friend was introduced and sat down to play, I cringed and looked at the floor. Even a tone-deaf person could hear that many of the notes were pinched or flat. But as my friend played, we were enveloped by a beauty that made us forget the mechanical problems. In the hands of a master musician, even that crusty old piano produced transforming music.

After the banquet, I apologized to my friend about the piano. He grinned, lovingly patted the battered old instrument and said, "Every piano dreams of an evening like this. I'm glad we could make music together."

There are days in my life when I feel like that old piano: out of tune with the Spirit of God, dented, scratched and squeaky in the joints. I cannot play God's music. But sometimes, when I'm faced with a friend's grief or a neighbor's need for encouragement, the hands of the Master begin to move across the chipped keys of my life and a music that is beyond my ability is heard for just a moment.

Father, I am not an instrument worthy of Your music, but use me as You will. Amen.　　　　　　　　　　　　　　　　—SCOTT WALKER

20 | W E D

Unto you is born this day in the city of David a Saviour, which is Christ the Lord.　　—LUKE 2:11

Hung with pine branches and scarlet bows, Victorian-style lampposts glow in Lander, our little Wyoming town, at Christmastime. Residents eagerly participate in the annual Christmas-lighting contest. Shop windows glitter and blink in the Rocky Mountain darkness; spotlights frame horses and sleighs; candles shine against frosty windows. Surrounded by split-rail fences, whole stands of spruce trees thrust through the snow, garlanded in twinkling light.

Our family always reserves one night before Christmas for a slow drive through the town, savoring the brilliance. But our favorite display will never win a prize. Few folks know about "Jesus of the Junk Pile."

My son Tom and I discovered this unlikely crèche the winter we delivered newspapers to a cramped trailer court on the edge of town. The last row of trailers faced a dirt road with nothing across it save the brush along the riverbank. But there, wedged against a chain-link fence, a small manger scene about three feet tall huddled in the snow. No cherubs here, only rusty saw blades, tangled chains and dried-up thistles. A single bare lightbulb "star" marked the lowly place where plastic figures of the Holy Family crouched. The lights were dim, the painted detail faded. There, where very few would ever notice, someone had tenderly wrapped the plastic Christ Child in a small tartan blanket to protect him from the bitter cold.

Lord, even in the unlikeliest places, help me to see the glory of Your presence.
—GAIL THORELL SCHILLING

21 T H U *"Give, and it will be given to you. A good measure, pressed down, shaken together and running over, will be poured into your lap. . . ."* —LUKE 6:38 (NIV)

When I was nine years old, my mother died, and my Dad's sister, Aunt Helen, stepped right in to help. Two days after our mother's funeral, she made my sister Susan a birthday cake, and insisted we celebrate as Mom would have. And how she brightened the sad holidays! I can still hear her exclaiming, "Howdy, Doody!" as she came through the door carrying shopping bags full of presents. Before Christmas we spent hours in her kitchen baking and decorating cookies—Aunt Mary's sugar, Aunt Jean's anise and Dad's favorite icebox cookies. Even while working full-time to support her own family, Aunt Helen cared for us. She took us girls shopping for school clothes and gave us home permanents in her kitchen.

To her grandson Danny, she was a bright star in his life after his mother died. He once told her, "Nana, I've never seen you cry." She answered, "If I started crying, I might never be able to stop." To lighten her burdens—her husband's alcoholism and constant sickness, losing her daughter, helping raise her nieces and nephews and grandchildren—she found humor and joy wherever she could, and kept giving.

When my dad died, Aunt Helen stood with us around her dear brother's coffin and whispered, "The Lord is my shepherd," then led us in praying Psalm Twenty-three together. That's when I began to glimpse the source of her strength. Years later, at her own funeral, we sang her favorite hymn, "What a Friend We Have in Jesus," and I knew. Her Friend walked with her through every suffering, and gave her the love and joy she poured out to us.

Oh, Lord, when I feel I have nothing to give, please fill my heart with love. Help me find simple ways to bring joy to others.

—MARY BROWN

22

F
R
I

Freely ye have received, freely give.

—MATTHEW 10:8

It was only a couple of days before Christmas, and I was working through lunch at the office, trying to get some work accomplished before I flew across the country to be with my family for the holidays. Caught in the seasonal rush, I half-wished that I didn't have to travel so I would have more time to finish all I needed to do. Just then, the receptionist at the front desk called me, saying, "There's a man here who says you don't know him, but he wants to see you anyway."

Indeed, a short, graying gentleman in a sports jacket introduced himself. "Rick, you don't know me, but for years I've been enjoying your pieces in *Daily Guideposts.*"

I took to the fellow immediately (flattered, of course, by his kind words). He lived in upstate New York and was in town for a *Messiah* sing-along at Carnegie Hall. For several minutes we talked about our mutual love of music, the chorus he sang in, the house where he lived and the recent troubles he'd been through. After a brief talk, we shook hands and he hurried on.

Back in my office I was thinking of all the efforts we make in the holidays—sending Christmas cards to people we haven't seen in years, buying presents for relatives we visit all too briefly, traveling across the country to gather for a day around tree and hearth. I understood then what makes it worthwhile: the love that motivates us out of selfishness, the desire to make someone else happy. Just like my unexpected visitor. He made my day.

Dear Lord, when I give, let me give of myself. —RICK HAMLIN

A PLACE OF MY OWN

23 | S
A
T *Bless the Lord, ye his angels. . . .* —PSALM 103:20

I pulled open the odds-and-ends drawer in the buffet and rooted around until I found the painting kit, with a brush and eight watercolors. "Hello there. Ready for another Christmas?" I said out loud to the familiar kit. "And you, too," I said to the large mirror over the fireplace. How many Christmases had I been painting a tree on this glass? Twenty-five in this Upper West Side apartment and all those years in Greenwich Village; I shook my head in disbelief.

With a glass of water in one hand and the brush in the other, I steadied myself on the ladder, dabbed at the green and then started in. I drew a great swab for a lower limb, then, with utter abandon, I added swirl upon swirl, decreasing in size, until I reached the top. A bit of brown would do for the trunk, and now I stood back to admire what I had done. Every year it looked different, and I, no painter, couldn't care less. It was the tradition that counted.

It was time for the trimmings. I dug into a drawer and pulled out a miniature glass horse. Ah, yes, I remembered the day Elizabeth gave it to me. Then a little cloth figure (embroidered supposedly by Lydia, but mainly, I suspect, by her mother Valerie), and a small American flag; a razzmatazz blower-thing from Diffy's birthday; a Lilliputian red stocking (Where from? Who knows?); an I LOVE POINTERS button left over from Clay, my dog before Shep; a Christmas medallion from Guideposts with 1980 at the top. These, and more, I affixed with Scotch tape to the mirror's tree. Then, as a last gesture, at the very summit I placed the figure of an angel. It had been there before, many times, and it said with all the fripperies of the holiday, "Peace."

The tree might be fun, and a collector of memories both beautiful and sad, but the angel would reign over it, and my household, a protective force throughout the rush of the season.

I trust You, Lord, and Your angels.   —VAN VARNER

24 | S u N | A CHRISTMAS FOR THE HEART
Christmas Eve
And she gave birth to her firstborn. . . .
—LUKE 2:7 (NIV)

The year is 1956. The time, 3:00 A.M. The place, St. Catherine's Hospital, McCook, Nebraska. I am about to give birth to our first child. My heart is filled with anticipation and hope, but as the contractions grip my body, fear introduces anxious thoughts. *Will this unbearable pain ever end? And if it does, will I survive it? What if my child isn't perfect, Lord? Or what if my baby dies? What suffering will life bring this child of mine?*

As I fade in and out of consciousness, a scene appears behind my eyelids. It's a starlit night in a town called Bethlehem. A young woman is doubled over in pain as her husband wipes the moisture from her face. Does she, too, hold fearful questions in her heart? Does she wonder if she'll survive this night in the cold barn, or if her Child will fail to be all the angel promised? Will His life be hard? What suffering will He bear? If she has such fears, she releases them to God, giving birth in joy. With great thanksgiving, Mary and Joseph offer the newborn Child to His heavenly Father. From somewhere in mists of timelessness, I hear an angel song echoing down the years into my hospital room, and a prayer forms in my heart beyond all pain.

> I've held this child so long within my womb,
> I hardly know that we are two, not one.
> But now the time has come to set her free,
> O Lord my God, I trust her life to Thee.

One last contraction now, a final push and Karen Jen Helleberg is born. In that moment I know that, even in the midst of pain, it is possible to let go to God. And, oh, the blessing of that surrender is greater than mountains and rivers, more precious than a thousand beating hearts.

Your birth is always now, Lord Jesus. I let go of doubts and fears about the future. Let Your living presence be the heartbeat of this newborn century. Amen.

—MARILYN MORGAN HELLEBERG

25 | M O N | A CHRISTMAS FOR THE HEART
Christmas Day
And suddenly there was with the angel a multitude of the heavenly host praising God. . . . —LUKE 2:13

This morning as I sit in my living room surrounded by empty boxes, crumpled red and green gift wrap, and happily playing grandchildren, I mentally revisit a hillside in Bethlehem. There I see grown men gazing skyward, leaning on shepherds' crooks, their faces bright with an unearthly light. Presently they fall to their knees, seeing and hearing a spiritual reality now revealed in time and space, a sky filled with "a multitude of the heavenly host" singing praises to the newborn King.

Could it be that right here in my Colorado home and right there in your home, in this first year of the twenty-first century, you and I are also in the presence of another world that is just as real, though unseen and unheard, as the one the shepherds knew that glorious night in Bethlehem? And could it be that the Child born in that manger is the link between that reality and this? Could it be that at this very moment, you and I are surrounded by singing angels and archangels and all the company of heaven?

I believe it is so, "For God, who commanded the light to shine out of darkness, hath shined in our hearts, to give the light of the knowledge of the glory of God in the face of Jesus Christ" (II Corinthians 4:6). So with brimming hearts let us join now in heaven's eternal song:

Glory to God in the highest, and on earth peace, good will among all people. Amen and amen.   —MARILYN MORGAN HELLEBERG

26 | TUE

And the light shineth in darkness; and the darkness comprehended it not.   —JOHN 1:5

Last Christmas we reluctantly decided that it had become too hard on my mother to transport her from her Alzheimer's unit to Christmas dinner with the family. Osteoporosis and heart problems had set in, and she was growing increasingly feeble.

December 25 was very bright and very cold, the way it should be in Michigan. My brother Joe, my sister Mary Lou and I, along with my teenage nieces Clare and Rachel, my cousin Carol, and my wife Julee, bundled up and piled into our cars and headed to Clausen Manor to see Mom. "Does she even know it's Christmas?" I asked Julee on the way.

Clare and Rachel brought chocolates. Julee and I had a plant, which I knew Mom would water to death before the new year. Carol brought an elaborate Twelve Days of Christmas pop-up book. It was this last that captured Mom's flickering attention as she sat silently in her wheelchair. We were all chatting when out of nowhere Mom began to read aloud: "On the . . . first . . . day of . . . Christmas, my true love gave . . . to me . . ."

We stared at her in astonishment. Mom had long since lost the ability to read. Yet she forged on, "On the . . . second day of . . . "

She stumbled and struggled. Turtledoves changed into turtle dolls, hens into hills, maids into moms. By the tenth day she was clearly weary. I started to help her with a passage when she suddenly shot me a look I hadn't seen for quite some time and snapped, "Are you going to let me do it myself?"

An instant of stunned silence gave way to laughter, save for Mom, who cast us a strangely knowing look. Then she let the book close, apparently having forgotten she'd been reading it.

Did Mom know it was Christmas? For that one bright shining moment, we all knew it.

Lord, You brought eternal light into the world. As our bodies grow old and feeble, give our souls strength, burning with that light.

—EDWARD GRINNAN

27 | W E D   *"Choose this day whom you will serve. . . ."*
—JOSHUA 24:15 (RSV)

The alarm buzzed loudly. I sleepily opened one eye and glanced at the clock. It was 5 A.M. I nudged my husband. "Roy," I said softly, "Merry Christmas."

We quietly walked downstairs, the scent of evergreen in the air. We lit candles and plugged in the Christmas tree lights. The room had a pristine look, like the first peek outside after an overnight snowfall. The stockings hung on the fireplace, still holding their surprises. The gifts under the tree were untouched, ribbon and tissue still intact. We stood for a moment and listened to the stillness.

In years past, Christmas had been different. The children had raced down the stairs, rushed to their stockings and torn into their presents. This year, we had promised to focus more on the birth of Jesus, the true gift of Christmas, and less on buying expensive presents for one another.

When the kids woke up they joined us in front of the fireplace for a breakfast of muffins and orange juice. Thirteen-year-old Kevin read the story of the birth of Jesus from Luke's Gospel. Then we exchanged gifts, taking time to watch as each of us opened our presents. We had stuck to a budget this year, and when our oldest daughter Misty opened her gift from her sister Kristen—two small tins of loose tea, a tea ball and a ceramic mug—she said, "Shopping with a smaller budget required a lot more thought. These gifts mean so much more."

I looked around at my family, thankful that despite those hectic Christmas mornings when they thought only of gifts, my children value the true gift of Christmas.

Thank You, Lord, for Your most precious gift, the gift of Your Son. Thank You for our most precious gift we can give each other, the gift of ourselves. —MELODY BONNETTE

28 | T H U | *Those who mourn are lifted to safety.*
—JOB 5:11 (RSV)

When I got the news on Christmas Day that my brother had died, my heart broke. Arriving at the Columbus, Ohio, airport, where he'd met me so often, triggered more pain. We would never meet on earth again. I prayed, but I couldn't be comforted. As children we had been inseparable. Now he was gone.

After the funeral, my father and I saved some of the flowers that had not been taken to the cemetery. "What should we do with them, Dad?" I asked. "I don't want them to be wasted."

My father put his arm around my shoulder and said, "I think he might like it if we put them in that field." He pointed out the window toward a field where corn had been harvested a few months earlier. In one of the last pictures I had of Bud, he was walking through the field, inspecting the fresh green rows. Now the brown stalks waved in the winter light like ghosts.

We put on our coats and carried bouquets of flowers to the spot where my brother had walked. We piled the flowers in a mound and stood over them. Wind blew across the field, stinging our faces. "Why did God have to take him?" I asked. All around us the empty husks showed the harvest that was gone. I took my father's hand and we bowed our heads.

Suddenly, I felt a warmth enter my heart. This field would be filled with growing things again, breaking through the earth. The flowers would nurture another harvest.

We began to pray:

Our Father, Who art in heaven, give us this day our daily bread.
—SUSAN SCHEFFLEIN

29

F
R
I

Behold, now is the accepted time; behold, now is the day of salvation. —II CORINTHIANS 6:2

This is the time of year when presidents and CEOs gather with their boards of directors to review the previous twelve months and to set strategy on the year ahead. According to one imaginative mind, the end of December is also the time that the devil convenes his associates to assess how they have been doing.

Last year, according to my source, the devil was not happy. "Our numbers are way off," he said with a scowl. "We need to figure a way to attract more people to hell." Then, turning to his dark-cloaked assistants, he asked, "Do you have any suggestions?"

One junior devil thought they might do better if they told people there is no heaven. "No, we've tried that before, and it doesn't work," Satan replied.

Another director suggested the opposite; tell people there is no hell. But that idea was rejected also.

Then the devil's chief assistant spoke. He is reportedly as wily as the old man himself. "If you want to get more people into hell," he confided, "just whisper in their ears, 'Relax, you've got plenty of time to change your ways. There's no hurry.'" And everyone in the room applauded.

Whatever your goals for the coming year—learning a new skill, losing weight, exercising more, watching less TV, finding a new job, becoming a volunteer, spending more time with your kids, growing in spiritual matters—your success will be determined by the strength of your commitment. Go at anything halfheartedly, and you will surely achieve a half-hearted harvest. Dedicate yourself fully to an endeavor, be willing to sacrifice time, money and effort, and you can expect to be rewarded in kind. With God's help, we can do miraculous things. We can even overcome our inclination toward procrastination when a tempting voice whispers, "Relax, you've got plenty of time. Wait until tomorrow to begin."

In the new year, God, teach us,
Time's the stuff that life is made of,
Too fleeting for acts other than love. —FRED BAUER

30
S
A
T

Many are the plans in a man's heart, but it is the Lord's purpose that prevails.

—PROVERBS 19:21 (NIV)

When I left Mississippi to attend school in California, I had no thought of coming back to my home state to live. God had other ideas. He brought me back to help develop Mendenhall Ministries. I planned to stay with that work for the rest of my life. But again, God had other ideas, and He moved me to work for reconciliation through Mission Mississippi.

It was hard for me to let go of my plans to stay in California, but it has been even harder to let go of my work in Mendenhall. I saw the ministry grow from three people and an after-school tutorial program to a staff of forty working in eight different programs. I had to struggle between my feeling of ownership—this was *my* ministry—and the reality of stewardship, knowing that, in fact, it was God's.

But after twenty-six years, God is reminding me that He is in control, and that it's okay to let go. It may be hard for some people to understand, but it's just as hard to let go of a ministry as it is to let go of a child. But in both cases, I've got to trust that God can keep things going without me. And as I celebrate the ways He's used me in the past, I've got to trust that He'll enable me to stretch forward to the future. I can—and I should—plan for my life and my family. But His purpose will prevail in the end.

Lord, help me always to be ready to move on, trusting in Your perfect plan.
—DOLPHUS WEARY

31
S
U
N

Enlarge the place of thy tent. . . . For thou shalt break forth on the right hand and on the left. . . .
—ISAIAH 54:2-3

Over the past several years, our New Year's Eve celebrations have grown smaller. Most often, my husband Don and I spend the evening with one or two couples we've known for decades—comfortable, familiar, simple celebrations. But last year we were invited to attend an elegant dinner party with my sister Amanda and her husband Tim.

"Thanks, but no thanks," I told Amanda. Although I hate to admit it, I'm often uncomfortable in unfamiliar situations. What if I used the wrong fork? Would I be able to make conversation? What if they played a game I didn't know?

Amanda wouldn't take no for an answer. "I've already told our hosts you're coming," she said. "You know and like some of the people who'll be there. You'll get to know and like the others."

We went, and I had a wonderful time. I made new friends and gained a deeper appreciation for the talents of others. I knew our hostess Beverly was a gracious hostess, but I didn't know she was a gourmet chef. I loved her spinach-strawberry salad! I'd heard about Cissie's prowess as a jigsaw puzzler (she was the only person with the courage to try the three-dimensional puzzle we gave Tim for Christmas), but I came away inspired by her courage. Despite being in a wheelchair, she takes care of her elderly mother. In fact, every guest had a unique talent—and each used his or her talent to help others.

This year we're again spending New Year's Eve with old friends, but we've included new faces as well. It's the perfect way to end an old year and prepare for a fresh new one filled with challenges, opportunities and friends—old and new.

Lord of the ages, You know I like my comfortable rut. Thank You for nudging me toward new people and new experiences.

—PENNEY SCHWAB

My Renewal Journal

1 _____

2 _____

3 _____

4 _____

5 _____

6 _____

7 _____

8 _____

9 _____

10 _____

11 _____

12 _____

13 _____

14 _____

15 _____

16 _____

17 _____

18 _____

19 _____

20 _____

21 _____

22 _____

23 _____

24 _____

25 _____

26 _____

27 _____

28 _____

29 _____

30 _____

31 _____

Fellowship Corner

On the threshold of this new millennium, we're opening our hearts to all the ways in which God is making us new. Our fifty old friends and three new ones are waiting to catch you up on all the new things that have been happening in their lives this past year. Come on in and join the conversation and fellowship. It's good to have you with us!

 "This has been another incredible year for me, filled with so many blessings," writes LIBBIE ADAMS of Richlands, North Carolina. "I'm married to my best friend Larry, and we share a wonderful life together. Here in the South, where families tend to grow up and settle down in or around their hometowns, I feel fortunate that my family has done the same. Our children, my parents, my brother and two sisters, and their extended families all reside near Richlands. It's a Pittman family tradition to gather once a month for Sunday dinner on Mother and Daddy's farm, where they still raise hogs, turkeys and cattle. I've grown to appreciate just what it means to have the unconditional love of all these family members who are so dear to me and who accept me without regard to my shortcomings. This year, when every day is a new page to be filled, my spiritual goal is to follow my family's example by disregarding others' shortcomings and allowing God's unconditional love to make all things new in my life."

 MARCI ALBORGHETTI of Hartford, Connecticut, joins the *Daily Guideposts* family this year. "I received my first *Daily Guideposts* from my mother for Christmas more than ten years ago," Marci says, "and I can't wait to return the favor this year. God has truly made things new for me this year in other ways as well: My first children's book has been accepted for publication, and I visited the West Coast for the first time, spending a week in Sausalito, California, climbing my first real mountain and driving along the spectacular Pacific West Coast Highway. The striking beauty of the ocean crashing into the mountains had me thanking God!" Marci confesses to "shedding a few tears" when she boarded the plane that flew her back to the first New England snow and ice storm of the season.

FAY ANGUS of Sierra Madre, California, writes, "This was a whirlwind year, a dizzy spinning of days that had me constantly checking my calendar to be sure of just where I was, when! Ireland, England, Italy, Switzerland, France, culminating in a glorious dinner cruise down the Seine in Paris where thousands of lights from the Eiffel Tower danced rainbows through windows of the restaurant barge that drifted us along. *'Qu'est-ce que tu dis?'* my husband said, grinning. *'Je t'aime!'* I replied. It was a dream come true and, for me, a major miracle! Just months before, the spinning was around doctors' offices, blood labs, frighteningly low platelet counts and the possibility of a bone marrow transplant. In His mercy, the Lord sorted it all out, and here I am, still on the run and rarin' to go! A new beginning? Way more than that . . . a new lease on life itself. Thanks be to God, I am most enormously grateful."

"God has certainly done something new in our lives," writes *Daily Guideposts* editor ANDREW ATTAWAY of New York City. "He's given us a brand-new baby, Mary Frances, born on Veterans Day last year. It hasn't been that long since Elizabeth and John were babies, but I had forgotten most of the things that come with an infant. After a week or two, I readjusted to the routine of 3:00 A.M. feedings, frequent diaper changes and all the rest. But nothing had prepared me for the smiles. Unlike her siblings, Mary has been smiling from the very beginning. And in a few weeks, her smiles had developed into giggles and then deep, hearty laughter. It's amazing how a happy baby can light up even the tiredest parent's day (or night)—but Julia knows more about *tired* than I ever will."

"A baby is so obviously the handiwork of the Lord, who makes all things new," says JULIA ATTAWAY, Andrew's wife. "But this year I've also been keenly aware of how God re-creates our entire family as He enlarges it. We all change when a soul is born into the world." Older siblings Elizabeth and John seem to have adapted well to the change and eagerly await the day that Mary can be more than a prop in their homemade shows and dramas.

When you ask KAREN BARBER of Alpharetta, Georgia, "What's new?" for the millennium, you might expect that she and her husband Gordon would tell about their three sons: Jeff is a member of the class of 2000 at Duke University; Chris has joined the class of 2003 at college; and John, a fourth-grader, will be a member of the high school class of 2008. But this year Karen found inspiration for facing strange new times from members of the previous generation. "Both of my parents, Bob and Sue Brown of Pumpkintown, South Carolina, are in their seventies. Following my mother's stroke, I have marveled at my father's can-do attitude toward his new responsibilities as Mom's caregiver. And Mom has surprised us by developing something new herself—a sense of humor. Recently, Dad asked for my e-mail address. Why? Because at seventy-six, he's just purchased his first home computer."

"As an elementary student during the 1940s," says ALMA BARKMAN of Winnipeg, Canada, "I used to doodle in the margins of my exercise books, trying to get a feel for the future by writing 1975, or 1985, or even 1995. But I can't recall ever writing the year 2000! It just seemed so distant as to be unimaginable. Now the years have slipped away, and here I am as the curtain goes up on the new millennium. Leo and I have enjoyed an uninterrupted run of forty-three years of marriage. My role has expanded to include that of mother to four grown children and grandmother to seven. A creative bunch, their impromptu phone calls continue to surprise us with news of their latest endeavors, which range from composing music to writing scripts to selling pianos to baking big sticky cinnamon buns. As I applaud their efforts, I continue to ask God for guidance as to the part He wants me to play, and thank Him for His faithfulness in directing me in the past."

FRED BAUER and his wife Shirley divide their time between Englewood, Florida, and State College, Pennsylvania. "When I was told the theme for *Daily Guideposts, 2000* was 'Behold, I make all things new,' I was in real need of renewal. I was diagnosed with non-Hodgkin's lymphoma a couple of years ago, and after a series of chemotherapy treatments had a re-mission. It lasted only a few months, so a stronger, risky regimen of high-dose chemicals was prescribed, culminating with a three-week stem cell transplant at the University of Pennsylvania Hospital in Philadelphia. Much of that time I was in isolation, without a protec-tive immune system. I did not know whether I would live or die, only that I was in the hands of the One Who will never leave me nor for-sake me. Because of God's grace and mercy, some dedicated doctors and nurses, and a huge outpouring of intercessory prayer by family and friends, I am celebrating one year of good health. And every day I give thanks to God for another day of life. He can, indeed, make things new."

"This has been a year that presented a lot of new challenges to my husband Keith and me," RHODA BLECKER of Los Angeles, California, says. "Keith is returning to school (many years after high school) to study computer networking, and it has been richly rewarding for me to see him learning study habits and coming back from classes excited about what he is learn-ing. As for me, although I recently lost my best friend, I have found that the comfort I received from my community helps to fill the gap her death left in my life. I have begun teaching classes in short story and fiction writing. I love to nurture the new talent of my students. And I wrote my very first fantasy short story. Since fantasy sells far better than science fiction, which I write as Roby James, I have some hopes of future publication!"

MELODY BONNETTE of Mandeville, Louisiana, was chosen the 1999 Louisiana Teacher of the Year. "I went to Washington and met President Clinton," she says. "As a historian, shaking the hand of our president was a very powerful moment indeed." She will also participate in International Space Camp in Huntsville, Alabama, and the National Teacher Forum in Washington, D.C., this year as part of her Teacher of the Year agenda. Husband Roy recently completed his Ph.D. Daughter Misty and son-in-law Indelethio are doing well in New York City. Kristen continues to pursue her degree in psychology. Christopher is working in New Orleans, and Kevin has completed his freshman year in high school. "Throughout this activity-filled year, Isaiah 40:31 has been a source of strength: 'But they that wait upon the Lord shall renew their strength; they shall mount up with wings as eagles; they shall run, and not be weary; and they shall walk, and not faint.' "

"What could be newer or more exciting than adding a few more hours to each day?" asks GINA BRIDGEMAN of Scottsdale, Arizona. "That's how I feel now that both kids are in school all day. I'm enjoying the extra time both to work and play, but it still feels a little strange to be entering this new phase in life." Ten-year-old Ross is in fifth grade and has added Little League baseball to a full schedule that includes Cub Scouts and piano. "He wants to be the first major leaguer to play the National Anthem and first base in the same game! Meanwhile, Maria, 5, is following in her brother's footsteps with piano lessons. Paul and I love how our house is always filled with music." Paul is beginning his tenth year teaching theater at Grand Canyon University in Phoenix and looks forward to designing scenery for his fiftieth show. Gina begins her ninth year teaching writing and genealogy classes for Elderhostel. "This has been a year to rejoice in God's gifts of love, life and new beginnings."

For MARY BROWN and family of Lansing, Michigan, the high point of last year was coming home after a year's sabbatical overseas. Elizabeth, 11, described arriving home as "when you forget about something and find it again, it seems brand-new." For Elizabeth and Mark, 6, those first days home were like opening a big present—riding bikes around their own neighborhood, playing again with toys and friends they hadn't seen for a year. Mary says, "Now that we're settled in and the daily routine feels more stressful than exciting, I want to keep that fresh appreciation and gratitude for home, friends and family."

"New has become my watchword this year," says MARY LOU CARNEY of Chesterton, Indiana. New offices, new employees and a brand-new magazine to edit, *Guideposts for Teens.* Mary Lou also continues editing *Guideposts for Kids,* the award-winning children's magazine. But *new* has been the word in other areas of Mary Lou's life, too. She helped daughter Amy Jo move into a new apartment (she's renting from her brother) and cheered her as she began a new challenge: law school. Son Brett continues to build, adding a new two-unit to his rentals. Gary and Mary Lou took a vacation to a new part of the world for them: Hawaii. And Mary Lou had a new book published, *Absolutely Angels: Poems for Children and Other Believers* (Boyds Mills Press). "When God is the architect of your life, you never know what new additions or renovations He will bring your way, but the final result is always exciting!"

"We are Texans again," writes KENNETH CHAFIN. "For years Barbara and I have flirted with moving back to Houston in order to be closer to our children. Sorting through forty-four years of accumulation as we downsized into a patio house was both painful and renewing. But the possibility of being with our children more excites us. In the middle of preparation for the move, our first grandchild was born—Daniel Kenneth. Before he was thirty minutes old, we were standing in the delivery room watching him at his mother's breast. His arrival has created for our whole family a new awareness of the potential of God's newness in the world."

MARY JANE CLARK and husband Harry continue to make Durango, Colorado, their home. "Our home has a lovely view of the nearby mountains. It's a peaceful, restful place. We also want it to be a welcoming place for guests and family, especially our six kids with their spouses and friends: Kennedy and wife Deb in Vienna, Virginia; Todd and wife Angie in High Point, North Carolina; daughter Wynne in Durham, North Carolina; Jeff and wife Jessica in Fort Collins, Colorado; daughter

Jess in Ann Arbor, Michigan; Ethan in Boulder, Colorado. One new adventure we're anticipating with great eagerness is the birth of our first grandchild. Still sometimes new things come to us unbidden: I have just been diagnosed with cancer. While this is not a path I would have chosen, my fears are tempered with the confidence of God's all-knowing, all-loving presence with us as we set out on this new journey."

MARK COLLINS of Pittsburgh, Pennsylvania, returns to *Daily Guideposts* after a year's hiatus. Turning forty, Mark thought, would be a good time for quiet contemplation. Of course, that's not what happened. His three children, Faith, 8, Hope, 7, and Grace, 3, made sure of that. Adding to the family's busy schedule, Mark's wife Sandee is working toward her Ph.D. in religion. In lieu of quiet contemplation, Mark has opted for harried-but-heartfelt supplication between the lines of the spontaneous script of life: "Lord, I promise to offer a full-fledged prayer to You—as soon as I turn off the buzzer on the dryer. Amen."

"This year my husband Bob and I have been a real stay-at-home pair," says DRUE DUKE of Sheffield, Alabama. "His Parkinson's disease continues to weaken his muscles. It caused him to fall in the middle of our living room floor in October, resulting in five broken ribs. By getting him a lift-chair and having the home health nurses assist us, we were able to keep him at home and avoid hospitalization. With bookshelves filled with good reading material, beloved long-playing phonograph records and wonderful friends popping in, we feel very blessed. Even as good health diminishes, we know we are in God's hands and that He makes everything new—in time."

The new millennium has KJERSTIN EASTON thinking about her future. Now a senior at the California Institute of Technology (Caltech) in Pasadena, she plans to graduate in June, then pursue her master's in electrical engineering in the fall. Wherever her engineering career may take her, she plans to keep writing. Looking back over her first four years with *Daily Guideposts,* she marvels, "One of the neatest things is meeting people who read the book. It's as if we already know each other, and we share an amazing fellowship. This year, I met a reader about my age. We talked about some of my devotionals, and she shared some inspirational stories of her own. We realized that, in a way, we had done a lot of growing up together."

"With all the changes in our family life this year, you might think that our new city, new home, new careers, new schools and a new car would be the source of reflection on this year's theme, 'Behold, I make all things new,' " says ERIC FELLMAN of Falls Church, Virginia. "However, those things don't come to mind first. My wife Joy thinks of the newness of rediscovered friends who mean more to us now. My son Jason points out a new awareness of how when everything else changes, it is the love of family that pulls you through. Nathan has a newfound independence as he focuses on life outside the family nest, and Jonathan looks ahead to new experiences as he leaves high school to spend a semester in South America. And I am deeply thankful that the One Who makes all things new never changes, and offers me a new chance each day to know Him, trust Him, love Him and share His story with each person who touches our lives."

"I feel like the poster child for 'all things new,' " writes SHARON FOSTER of Glen Burnie, Maryland. "*Daily Guideposts* welcomed me into the family just about the same time I completed my first novel. *Passing by Samaria,* published by Multnomah Publishing, will be available in bookstores in the spring. My daughter Lanea is graduating from Grambling State University in Louisiana, while my son Chase is graduating to an electric shaver. In the midst of change, I am still a single mom employed as a civilian instructor at the Defense Information School, Fort Meade, Maryland, where I train military instructor-candidates."

"When someone asks me, 'What's new?' " says *Daily Guideposts* newcomer DAVE FRANCO, "my tendency is to ask, 'How much time do you have?' This year God has given us a new apartment, a new job and a new child, all in the same month! But it has been a great opportunity to feel God holding us close during uncertain times, just as He has promised." Dave lives in New York City with his wife Nicole and children Julian, 4, and Noelle, 1. A transplanted Californian, Dave has dreams of returning to the West Coast someday, but he's happy to be where the Lord wants him and, for now, that's New York.

ARTHUR GORDON of Savannah, Georgia, writes, "Perhaps the newest thing that happened was the decision my wife Pam made to spend three weeks in Siberia and Mongolia under the auspices of an organization called The Friendship Force, which arranges for American citizens to visit foreign lands and stay in the homes of natives. I had to stay in our own home and look after the cats. The idea behind The Friendship Force is that people everywhere have so much in common that they should never let superficial differences come between them. Pam found this to be true and became very fond of the married couple she stayed with in Irkutz. Olga was looking forward to the birth of a grandchild, and all seemed to be well, but news reached us later that the child had been born without feet. This handicap can be corrected to some degree, but it made us realize how sadness can leap across half a world in an instant. And also how love and sympathy can flow right back."

OSCAR GREENE of West Medford, Massachusetts, was reappointed to the Medford Cultural Council that awards grants to local artists, musicians, educators and community workers. He also appeared in *Voices of West Medford*, a publication featuring the roots of nine black West Medford senior citizens. Oscar served as a greeter at the Grace Episcopal

Church's 150th anniversary church tour and English tea. In September, Oscar and Ruby quietly acknowledged their 56th wedding anniversary. "Behold, I make all things new" was revealed to Oscar through comforting insights gained from the Monday evening Bible study of Genesis and Exodus. "These Scriptures pictured God as seeking those who believe in Him and those who worship Him, rather than those who were striving to become perfect."

Talk about new beginnings! EDWARD GRINNAN was recently named editor-in-chief of *Guideposts* magazine, where he has worked since 1986 under predecessors Van Varner and Fulton Oursler, Jr. "They were the two best editors I could have had," says Edward. "Van taught me how to edit a *Guideposts* story—and write a *Daily Guideposts* devotional, by the way—and Fulton showed me how to edit a magazine." On the home front, Edward and wife Julee Cruise split their time between an apartment in New York City and a vacation cabin in the Berkshire Hills of Massachusetts. "I thrive in the city, and Julee, who's from a small town in Iowa, likes to retreat to the country. So we compromise and do a lot of driving." Their two dogs, Sally and Marty, keep them company on the drives.

RICK HAMLIN of New York City says, "I mark the passing years by the ages of my children. Will is now in seventh grade and Timothy is in fourth. So where does that put me? In an effort to keep up with Tim, I teach his Sunday school class, and Will and I bond by making frequent trips to the movies. I've seen more than my quota of disaster films. Last spring, Will and I were in a production of *HMS Pinafore,* where he stole the show, and Carol tolerated our late nights out at rehearsals. Tim remains the star soprano in the choir at church, and Carol and I give some support in the alto and tenor sections. I'm pleased to be enjoying my fifteenth year on staff at *Guideposts* magazine, and was recently promoted to the position of managing editor. This spring I have a novel, *Mixed Blessings,* being published by Bethany House, and my wife has been writing a book of names for Penguin Books."

"I look forward with excitement to the challenges that lie ahead in this time of new beginnings," writes MADGE HARRAH of Albuquerque, New Mexico. "Interacting with my children and grandchildren who continue to amaze me with their insights, their humor, their triumphs and their mistakes; working in a church that explores God's mystery in thought-provoking ways; appearing as a children's book author in schools to support writing and reading programs; traveling to Ireland with my husband Larry, whose grandmother emigrated from County Antrim when she was a child in 1884. One thing Larry's tiny leprechaun of a grandmother, lovingly called 'Big Grandma,' brought with her to her new homeland was a staunch faith, which she shared with family and friends throughout her long productive life. Big Grandma's faith continues to inspire me as I forge into the twenty-first century where opportunities abound and God makes all things new!"

MARILYN MORGAN HELLEBERG has been living a made-in-heaven love story for the past two years. She and Robert King renewed their friendship, fell in love, and decided to become husband and wife. Their wedding began on New Year's Eve, and when it was complete, they walked arm-in-arm into the new year and into their new life together. Following their wedding trip to France, construction began on their new home, built near the family cabin in Green Mountain Falls, Colorado. Robert is a former college professor and dean, as well as a writer. "For many years," says Marilyn, "I have prayed for a partner who shares my spiritual path. This has been a year of grace for me, as that prayer has been answered and all things truly have become new." It's also been a good year for Marilyn's children: Karen has a new relationship; Paul has gone back to college; John is working toward his Ph.D. at the University of Illinois in Champaign/Urbana.

PHYLLIS HOBE of East Greenville, Pennsylvania, writes, "Earlier this year I realized that I had lost touch with a very important part of my life: my friends. I had been too busy to see them or call them, and I had missed a few birthdays. When I began calling around, I was surprised to learn how many other things I had missed. There were new grandchildren, a few graduations and two retirements. Jobs had been lost, and some new ones started. There had been illnesses and, blessedly, there had been recoveries. What I also discovered was that I had been missed, too. My dear old friends were not the same as I remembered them, but neither was I. No matter. Friendships, like each of us, change over the years, and we keep needing each other in new ways."

 MARJORIE HOLMES of Manassas, Virginia, says, "I will be ninety this year and can honestly say that I've achieved almost all my goals. Thirty-three books, many of them best-sellers, and wonderful friendships with people who were inspired by what I'd written and wrote to me. My mother said that I was born with a pencil in one hand and a piece of paper in the other. But it was a wonderful teacher, who saw promise in the little girl I was, who encouraged me. 'Marjorie, you must make the most of your talent,' she told me. 'You have been endowed with so much. You must write beautiful things for people who crave beautiful things. There is a duty.' As we head into a thrilling new century, it's a message I want to pass along. Encourage talent and goodness whenever you find it. There is a duty!"

 BROCK KIDD of Nashville, Tennessee, says, "Owning a home, pursuing a career as a financial consultant and being a contributing member of my community began to feel stale. My kitchen was beginning to look like an appliance junkyard. I could hardly see the countertop. My Saturdays were being spent in a couch potato-type stupor, rebelling from the long hours that I work during the week. Dealing with a certain client began wearing on my patience. That's when I realized that everything in my life has the potential of becoming old unless I actively work to keep making all that each day brings new. I tackled the kitchen first. I gave a number of items that were cluttering up the room to a friend who was just moving into her first apartment. I took my mountain bike to the service station and had the tires pumped up, ready for the next pretty Saturday. And I called that certain client and asked him to lunch. Getting to know him again reminded me of the things I enjoy about my work."

"Behold, God does indeed make all things new for the Kidd family!" writes PAM KIDD of Nashville, Tennessee. "With Brock using his investment skills and his knack for financial planning, David and I find ourselves in the rather surprising position of being led by our son to look more carefully to our future. It's a delightful, new way of living, having a son who so willingly watches out for his financially challenged parents! And there's always something new to learn from Keri, as she works her way through the University of Tennessee School of Social Work in Memphis. She brings us lessons of compassion and caring, and makes sure we stay on the cutting edge of social justice issues. We have also been blessed with a wonderful new home, which is within easy walking distance of one of Nashville's best parks. And the views of nature from our new house-on-the-hill renew our souls every single morning, and again each evening!"

"Our son Derek got married," reports CAROL KUYKENDALL of Boulder, Colorado, "so this has been a wedding year for us. And in the delightful process, God has made many things new in our lives. The preparation started in January with a diet (wedding pictures last forever, so my husband Lynn and I wanted a 'new' look). Then the four-day wedding weekend in May gave us an opportunity for a family reunion. (We've never had that many relatives all together in one place.) Since then, we've been savoring memories and sorting photographs in our empty nest, which makes our love new again as we realize how a wedding marks the beginning of a relationship that grows and deepens through the years. We celebrated the millennium with our daughters Kendall and Lindsay who live in California, and Derek and his bride Alexandra who live in Portland, Oregon."

For PATRICIA LORENZ of Oak Creek, Wisconsin, the year 2000 means feeling new in a number of ways. "The past year as an empty nester has made me feel like a woman with a new set of wings. My new adventures include driving across the state in my trusty thirteen-year-old red station wagon or flying across the country to do more professional speaking. The new people I meet are marvelous and often become e-mailing buddies. I also feel newly energized because I've quit grousing about the long winters in Wisconsin and enjoy the fact that I get so much done in my writing room during these months. My four children, their spouses and four grandchildren live in New York, Arizona and in different parts of Wisconsin, which also gives me lots of travel opportunities. As I step into the new millennium, everything in my life seems to be brimming with opportunity and adventure. I hope this feeling of newness lasts for another fifty years, at least. *Whoo-ha!* Life is good."

This past year, ROBERTA MESSNER of Huntington, West Virginia, began restoring an old log cottage, which was once a fishing lodge. "With all the needed repairs, I've gained a new appreciation for those two little words in the contract: *As is.* It reminds me of the condition I'm often in when I go to the Lord for help. But I'm learning that with houses and with people, *making all things new* means perfecting the past. Despite that cottage's crumbling mortar, peeling paint and the-sky-is-falling ceilings, the renovations have built on the past, not replaced it. And, strangely, the very things that once were eyesores are reaping the most compliments now. That's how it is with the Lord, too. When we entrust our past to Him, He transforms our greatest weaknesses into our finest strengths."

KEITH MILLER and his wife Andrea, both writers, speakers and consultants, live in Austin, Texas. Keith's three married daughters and their husbands live in different cities in Texas, and each has two children—an older boy and younger girl—between 7 and 15. "My own devotional life has gotten longer and quieter," Keith writes. "My faith-world is quieter and more focused on the people closest to me—on my better days. And I am very grateful about that. I am writing two books about what I am learning about the adventure God offers us. The first is titled *Coming Home,* and the second is about the different ways of sharing faith, *Invitation to Life.*"

LINDA NEUKRUG of Walnut Creek, California, loves the theme of this year's *Daily Guideposts,* "Behold, I make all things new." This year, Linda has enjoyed forming new relationships by phone, by mail and in person with her nephews Adam and Glenn and her niece Jamie, and Linda is looking forward to a new year (and a new millennium) of continuing relationships with old friends from Brooklyn, New York. Linda is learning to enjoy what she has, and she is teaching a fun workshop on "clutter" (getting rid of it, not collecting it!). "I've learned more from my students than they've learned from me," she says. "Clearing out junk—whether it's old calendars or old resentments—is a good way to thank God for all the good things that are so abundant in my life." Something else new is that she has become an Oakland A's fan—*very* new for someone who last year didn't know whether they were a baseball or football team!

Continuing change keeps life interesting for MARJORIE PARKER and her husband Joe. They've assumed new roles with older daughter Joanna, a student at Texas Tech University, now living in her own rented house, and younger daughter Sarah, driving herself everywhere as she embarks on her junior year in high school, where she is on the golf team. Marjorie is enjoying another new role as next-door neighbor to her own widowed mother, who moved from Fort Worth, Texas, to Wichita Falls in 1999. With the loss of Joe's father last year, Marjorie and Joe hope to be helpful to (and keep up with) one more widowed, but very active mother. Marjorie continues to delight in freelance writing, church work and Bible study fellowship, where she says, "I've learned so much more about the character of God and the endless depth of His Word. There is always something new to learn about our Father!"

"One of the great blessings in my life is my home on Quaker Hill," says RUTH STAFFORD PEALE of Pawling, New York. "It's just four miles from my office at the Peale Center for Christian Living, the outreach division of Guideposts. Part of my daily routine is a one- to two-mile walk around the hill.

The fresh air, the invigorating breeze and the beautiful sunshine bring feelings of thanksgiving for God's loving care. I felt that care in a special way last year when my two daughters and their husbands, my son and his wife, my eight grandchildren (five of them with spouses), and six great-grandchildren—a total of twenty-five—were all together to celebrate the one hundredth anniversary of Norman Vincent Peale's birth. The blessings of family are so many that one cannot name them all. God has given me abundance beyond measure."

"God has been 'making all things new' this year—literally!" says ROBERTA ROGERS of White Plains, Maryland. "After fifteen years here, raising four boys, we are repairing and restoring our house, and thinking about moving on. Our youngest, David, graduated with many honors from Western Maryland College and is headed into Army aviation (flying helicopters). Tom earned his MBA and plans a move, maybe to Atlanta. John is still in the Shenandoah Valley and Pete on Cape Cod. I pray often for our yet-to-be-seen daughters-in-law, whomever and wherever they are. In addition to being part of several prayer groups, teaching 'the joy of writing' to home school students and article-writing, I am drafting my first book. The working title is *"Is That YOU, Lord?"—Practical Methods for Learning Spiritual Discernment.* Bill is retired and busier than ever. We have been blessed."

Besides a few new wrinkles, DANIEL SCHANTZ of Moberly, Missouri, and his wife Sharon should have a new grandchild soon, born to their older daughter Teresa Williams of Kansas City. Central Christian College, where Dan teaches education courses, is getting a new president, a new dean and a new business manager. This means some adjustments for Dan. This year, as always, Dan tried some new crops in his garden: ambrosia cantaloupe, Ozark Beauty strawberries, Angel Face roses and arugula. "I'm always surprised by new wonders from the plant kingdom," he says. Each spring Dan has a series of essays in *The Lookout* titled, "A

Slice of Heaven," in which he develops the theme of "All this which now we see is but the childhood of eternity." He hopes to put these essays about the New World into a book someday. One of Dan's favorite Scriptures is "The Lord's mercies . . . are new every morning" (Lamentations 3:22–23).

"It's exciting to be part of a new century," writes SUSAN SCHEFFLEIN of Putnam Valley, New York. "And yet, there are days when life feels a little too routine. When I get those 'been there, done that' feelings, I try to remind myself that I'm never too old to learn something new. God wants me to keep growing, all my life. I try to have adventures each day. Last week I volunteered to judge 4-H presentations and ended up holding a spitting cockroach from Madagascar. This week I signed up for a drawing class at the local high school and discovered an untapped talent. When I open myself to the new, God renews my spirit. Just as we have new bodies every seven years because our cells grow and change, so, too, we have new souls because God is always with us, transforming our lives."

"This past year, all of us began new schools," reports GAIL THORELL SCHILLING of Lander, Wyoming. Tess completed certified nursing assistant training at Central Wyoming College; Tom moved up to high school and Trina to junior high; Greg chose to attend high school in Valencia, California, closer to his dad. Even Gail began her rookie year teaching fifth grade at Wyoming Indian Elementary School on the Wind River Reservation. "New situations and life changes sometimes make me anxious," she admits. "When my mom, who lives in New Hampshire, suffered a stroke last year, lost her vision in one eye and developed serious health problems, I worried long-distance for both her and Dad. As if first-year teaching in a foreign culture wasn't enough! But our Lord has promised that He will neither forsake us nor give us more than we can handle. He keeps His promises. I just need to remember them!"

"I'm so grateful that God made me 'new' through His Son Jesus Christ," says PENNEY SCHWAB of Copeland, Kansas. "His Holy Spirit leads, guides and often pushes me to experience the abundant life He has promised. Grandchildren Ryan, David, Mark, Caleb and Olivia let me see the world through young and enthusiastic eyes. The clinic staff at United Methodist Mexican-American Ministries, where I work, moved into a new building—the culmination of years of dreaming and planning. My husband Don and I visited England and France last June, another exciting new experience."

Once again, ELIZABETH (Tib) SHERRILL of Chappaqua, New York, and her husband John spent part of the year on writing projects in Europe. A new experience on this trip, Tib says, was giving the prices of things in euros. Actual euro coins and bills won't be in circulation for several years, so transactions were made "in faith," exchanging dollars for an unseen currency. "It reminded me a little of what happens when we exchange the world's norms for spiritual values that we believe in but can't see and touch. The difference is that belief in the new euro is based only on the promises of the European Union, while faith in the new life in Christ is based on the promises of God!"

Traveling in Italy with his wife Elizabeth last year, JOHN SHERRILL of Chappaqua, New York, disproved the saying, "Traveler, beware!" One blustery day he was loading their rental car when a wind gust slammed the trunk lid down on his glasses, breaking the frame. Practically blind, John groped his way to the nearest optician. For half an hour the white-smocked optometrist searched unsuccessfully for a frame to fit John's lenses. For another thirty minutes she applied various professional adhesives in an effort to glue the frame back together. When at last one of the glues held, John asked what he owed. *Niente, signore, niente!* Nothing at all! "Thanks to the kindness of a stranger who knew I would never become a regular customer," John says, "for the rest of the trip I saw 'all *people* new.' "

"This year has found me more involved with the children at church," writes SHARI SMYTH of Kingston Springs, Tennessee. "Sunday mornings and Wednesday nights, from our circle of 'magic carpets,' we enter the exciting land of the Bible. An ark of safety. A boy facing a giant. An empty tomb. 'The same God is in the room with us today. He goes with you everywhere. He's your friend,' I tell the children after each story. 'Do you know that for a fact?' an eight-year-old challenged me recently. Controlling a smile, I said, 'No. But I know it by faith, which runs deeper than fact.' 'Oh,' he said, settling back on his carpet square. It's an awesome responsibility, this passing of faith from one generation to the next. Meanwhile, my own four grown children are doing wonderfully, which fills me with joy. As does our three-year-old house in the woods. It's a fine place for my husband Whitney and me to work and play and live."

"The subject this year is apparently *new*. That goes for me," says VAN VARNER of Manhattan, "in that I retired as of March 1999 and went off in a brand-new direction. I don't think it was any better, mind you, but there was less responsibility and a signal for trying new things. My dog Shep has profited, in that I'm around for longer walks, but alas, I spend more time away, which means she has dog-sitters. Come to think of it, she does very well with them. In fact, I sometimes think she is just as happy with them as with me. (*Naw*, not on your life!) The trip I took to *New* Zealand was great, plenty of beautiful sights and fabulous dogs (Shep is a Belgian sheep hound), sheep, and racehorses. When I returned, it was to *New* York, but although I hate to say this, I did not put on a 'new man.' You'll find me the same curmudgeon as of old!"

SCOTT WALKER of Waco, Texas, writes, "My oldest son Drew will graduate from high school in May 2000. My 13-year-old son Luke is an avid *Star Wars* collector. Jodie, 10, will be entering middle school—I can't believe that my youngest is growing up so quickly. My wife Beth continues to work with international students at Baylor University, and I very much enjoy my ministry at First Baptist Waco and teaching at the George W. Truett Theological Seminary. I find that the interaction with students is one of the most vitalizing parts of my life. A book that I published some ten years ago with Guideposts, entitled *Life Rails*, was republished last summer in a new and expanded form. I am excited about this and hope that it will bring help into the lives of many. One of the best parts of last year was meeting people who read *Daily Guideposts*. Even though we'd never met before, it often felt like a family reunion, and I am always thrilled by that experience."

DOLPHUS WEARY now resides in Richland, Mississippi, ten miles south of Jackson and twenty-five miles north of his old hometown, Mendenhall. He is excited about the challenge of taking his reconciliation and unity message throughout the state with Mission Mississippi. His wife Rosie is working from their home, helping to build R.E.A.L. Christian Foundation— a concept they developed by selling Dolphus's book, *I Ain't Comin' Back*, and using the proceeds to build the foundation that will one day support rural ministries in Mississippi. Danita is in her fourth and final year of medical school; Reggie graduated from Tougaloo College and is looking for a business career; Ryan, 12, is in his first year of junior high school. Says Dolphus, "God wants to use us to make all things new by helping to change Mississippi one relationship at a time."

BRIGITTE WEEKS tells us that moving to a small apartment in Manhattan seems to have set off a chain of other changes, both at home and at work. She and her family, all five of them, took a second exciting voyage this year. "We spent the Fourth of July amongst the islands of the Galapagos, off the coast of Ecuador, where my adopted son was born twenty-four years ago. We saw animals that have lived undisturbed and unchanged for thousands of years. And at Guideposts we continue to reach out across the world, especially via the Internet and through Prayer Fellowship. *Daily Guideposts* now reaches more readers than ever before in its history, making us all tremendously proud."

"I adore the way God makes all things new," says MARION BOND WEST of Watkinsville, Georgia. "Mornings, relationships, hopes, feelings. I'm grateful He's still doing new works in my life, such as showing me that I don't have to speak every opinion I have. He cares about such smaller 'new works,' too, like a piece of furniture. Since Gene and I married twelve years ago, I've hounded him to agree to buy an old-fashioned bed. Finally, he agreed. It's a very high, stick-canopied, chestnut bed, and I feel just like a princess in it, especially when Gene brings me morning coffee. He says he's having to adjust to the bed, that it's really not practical for someone with a fear of heights. Our aged cat Minnie hasn't made the adjustment either. She misjudged her routine jump on the first night and fell back onto the floor, mortified. My ninety-year-old mother 'Goge' continues to make her home with us and recounts what life was like in the early 1900s."

"If there ever was a year of 'all things new,' this has been it," writes BRENDA WILBEE of Bellingham, Washington. "Last August my son Phil was married, and a scant six hours later my son Blake flew off to college—Chicago, two thousand miles away. In less than a day I was left with an empty house, with a lonely heart and, after I got over the shock, in search of new direction. The months have been good. After years of inward focus on my children, so necessary as a single parent, I'm able to look outward again and I'm having a good time reconnecting with the world. I'm rediscovering time and energy. Wow! Some of the excitement? A new job, one outside my house, with real people I can talk to; new friends; a new church; restored confidence; and new hope. Truly, with God—even in an Empty Nest—behold, all things are made new!"

"My husband Roland died in the midst of my writing for *Daily Guideposts, 2000*," reports ISABEL WOLSELEY. "Thus, this has been a year of change, and the theme for this year's volume, 'Behold, I make all things new,' has taken on a deeper significance than when I started. God's love and mercy now have greater depth. Supportive friends are dearer. So are my sons

John and Kelly Champ and their wives and my six grandchildren, plus a great-grandchild, too. Syracuse University, where my husband taught for more than a quarter century, has established the Wolseley Award in his memory, and is giving me the honor of presenting it to the outstanding journalism student each spring. I plan to remain in Syracuse, New York, where I'm a newspaper columnist."

Scripture Reference Index

An alphabetical index listing the Scripture references to verses appearing either at the top of devotionals or, on occasion, within the text. Chapter and verse numbers are in bold type on the left. Numbers in regular type, on the right, refer to the Daily Guideposts *page(s) on which the complete verse or reference can be located.*

Authors, Titles and Subjects Index

An alphabetical index to devotional authors; titles of special series; poems and songs; proper names of people, places and things; holidays and holy days; biblical persons and events appearing in the text; and subjects with subheading breakdowns that will help you find a devotional to meet that special need. Numbers refer to the Daily Guideposts *page(s) on which these can be located.*